Towards Learning and Instruction in Web 3.0

Pedro Isaias · Dirk Ifenthaler · Kinshuk
Demetrios G. Sampson · J. Michael Spector
Editors

Towards Learning and Instruction in Web 3.0

Advances in Cognitive and Educational Psychology

 Springer

Editors
Pedro Isaias
Universidade Aberta
Lisbon, Portugal
pisaias@univ-ab.pt

Kinshuk
School of Computing
and Information Systems
Athabasca University
Athabasca, AB, Canada
kinshuk@athabascau.ca

J. Michael Spector
University of Georgia
Athens, GA, USA
mspector@uga.edu

Dirk Ifenthaler
Department of Educational Science
University of Mannheim
Mannheim, Germany
ifenthaler@uni-mannheim.de

Demetrios G. Sampson
Department of Digital Systems
University of Piraeus
Piraeus, Greece
sampson@unipi.gr

ISBN 978-1-4614-1538-1   e-ISBN 978-1-4614-1539-8
DOI 10.1007/978-1-4614-1539-8
Springer New York Dordrecht Heidelberg London

Library of Congress Control Number: 2011941215

Printed on acid-free paper

Springer is part of Springer Science+Business Media (www.springer.com)

Preface

This edited volume contains selected expanded papers from the CELDA (Cognition and Exploratory Learning in the Digital Age) 2010 Conference (www.celda-conf. org). It addresses the main issues concerned with problem solving, evolving learning processes, innovative pedagogies, and technology-based educational applications in the digital age. There have been advances in both cognitive psychology and computing that have affected the educational arena. The convergence of these two disciplines is increasing at a fast pace and affecting academia and professional practice in many ways. Paradigms (such as just-in-time learning, constructivism, student-centered learning and collaborative approaches) have emerged and are being supported by technological advancements such as simulations, virtual reality and multi-agent systems. These developments have created both opportunities and areas of serious concern. Hence, this volume aims to cover both technological as well as pedagogical issues related to these developments.

We organized the papers included in this volume around five themes: (a) Student-centered Learning, (b) Collaborative Learning, (c) Technology, Learning and Expertise, (d) toward Web 3.0 in Education, and (e) Exploratory Technologies. Each of the editors took lead responsibility for reviewing and editing the papers associated with one theme.

In Part I, student-centered learning, several issues are described and discussed. The authors address the issue of technology enhanced learning environments and propose an architecture to dynamically identify students' learning styles from their behaviour in a learning system, and updating their learning styles based on their behaviours. These learning styles' information is later accessed by an adaptivity module to provide students with customize feedback about their learning styles as well as about how to improve their learning processes (Graf, Kinshuk, Zhang, Maguire & Shtern, Chap. 1). Other way to enhance learners' efficiency is through the proposal on an annotation-based pedagogical process called SQAR (Survey, Question, Annotation and Review). SQAR aims to help the learners to enhance their learning activity and fosters learners' evolution (Mostefai, Azouaou & Balla, Chap. 2). Also an important issue in student-centered learning is the students' assessment. A survey is presented to analyse and infer from current and future online formative assessments. The results provide insights on how to better plan online formative assessments having into account the expectancies of both students and tutors (Minder, Schmitz & Schär, Chap. 3). Lastly, informal learning and assessment has also been addressed by authors that investigated learners' performance and attitude toward a community-based project management learning system and the role of participatory media and Web 2.0 technologies in the whole process (Mohamed & Koehler, Chap. 4).

In Part II, chapters focus on collaborative learning issues. One way to achieve collaborative learning is through the use of games. A game has been devised specifically to accomplish this goal using mobile technologies (Sultana, Feisst & Christ, Chap. 5). Other authors propose a generic framework that complies with the rules of both higher education and life-long learning, and propose a virtual collaboration prototype (Porumb, Orz & Vlaicu, Chap. 6).

In Part III, chapters address technology, learning and expertise issues. Authors start by reporting the results of a survey conducted in an Australian University to explore the types of learning outcomes academics target in their curricula. This is assessed in lign with having in consideration how technologies are used to assess the referred outcomes (McNeill, Gosper & Hedberg, Chap. 7). The next chapter introduces mashups as a realistic method to develop new educational tools. The educational mashups can operate as a tool that combines data from an extensive variety of sources on the web, which can motivate students to share their learning experiences (Karavirta & Korhonen, Chap. 8). After that, three projects are presented to draw attention to several e-mentoring issues for example the nature of the mentoring process and the timing of the mentoring intervention. These projects demonstrate that a successful communication is critical to the improvement of the interaction between mentor and mentee (Lord & Coninx, Chap. 9). Finally, the authors recommend a new instructional design framework called IPTEACES (Involvement, Preparation, Transmission, Exemplification, Application, Connection, Evaluation and Simulation), which propose a suitable learning strategy for different learners in order to fit different learning profiles (Pena & Isaías, Chap. 10).

In Part IV, the chapters focus the issues of Web 3.0 in Education. Firstly, the authors compare two different representation methods that can encourage interaction behaviors between students within Virtual Learning Environments (VLEs). They believe that learning is a dynamic process of knowledge creation made by the learners' community with the help of the teacher (Pasqualino, Barchiesi & Battistoni, Chap. 11). Next, it is presented the results of a learning exercise in which students from two universities in the United States create a Website to promote a fictitious product online. In this exercise they must apply several different Search Engine Optimization (SEO) techniques to establish those which are the most useful (Frydenberg & Miko, Chap. 12). Other authors explore 3D Virtual Worlds (VWs) as an environment, which can introduce new educational benefits. By using 3D VWs, teachers can foment more interactive learning experiences to their students through the high representation fidelity that 3D Virtual Worlds can offer (Sampson & Kallonis, Chap. 13). In order to establish more adaptive e-learning environments, it is critical to focus on the user as an individual with his own characteristics. To finish, it is described an exploratory study, which examine several cognitive processes of undergraduate students throughout mental rotation tasks (Mazman & Altun, Chap. 14).

In Part V, exploratory technologies are presented. Educational games are described as potential successful learning environments, due to the fact that they can stimulate the player by mixing casual and familiar content with educational content. It is described a solution on how motivation can be calculated and assessed during the game play (Ghergulescu & Muntean, Chap. 15). Other authors show that there is a common tendency of using merely acceptable-answer frequencies to evaluate if a student learning is both mathematically and psychologically unacceptable (Powell, Bernauer & Agnihotri, Chap. 16). Next, it is explored how an interactive cubic user-configurable modular robotic system, called Number Blocks, can facilitate the learning by 7–8 year old children regarding numbers and their pronunciation. This system merges physical interaction, learning and immediate response (Majgaard, Misfeldt & Nielsen, Chap. 17). Last, it is explored several reasonable ideas to produce devices for children through Computer-controlled Fabrication. The design and printing of physical objects has been growing and can be used for numerous educational purposes (Eisenberg, Ludwig & Elumeze, Chap. 18).

This is the third edited volume to result from a CELDA conference. We are convinced that this work covers the current state of research, methodology, assessment, and technology. When we have so many outstanding papers as were presented in Freiburg, Germany 2008, Rome, Italy 2009, and Timisoara, Romania, 2010 we will certainly seek to also have future edited volumes, as this benefits the entire professional community.

Lisbon, Portugal   Pedro Isaias
Mannheim, Germany   Dirk Ifenthaler
Athabasca, AB, Canada   Kinshuk
Piraeus, Greece   Demetrios G. Sampson
Athens, GA, USA   J. Michael Spector

Acknowledgements

We would like to acknowledge the vital role played by the International Association for Development of the Information Society (http://www.iadis.org) and for its continuing sponsorship of CELDA conferences. In addition, we owe our thanks to the over 90 international CELDA committee members for providing thoughtful reviews for all papers submitted to the CELDA 2010 conference.

Lisbon, Portugal	Pedro Isaias
Mannheim, Germany	Dirk Ifenthaler
Athabasca, AB, Canada	Kinshuk
Piraeus, Greece	Demetrios G. Sampson
Athens, GA, USA	J. Michael Spector

Introduction
Is Web 3.0 Changing Learning and Instruction?

Dirk Ifenthaler

Abstract This chapter addresses the evolution of Web generations and their influence on learning and instruction. The development of current Web generations and their major distinguishing functions are addressed. Next, implications for learning and instruction will be discussed. This chapter concludes with remarks about future perspectives of Web generations and how they might influence learning and instruction.

Keywords Web generation, Web 2.0, Web 3.0, Semantic Web

Introduction

Almost 20 years ago, Rheingold (1993) described virtual communities as social aggregations of people which form webs of personal relationships by sharing interests and human feeling. Since then, the Web evolved from a primarily read-only information medium to a collaborative information vehicle (Lassila and Hendler 2007). The next evolution of the Web will include *intelligent technological behavior* which enables meaningful interaction between human users and the Web technology (Ifenthaler 2010). In this way, the Web could provide the basis for *free learning environments*, which have been regarded by educational theorists as the quintessential form of learning environment for decades.

This rapid development of information and communication technology has strongly influenced advances and implications for learning and instruction. A review of scientific databases (ERIC, PsychINFO) shows the development of publications focusing on Web generations and learning and instruction (see Fig. 1).

Interestingly, almost 4,000 publications focusing on Web 2.0 and learning and instruction were found. They increased from less than 20 publications (2005) to over 1,200 publications (2010). A query regarding Web 3.0 and learning found less than 200 publications in total with a slow increase so far. As technology is rapidly

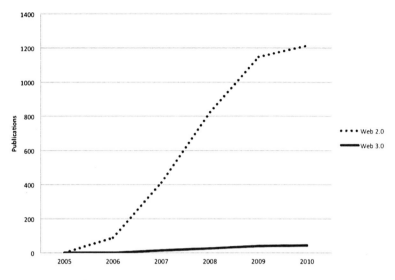

Fig. 1 Development of publications focusing on Web 2.0 and Web 3.0

advancing towards Web 3.0 applications, an increase of publications focusing on the new technological possibilities for learning and instruction is expected for the next 5 years.

In this introductory chapter, we address the evolution of Web generations. The reflection of Web generations (Web 1.0, Web 2.0, Web 3.0) provides a short overview of their technological functions and limitations. Next, implications for learning and instruction will be discussed. Clearly, it is difficult to predict new developments in the domain of learning and instruction, however, new developments of information and communication technology will continue to guide them in a sustained manner. We conclude with remarks about future perspectives of Web generations and how they might influence learning and instruction. Future CELDA conferences will provide the research community a perfect podium to discuss latest developments of learning and instruction in the digital age.

Web Generations

A common misconception regarding Web generations is that the newest Web generation will replace or suppress previous ones (Blumauer & Pellegrini 2009). In order to overcome this misconception, Fig. 2 illustrates the development of current Web generations and their major distinguishing functions.

Clearly, the core of the Web mainly consists of (X)HTML documents which contain static information (e.g., text, pictures, animations, etc.). The architecture of an individual website is usually represented in a tree structure including a hierarchical

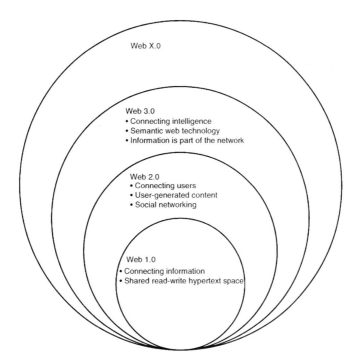

Fig. 2 Web generations and their key functions

array of (X)HTML documents. Further, specific information is connected through hyperlinks which refer to other documents all over the Web. Accordingly, the Web 1.0 generation connects information which is predominantly offered by a small group of experts who are able to develop these (X)HTML documents. The larger number of Web 1.0 users are passive, i.e. they browse and read single websites but are not able to add additional information to the Web.

One of the main strengths of Web 2.0 is the increased possibilities for *user generated content* (Ifenthaler 2010). Further defining characteristics of Web 2.0 are information sharing and a decentralization of its management and use. Accordingly, Web 2.0 represents a shift toward a *read and write* environment, inasmuch as the users themselves can participate actively in the creation and management of content. Web 2.0 already offers many so-called APIs (application programming interfaces) which allow users to use and exchange available data and services. Essential characteristics of Web 2.0 are (a) community, (b) tools, and (c) collaboration (Knappe & Kracklauer 2007). *Community* stands for the virtual union of users sharing common interests (e.g., XING, LinkedIn). This is where specific interest groups actively share their knowledge (e.g., Wikipedia). *Tools* are the technological foundations which enable users to interact with other users or groups of the Web. Vitally important is the high usability of the tools and low computer skills (e.g., no programming) needed for using them. *Collaboration* provides the basis for closed communities working on specific projects using specialized applications and virtual workflow (e.g., Google Docs, WebLogic). Information of Web 2.0 is therefore self-organized, user generated, and primarily open source. Last, quantity is an additional characteristic. The more users actively participate in a Web community the more people get attracted. Accordingly, certain information gain in importance and quality (e.g., Wikipedia).

Web 3.0 has now been coined to describe the coming wave of innovation (Yu 2007). Accordingly, Web 3.0 will go a step further and will understand or rather learn what the user wants and suggests the information fitting to the users' needs. This requires that all information which is available in the Web is accessible by a certain standard and that the technology is able to *understand its meaning*. Thus, Web 3.0 is intelligent offering a data network consisting in a collection of structured data records published in the Web in repeatedly reusable formats (e.g., XML, RDF). Besides the service-oriented architecture, Web 3.0 will be the realization and extension of the concept of the Semantic Web (Lassila and Hendler 2007; Yu 2007). Web 3.0 operations will be designed to perform logical reasoning using a multitude of rules which express logical relationships between semantic meaning and information available in the Web.

What about Web X.0? There are of course many opinions as to the course further development of the Web will take – starting with concepts like *emergent technologies* or the *Semantic Web*, which will change the way we use the Web and constitute a step in the direction of artificial intelligence, and ranging all the way to the prediction that due to the increasing amount of connections to the Internet modular Web applications and improved computer graphics will play a key role in its further evolution. The next Web X.0 generation will be imminent.

Implications for Learning and Instruction

Although the advantages of current and future Web generations for learning and instruction are all beyond question, the pedagogically significant question as to how learning can be supported effectively is sometimes left out of the picture (Ifenthaler 2010).

When defining Web 3.0 as intelligent, one could assume that the future technology will take on the part of the instructor. Still, we assume that Web 3.0 learning environments do not make the instructor redundant. Although, it is expected that the role of the instructor is changing (Devedžic 2006; Morris 2011). The possibility of Web 3.0 will assist the instructor by creating reusable learning objects and providing immediate feedback to a learner at a specific stages of the learning process (Ifenthaler 2011).

Considering the inseparable interaction between the learner and the learning environment, three factors may be distinguished:

1. The learner's beliefs and expectations before the learning experience.
2. The learning experience itself and the inherent change of the learner's cognitive structure (both intended and incidental).
3. The learner's beliefs and expectations after the learning, both considering attitudes towards the learning experience and the content.

These factors may be supported by personal learning systems (PLS) which are regarded as intelligent learning environments in Web 3.0. In PLS, learners develop their individual learning by selecting various Web tools to meet their specific learning goals (Ifenthaler 2010). So far, PLS are expected to include four major characteristics: (a) portal, (b) integration, (c) neutrality, and (d) symbiosis. A PLS is an open portal to the Web which is connected with various tools and collects and structures information from sources of the Web. The content can be created by both learners and instructors using simple authoring tools. The required information is accessible in standardized formats which learners can subscribe to and synchronize with their mobile desktop applications. In this way, the learning environment is integrated into the user's daily working environment and connected to it. Individualized tasks are designed in such a way that the learners themselves can choose which application they wish to use to work on them. Also, PLS allow learners to collaborate with others on a specific topic under study (Oliver 2007). The PLS can make recommendations and provide meaningful support. Instead of creating new spaces, a PLS uses existing resources and information. The PLS works with existing free static content, social networks, reusable learning objects, databases, wikis, blogs, etc. All in all, PLS require increased personal responsibility, both from the learner and from the instructor. At the same time, however, they offer more freedom for individual learning.

Future Perspectives

A practical taxonomy for Web features might help instructors to develop meaningful learning environments for the digital age. Such a taxonomy may contain (1) the name of the Web feature, (2) a short description of the Web feature, (3) a classification of the Web feature with regard to the three design elements *information*, *instruction*, and *learning*, (4) the Web feature's association with instructional functions, and (5) exemplary recommendations for instructional use (Ifenthaler & Pirnay-Dummer 2011).

However, the development of such a taxonomy requires empirical research. This will enhance the understanding of the underlying psychological and educational principles of online learning. On the basis of these results, new instructional design principles for online learning could be introduced for classroom practice.

Closely linked to the demand of new approaches for designing and developing up-to-date learning environments in Web 3.0 is the necessity of enhancing the design and delivery of assessment systems (Spector 2010). Recently, promising methodologies have been developed which provide a strong basis for applications in research and instruction for the Web 3.0 generation (Isaias and Ifenthaler 2011). However, only a few assessment methodologies are available which have the potential to meet the requirements of future Web 3.0 learning environments so far. Future systems need to accomplish specific requirements, such as (1) adaptability to different subject domains, (2) flexibility for experimental and instructional settings, (3) management of huge amounts of data, (4) instant or rapid analysis of specific data,

(5) immediate feedback for learners and educators, and (6) generation of automated reports of results (Isaias and Ifenthaler 2011).

The CELDA conferences have been and definitely will be a perfect podium to discuss these highly important developments for learning and instruction in the digital age.

References

Blumauer, A., & Pellegrini, T. (2009). Semantic Web Revisited – Eine kurze Einführung in das Social Semantic Web. In A. Blumauer & T. Pellegrini (Eds.), *Social Semantic Web* (pp. 3–22). Heidelberg: Springer.

Devedžic, V. (2006). *Semantic Web and education*. New York: Springer.

Ifenthaler, D. (2010). Learning and instruction in the digital age. In J. M. Spector, D. Ifenthaler, P. Isaías, Kinshuk & D. G. Sampson (Eds.), *Learning and instruction in the digital age: Making a difference through cognitive approaches, technology-facilitated collaboration and assessment, and personalized communications* (pp. 3–10). New York: Springer.

Ifenthaler, D. (2011). Intelligent model-based feedback. Helping students to monitor their individual learning progress. In S. Graf, F. Lin, Kinshuk & R. McGreal (Eds.), *Intelligent and adaptive systems: Technology enhanced support for learners and teachers*. Hershey, PA: IGI Global.

Ifenthaler, D., & Pirnay-Dummer, P. (2011). States and processes of learning communities. Engaging students in meaningful reflection and elaboration. In B. White, I. King & P. Tsang (Eds.), *Social media tools and platforms in learning environments: Present and future*. New York: Springer.

Isaias, P., & Ifenthaler, D. (2011). *Challenging the assessment in Web 3.0*. Paper presented at the AECT International Convention, Jacksonville, FL, 08-11-2011.

Knappe, M., & Kracklauer, A. (2007). Von Web 1.0 zu Web 2.0 — eine neue Ôra? *Verkaufschance Web 2.0* (pp. 15–28). Wiesbaden: Gabler.

Lassila, O., & Hendler, J. (2007). Embracing "Web 3.0". *Internet Computing, 11*(3), 90–93.

Morris, R. D. (2011). Web 3.0: Implications for online learning. *TechTrends, 55*(1), 42–46.

Oliver, K. (2007). Leveraging Web 2.0 in the redesign of a graduate-level technology integration course. *TechTrends, 51*(5), 55–61.

Rheingold, H. (1993). *The virtual community: homesteading on the electronic frontier*. Reading, MA: Addison-Wesley.

Spector, J. M. (2010). Mental representations and their analysis: An epestimological perspective. In D. Ifenthaler, P. Pirnay-Dummer & N. M. Seel (Eds.), *Computer-based diagnostics and systematic analysis of knowledge* (pp. 27–40). New York: Springer.

Yu, L. (2007). *Introduction to the Semantic Web and Semantic Web Services*. Boca Raton, FL: Chapman & Hall.

Contents

Contributors

Vishnuteerth Agnihotri Test Development, Educational Initiatives Pvt. Ltd.,
Bangalore, India
vishnu@ei-india.com

Arif Altun Department of Computer Education and Instructional Technologies,
Hacettepe University, Ankara, Turkey
altunar@gmail.com

Faiçal Azouaou National High School for Computer Science (ESI),
Algiers, Algeria
f_azouaou@esi.dz

Amar Balla National High School for Computer Science (ESI),
Algiers, Algeria
a_balla@esi.dz

Maria Assunta Barchiesi Department of Enterprise Engineering,
"Tor Vergata" University of Rome, Rome, Italy
barchiesi@dii.uniroma2.it

Elisa Battistoni Department of Enterprise Engineering,
"Tor Vergata" University of Rome, Rome, Italy
battistoni@dii.uniroma2.it

James Bernauer Robert Morris University, Moon Township, PA, USA
bernauer@rmu.edu

Andreas Christ University of Applied Sciences Offenburg, Offenburg, Germany
christ@hs-offenburg.de

Nele Coninx Fontys University of Applied Sciences, Eindhoven, The Netherlands
ns.coninx@fontys.nl

Michael Eisenberg University of Colorado, Boulder, CO, USA
duck@cs.colorado.edu

Nwanua Elumeze University of Colorado, Boulder, CO, USA
nwanua@aniomagic.com

Markus Feisst University of Nottingham, Nottingham, UK
Markus.Feisst@nottingham.ac.uk

Mark Frydenberg Bentley University, Waltham, MA, USA
mfrydenberg@bentley.edu

Ioana Ghergulescu National College of Ireland, School of Computing,
Dublin, Ireland
ioana.ghergulescu@student.ncirl.ie

Maree Gosper Macquarie University, Sydney, Australia
maree.gosper@mq.edu.au

Sabine Graf School of Computing and Information Systems,
Athabasca University, Athabasca, AB, Canada
sabineg@athabascau.ca

John Hedberg Macquarie University, Sydney, Australia
john.hedberg@mq.edu.au

Dirk Ifenthaler Department of Educational Science, University of Mannheim,
Mannheim, Germany
ifenthaler@uni-mannheim.de

Pedro Isaias Universidade Aberta, Lisbon, Portugal
pisaias@univ-ab.pt

Pavlos Kallonis Department of Digital Systems, University of Piraeus,
Piraeus, Greece

Centre for Research and Technology Hellas (CERTH), Informatics and Telematics
Institute (ITI), Thessaloniki, Greece
pkalloni@iti.gr

Ville Karavirta Department of Computer Science and Engineering,
Aalto University, Aalto, Finland
ville.karavirta@aalto.fi

Kinshuk School of Computing and Information Systems, Athabasca University,
Athabasca, AB, Canada
kinshuk@athabascau.ca

Thomas Koehler TU-Dresden, Dresden, Germany
thomas.koehler@tu-dresden.de

Ari Korhonen Department of Computer Science and Engineering,
Aalto University, Aalto, Finland
ari.korhonen@aalto.fi

David Lord University of Huddersfield, Huddersfield, UK
d.lord@hud.ac.uk

Kyle Ludwig University of Colorado, Boulder, CO, USA
rushk144@gmail.com

Paul Maguire School of Computing and Information Systems,
Athabasca University, Athabasca, AB, Canada
paul@pmetal.ca

Gunver Majgaard The Maersk Mc-Kinney Moller Institute,
University of Southern Denmark, Odense M, Denmark
gum@mmmi.sdu.dk

Sacide Güzin Mazman Department of Computer Education
and Instructional Technologies, Hacettepe University, Ankara, Turkey
s.guzin@gmail.com

Margot McNeill Macquarie University, Sydney, Australia
margot.mcneill@mq.edu.au

John S. Miko Saint Francis University, Loretto, PA, USA
jmiko@francis.edu

Stefan P. Minder Institute of Medical Education, Medical Faculty
of the University of Bern, Bern, Switzerland
minder@iml.unibe.ch

Morten Misfeldt The Danish School of Education, Aarhus University,
Copenhagen, Denmark
mmi@dpu.dk

Bahaaeldin Mohamed TU-Dresden, Dresden, Germany
bahaa_i@yahoo.com

Belkacem Mostefai National High School for Computer Science (ESI),
Algiers, Algeria
b_mostefai@esi.dz

Cristina Hava Muntean National College of Ireland, School of Computing,
Dublin, Ireland
cmuntean@ncirl.ie

Gianluca Murgia Department of Information Engineering, University of Siena,
Siena, Italy
murgia@unisi.it

Jacob Nielsen Center for Playware, Technical University of Denmark,
Lyngby, Copenhagen, Denmark
jn@playware.dtu.dk

Bogdan Orza Technical University of Cluj-Napoca, Cluj-Napoca, Romania
bogdan.orza@com.utcluj.ro

Paola Pasqualino Department of Enterprise Engineering,
"Tor Vergata" University of Rome, Rome, Italy
paola.pasqualino@uniroma2.it

Nuno Pena Universidade Aberta, Lisbon, Portugal
nuno.raposo.pena@gmail.com

Cosmin Porumb Technical University of Cluj-Napoca, Cluj-Napoca, Romania
cosmin.porumb@com.utcluj.ro

Sanda Porumb Technical University of Cluj-Napoca, Cluj-Napoca, Romania
sanda.porumb@com.utcluj.ro

Jay C. Powell Better Schooling Systems, Pittsburgh, PA, USA
jpowell@tir.com

Demetrios G. Sampson Department of Digital Systems, University of Piraeus,
Piraeus, Greece

Centre for Research and Technology Hellas (CERTH), Informatics and Telematics
Institute (ITI), Thessaloniki, Greece
sampson@unipi.gr

Sissel Guttormsen Schär Institute of Medical Education,
Medical Faculty of the University of Bern, Bern, Switzerland
guttormsen@iml.unibe.ch

Felix M. Schmitz Institute of Medical Education,
Medical Faculty of the University of Bern, Bern, Switzerland
schmitz@iml.unibe.ch

Victoria Shtern School of Computing and Information Systems,
Athabasca University, Athabasca, AB, Canada
vika_shtern@yahoo.com

J. Michael Spector University of Georgia, Athens, USA
mspector@uga.edu

Razia Sultana University of Applied Sciences Offenburg, Offenburg, Germany
razia.sultana@hs-offenburg.de

Aurel Vlaicu Technical University of Cluj-Napoca, Cluj-Napoca, Romania
aurel.vlaicu@com.utcluj.ro

Qingsheng Zhang School of Computing and Information Systems,
Athabasca University, Athabasca, AB, Canada
qzhang@athabascau.ca

Maiga Chang Athabasca University, Athabasca, Canada
maigac@athabascau.ca

Eva Grundl Department of Educational Science, University of Mannheim,
Mannheim, Germany
egrundl@rumms.uni-mannheim.de

Sheng-Hui Hsu National Cheng Kung University, Tainan, Taiwan
obs945@gmail.com

Ming-Chi Liu National Cheng Kung University, Tainan, Taiwan
liumingchi@gmail.com

Imran Zualkernan American University of Sharjah, Sharjah,
United Arab Emirates
izualkernan@aus.edu

Part I
Student-Centered Learning

Chapter 1
Facilitating Learning Through Dynamic Student Modelling of Learning Styles

An Architecture and Its Application for Providing Adaptivity

Sabine Graf, Kinshuk, Qingsheng Zhang, Paul Maguire, and Victoria Shtern

1 Introduction

Technology enhanced learning environments provide many new ways of facilitating learning as well as teaching. One of the possibilities that are available in such learning environments is to get information about how students learn and use online courses by tracking their learning paths and activities in the system. Such information can be very valuable in many ways and can be used, for example, for identifying when students have difficulties in learning and to get feedback about the course materials such as whether particular types of learning objects/activities (e.g., videos, exercises, etc.) are actually used by students as well as which learning objects/activities seem to be difficult for students, indicating the need for improvement of the respective learning materials. Furthermore, information from students' behaviour in an online course can be used to identify students' characteristics such as their learning styles (e.g., García et al. 2007; Graf et al. 2009; Özpolat and Akar 2009), cognitive abilities (e.g., Kinshuk and Lin 2004; Lin 2007), and affective states (e.g., Khan et al. 2010).

In this chapter, we focus on the consideration of students' learning styles in technology enhanced learning environments as well as on the dynamic identification of learning styles from students' behaviour in an online course. Knowing students' learning styles and considering this information in the learning process can lead to many benefits for students. First, students can be made aware of their learning styles as well as the implications of their learning styles for learning, including general strengths and weaknesses of students in the learning process. Such information can help students to understand why learning is sometimes difficult for them and builds the basis for developing their weaknesses. Second, the

S. Graf (✉) • Kinshuk • Q. Zhang • P. Maguire • V. Shtern
School of Computing and Information Systems, Athabasca University, Athabasca, AB, Canada
e-mail: sabineg@athabascau.ca; kinshuk@athabascau.ca; qzhang@athabascau.ca;
paul@pmetal.ca; vika_shtern@yahoo.com

P. Isaias et al. (eds.), *Towards Learning and Instruction in Web 3.0: Advances in Cognitive and Educational Psychology*, DOI 10.1007/978-1-4614-1539-8_1,
© Springer Science+Business Media, LLC 2012

information about students' learning styles can be used to match the teaching style with the students' learning styles. Providing students with learning material/activities and personalized recommendations that fit their preferred ways of learning can make learning easier for them. This matching hypothesis is supported by educational theories. Moreover, studies such as those by Bajraktarevic et al. (2003), Graf and Kinshuk (2007), and Popescu (2010) demonstrated supportive results and showed that students can learn easier and faster if their courses are adapted to their learning styles.

To consider learning styles in education, the students' learning styles need to be known first. Brusilovsky (1996) distinguished between two different ways of student modelling: *collaborative* and *automatic*. In the collaborative approach, the students provide explicit feedback which can be used to build and update a student model, such as filling out a learning style questionnaire. In the automatic approach, the process of building and updating the student model is done automatically based on the behaviour and actions of students while they are using the system for learning. The automatic approach is direct and free from the problem of inaccurate self-conceptions of students. Moreover, it allows students to focus only on learning rather than additionally providing explicit feedback about their preferences. In contrast to learning style questionnaires, an automatic approach can also be more accurate and less error-prone since it analyses data from a time span rather than data which are gathered at one specific point of time.

Additionally, student modelling can be classified as *static* or *dynamic*. Static student modelling refers to an approach where the student model is initialised only once (mostly when students register in the system). In contrast, a dynamic student modelling approach frequently updates the information in the student model and therefore allows responding to changes of the investigated student characteristic. A dynamic approach has two advantages over a static one in the context of identifying learning styles. First, dynamic student modelling can consider exceptional behaviour of students and can extend static student modelling by incrementally improving and fine-tuning the information in the student model in real-time, learning students' learning styles until the learning styles have been identified reliably. Therefore, dynamic student modelling can contribute to identify students' learning styles with higher accuracy, considering new data whenever students use the system for learning. Second, since many of the major learning style models argue that learning styles can change over time, dynamic student modelling allows monitoring students' behaviour, identifying changes in their learning styles, and updating the learning styles once they changed.

When looking at the student modelling approaches that are used by adaptive learning systems that aim at providing adaptivity based on learning styles, it can be seen that a lot of these systems use questionnaires (a static and collaborative approach). Examples of such systems are CS383 (Carver et al. 1999), IDEAL (Shang et al. 2001), and LSAS (Bajraktarevic et al. 2003). Recently, more and more research has been done on developing automatic student modelling approaches by considering students' behaviour in a course. However, these approaches typically use a predefined amount of behaviour data for identifying students' learning styles at one point of time and are therefore automatic but still static approaches (Cha et al. 2006; García et al. 2007; Graf et al. 2009; Özpolat and Akar 2009). Very little research has been conducted so far on developing approaches which aim at dynamic and automatic student modelling of learning style, where the system monitors a students' behaviour and uses this behaviour data to frequently update learning styles of students.

In this chapter, an architecture is introduced which integrates dynamic student modelling into existing learning systems, enabling them to monitor students' behaviour, analyse these data for detecting and frequently updating students' learning styles, and storing the information about students' learning styles in a student model which can be accessed by the system in order to provide adaptive and personalized support for students. The introduced architecture has been integrated in a learning system and a module for providing students with adaptive support has been developed in order to demonstrate the benefits of dynamic student modelling of learning styles and the introduced architecture.

This research is based on the Felder-Silverman learning style model (FSLSM) (Felder and Silverman 1988). FSLSM is a learning style model that describes learning styles in detail and is therefore highly appropriate for providing adaptivity in learning systems. Furthermore, the FSLSM is based on the concept of tendencies, allowing handling of exceptional behaviour by considering learning styles as a main tendency rather than as an obligatory type. FSLSM assumes that these tendencies are "flexibly stable", meaning that they are more or less stable but can change over time, for example, if a student is training his/her weak learning preferences. Moreover, FSLSM is used very often in technology enhanced learning and some researchers even argue that it is the most appropriate learning style model for the use in adaptive learning systems (Carver et al. 1999; Kuljis and Liu 2005). According to FSLSM, each learner has a preference for each of its four dimensions (active/reflective, sensing/intuitive, visual/verbal, sequential/ global). *Active* learners prefer to learn by trying things out and working with others, whereas *reflective* learners prefer to learn by thinking things through and working alone. *Sensing* learners like to learn from concrete material like examples and tend to be more practical and more careful with details, whereas *intuitive* learners prefer to learn abstract material, tend to be more innovative, and like challenges. *Visual* learners remember best what they have seen, whereas *verbal* learners get more out of words, regardless of whether those words are spoken or written. *Sequential* learners learn in linear steps and prefer to be guided through the learning process, whereas *global* learners learn in large leaps and prefer more freedom in their learning process.

In the next section, the architecture for dynamic student modelling is described. Section 3 deals with the integration of the architecture into a learning system and describes the adaptivity module used for providing students with personalized recommendations based on their learning styles. Section 4 concludes the chapter and provides some directions for future work.

2   Architecture for Dynamic Student Modelling

In this section, an architecture is presented that aims at enabling existing learning systems to build and frequently update a cognitive profile of their students, which is stored within the student model and includes information about students' learning styles based on the FSLSM. The architecture is illustrated in Fig. 1.1. In order to integrate the architecture into a learning system, a *Notification Mechanism* needs to be added to the learning system, which notifies the *Dynamic Student Modelling Module* about students' actions. After a student has performed a predefined number of actions, the *Dynamic Student Modelling Module* requests the *Learning Style Calculation Module* to recalculate the learning styles of the particular student based on his/her recent behaviour in the system. The *Learning Style Calculation Module* requests the relevant data for calculating learning styles from the *Data Extraction Module* which connects to the data sources of the learning system, extracts the requested data and delivers them to the *Learning Style Calculation Module* where the current learning styles of the student are calculated and then stored in the *Student Model* as intermediate result. Once this process has been completed, the *Learning Style Calculation Module* reports back to the *Dynamic Student Modelling Module* which requests the *Dynamic Analysis Module* to check whether the results of the *Learning Style Calculation Module* differ significantly from the currently stored learning styles of the student in his/her cognitive profile and update the learning styles if required.

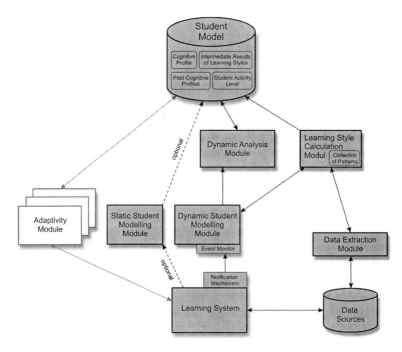

Fig. 1.1 Architecture for dynamic student modelling

In addition to dynamic student modelling, static student modelling is integrated in the architecture for providing an option to initialise the cognitive profile in the *Student Model* from the data of a questionnaire. The *Static Student Modelling Module*, which administers the learning style questionnaire, is called directly from the learning system, for example, when students register the first time, and stores the results of the questionnaire in the cognitive profile of the *Student Model*. These results are then used as the student's learning styles until information from the student's behaviour is received for fine-tuning and updating the learning styles.

The modules of the architecture are designed to be as independent as possible with respect to the learning system, so that they can be integrated in different systems. Only two modules are system-dependent: the *Data Extraction Module* aims at extracting relevant data from the data sources of the learning system (e.g., a database that includes logs of students' behaviour) and therefore has to consider the different structures of data sources in different learning systems. Furthermore, the *Notification Mechanism* has to be directly integrated in the learning system for sending notifications whenever a student performs an action in the learning system. In addition, a link to the *Static Student Modelling Module* has to be provided within the learning system for integrating static student modelling.

In order to use the information about learning styles identified through the proposed architecture for dynamic student modelling, adaptivity modules can be added to the learning system. These adaptivity modules can access the cognitive profile in the *Student Model* and use the information about students' learning styles, for example, for providing students with personalized recommendations and/or adaptive courses based on students' learning styles. The implementation of such an adaptivity module is described in Sect. 3.

In the following subsections, the modules of the architecture are described in more detail.

2.1 Static Student Modelling Module

The *Static Student Modelling Module* aims at providing an option for initialising the cognitive profile through the use of a questionnaire. Such a questionnaire enables a system to quickly gather information about students' learning styles, which can then be refined and updated through dynamic student modelling once students use the system for learning. Therefore, by combining static and dynamic student modelling, adaptivity can be provided right after a student filled out the questionnaire rather than having to wait until enough information from student's behaviour is available for calculating his/her learning styles.

The *Static Student Modelling Module* is called through a link that can be added in the learning system, for example, when students register in the system or for their first course. Once students click on this link, the *Static Student Modelling Module* presents them with the Index of Learning Styles questionnaire (Felder and Soloman 1997), a 44-item questionnaire that has been developed by Felder and Soloman in order to identify learning styles based on FSLSM. Once students filled out this questionnaire, the results, four values between +11 and −11 indicating the preference on each of the four learning style dimensions of FSLSM, are normalised to values between 0 and 1 and stored in the cognitive profile of the *Student Model*. These values are used as currently identified learning styles which are later refined and updated through dynamic student modelling. Students can choose not to fill out the questionnaire. In that case, no information is stored in the cognitive profile and dynamic student modelling is used to build and update information about students' learning styles from students' behaviour in the learning system.

2.2 Notification Mechanism

The *Notification Mechanism* is a system-dependent component which is integrated in the learning system and can be seen as the interface between the learning system and the *Dynamic Student Modelling Module*. The *Notification Mechanism* is responsible for notifying the *Dynamic Student Modelling Module* when a student is performing an action in the learning system. Actions are defined as visits of learning objects/activities so that when a student is going through the course, each learning object/activity that he/she is visiting is considered as an action. Whenever such an action occurs, the *Notification Mechanism* sends a message with the student ID and the course ID to the *Dynamic Student Modelling Module*.

2.3 Dynamic Student Modelling Module

The *Dynamic Student Modelling Module* is responsible for managing the dynamic student modelling process. This includes two activities. First, the *Dynamic Student Modelling Module* monitors students' activity levels, in terms of how many actions they perform, based on the messages received from the *Notification Mechanism*. Second, the *Dynamic Student Modelling Module* requests recalculations of students' learning styles once a student performed a predefined number of actions since the last recalculation of his/her learning styles. Such recalculations aim at considering students' recent behaviour in the calculation process of their learning styles and checking whether their behaviour still reflects the students' learning styles as stored in the cognitive profile of the *Student Model* or whether updates in the cognitive profile are required. Therefore, the *Dynamic Student Modelling Module* first requests a recalculation from the *Learning Style Calculation Module* and subsequently requests the *Dynamic Analysis Module* to check whether the newly calculated learning styles from the *Learning Style Calculation Module* differ significantly from the learning styles that are currently stored in the cognitive profile, considering cases of exceptional behaviour in students' actions, and update the learning styles in the cognitive profile if required.

2.4 *Learning Style Calculation Module*

The *Learning Style Calculation Module* aims at calculating students' learning styles from their behaviour in a learning system. This calculation is based on certain patterns of behaviour, which provide indications of students' learning styles. Such patterns can be, for example, the number of visits of particular types of learning objects/activities such as content, exercises, and quizzes, and the time spent on such types of learning objects/activities.

The *Learning Style Calculation Module* includes a collection of patterns where each pattern provides indications for identifying learning styles based on a particular learning style dimension of the FSLSM. Furthermore, information for each pattern is included that states how the pattern affects a certain learning style dimension (e.g., whether a high number of visits of exercises is an indication for an active or reflective learning style). Since different learning systems support different types of learning objects/activities, not all patterns can be used for each learning system and only the patterns that deal with types of learning objects/activities that are considered in the respective learning system are used in the calculation process. The collection of patterns can be extended in the case that a learning system considers types of learning objects/activities that are not included so far.

In order to get data about a student's behaviour with respect to each pattern that is considered in the learning system, the *Learning Style Calculation Module* sends a request to the *Data Extraction Module*, which then returns raw data for each available pattern. These raw data (e.g., the amount of times a student visited a certain type of learning object or the number of minutes a student spent on average on certain types of learning objects) are then transformed to ordered data based on predefined thresholds from literature. Ordered data are used to indicate whether the occurrence of a particular behaviour pattern is high, medium or low (or information about this pattern is not available). Subsequently, these ordered data are related to how the pattern affects a learning style of a student by using four values: 3 indicates that the student's behaviour gives a strong indication for the respective learning style, 2 indicates that the student's behaviour is average and therefore does not provide a specific hint, 1 indicates that the student's behaviour is in disagreement with the respective learning style, and 0 indicates that no information about the student's behaviour is available.

By summing up these values for each pattern that is relevant for a particular learning style dimension and dividing these values by the number of patterns that include available information for that dimension, a measure for the respective learning style dimension is calculated. This measure is then normalised on a range from 0 to 1, where 1 represents one pole of the dimension (e.g., active) and 0 represents the other pole of the dimension (e.g., reflective).

This calculation process is very similar to how learning styles are calculated in the learning style questionnaire but uses information from students' behaviour instead of asking students explicitly about their preferences. The approach has been introduced and successfully evaluated by Graf et al. (2009), using a predefined set of patterns for detecting learning styles in learning management systems.

The results of the *Learning Style Calculation Module* are four values between 0 and 1, each value representing the calculated learning style on each of the four dimension of the FSLSM. These results are stored in the Student Model as intermediate results, representing the students' current learning styles identified at one particular point of time from their behaviour while learning in the system. In the subsequent sections, these values will be referred as *ls_behaviour*. After the calculation and storage of these values is completed, the *Learning Style Calculation Module* notifies the *Dynamic Student Modelling Module*.

2.5 Data Extraction Module

The *Data Extraction Module* connects to the learning systems' database (or other sources of log data) and extracts data of available patterns in the learning system. Since the data extraction is dependent on the structure of the learning system's data sources and where particular data are located, this module is system-dependent and has to be adjusted to each learning system that integrates the introduced architecture.

Once the *Data Extraction Module* receives a request from the *Learning Style Calculation Module* to collect data from a particular student, it extracts and returns the data of the available patterns to the *Learning Style Calculation Module*.

2.6 Dynamic Analysis Module

This module is responsible for analysing how the learning styles calculated from students' recent behaviour by the *Learning Style Calculation Module* change over time and whether these changes should lead to a change in the learning styles stored in the students' cognitive profiles. For deciding whether such a revision should be done, two partially conflicting objectives have to be reached. On one hand, the currently stored information in the cognitive profile should reflect the current learning styles of students as good as possible and therefore should be updated as soon as a revision can be done. On the other hand, deviations of students' behaviour have to be considered and the student modelling approach should avoid situations where the learning styles of students are revised and then briefly afterwards this revision has to be reversed.

The *Dynamic Analysis Module* integrates an approach that has been introduced and evaluated by Graf and Kinshuk (2009). This approach uses the intermediate results (*ls_behaviour*) identified by the *Learning Style Calculation Module* as input data, representing the students' learning styles over time calculated based on their behaviour. In order to decide whether a learning style stored in the cognitive profile needs to be updated, three conditions have been formulated that have to be fulfilled. The first condition aims at updating students' learning styles as soon as a change in students' behaviour is noticed and therefore compares the currently stored learning style in the cognitive profile and the mean value of the last A identified learning styles (ls_behaviour), where an experiment by Graf and Kinshuk (2009) identified that 3 is a suitable number for A. The second and third conditions focus on detecting and considering deviations in terms of exceptional behaviour of students. The second condition looks into the difference between the currently identified learning style ($ls\_behaviour_t$) and the previously identified learning style ($ls\_behaviour_{t-1}$) in order to detect exceptional behaviour. Once exceptional behaviour has been detected, the third condition investigates whether the next identified learning style goes significantly towards the learning style stored in the cognitive profile or shows again exceptional behaviour (which then can indicate a change in a student's learning style rather than exceptional behaviour). If all conditions point to a change in the student's learning style rather than exceptional behaviour, the stored learning style in the cognitive profile is updated by the mean value of the past A identified learning styles.

2.7 Student Model

The *Student Model* aims at storing several types of information about students. First, it stores the cognitive profile of students, which includes the four values of students' learning styles based on the four dimensions of FSLSM. This information can be used by adaptivity modules, which can access the students' cognitive profiles and use the information in these profiles, for example, to provide students' with adaptive and personalized recommendations as well as with courses, learning objects, and/or learning activities that match students' learning styles.

Besides the cognitive profile, the *Student Model* also stores data about students' activity level, past data from the cognitive profile, intermediate results from the *Static Student Modelling Module* including data from the questionnaire, and intermediate results from the *Learning Style Calculation Module* which represent the identified learning styles over time based on students' behaviour.

3 Application of the Architecture in a Learning System

The above described architecture has been implemented for an online learning system. A *Notification Mechanism* has been integrated in the learning system and the *Data Extraction Module* has been adjusted to the learning system's data sources and the available patterns that can be extracted in the learning system. Furthermore, an *Adaptivity Module* has been developed that uses the information from the cognitive profile in order to make students aware of their learning styles as well as provide them with personalized suggestions on how to improve their learning based on the elements available in their courses.

In the following subsection, the types of courses and course elements of the learning system are described. The next subsection describes how the information in the cognitive profile is used to provide students with adaptive feedback.

3.1   Course Structure and Available Behaviour Patterns

The learning system includes two types of courses: courses that focus on assessment only and courses that focus on learning and assessment. The assessment-only courses consist of exercises, quizzes and a study guide. *Exercises* are mainly for practicing the learned material through theoretical or practical questions which are randomly composed and can therefore be used by the students as often as they want to practice. An exercise can consist of multiple parts where each part includes a question. After a student answered the question, his/her answer is automatically marked and feedback about the correct answer is provided. *Quizzes* are more comprehensive tasks which are intended to be solved by students at the end of a section or course. Students are usually given a certain time limit (e.g., 60 min) for solving all the theoretical and practical questions within the quiz. Once a student submitted the quiz, his/her answers are automatically marked and feedback about the correct answers is provided. The *study guide* is a page that includes information about a student's progress in the context of all the concepts of the course.

The courses for learning and assessment also include exercises, quizzes and a study guide but they additionally use elements for presenting learning material. Therefore, each course has chapters and each chapter consists of sections. Each chapter and section includes an *outline*, which consists of a short introduction, and chapter outlines additionally include a description of the learning objectives. Each section has a *lesson* which consists of several *pages of learning material, applied self-assessment questions* which are very practical oriented questions that allow students to apply the learned knowledge in practise, and *theoretical self-assessment questions* which are theoretical questions about the learned material. Furthermore, a section can include *activity-related questions* which facilitate experimentation by providing immediate feedback even to parts of students' answers. In addition, a section can have a *case study* which is a large practical problem with several steps to solve.

Table 1.1 provides an overview of the considered patterns based on the course elements mentioned above. The first column includes the names of the patterns and the second column provides a brief description of the patterns. The last three columns indicate which learning style is related with a high occurrence of the respective pattern. For example, an active learning style is associated with the pattern exercise_visits, meaning that a high number of visits of exercises indicates an active learning styles. The patterns and their indications are based on the learning style literature (Felder and Silverman 1988) as well as on the literature about detecting learning styles from behaviour patterns (Graf et al. 2009).

The patterns in Table 1.1 were considered in the collection of patterns in the *Learning Style Calculation Module* and the *Data Extraction Module* was built based on those patterns.

Table 1.1 Patterns of behaviour from course elements of the learning system[a]

Pattern name	Description of patterns	act/ref	sen/int	seq/glo
exercise_stay	avg. time spent on solving an exercise question	ref	sen	
exercise_visits	avg. number of attempts to solve an exercise question	act		
exercise_performance_ increase	avg. rate of grade increase on exercise questions	ref	sen	
exercise_performance	avg. final grade on exercise questions		sen	
exercise_stay_results	avg. amout of time spent for studying the feedback of exercise questions	ref	sen	
exercise_sequence_skip	number of time of skipping an exercise question[a]			glo
exercise_sequence_back	number of times of going back to a previous exercise question[a]			glo
quiz_sequence_revise	number of times of re-entering a quiz[a]		sen	
quiz_stay	percentage of time took on avg. for submitting a quiz		sen	
quiz_stay_results	avg. amount of time for studying the feedback of a quiz	ref	sen	
studyguide_visits	number of visits of the study guide[a]			glo
outline_visit	number of visits of outlines[a]			glo
outline_stay	avg. amount of time spent on outlines	ref		glo
content_visit	number of visits on content pages[a]	ref		glo
content_stay	avg. amount of time spent on content pages	ref		
content_back	number of times of re-visiting a content page[a]			glo
content_skip	number of times for skipping content pages[a]			glo
asa_solution_visit	number of visits of solutions of applied self-assessment questions[a]		sen	
asa_solution_stay	avg. amount of time spent on solutions of applied self-assessment questions	ref	sen	
tsa_solution_visit	number of visits of solutions of theoretical self-assessment questions[a]		sen	
tsa_solution_stay	avg. amount of time spent on solutions of theoretical self-assessment questions	ref	sen	
tsa_solution_back	number of re-visits of a solution in the same theoretical self-assessment page[a]		sen	glo
activityquestions_visit	number of visits of activity pages[a]	act	sen	
activityquestions_ instances	avg. number of attempts tried for each activity page	act	sen	
activityquesitons_stay	avg. amount of time spent on an attempt of activity-related question	ref	sen	
casestudy_visit_same	avg. number of visits of a case study question	act		
casestudy_visit_diff	percentage of solved case study questions		sen	seq
casestudy_stay	avg. amount of time spent on a case study question	ref	sen	

[a] Patterns marks with a which are related to parameters such as overall number of actions, solved questions etc

3.2   Providing Adaptive Feedback Based on Learning Styles

The purpose of student modelling is to identify and frequently update information about students which can then be used to provide students with personalized courses, learning material, learning objects/activities, and/or recommendations based on this identified information. Therefore, the introduced architecture is intended to be combined with *Adaptivity Modules* which access the student model, retrieve students' learning styles and use the information about students' learning styles to provide students with adaptivity. Such modules have strong interdependence with the learning system since they have to consider the characteristics of a course, such as the available types of learning objects/activities, in order to provide students with adaptive courses and/or recommendations.

An *Adaptivity Module* has been developed that aims at providing students with adaptive feedback based on their learning styles. This feedback is shown within the *study guide* and consists of three parts. First, students are presented with their learning styles on each of the four dimensions of FSLSM, as they have been identified through static and dynamic student modelling. A five-item scale is used for each learning style dimension, distinguishing for example between a strong active, moderate active, balanced, moderate reflective and strong reflective learning style. Second, each of the learning styles of a student (i.e., active or reflective; sensing or intuitive, etc.) is explained in more detail, pointing out typical characteristics, strengths and weaknesses of students with the respective learning style in a general learning context. Third, students are provided with personalized learning advices, dealing with suggestions on how to learn more effectively based on their individual learning styles and considering the types of learning objects available in the student's course, distinguishing between assessment-only courses and courses that focus on learning and assessment.

4   Discussion and Conclusions

This chapter introduced an architecture for dynamic student modelling of learning styles based on the Felder-Silverman learning style model, aiming at building and frequently updating a cognitive profile of students' learning styles based on students' behaviour in an online course. For a faster initialisation of the cognitive profile, a static student modelling approach in form of a learning style questionnaire has been added to the architecture which can be used by students optionally.

The architecture is developed in a generic way so that it can be integrated into different learning systems. Only two of the modules in the architecture require modifications if integrated in different learning systems. These two modules are the *Notification Mechanism* which sends notifications to the dynamic student modelling approach once a student conducts an action in the learning system as well as the *Data Extraction Module* which requires information on how and where data are stored in the learning system. Furthermore, *Adaptivity Modules* can be added to the architecture which aim at providing adaptivity and personalization in the learning system based on the identified learning styles of students, and are therefore system-dependent as well.

The application of the introduced architecture has been demonstrated for an online learning system, considering the different types of courses and types of learning objects/activities within this system. Furthermore, an *Adaptivity Module* has been developed which presents students with adaptive feedback by making students aware of their learning styles, providing explanations on each learning style of a student in a general learning context, as well as presenting students with personalized advices on how to learn more effectively given the learning styles of the student and the available learning objects/activities in the student's course.

Adding dynamic student modelling of learning styles to learning systems has two advantages over using a static approach: (1) it enables the system to incrementally learn students' learning styles and identify exceptional behaviour of students which can be excluded from the updating process, and (2) it makes it possible to identify changes in students' learning styles over time and updating the cognitive profile respectively. Both advantages lead to more accurate information about students' learning styles and therefore facilitate more effective adaptivity in learning systems. By developing an architecture that can be easily used by different learning systems with few adjustments to the respective systems, dynamic student modelling can enable these systems to provide adaptivity based on students' learning styles, for which benefits such as less study time to achieve on average same grades (e.g., Graf and Kinshuk 2007) and higher student satisfaction (e.g., Popescu 2010) have been demonstrated.

Future work will deal with developing and providing additional adaptivity modules for the online learning system described in this paper, such as automatically modifying courses, learning objects, and/or learning activities in order to make them fit to students' learning styles. Furthermore, the collection of patterns is planned to be extended (e.g., with patterns about students' navigational behaviour in a learning system as well as with patterns related to additional types of learning objects/activities) and the application of the architecture to other learning systems such as learning management systems is planned. In addition, a qualitative evaluation is planned in order to investigate students' satisfaction with the provided adaptivity.

Acknowledgements   The authors acknowledge the support of NSERC, iCORE, Xerox, and the research related gift funding by Mr. A. Markin.

References

Bajraktarevic, N., Hall, W., & Fullick, P. (2003). Incorporating learning styles in hypermedia environment: Empirical evaluation. In P. de Bra, H. C. Davis, J. Kay & M. Schraefel (Eds.), *Proceedings of the Workshop on Adaptive Hypermedia and Adaptive Web-Based Systems* (pp. 41–52). Nottingham, UK: Eindhoven University.

Brusilovsky, P. (1996). Methods and techniques of adaptive hypermedia. *User Modeling and User-Adapted Interaction, 6* (2–3), 87–129.

Carver, C.A., Howard, R.A., & Lane, W.D. (1999). Addressing different learning styles through course hypermedia. *IEEE Transactions on Education, 42* (1), 33–38.

Cha, H.J., Kim, Y.S., Park, S.H., Yoon, T.B., Jung, Y.M., & Lee, J.-H. (2006). Learning style diagnosis based on user interface behavior for the customization of learning interfaces in an intelligent tutoring system. In M. Ikeda, K. D. Ashley & T.-W. Chan (Eds.), *Proceedings of the 8th International Conference on Intelligent Tutoring Systems, Lecture Notes in Computer Science* (pp. 513–524). Berlin, Heidelberg: Springer, Vol. 4053.

Felder, R.M., & Silverman, L.K. (1988). Learning and teaching styles in engineering education. *Engineering Education, 78* (7), 674–681.

Felder, R.M., & Soloman, B.A. (1997). *Index of Learning Styles questionnaire.* Retrieved 14 March, 2011, from http://www.engr.ncsu.edu/learningstyles/ilsweb.html.

García, P., Amandi, A., Schiaffino, S., & Campo, M. (2007). Evaluating Bayesian networks' precision for detecting students' learning styles. *Computers & Education, 49* (3), 794–808.

Graf, S., & Kinshuk (2007). Providing adaptive courses in learning management systems with respect to learning styles. In G. Richards (Ed.), *Proceedings of the world conference on e-learning in corporate, government, healthcare, and higher education (e-Learn 2007)* (pp. 2576–2583). Chesapeake, VA: AACE Press.

Graf, S., & Kinshuk (2009). An approach for dynamic student modelling of learning styles. *Proceedings of the International Conference on Exploratory Learning in Digital Age (CELDA 2009)* (pp. 462–465). Rome, Italy: IADIS press.

Graf, S., Kinshuk, & Liu, T.-C. (2009). Supporting teachers in identifying students' learning styles in learning management systems: An automatic student modelling approach. *Educational Technology & Society, 12* (4), 3–14.

Khan, F.A., Graf, S., Weippl, E.R., & Tjoa, A.M. (2010). Identifying and Incorporating Affective States and Learning Styles in Web-based Learning Management Systems. *International Journal of Interaction Design & Architectures, 9–10*, 85–103.

Kinshuk, & Lin, T. (2004). Cognitive profiling towards formal adaptive technologies in web-based learning communities. *International Journal of WWW-based Communities, 1* (1), 103–108.

Kuljis, J., & Liu, F. (2005). A comparison of learning style theories on the suitability for elearning. In M. H. Hamza (Ed.), *Proceedings of the IASTED Conference on Web Technologies, Applications, and Services* (pp. 191–197). Calgary, Alberta: ACTA Press.

Lin, T. (2007). *Cognitive Trait Model for adaptive learning environments.* PhD thesis, Massey University, Palmerston North, New Zealand.

Özpolat, E., & Akar, G.B. (2009). Automatic detection of learning styles for an e-learning system. *Computers & Education, 53* (2), 355–367.

Popescu, E. (2010). Adaptation provisioning with respect to learning styles in a web-based educational system: An experimental study. *Journal of Computer Assisted Learning, 26* (4), 243–257.

Shang, Y., Shi, H., & Chen, S.-S. (2001). An intelligent distributed environment for active learning. *ACM Journal of Educational Resources in Computing, 1* (2), 1–17.

Chapter 2
SQAR: An Annotation-Based Study Process to Enhance the Learner's Personal Learning

Belkacem Mostefai, Faiçal Azouaou, and Amar Balla

1 Introduction

Adding annotations to learning objects has grown into a habit at learners. The main goal of most learners for annotating is to memorize his ideas directly on the learning objects to reuse them later. Available annotation tools were not conceived with the aim of assisting learners to succeed in their learning activities. In our approach, the annotation tool can be designed to help the learner to learn more efficiently and to make sure his learning evolution in both knowledge and ability. The target is to study, propose and carry out a new process that use the learner's personnel annotations to enhance his learning activity. So, in order to provide students with such process, we integrate a learning process SQAR steps into a web-based annotation tool WebAnnot. This will enable learners to create their personal annotations directly on their pedagogical documents within their web based learning environment.

This paper is organized as follows: in first section we present the annotation practice, then we describe the learner's personnel annotation. After, the web annotation tools are briefly presented. In the fifth section, we present our approach: the formalism of learner's personnel annotation, the architecture of SQAR process and its modeling. Subsequently, we describe, in the sixth section, the implementation of WebAnnot as a prototype of SQAR process. Then we present, in the seventh section, the experimentation participants, materials, method and disputed results. Next, we give a brief overview of related work. We finish with a summary and an outlook on future research tasks with respect to this topic.

B. Mostefai (✉) • F. Azouaou • A. Balla
National High School for Computer Science (ESI), Algiers, Algeria
e-mail: b_mostefai@esi.dz; f_azouaou@esi.dz; a_balla@esi.dz

P. Isaias et al. (eds.), *Towards Learning and Instruction in Web 3.0: Advances in Cognitive and Educational Psychology*, DOI 10.1007/978-1-4614-1539-8_2, © Springer Science+Business Media, LLC 2012

2   The Annotation Practice

In common parlance, the annotation is a critical or explanatory note, which is written on a text. In computing, the annotation is a concept (predefined) attached to a piece of paper used for search and retrieval information. Formally, annotation can be defined as a value adding note or marking that is linked to an existent information object, representing a record of interaction between the reader and the information object (MacMullen 2005). In the web environment, annotation is a fundamental aspect of hypertext, it increases not only the overall girth of the hypertext, but also its value (Marshall 1998a).

Several studies examined the practice of making annotations on paper as well as the use of annotations and their functionality in the context of hypertext. For example, (Ovsiannikov et al. 1999) carried out a survey to study how people make annotations in an academic research environment. They summarized the joint uses of annotations as "to remember, to think, to clarify and to share".

3   Learner's Personnel Annotation

In pedagogical context, there is no formal definition about the learner's personal annotation, but we find that few authors, like (Marshall 1998b), have attempted to study the characteristics of annotations among students. We also find the work of (Mille 2005) documents; the author considers the annotation as a set of attributes organized in distinct but complementary categories.

Another study of the annotation (Azouaou 2006) which isn't dedicated to learners, but it more relevant and closer to our context, it is the teacher's annotation, where the author concludes that the annotation can be an activity and an object added by the user in a material and also a creative activity of the object annotation.

4   Web Annotation Tools

Generally, according to a study (Xin et al. 2005) that focuses on Web users' explicit needs for personal annotation tools, the users' annotation (especially learners) needs in the Web environment are similar to those in the paper environment. Thus, to harness the power of new technologies and give electronic documents some of the same note-taking possibilities as paper documents, various kinds of annotation tools and many annotation systems are developed. So, the personal annotations constitute the vast majority of the annotations that Web users, learners included, currently make on the Web (Marshall and Brush 2004).

Considering leaner's annotation's activity in educative application can have many benefits for learners such as providing them with personalized annotation. However, in order to enhance learners' personal learning – firstly by leading theme to more undressing and making good annotations on the work's pedagogic document, secondly by providing them with personalized recommendations and advice – we proposed, in our approach, the process SQAR that supply such functionalities in WebAnnot a web annotation tool.

5   SQAR Process: An Annotation Based Pedagogical Process

Our approach comes from the perspective that annotation, created by the learner on his documents during his pedagogical documents, is beneficial and can be used to enhance his learning. Our goal is to propose a pedagogical process based on the learner's personal annotations. To achieve this, we started by analyzing earlier works related to the use of annotation in pedagogical activities and we have identified two kinds of problems:

- The first problem is how to design a learner's dedicated annotation formalism.
- The second one is how to use the annotation activity as a pedagogical activity in a learner process in order to enhance the learning efficiency.

In order to give a solution for the first problem, we reuse the learner's personal annotation formalism proposed by Azouaou (2006) (see Sect. 5.1), while for the second one we reuse the functionalities proposed by other personal annotation systems. In particular, we are interested by the teaching aspect functionality, so we propose a new architecture of an annotation tool that integrates the SQAR process steps (see Sect. 5.2).

5.1   Learner's Personal Annotation Formalism

The following table shows our learner's personal annotation formalism. We identify three facets with their attributes, the categorization of the annotation attributes in facets is inspired from Mille (2005), and then the facet's attributes are inspired from Azouaou (2006).

5.2   Architecture of SQAR Process

We believe that the annotations made by learners do not only reflect their personal interpretation of the document content, but can be adopted by learners within the context of a global process to learn more efficiently and to make sure their learning evolution in both knowledge and ability. Starting from this, we conceive the SQAR process.

To highlight the main expected features in SQAR process, we study some annotation systems among the most popular (YAWAS (Denoue 2000), Amaya (Koivunen and Swick 2001), iMarkup (2004) … etc.). The result of this study shows that no annotation system is dedicated to the learners, however, these systems offer functions related to the annotation's management (creation, sharing, research … etc.). Consequently, we distinguish two modules in the architecture of our process:

- The *"Annotation's Management"* module. The functions included in this module are generic ones such as research and sharing annotations …, these functions usually exist in several annotation systems.
- The *"Assisted Annotation"* module. This module deals with the pedagogical aspect.

To introduce the pedagogical aspect in the *"Assisted Annotation"* module, we propose the pedagogical *SQAR process* (Survey, Question, Annotation and Review). It is an adaptation of the famous study method *SQ3R*, an individual learning technique (Huang et al. 2008). First we will model the SQAR process' steps (see Sect. 5.3) then include it into the *"Assisted Annotation"* module. We present here the architecture including SQAR process.

Our model consists of these main entities: (a) the user who is also the annotator (learner), (b) the document (web page),(c) the annotation interface which includes the two modules: "Assisted Annotation" and "Annotation Management", (d) local and distant database.

5.3 Modeling of SQAR Process

To make sure that learners could effectively get knowledge and progress in their learning during the learning activities, we propose the SQAR process for enabling students to access and familiarize themselves with course content and enhance the quality of their annotations. Definitions and modeling steps of SQAR are listed below:

Step 1 – Survey: In this step, learners quickly survey the material, to get an overview of the assigned topic. For modeling this step, we use the online free web service (GreatSummary online web service), which can automatically generate a short summary of a web page. This summary presents a significant gain of time and efficiency when the learner must regularly fly over some texts or documents when he doesn't have enough time to read all sites that he/she is interested on.

Step 2 – Question: Once students have completed their survey, they use their general understanding of the topic to generate a list of questions, which should serve to direct their efforts and focus their attention during a more thorough reading of the material. For modeling this task, we have two choices,

- In the first one, the system automatically generates questions, which are related to the text.

– In the second one, learner is free to put (use his intellectual efforts) the questions which help him to focus his attention.

Step 3 – Annotation: In this step, learners read the material more thoroughly, making a concerted effort to find the answers to questions they generated in step 2. During the reading phase, students can and should make annotations (such as highlighting, underlining, emphatic text or answers to their questions within the text….). By annotating the text with notes based on paraphrasing or summarizing, students not only increase their ability to recall key pieces of information, but also deepen their understanding. For modeling this task, we propose that the annotation system provides the learner with annotation forms in a single bar.

Step 4 – Review: In the last step, in order to consolidate their knowledge, students need to review it thoroughly. This step can also help learners to find any gaps in their knowledge and to refine any annotations completed earlier. With an aim of helping learners to check and evolve themselves in theirs knowledge, we propose to automate this step by using a questionnaire for evaluation of learner, afterwards we give him automatically the adequate recommendations. For learner's evaluation, the questionnaire used is composed of both **survey** and **quiz** questions. The reason for using a composite questionnaire was to accurately assess learner's knowledge and to which extent he can use it to answer the given questions. Indeed, a questionnaire compound is considered as an "advanced organizer (AO)" used to measure the degree of understanding of an individual of an e-learning course (Huang et al. 2008). The survey questions are depending on the possible choice in second step quoted above:

– If we opt for the first choice (see *step2 – Question*), the system will answer questions and generate *survey questions* obtained from the document's content on which the learner is working, so the learner's responses of the survey questionnaire were classified into one of the three groups: does not understand, understands to some extent (medium), and fully understands. Each group was assigned a score, "does not understand" was worth one point, "medium" was worth three points, and "understands fully" was worth five points. The score of a survey type questionnaire was calculated using the following formula:

$$x = \frac{No\_Understand\_Items \times 1 + medium\_understand\_Items \times 3 + Full\text{-}understand\_items \times 5}{The\ number\ of\ the\ survey\ items \times 5}$$

– Otherwise (second choice), where there is no questionnaire, the system asks the learner to point out his own understanding degree by checking one of the three choices: "does not understand", "understand to some extent" or "fully understands". So the value of score x is assigned directly.

– The other type of questionnaire (quiz questions) examines the learner with a set of questions on the area of reading material. Then there is no effective strategy to make a good quiz questionnaire covering the topic's content.

Table 2.1 Learner's personal annotation formalism

Personal annotation's facets for learner	– Episodic	– User (Learner)
		– Date
		– Place
		– Remembrance situation
		– Learning situation
		• Domain
		• Studied notion
		• Level of study
	– Cognitive	– Physical Anchor
		• Document URL
		• Location of annotation in the document
		– Visual form
		– Syntactic Anchor
	– Semantics	– Free Content
		– Objective (s)
		• Objective (s) of active reading
		• Objective (s) of memory
		– Strength
		• Importance
		• Confidence
		– State
		– Lifetime

Furthermore, we believe that it is better to replace the score calculated from a quiz questions by another annotation score that will be calculated according to the learner's annotation. More precisely, we propose to combine the attributes "*Confidence and Importance*" in each annotation (See Sect. 5.1, Table 2.1, semantics' facet) by a value reflecting its semantics (such as *absolute-confidence* by value 5, *null-confidence* by value 1, *average-confidence* by value 3…). Then the score concerning the quiz questions can also be calculated using the following formula:

$$y = \frac{1}{(annotations\ number)^2} \times \sum_{One\ annotation}^{All\ Annotation} \left(Value_{Confidenace} * Value_{Importance} \right)$$

Depending on the score **x** and **y** with α coefficient, which is adjusted to the desired precision, the composite score **r** is calculated as follows:

$$r = a * x + (1 - a) * y$$

Depending on the value of "*r*", the system determines the exact learner's familiarizing degree with the document's topic, and it provides him with appropriate recommendation. Information's recommendation technique can identify and provide

Table 2.2 The recommendation's strategy according to the score r in PAML model

Value of score "r"	Interpretation (understanding degree the topic)	Recommendations based on		
		Expert annotations	Public annotations: annotator/ numbers of these annotations	Cloud (tag) of words from annotated texts
$0.2\alpha \leq r <0.3$	The learner is very unfamiliar with the given topic	Links to similar documents annotated with **abounding annotations**	Shows **ten** annotators sorted by number of published annotations	Large cloud
$0.3 \leq r <0.7$	The learner has some understanding and knowledge about the topic	Links to similar documents annotated with **medium annotations**	Shows **five** annotators sorted by number of published annotations	Medium cloud
$0.7 \leq r \leq 1$	The learner fully understands the given topic	Links to similar documents annotated with **brief annotations**	Shows annotators who publish less annotations	Small cloud

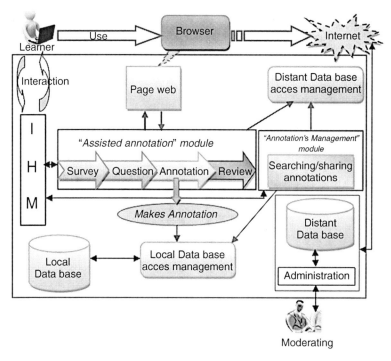

Fig. 2.1 The architecture of SQAR process

automatically useful information for the learner. There are two different cases to assess the learner's knowledge, the first one is to use annotation system with a moderator and the second one is to use an independent annotation system (autonomous system).

Case 1 – Annotation system with moderator: When reviewing the learners shared notes, the moderator (see Sect. 5.2, Fig. 2.1) may add links to the learner's documents, the links themes vary according to the different fields of knowledge relevant to the learners. The annotations can be classified according to their scope and depth as being either *brief, medium and abounding:*

- The knowledge in brief annotations is dense-based information, rich in implication and concise.
- The knowledge in abounding annotations is more detailed, more fully explained, expansive and would be easier to understand by readers who are less familiar with the topic (Huang et al. 2008).
- The knowledge in medium annotations is between the brief en abounding annotations according the suggestion of the expert annotators.

Then the moderator can make an agreement with experts in each field to explicitly annotate on the meantime the interesting documents on each area so that each document will be annotated in three versions: brief, medium, and abounding annotations.

Thus, based on each learner's performance (according to the value of score r), student would then be automatically provided with appropriates recommendations. The recommendation will be sent to the learner according to the strategy presented in the following table:

Case 2 – Autonomous annotation system (without moderator): In this case, the documents would not be annotated by experts, so the recommendations will be made in the same way except that there are no brief, medium or abounding annotations.

6   Webannot a Prototype of PAML

To validate our proposals, we have developed WebAnnot a prototype of SQAR as an extension for the Firefox browser. Then, Firefox's browser interface will incorporate the annotations' WebAnnot tool bar (see Fig. 2.2). The learner clicks the button named "WebAnnot" to start an annotation session (session is used to identify user's activities in the process with date, time and page's URL) providing information on the context learning (assess the attributes of episodic facets, see Table 2.1). Then, new buttons are displayed as shown in Fig. 2.3. The button "Start" enables to

Fig. 2.2   The toolbar WebAnnot interface

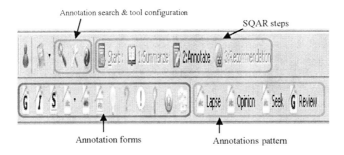

Fig. 2.3   WebAnnot: learner's annotations tools

begin the SQAR process, the other buttons are relating to other functions such as annotation searching and sharing.

To annotate with WebAnnot, the learner must click on the buttons "start", so other buttons corresponding to the different SQAR steps are displayed. Then, the button "summarize" provides in new page an automatic summary of the current page, the second step involves the questioning is letting for learner's intellectual effort, the third button displays annotation's forms, and the last button will open a new tab containing the recommendations suitable for learners. To create an annotation manually learner selects the transition to annotate. Then, he chose the shape and form semantics appears, the student completed the form and record annotation (see Fig. 2.4). If a pattern exists learner may create an annotation-based pattern (semi-automatic annotation), to make it pass the selection then selects the pattern annotation. To create a pattern annotation learner chooses the form and the target patron, it is recorded last. The intended use of patterns uses is to allow the learner to create patterns (models) annotations and use them immediately to annotate documents.

Regarding recommendation, the system will first calculate the score of the learner to evaluate his level. Subsequently, it queries the server to recover the recommendations according to the score calculated, and then a new page will open with appropriate recommendations (see Fig. 2.5).

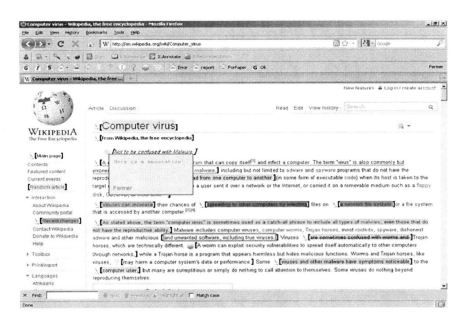

Fig. 2.4 A web page annotated with WebAnnot

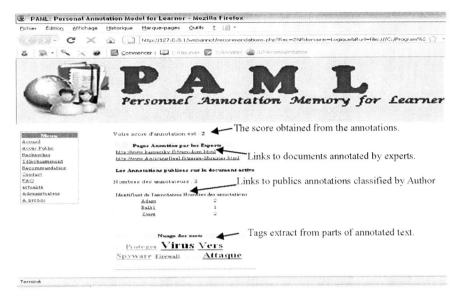

Fig. 2.5   Recommandation page automatically generate by WebAnnot

7   Experimentation

The experimentation goal is to compare the results of learners after studying the same documents (lessons in web format) in three different situations:

– *Situation 1:* studying with annotation by using of WebAnnot tool (in this case the annotation activity is a part of the SQAR process steps).
– *Situation 2:* studying with annotation without using WebAnnot (no SQAR process), so we have developed a simple annotation tool made for making textual annotations.
– *Situation 3:* studying without annotations.

7.1   Participants, Materials and Method

Thirty undergraduate students participated in various tests of this experimentation; we separated the students into three groups of ten persons in order to examine them in the three situations described above. Thus:

– Group A: Studying in the *Situation 1*.
– Group B: Studying in the *Situation 2*.

– Group C: Studying in the *Situation 3*. This Group is constituted of learners who
  are not used to annotate during their learning activities.

We trained the group of students that meet the Group C learners who are not or
rarely used the annotation activity during their learning while the rest of the students, whom identified their annotation habit as medium or high, were assigned
randomly to their groups.

To give more value to the experimentation, each group is examined in his situation several times using several tests, therefore we have prepared some documents related to different subjects but they are all in linked to the learners' study
themes. For each document we prepared a combined "multiple choice quizzes"
with maximum score of 20. In regard to the group A which needs access to the
distant database server (see Fig. 2.1), we have already alimented it using annotated documents which are similar to documents that students are used during the
experimentation.

8   Results

During the experimentation, five different tests are performed. First, students read,
a single document, depending on the situation we have previously set for each
group. Then they are asked to answer the related QCM.

We present below the results of a single test and then the overall results.

In the first test, the following table shows the number of learners in groups
according to their results (note/20: score obtained after replying the QCM questions
concerned the studied document), Thus, each result is considered:

– Good: if the score is higher than fifteen,
– Middle: if the score is between ten and fifteen,
– Weak: if the score is less than ten.

Most of the learners in Group A have obtained good results, while less than half
of students in group B, have good results, while in group C only one learner has
good results.

Similarly, if we analyze the results for all the tests (see Table 2.3) we note that
group A has better results, in many good and/or average scores, than the group B
and C. The latter has the worst scores.

Figure 2.6 shows the number of learners by group according to their results, but
this time we took for each learner, his average score in all tests, then we conduct a
classification according to his average score.

The figure below shows the consensus of sorted out average scores in each group,
this graph displays a comparison between the students according to the method followed during this investigation.

Table 2.3 Number of students by group depending on the results type

Results	Number of students		
	Group A	Group B	Group C
Good (score ≥ 15)	6	4	1
Middle (10 ≤ score < 15)	3	4	4
Weak (score < 10)	1	2	5

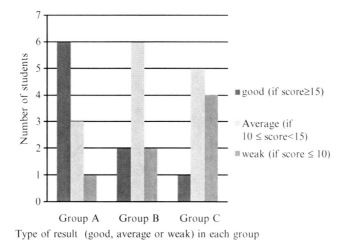

Type of result (good, average or weak) in each group

Fig. 2.6 Number of students classified according result type

9 Discussion

An interesting result comes out from our experimentation, is that the way followed by the learner to study (read) a handout has an important role on its concentration and its general understanding of the document to be studied:

- Group C learners, who don't use any technique or method for reading the documents offered in different tests, are less effective comparing to Group B learners who use the annotation activity.
- Group B learners are often less effective comparing to Group A learners who follow the SQAR process.

In general, we can explain the advantage of Group A versus Group B, and both versus Group C, either in terms of numbers of students who are classified good (Table 2.3 and Fig. 2.6) or in terms of overall consensus of their average scores (Fig. 2.7), by the following arguments:

- Group B learners use annotation activity by putting annotations on several passages and/or paragraph.... These annotations allow them to concentrate better

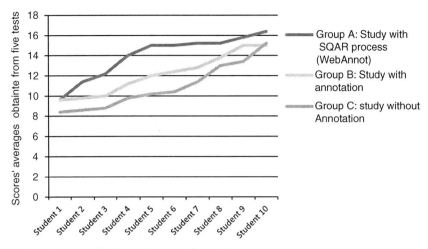

Students classified by order ascending to theirs averages scores

Fig. 2.7 Consensus of scores averages at students according to group study method: SQAR process, with and without annotation activity

and learn more concepts and ideas during the document reading, so they are better memorized comparing to Group C learners.

– The results of Group A are better than of Group B, because the learners of the first one are studying their documents in a more detailed and efficient way compared with those of the second group, they followed the SQAR process steps that requires them a lot more effort:

- Reading the summary of the studied document
- Answering the related questions
- Annotating the document
- Consult the recommendation page (see Fig. 2.5) that enable them to see their colleagues shared annotations (see Sect. 5.3 – step 5).

Finally, we can confirm that the process SQAR helps learners to work handouts effectively for their learning. This is due to the fact that that this process is inspired by the validated pedagogical method QA3R method (Marshall 1998a).

10   Related Work

In this section, we first compare the SQAR process with two other similar models, which use the annotation within a learning framework. Then we compare WebAnnot with some other prototypes and tools of annotation system. Several Models have been based on annotations; the most relevant to our project are Mille (2005) and Azouaou (2006).

Table 2.4 Comparison between WebAnnot and some prototypes

Prototype Canon	IMarkup (Marshal 1998b)	Amaya 2001 (Mille 2005)	Yawas for IE 2000 (Ovsiannikov et al. 1999)	WebAnnot 2010
Pedagogic aspect	✗	✗	✗	✓
Typing of annotation	✓	✓	✗	✓
The sharing of the annotations	✗	✓	✗	✓
The research by annotations	✓	✓	✓	✓
Semiautomatic annotation	✗	✗	✗	✓

The model of (Azouaou 2006) focuses on teacher's annotation in order to use it as knowledge's management tool for the teacher. This model has several similarities with our model (architecture of SQAR process); first, they both are dedicated to educational. Secondly, they both are aimed to document annotation, the two approaches aim at providing semantic annotation. Thirdly, they are both designed to a personal use. In the other hand, there are the following differences; first, whereas teacher's annotation model is dedicated for teachers, then SQAR is dedicated for learners. Secondly, the model of teacher's annotation is based only on the annotation, while SQAR is a specific process to improve the efficiently of the learners learning.

In (Huang et al. 2008) the authors propose a cooperative learning environment that uses the annotation services on handheld devices. The similarities between SQAR and ubiquitous is the use of pedagogical method, in Ubiquitous the SQ3R study method is introduced during the individual study phase of cooperative learning activities, but we use and modeling the same method improved to SQAR.

To compare our prototype WebAnnot with other prototype and annotation tools we studied some annotation system among the most popular (YAWAS (Denoue 2000), Amaya (Koivunen and Swick 2001), iMarkup (2004) .... etc.). The result of this study (see Table 2.4) shows the novelty and the advantage provided by our prototype over some existing prototypes.

11   Conclusion and Future Work

The purpose of this paper is to describe SQAR a new annotation-based study process to support the learner in his learning. We implemented this process as a personal web annotation tool, WebAnnot, by reason of enhancing the learner personal learning in the web environment. The evaluation and the comparison of our process with other study methods showed its very important aid and positive effect on the learner personal learning efficiently.

With the SQAR process the learner will become an active reader of his web based pedagogical documents. The practice of interactive annotation (third step of

SQAR process) allows more powerful and more effective reading for a better understanding such as the annotation is based on a specific formalism, which describes perfectly the characteristic of learner's annotation at three different facets: episodical, cognitive, and semantic.

WebAnnot (the initial prototype of SQAR) shows interesting results to allow supporting the learner abilities at best. Annotation will help the learner to develop his capacity of memorizing and reflective reading, while the recommendations (see Sect. 5.3 – Table 2.2) ensure the assistance of learner for evolving most quickly in his learning activities. Indeed, the architecture of SQAR process has a specific annotation system that is based on four principal parts: User (annotator), document (web page), annotation's interface (SQAR steps, research, sharing…), local and distant databases.

Generally, the findings of the superiority of the students' whom guided by SQAR process showed several factors, such as personal annotation and recommendation, that enhance the learner's personal learning. The main advantage of our process is that it enables the learner's improvement of understanding and memorization of the document they are working on, indeed, according to the experiment results of students whom used the Web annotation, the proposed process study methods can enable learners to engage with documents in a way that aligns with observed practice.

The appreciation of our study process SQAR and its prototype will continue, with more longitudinal studies for better understanding the learner's activity. This will also build up an effective resource for use in the teaching activity as well as for those studying the teaching methods and processes. Therefore, in the next phase of our research, we aim to reach a larger learner population in the experimentation to generalize the obtained results. Further work would include also the integration of our model in an e-Learning platform such as moodle.

References

Xin Fu Tom Ciszek, Gary Marchionini, Paul Solomon; "Annotating the Web: An Exploratory Study of Web Users" Needs for Personal Annotation Tools ASIST Annual Meeting, Charlotte, NC (October 28–November 2, 2005).

Marshall, C., Brush, A. J. (2004). Exploring the relationship between personal and public annotations. JCDL '04 (pp. 349–357).

MacMullen, W. J. (2005). Annotation as Process, Thing, and Knowledge: Multi-domain studies of structured data annotation. ASIST Annual Meeting, Charlotte, NC (October 28–November 2, 2005).

Marshall, C. (1998a). Toward an ecology of hypertext annotation. Proceedings of ACM Hypertext '98, Pittsburgh, PA (June 20–24, 1998) pp. 40–49.

Ovsiannikov, I. A., Arbib, M. A., McNeill, T. H. (1999). Annotation Technology. International Journal of Human-Computer Studies, 50(4): 329–362.

Mille, D. "Modèles et outils logiciels pour l'annotation sémantique de documents pédagogiques", Thèse. Département informatique. Grenoble, Université Joseph-Fourier.p. 173 pages. Sous la direction de C. Desmoulins et J.-p. Peyrin.2005.

Marshall, C. (1998b) "The future of annotation in a digital (paper) world". Paper presented at the 35th Annual GSLIS Clinic: Successes and Failures of Digital Libraries, University of Illinois at Urbana-Champ.

Azouaou, F. " modèles et outils d'annotations pour une mémoire personnelle de l'enseignant", Thèse de doctorat de l'Université Joseph Fourier de Grenoble, octobre 2006.

Huang, Y.-M., Huang, T.-C., & Hsieh, M.-Y. (2008). "Using annotation services in a ubiquitous Jigsaw cooperative learning environment". Pedagogical Technology & Society, 11 (2), 3–15.

GreatSummary online web service, Url: http://www.greatsummary.com/.

Denoue. L, "De la création à la capitalisation des annotations dans un espace personnel d'informations", Université de Savoie. 159. Sous la direction de L. Vignollet. 2000.

Koivunen & Swick (2001) "Metadata Based Annotation Infrastructure offers Flexibility and Extensibility for Collaborative Applications and Beyond" Marja-Riitta KOIVUNEN, Ralph R. SWICK World Wide Web Consortium MIT Laboratory for Computer Science. Url: http://www.ra.ethz.ch/CDstore/www6/Technical/Paper189/Paper189.html.

iMarkup-Solutions-Inc. (2004) iMarkup Client. Vista, California, USA. Url: http://www.imarkup.com/.

Chapter 3
Online Formative Assessment in a Medical PBL-Curriculum

Building a Didactic Metadata Layer

Stefan P. Minder, Felix M. Schmitz, and Sissel Guttormsen Schär

1 Introduction

Assessments are formative if, on the one hand, they influence the way of learning by iteratively validating the learning activities with the learning goals by one's self (Black and Wiliam 1998; Leung and Mohan 2004). In that respect, the achievement of self-regulated learning is a desirable goal (Mc Donald and Boud 2003). On the other hand, the formative aspect also aims at adequate teaching: Tutors need to be aware of their students' performances at formative assessments (FAs), and given that they are informed, they should modify their teaching by addressing knowledge and comprehension deficits (Bell and Cowie 2001). Crucial are also the cognitive processes induced by the feedback on a student's performance (Buck et al. 2010). This feedback is conventionally given by the tutor in written or spoken form. In aiming for the effects conducive to learning, Nicol and Macfarlane-Dick (2006) place feedback quality at the center of their considerations, and differentiate between seven feedback principles holding different formative impacts, i.e. clarify how good performance is, facilitate self-assessment, deliver high quality feedback information, encourage teacher and peer dialogue, encourage positive motivation and self-esteem, provide opportunities to close the gap, and use feedback to improve teaching.

The current FAs in the medical curriculum at the University of Bern (Switzerland), however, do not meet these requirements for two reasons. Firstly, our current FAs only take place in the form of paper and pencil based self-tests with open questions accompanied by standard solutions. Therefore a particular iterative validation of the learning process is not really supported. Secondly, the tutors have no access to how their students score in these assessments, and therefore, cannot give any feedback.

S.P. Minder (✉) • F.M. Schmitz • S.G. Schär
Institute of Medical Education, Medical Faculty of the University of Bern,
CH-3010, Bern, Switzerland
e-mail: minder@iml.unibe.ch; schmitz@iml.unibe.ch; guttormsen@iml.unibe.ch

P. Isaias et al. (eds.), *Towards Learning and Instruction in Web 3.0: Advances in Cognitive and Educational Psychology*, DOI 10.1007/978-1-4614-1539-8_3,
© Springer Science+Business Media, LLC 2012

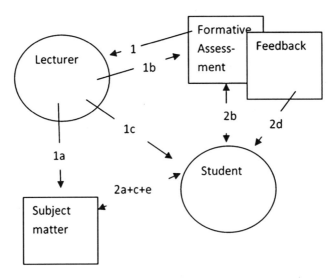

Fig. 3.1 The lecturer prepares the learning material (1a), writes questions for FA as well as their ready-made feedbacks (1b) and later gives the lecture (1c). The student processes the learning contents (2a), answers the FA (2b), again interacting with the learning contents (2c), receives automated feedback on his/her performance in the FA (2d) which again confronts him/her with the learning contents (2e)

We pose the question of how the requirements for FAs, can be expressed in our medical curriculum, with its special circumstances: its problem-based approach with tutorials in small groups as well as plenary lectures with over 100 students. In order to set the stage for how to optimize our FAs, both the tutors and the bachelor students at our medical faculty were questioned about the use and the perceived effects of current FAs, as well as expectations for future FAs.

The individual grading of the performance in FAs by personal feedback is – given the sheer number of students per academic year exceeding 100 by far – difficult to implement. That is why the introduction of online and, among others, multiple-choice-based FAs is evaluated. With a standardized answer-format it is possible to provide the students with ready-made feedback and the tutors with anonymous performance data (Pachler et al. 2010), giving them the possibility to make educational changes (see Fig. 3.1). The change from paper-and-pencil to online FAs opens the door to data collection and analysis not only concerning students' learning progress, but also in reference to students' learning behavior. This data contributes to the creation of a didactic metadata layer leading to potential new insights in curriculum mechanics as discussed in the outlook section.

This chapter presents the results of a survey study comparing perceptions of students and tutors regarding our current paper-and-pencil FAs as well as expectations regarding future online FAs. These results should help us improve the quality of content, technology and didactical setting. Furthermore (in the outlook), we go beyond our primary results of this study and present an approach to online FAs that could be part of the medical curriculum at the University of Bern in the future.

2 Method

During the 2010 spring-semester, 477 bachelor students (60.4% women) and 131 lecturers (75.6% men) of the medical faculty at the University of Bern were questioned with paper-and-pencil questionnaires. The students' edition of the questionnaire was handed out during the last 15 min of an exam-related lecture (return rate: 78.6%). Tutors received their questionnaire by mail with an enclosed reply envelope (return rate: 48.3%).

41.6% of the students' sample was freshmen (first year of training), 33% sophomores (second year of training), and 24.4% juniors (third year of training). Over 80% of the lecturers' sample represents lectures where FAs are given as traditional paper and pencil form without individual feedback. Both the students' and lecturers' questionnaires contained multiple-choice items focusing on the following areas:

Current FAs

- Students: frequency of use, learning benefit, usefulness for exams, amount and quality of questions asked in FAs
- Lecturers: same areas as students with the perspectives what lecturers expect from students concerning the usage of FAs

Future online FAs

- Students: same areas as for ‚current FAs' with further questions concerning prospective usage frequency of online FAs and willingness to give lecturers access to anonymized performance data
- Lecturers: same areas as for, current FAs' with further questions concerning willingness for online authoring and online consulting of students' performance data

Except for the question concerning FA-usage frequency, the students and lecturers evaluated statements concerning the current/future FAs using a four-point Likert scale ranging from (1) "no" to (4) "yes". In order to prevent the forcing of irrelevant answers, all participants were given the option to state that they could not answer the question sensibly (referred to below as (0) "do not know"). The statements in the questionnaire for students and in the one for lecturers regarding the rating of the current FAs as well as requests and expectations imposed on future FAs were formulated in a way enabling comparisons between current and targeted states, as well as between students and lecturers.

3 Results

3.1 Current FAs

Over 60% of the student sample reported that they either use the FAs less than once a month (48.1%) or never (15.2%) during the semester. The data about the current use of the FAs shows that the monthly or more frequent use of FAs by freshmen is

Table 3.1 Students' stated usage of current FAs and lecturers' expected usage of current FAs by students

	Answers[a]					
	Students (n = 462)		Lecturers (n = 98)			
Item	M	SD	M	SD	t	df
How often do you/should students use FA?	2.25	0.84	3.2	0.72	−10.53*	558

*p < 0.01

[a] Scale: (1) "never", (2) "<1×/month", (3) "≥1×/month & <weekly", and (4) "weekly"; answers (0) "do not know" excluded

Table 3.2 The current FAs' quality, conformity, necessity, complexity of questions and solutions perceived by students and lecturers

	Answers[a]					
	Students (404 ≤ n ≤ 432)		Lecturers (65 ≤ n ≤ 104)			
Item	M	SD	M	SD	t^b	df^b
The FA-quality is good	2.47	0.77	2.88	0.48	−5.66*	122.74
The FAs match the subject matters of the lectures	2.32	0.81	2.85	0.64	−5.90*	98.93
The FAs are unnecessary	1.64	0.84	1.38	0.73	3.15*	176.02
The FAs are too complex	1.42	0.51	1.86	0.71	−6.48*	476
The solutions provided are too complex	2.95	0.77	1.90	0.65	10.67*	486

*p < 0.01

[a] Scale: (1) "no", (2) "rather no", (3) "rather yes", and (4) "yes"; answers (0) "do not know" excluded

[b] Rectified where $p_{Levene} < 0.05$

59.6%, but that its frequency declines during the sophomore (14.0%) and junior (12.0%) years. The lecturers' expectations differ: 39.7% of them report that students should use FAs on a monthly basis, 23.7% say weekly and another 23.7% indicated that they could not answer this question (furthermore, 2% say daily, 9.2% less than once a month, 0.8% never, 1.5% missing). Table 3.1 shows that this discrepancy is highly significant.

Less than half of the students (47%) and lecturers (42%) rate the quality of current FAs as high while more than 80% of students find that especially the proposed answers to the problems are too difficult to comprehend.[1] Notably, 48% of the lecturers indicated that they could not judge the quality of the self-test questions ("do not know"). However, roughly three fourth of both groups underline the necessity of FAs. Table 3.2 shows that the students rate the current FAs significantly worse than the tutors, but underline their necessity.

---

[1] Quite a few of them consist of a text filling an A4 page.

Table 3.3 Comparison between students' and lecturers' point of view regarding current FAs: do they foster knowledge acquisition activities and when are they actually used?

	Answers[a]					
	Students (445 ≤ n ≤ 450)		Lecturers (95 ≤ n ≤ 102)			
Item	M	SD	M	SD	t[b]	df
I/students consult lecturers because of FA (face to face or online forum)	1.16	0.41	2.37	0.76	−15.02**	105.74
I/students consult literature because of FA	2.03	0.95	2.66	0.66	−7.69**	190.80
I/students use the FAs synchronized with the respective lectures	2.09	1.05	3.08	0.61	−12.45**	235.67
I/students use FA to prepare exams	3.14	0.95	3.32	0.66	−2.37*	206.85

*$p < 0.05$
**$p < 0.01$
[a]Scale: (1) "no", (2) "rather no", (3) "rather yes", and (4) "yes"; answers (0) "do not know" excluded
[b]Rectified where $p_{Levene} < 0.05$

The differing views – students vs. lecturers – become apparent in the optional free-text answers of our survey, too. The option to enter free answers regarding the issues "current FAs", "future FAs", and "further comments" was used by less than one fourth of the participants; their answers underline their positions: Some lecturers repeatedly noted that the current system was helpful, while others noted that they were left out of the loop regarding the creative process and maintenance of FAs. Students noted that the FA-quality was heterogeneous – depending on the FA-authors. The following problems were noted by the students: missing exam relevance; poor coverage of the subject matters taught in the lectures; not enough accurate solutions provided; too complex solutions provided; types of questions/answers different from the ones used in the exams (the current FAs are based on short-answer questions and multiple-choice questions, while Bachelor intermediate exams are oral, and final exams are multiple-choice complemented by a skills exam [Objective Structured Clinical Examination] in the senior year).

Table 3.3 shows how students judge the effects of current FAs on certain aspects of knowledge acquisition – the consultation of tutors and literature – (namely, marginal), and how they apply FAs (namely, frequently for the preparation of exams). The tutors are far more inclined than the students to take it for granted that the FAs are the cause of the formerly mentioned effects (consulting literature and tutors); the discrepancy between tutors' and students' opinions concerning that point is highly significant.

In their free-text entries, students repeatedly stressed that they use FAs mainly or exclusively for their preparation for the written exams, and therefore requested that FAs be tailored to the latter. Some lecturers noted that they would prefer to offer FA-support face-to-face. Table 3.3 at the top shows that – contrary to the lecturers' significantly more positive expectations – FAs hardly incite students to consult lecturers.

Table 3.4 Introduction of online FA in the near future: Students' compliance versus lecturers' expectations

	Answers[a]					
	Students (459≤n≤463)		Lecturers (106≤n≤115)			
Item	M	SD	M	SD	t^b	df^b
You/students would use online multiple choice FA regularly	3.12	0.84	3.01	0.61	1.88	231.37
You/students would use online short answer FA regularly	2.70	0.96	2.56	0.67	1.78	241.49
You/students wish the solutions to unhide only after giving answers	3.16	1.01	2.77	0.89	3.56**	562

$p < 0.05$
$**p < 0.01$
[a]Scale: (1) "no", (2) "rather no", (3) "rather yes", and (4) "yes"; answers (0) "do not know" excluded
[b]rectified because $p_{Levene} < 0.05$

3.2   Future Online FA: Students' and Lecturers' Expectations

An important feature of the new online FA to be introduced would be the anonymous backflow of the students' performance data to the tutors. Both, students ($M = 3.09$; $SD = 1.02$) and tutors ($M = 3.17$; $SD = .85$), agree similarly on the necessity of this backflow ($t_{(192.22)} = -0.76$; $p > 0.05$). The tutor's responses show us that the motivation to support a change is at hand: more than half of the tutors would basically be willing to co-create online FAs (50.4%), consult students' performance data (64.8%), and during their lectures pick up items (74.8%) that many failed to answer correctly. Table 3.4 shows that – given the introduction of online FAs – students would be willing to use them on a regular basis. There is one significant difference in opinions: While students are reporting that they do rather not want to see the correct answers before having performed the FA, lecturers expect the students to prefer having the possibility to consult the correct answers in advance.

A 2×2 ANOVA (*students vs. lecturers (between subjects) × current vs. future FA (within subjects)*) shows the within-factor main-effect: New online FAs compared to the current ones should better support all domains shown in Fig. 3.2, i.e. passing exams ($F_{(1, 475)} = 225.07$; $p < 0.01$), learning new subject matters ($F_{(1, 533)} = 17.57$; $p < 0.01$), detecting knowledge gaps ($F_{(1, 538)} = 175.90$; $p < 0.01$), knowing what to learn ($F_{(1, 536)} = 200.83$; $p < 0.01$), and knowing how detailed to learn ($F_{(1, 534)} = 351.08$; $p < 0.01$). Further, each interaction in the latter domains is highly significant ($13.78 ≤ $all $F ≤ 151.29$; all $p < 0.01$), which points out a distinct divergence between students and tutors concerning the qualities of current *and* future FAs (see figure on next page).

Analyzing these effects in detail, firstly, students rate the current FAs significantly worse than tutors in all domains, i.e. passing exams ($t_{(195.85)} = -9.66$; $p < 0.01$), learning new subject matters ($t_{(538)} = -4.00$; $p < 0.01$), detecting knowledge gaps

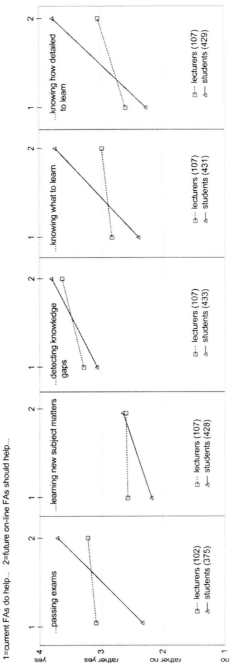

Fig. 3.2 Comparison of students' and lecturers' expectations concerning current FAs and future online FAs

Table 3.5 Students' wish for FA relevant to exams

	Answers from students[a]		
Item	N	M	SD
FA should only consist of questions relevant to exams	460	3.50	0.78
FA should deal with complex subject matters only	447	1.34	0.64
FA should consist of former exam questions	449	3.61	0.67
FA should contain special challenge questions beyond exam level	446	1.64	0.78

[a]Scale: (1) "no", (2) "rather no", (3) "rather yes", and (4) "yes"; answers (0) "do not know" excluded

$(t_{(541)} = -2.66; p < 0.05)$, knowing what to learn $(t_{(178.48)} = -4.55; p < 0.01)$, knowing how detailed to learn $(t_{(539)} = -3.30; p < 0.01)$. Secondly, for future online FAs, students expect significantly higher enhancements than lecturers in the following domains: passing exams $(t_{(164.66)} = 6.38; p < 0.01)$, detecting knowledge gaps $(t_{(171.01)} = 2.41; p < 0.05)$, knowing what to learn $(t_{(147.44)} = 8.40; p < 0.01)$, knowing how detailed to learn $(t_{(146.96)} = 8.54; p < 0.01)$.

Particularly striking is the fact that students rate the benefit from current FAs in helping them pass their exams as somewhat limited, expecting a substantial improvement in that respect. The data of control questions in Table 3.5 (two pages forward) underline the request of students for FAs that are more accurately aimed at their summative exams.

4   Discussion

Our analysis shows three main results. (1) The current FAs in the form of self-tests with open questions and standard solutions do not meet students' and tutors' expectations. (2) Consequently, both groups express improvements towards interactive and online future FAs. (3) Usually students have more pronounced attitudes and expectations than the tutors regarding current and future FAs, respectively.

The current FAs neither offer feedback for students nor data access for tutors. Both features are central parts of FA (see Black and William 2009; Bell and Cowie 2001). This is a theoretical link explaining why both, tutors and students, gave the current situation less than favorable reviews (especially the latter group). However, certain *asked* motivations for FAs differ: Students maintained that the FAs should be conductive to passing exams while tutors emphasize the establishment of a well-rooted and cross-linked body of knowledge, as gathered from remarks entered on the questionnaires. So, the students' focus on exams is very apparent in the data. They maintain that the current FAs offer little in that respect, and expect substantial improvements to be implemented in new assessment forms, e.g. the inclusion of problems that were used in former exams, but not of problems that go beyond the subject matter. Still, data show that the current FAs are indeed used in the preparation for exams even though students rated them as sub-optimal in that respect.

For the current assessments, there is no discrepancy in the views of tutors and students concerning the motivating effect on self-reliant knowledge research, be it through literature, or by consulting tutors. Both groups rated this effect as small; this stands in contradiction to the concept of problem-based learning for which self-reliant research is a fundamental mechanism of learning (Hmelo-Silver and Barrows 2006). Although the literature on problem-based learning lists primarily the tutorials as motivational source for self-reliant research, FAs are considered thematically interwoven with the tutorials and could well contribute to this end.

The survey shows the need for a change in the system. The results show that tutors would be willing to create FAs online, consult the performance data of their students, and make educational changes accordingly. Students affirmed their willingness to employ FAs online on a regular basis and would welcome plenary follow-up discussions (current FAs are used by students significantly less frequently than their tutors would like them to). However, the data also show that the new online FAs should be implemented differently, not only concerning the formal aspects (online, with automatic feedback and influence on teaching), but also taking into consideration that there are needs concerning the content (orientation toward exams and model solutions that are easier to comprehend for students and generation of profound knowledge for the tutors). That means that first of all, before the system is changed, the current self-test problems and their solutions must be revised with regards to content. However, the data of our survey is unclear about what direction to take, except that students request the inclusion of questions used in former exams.

As a subsequent step, quality standards for the new FAs must be defined that above all underline the term 'formative', but also connote attributes such as 'motivating', 'captivating', 'interesting', and 'inspiring' to activate the discourse between tutors and students (Pryor and Crossouard 2010; Gamulin et al. 2010). However, quality considerations are not confined to problems and their solutions, but also include feedback (Nicol 2010). In the new system, tutors would deposit a variety of feedbacks as text elements to be displayed to students according to their answers. The question of whether these ready-made feedbacks can satisfy the requirements for good FA, and whether and how tutors can be successful at creating feedback text elements that are not only didactically sound, but also with regards to software usability will be the subject of our further investigations. Furthermore, the usability qualities of the learning management system giving access to the FAs is crucial to students' learning success and motivation (Chen et al. 2010).

5   Outlook

5.1   Requirements for Online FAs

For the launching of new FAs online that are managed in a Learning Management System, six measures and goals can be identified:

1. The current paper-based FAs need to be revised regarding their content to meet tutors' and students' expectations in terms of their formative effects.

2. The current FAs need to be revised formally towards multiple choice questions since with many current FAs, students provide their solutions in the form of whole sentences or sketches, which cannot be automatically rated by a Learning Management System.
3. The system is to provide tutors access to students' anonymized (or more traceable: pseudonymized) performance data in order to address items during lectures at which students score particularly badly.
4. The system shall make the correct answers available to the students only after taking the respective FA.
5. The FA-authors must be able to deposit within the system precise feedback text elements depending on multiple choice answers checked by the student, as well as the solutions (correct answers with explanations). The solutions need to be revised (according to the results, students find the current solutions too complex).
6. The system must be easy to use for tutors and students, that is, must have a high usability (Wang et al. 2010). Usability has a direct influence on cognitive load: mental resources are limited and must not be absorbed by operating the Learning Management System (Patsula et al. 2010).

As a next step an analysis of how classic face-to-face feedback can be reconstructed to ready-made feedback based on text elements called up depending on the choices a student makes during the FA should be made. The central question is, whether similar effects – formative, and implied, motivational ones – can be achieved with feedback consisting of text elements. Furthermore, possible changes in the formative effects appearing as side effects of the transformation of essay or sketch tasks into multiple choice questions have to be investigated. There exist very few papers reporting the development *and* the evaluation of online FA (Costa et al. 2010).

These analyses will define the requirements for the system. Not only will the standard Learning Management Systems be evaluated; an in-house development is a possible perspective, too. In order to achieve good formative effects by means of FAs, they must have didactic qualities formed during their authoring process. So, it is assumed that the authoring process must be supported by a Learning Management System in a more dedicated way than the mere provision of entry masks for FAs. Current Learning Management Systems we have evaluated lack any option to allocate FA items to learning content stored in the system. Such allocations should enable tutors to perform a mapping of the weighting of FA vs. learning targets, thus controlling the FA authoring process (Su and Wang 2010). Therefore, the goal is to implement an FA authoring support in Learning Management Systems conducive to high-quality FAs.

5.2 Creating a Didactic Metadata Layer

The use of online technologies in a curriculum employing either centralized or distributed systems produces a huge amount of trackable usage data. If this data is to be interpretable on the level of individuals and/or cohorts, the systems employed must provide unique user IDs. In Switzerland, a centralized Authentication and Authorization Infrastructure (AAI) from the academic foundation SWITCH is providing this service. Hence, the technological structure for creating a didactic metadata layer is available. Four questions occur:

1. How can these data be incorporated in a didactic metadata layer describing aspects of a curriculum in a meaningful way, that didactic planning and activities can be operationalized?
2. How can data in the form of full sentences (human-written text) coming from formative assessments, exams, and online forum discussions be made machine-interpretable?
3. How can these data entities be semantically connected?
4. What is the legal situation of using such data for profiling individuals and/or cohorts?

There are different ways to investigate these data sources: e.g. by cluster analysis of various student performance data, or performing controlled goal directed studies.

Table 3.7 shows three possible characteristics of the data sources introduced in Table 3.6. Building a didactic metadata layer describing the students as individuals, the cohorts and the overall curriculum connotes building the ontology of the curriculum. And building the ontology has requirements of how to connect the data: it is not only about connecting them in respect of correlation and causality; it is about extracting their *meaning* and connecting these derived entities (Feigenbaum et al. 2008; Hitzler et al. 2009; Weller 2010). While correlation (the long way commuters missed morning lessons and many of them failed in the exams) and causality (the long way commuters missed morning lessons because of commuting, and that was the reason for exam failure) are calculated as direct relations and paths of relations, the ontology stands on a semantic network. The semantic network is the connected meanings introduced above, and it tries to catch the phenotypes as a whole and describes how the phenotypes interact. Our phenotypes are the individual student, the cohort, the knowledge domains (e.g. anatomy), the lecturers, and the curriculum as a whole. In other words, it is kind of profiling the phenotypes and drawing didactic conclusions: how to support students, how to develop the curriculum (and how to convince politicians for – may be costly – measures) (Fig. 3.3).

It is obvious that extraction of the meaning of data must be automated. For students, this can be operationalized by building classes of phenotypes. For example, a class can describe the curriculum compliance incorporating data from lecture attendance and formative assessment timing (formative assessments in the medical curriculum are assigned points in time at which they should be performed). Another class can describe the self-perception incorporating items, where this quality is asked for (we do this in online formative assessments and curriculum evaluation). In consequence, a student could belong to the class of "high self-esteemers" and/or to the class of "low compliance". These classes can be seen as equivalents to the meanings of data introduced above. In a similar way, the meaning

Table 3.6 Data types and sources

Data types	Data sources					
	Numerous clausus exam	Online lessons	Online discussion forums and video annotation	Online formative assessments	Exams (summative assessments)	Curriculum evaluation
Usage, activity, behavior	–	Frequency, time, duration, selection	Frequency, time, duration, quantity, asking vs. answering	Frequency, time, duration, selection	–	–[a]
Perceived performance	–	–[a]	–[a]	–[a]	–	–[a]
Measured performance	Score	–	–	Score	Score	–

[a]does not automatically capture this data type unless explicitly asked for. For example, in online lessons, forums and curriculum evaluations, questions concerning usage, activity, behavior and perceived performance can be asked

Table 3.7 Data Sources

Source	Examples		
	1	2	3
Log-files	Usage frequency (e.g. forums)	Score in multiple choice formative assessment	Score in exams
Questionnaires	Perceived performance	Learning behavior	Curriculum quality
Unstructured web	Input in forums	Full-sentence answers in formative assessments	Quality of laboratory log

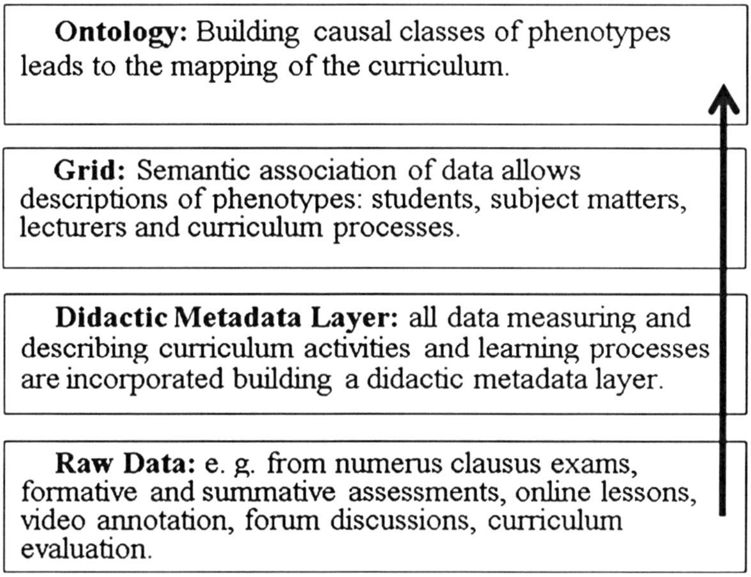

Ontology: Building causal classes of phenotypes leads to the mapping of the curriculum.

Grid: Semantic association of data allows descriptions of phenotypes: students, subject matters, lecturers and curriculum processes.

Didactic Metadata Layer: all data measuring and describing curriculum activities and learning processes are incorporated building a didactic metadata layer.

Raw Data: e. g. from numerus clausus exams, formative and summative assessments, online lessons, video annotation, forum discussions, curriculum evaluation.

Fig. 3.3 From raw data to the ontology. The meaningful connection of data creates a semantic network of relationships called Grid in the Web 3.0 jargon

of performance in formative assessments is machine-interpretable as long as it consists of multiple choice items whose scores can be calculated automatically.

With this approach, one does not only profile students concerning the domain, the domain itself got a profile. And that is the real serendipity effect: it is becoming predictable as to students of which profile could be appointed to teach which subject matters to other students. Students teaching students is not only a problem-based learning approach, it could become imperative when human resources at universities are becoming even more scarce.

6   Conclusion

This work examined students' and tutors' perceptions of current FAs conducted at the Medical Faculty of Bern, and their expectations regarding future online FAs. Results of the survey study show that especially according to students the current FAs are lacking in important properties such as overall quality and comprehensibility of the provided solutions. In addition, primarily students reported that the current FAs do not sufficiently match the subject matters of the lectures and are not very helpful for passing exams. Furthermore, for both tutors and students the current forms of the FAs do not seem to be a supporting tool for learning new subject matters and it does not indicate to what depth a particular item should be learned. It became apparent that both groups clearly agreed upon appropriate enhancements of the current FAs in form of online FAs. Students as well as lecturers affirmed their willingness to regularly work with online FAs in the future.

The introduction of online FAs provides important data describing aspects of the curriculum, in that on the one hand they evaluate the learning progress by means of multiple-choice questions, and on the other hand contain items such as learning behavior and students' self-assessments. Because these FA-records constitute only a fraction of the body of digital data concerning the (medical) curriculum, we introduced the construct of the didactic meta data layer which is the systematic but not-yet meaningful junction of all data sources. The semantic crosslinking creates a grid from which statements can be derived with the potential to create both the transparent student and the transparent curriculum.

This data whose handling must be lawful and in consent with the people involved has the potential for new effectiveness in education. The effectiveness of the access to these data and to the higher taxonomies "Grid" and "Ontology", respectively, needs to be high as well. Regarding future developments, effectiveness of data access means, above all, that context-relevant ontology-snippets must be available on the spur of the moment. We might boldly picture the following scenario: If students and lecturers of a university collaborate on-site (i.e. not virtually), this reality can be augmented through ontology-snippets being unhidden by means of goggles.

However, the question remains what the main goal in education is that universities should aim at. For the domain of medical education, we know the answer already: we want to produce good physicians. Success in this domain has several parameters: the doctors must be professionally sound, empathetic and efficient, and there must be an adequate number of degree holders in each area of expertise.

Acknowledgement   A big 'thank you' goes to Institute of Medical Education staff members Hans Holzherr for the translation into English, and to Dethardt Baumann for his support in processing the questionnaires. We also thank the students and the tutors for their participation in the survey and for the time we were given during the lectures, resulting in a high response rate.

References

Bell B., & Cowie, B. (2001). The characteristics of formative assessment in science education. *Science Education*, *85*(5), 536–553.

Black P., & Wiliam, D. (1998). Assessment and classroom learning. *Assessment in Education*, *5*(1), 7–74.

Black, P., & William, D. (2009). Developing the theory of formative assessment. *Educational Assessment, Evaluation and Accountability*, *21*(1), 5–31.

Buck G. A., Trauth-Nare A., & Kaftan, J. (2010). Making formative assessment discernable to pre-service teachers of science. *Journal of Research in Science Teaching*, *47*(4), 402–421.

Chen I., Shih D., & Hu S. (2010). Augmenting a web-Based learning environment through blending formative assessment services. *Journal of Web Engineering*, *9*(1), 48–65.

Costa D. S. J., Mullan B. A., Kothe E. J., & Butow P. (2010). A web-based formative assessment tool for Masters students: A pilot study. *Computers & Education*, *54*(4), 1248–1253.

Feigenbaum, L., Herman, I., Hongsermeier, T., Neumann, E., & Stephens, S. (2008). *Mein Computer versteht mich – allmählich* [My computer understands me – gradually]. Spektrum der Wissenschaft.

Gamulin J., Gugic J., & Gamulin, O. (2010). Improving classroom teaching in higher education environment using web-based formative assessment. *MIPRO, 2010 Proceedings of the 33 rd International Convention, Opatija, Croatia*, 1001–1006.

Hitzler, P., Krötzsch, M., & Rudolph, S. (2009). *Foundations of Semantic Web Technologies*. CRC Press.

Hmelo-Silver, C., & Barrows, H. (2006). Goals and strategies of a problem-based learning facilitator. *The Interdisciplinary Journal of Problem-based Learning*, *1*(1), 21–39.

Leung, C., & Mohan, B. (2004). Teacher formative assessment and talk in classroom contexts: Assessment as discourse and assessment of discourse. *Language Testing*, *21*(3), 335–359.

Mc Donald, B., & Boud, D. (2003). The impact of Self-assessment on achievement: The effects of self-assessment training on performance in external examinations. *Assessment in Education: Principles, Policy & Practice*, *10*(2), 209–220.

Nicol, D., & Macfarlane-Dick, D. (2006). Formative assessment and self-regulated learning: A model and seven principles of good feedback practice. *Studies in Higher Education*, *31*(2), 199–218.

Nicol, D. (2010). From monologue to dialogue: improving written feedback processes in mass higher education. *Assessment & Evaluation in Higher Education*, *35*(5), 501–517.

Pachler N., Daly C., Mor Y., & Mellar H. (2010). Formative e-assessment: practitioner cases. *Computers & Education*, *54*(3), 715–721.

Patsula P. J., Detenber B. H., & Theng Y. (2010). Structure processing of web-based menus. *International Journal of Human-Computer Interaction*, *26*(7), 675–702.

Pryor, J., & Crossouard, B. (2010). Challenging formative assessment: disciplinary spaces and identities. *Assessment & Evaluation in Higher Education*, *35*(3), 265–276.

Su, C., & Wang, T. (2010). Construction and analysis of educational assessments using knowledge maps with weight appraisal of concepts. *Computers & Education*, *55*(3), 1300–1311.

Wang J., Solan D., & Ghods A. (2010). Distance learning success – a perspective from socio-technical systems theory. *Behaviour & Information Technology*, *29*(3), 321–329.

Weller, K. (2010). *Knowledge Representation in the Social Semantic Web*. Berlin: De Gruyter Saur.

Chapter 4
The Effect of Project Based Web 2.0-Learning on Students' Outcomes

Bahaaeldin Mohamed and Thomas Koehler

1 Introduction

In recent years there has been considerable interest in the possibilities of Web 2.0 technologies for education. Sometimes these technologies are known as social media or social software, which are the platform for communication and social networking (Kear et al. 2010). Kear et al. (2010) state that the educators are "excited by possibilities such tools offer for making learning more shareable, collaborative and enjoyable" (2010: p. 2). Many people collaborate, create, share new information on the web in order to reshape their experiences. Web 2.0 tools mainly social bookmarking systems, wikis, blogs and video sharing platforms are used during leisure time too. Also many users are informally involved in various Web 2.0 communities just for being connected and deal with research opportunities and informal activities. Lai and Ng (2010) pointed out that there are very few empirical studies on how to assess students' learning in Web 2.0 environments. From this point of view explore this study the influences of using Web 2.0-based system for assessing postgraduate students to produce one-paper-research. In addition, this study also examines whether or not the Web 2.0-based system provides a good environment for changing learners' attitudes towards producing (writing, presenting, connecting) of scholarly research.

During last decade, ICT in Egypt and facilitating access to networks and services has been highly developed. Concerning Egyptian law 15 in 2004, the Information Technology Industry Development Agency ITIDA has been established as a governmental entity. This agency aimed to carry out the diffusion of the e-business services in Egypt. ITIDA facilitates increasing exports of ICT products and services and supports R&D in the ICT sector and implementation of its output. Accordingly, ICT events and services can be found in different places as IT-clubs, free internet, ICT training for universities staff members, the 'PC for Every Home'

B. Mohamed (✉) • T. Koehler
TU-Dresden, Dresden, Germany
e-mail: bahaa_i@yahoo.com; thomas.koehler@tu-dresden.de

P. Isaias et al. (eds.), *Towards Learning and Instruction in Web 3.0: Advances in Cognitive and Educational Psychology*, DOI 10.1007/978-1-4614-1539-8_4,
© Springer Science+Business Media, LLC 2012

initiative PCFEH, the DSL Digital Subscriber Line and some e-government applications (UNESCO 2007).

2 Project-Based Learning and Informal Learning

Project-Based Learning (PBL) is a comprehensive approach designed to engage students in the investigation of authentic problems and it is based on teaching and learning in the class environment. Accordingly, projects are complex tasks, based on challenging problems that involve students in design, problem solving, decision making, or investigative activities. It gives students the opportunity to work relatively autonomously over extended periods of time (Tuncay and Ekizoglu 2010). PBL is a constructivist pedagogy that intends to bring out deep learning by allowing learners to use an inquiry based approach to engage with issues that are real, rich and relevant to the topic being studied. It is designed to be used for complex issues that require students to investigate in order to understand. What makes PBL constructivist is cooperation and collaboration between team members and group-based learning (Milentijevic et al. 2008). Cooperation, as a term, refers to the practice of working in line with commonly agreed goals and possible methods, instead of working separately in competition. It is an altruistic sharing, while learners' collaboration refers abstractly to all processes wherein people actually work together at the same time. A project method in learning is always a challenging task due to the fact that projects can be complex and demanding for the management. Projects present what might be called a "learning paradox" on one hand, through their transience and interdisciplinary nature for creating knowledge in the context of its application. On the other hand the temporary natural of projects which seems to inhibit the sedimentation of knowledge (Bakker et al. 2010). Accordingly, projects suffered from project's amnesia (i.e. not retaining project insights) which shows that knowledge and experiences gathered from different projects are not being systematical and that there is a great discrepancy between the need for project debriefing and its actual deployment (Schindler and Eppler 2003).

3 Community-Based Project Management Learning Model

Community-Based Project Management CBPM learning model has been published by Mohamed and Köhler (2009) as a pedagogical attempt for describing how informal learning for postgraduate and novice researchers occurs, in order to accomplish their projects' scholarly research. Concerning to Fig. 4.1 study assimilated it as the plane which carries the knowledge. Our Jumbo Jet learning model, CBPM is structured based on three main parts: the main part is the middle part (The Body), which concerns of project's task workflow, the right and left parts (The Wings) related to communities of practice and the memory of the project (knowledge management) respectively. The body part of the model presents the tasks and activities workflow of scholarly research process. It should be considered by learners in order to accomplish and manage learning tasks. This construction

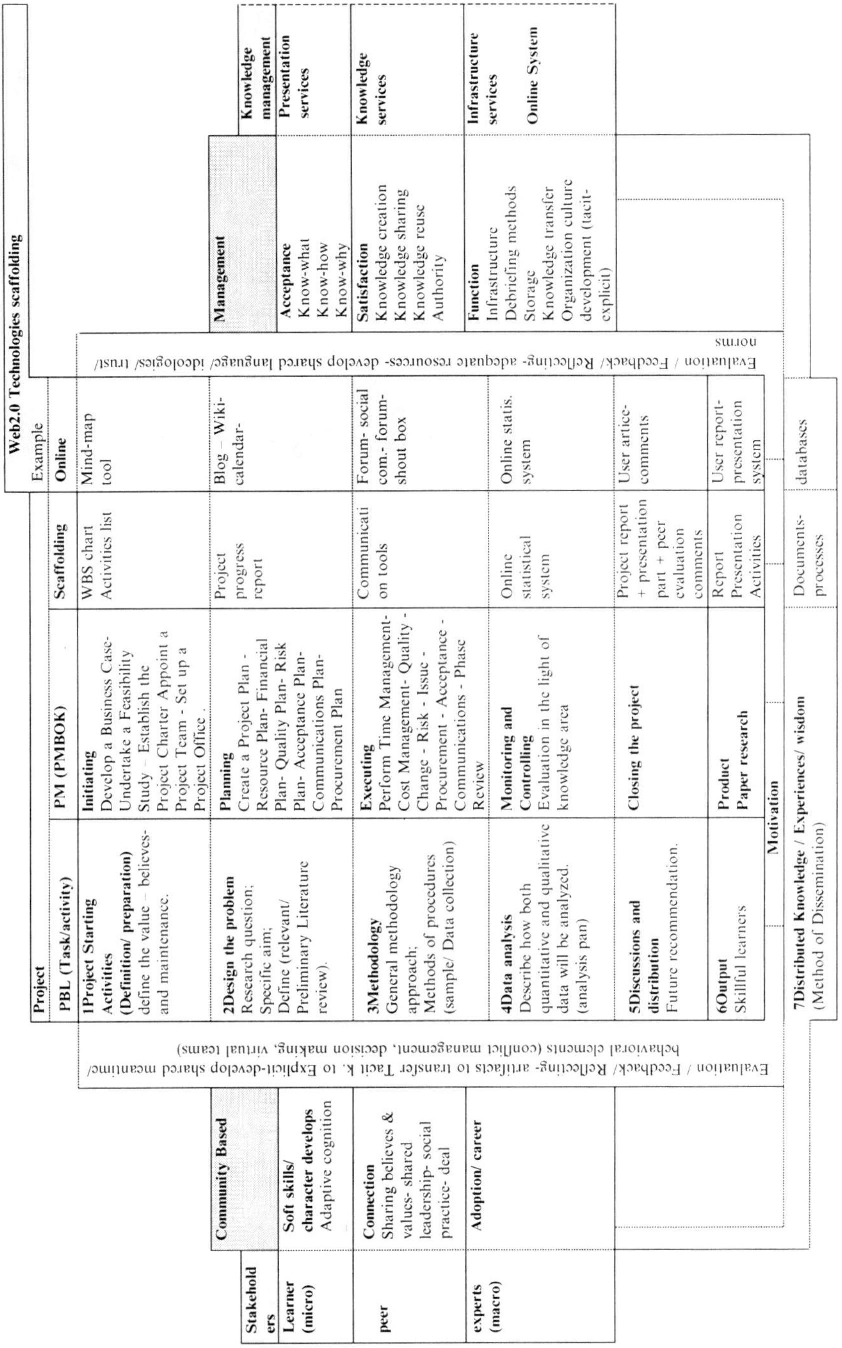

Project

	PBL (Task/activity)	PM (PMBOK)	Scaffolding	Example Online
1	**Project Starting Activities (Definition/ preparation)** define the value – believes and maintenance.	**Initiating** Develop a Business Case- Undertake a Feasibility Study – Establish the Project Charter Appoint a Project Team - Set up a Project Office .	WBS chart Activities list	Mind-map tool
2	**Design the problem** Research question; Specific aim; Define (relevant/ Preliminary Literature review).	**Planning** Create a Project Plan - Resource Plan- Financial Plan- Quality Plan- Risk Plan- Acceptance Plan- Communications Plan- Procurement Plan	Project progress report	Blog – Wiki- calendar-
3	**Methodology** General methodology approach; Methods of procedures (sample/ Data collection)	**Executing** Perform Time Management- Cost Management- Quality - Change - Risk - Issue - Procurement - Acceptance - Communications - Phase Review	Communication tools	Forum- social com- forum- shout box
4	**Data analysis** Describe how both quantitative and qualitative data will be analyzed. (analysis pan)	**Monitoring and Controlling** Evaluation in the light of knowledge area	Online statistical system	Online statis. system
5	**Discussions and distribution** Future recommendation.	**Closing the project**	Project report + presentation part + peer evaluation comments	User artice- comments
6	**Output** Skillful learners	**Product** Paper research	Report Presentation Activities	User report- presentation system
7	**Distributed Knowledge / Experiences/ wisdom** (Method of Dissemination)	Motivation	Documents- processes	databases

Evaluation / Feedback/ Reflecting- artifacts to transfer Tacit k. to Explicit-develop shared meantime/ behavioral elements (conflict management, decision making, virtual teams)

Community Based

Stakeholders	
Learner (micro)	**Soft skills/ character develops** Adaptive cognition
peer	**Connection** Sharing believes & values- shared leadership- social practice- deal
experts (macro)	**Adoption/ career**

Web2.0 Technologies scaffolding

Example Online

Management		
Management		Knowledge management
Acceptance Know-what Know-how Know-why		Presentation services
Satisfaction Knowledge creation Knowledge sharing Knowledge reuse Authority		Knowledge services
Function Infrastructure Debriefing methods Storage Knowledge transfer Organization culture development (tacit- explicit)		Infrastructure services Online System

Evaluation / Feedback/ Reflecting- adequate resources- develop shared language/ ideological/ trust/ norms

Fig. 4.1 CBPM learning model

of this tasks conducted by adopting EMRAD methods of writing research scholarly paper (introduction, method, analysis, and discussion). The Body part has been supported by Project Management Body of Knowledge (PMBOK), in order to manage, organize activities, map relationships and paths between activities mainstreaming. The PMBOK Guide is process-based which means that it describes work as it is being accomplished by processes. These processes are: initiating, planning, executing, monitoring/controlling and closing. This method has been used recently in learning researches to works as a scaffolding tool for project-based learning methodology. The first wing of CBPM concerns Communities of Practice (CoP), which means that each project's stockholder and team member is involved in one or more community of practice, in order to create, share, visualize and evaluate their knowledge. This process is known as collaborative informal learning. The second wing of CBPM is the memory of the project which is known – in the information system sciences – as Knowledge Management (KM), which are concerns the process of creation, sharing visualization and control of knowledge (Fig. 4.1).

4 Web-Based Learning System: PHD-LAB as a Social Community Project Management System

The PHD-LAB (http://phd-lab.com/ar) as a community-based project management learning system has been developed based on CBPM learning model, in order to assess the influences of Web 2.0 technologies on developing scholarly generic skills and attitude of novice researcher for conducting scientific research paper. PHD-LAB has been developed by adopting one of the open-source content management systems which is known as JOOMLA CMS (http://joomla.org). The system is structured conceptually as presented in Fig. 4.2 with three main tires: the tire of project management; the tire of community and the tire of project memory mainly knowledge management. Some special widgets mainly Jomsocial, Project-forg has been installed to the main CMS platform to make knowledge management, project management and activities easier for learners to manage. Fig. 4.3 PHD-LAB learning system (cp. http://phd-lab.com/ar): this screen presented the homepage which includes the recently news and announcements of projects and group-based work. additionally, the recent assessed projects by supervisor.

The PHD-LAB system has been tested for both technical and usability purposes. The results of technical test by w3c css validator tool figured out five sub errors concerning installing one incompatible widget Chat box. Therefore, the researcher uninstalled this component and reinstalled compatible software to make sure that system is without any conflict with the whole main system. Usability has been tested by 22 users (users who participated with the test group). The result of usability test show that all items of ease of use, usefulness and satisfaction of the system had high positive levels between (2.4 to 3) in the likert 3 level scale.

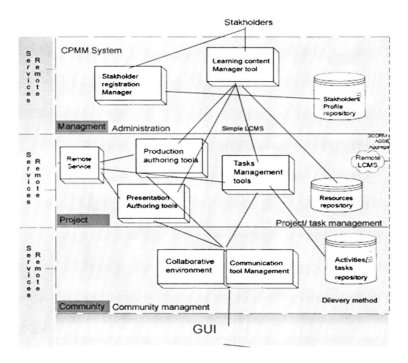

Fig. 4.2 Community Based Project Management (*CBPM*) system architecture

Fig. 4.3 PHD-LAB learning system (cp. http://phd-lab.com/ar)

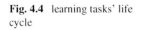 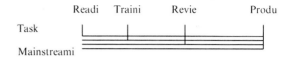

Fig. 4.4 learning tasks' life cycle

5   Learning Content and Activities via PHD-LAB

Learning material has been developed based on the number of tasks which have emerged from CBPM. CBPM learning model encompasses five main learning modules (Starting the project, Design the problem, Method, Analyzing data and Discussion), additionally four other referenced modules for helping and supporting (Writing references and citation, Instructional design, Active presentation and Academic writing).

   Learning task concerning Wertenbroch and Nabeth (2000) is the idea that learners "have to 'do' things and that 'doing' must be meaningful" (p. 6). From this point of view PHD-LAB web-based system facilitate five main tasks concerning CBPM learning model mainly (starting the project, design the problem, method, analysis, and discuss) scaffolded by project management method mainly PMBOK. For example, starting task includes sub-tasks which are PBL (define the value, believes and maintenance) and scaffolded by PMBOK (develop a business case, undertake a feasibility study, establish the project charter, appoint a project team and set up a project office). Learners deal with each sub-tasks through the tasks' life cycle concerning Fig. 4.4. The learner starts with reading the tasks learning content (learning module), in order to know "what" the task and dealing with accomplishing it. The second and third points (Training and Review) are both on the level of knowing "how". How learners can deal with it. The learners trains themselves by sharing the answer of some questions with peers. Finally, the learner is able to produce and accomplish the task and be able to know "why" the task. Around the concepts of knowing "what", "how" and "why" the learner deal deeply with the problem that can occure understanding and learning.

6   Aim of this Study and Hypothesis

The study intends to fulfill two expectations:

(a) To assess CBPM learning model in both the online version with PHD-LAB and the offline version with the accomplishment of tasks and project performance.
(b) To assess PHD-LAB as a web-based social project management system on learners' attitude towards web-based research activities.

6.1   Hypothesis 1: Learners' Performance Between Groups

The means of the two groups of the learners who are using online CBPM learning model (PHD-LAB system) in learning and those who are using offline CBPM learning model are significantly different in performance:

- The means of the two groups of the learners who are using online CBPM learning model PHD-LAB system in learning and those who are using offline CBPM learning model are significantly different in performance for writing research's report;
- The means of the two groups of the learners who are using online CBPM learning model PHD-LAB system in learning and those who are using offline CBPM learning model are significantly different in performance for sharing and social activities;
- The means of the two groups of the learners who are using online CBPM learning model PHD-LAB system in learning and those who are using offline CBPM learning model are significantly different in performance for presenting projects.

6.2   Hypothesis 2: Learners' Attitude Between Groups

The means of the two groups of the learners who are using online CBPM learning model PHD-LAB system in learning and those who are using offline CBPM learning model are significantly different in learners' attitude.

7   Method

7.1   Research Design

The study was conducted in the educational technology departments, Faculty of specific education, Menofia University in Egypt from 11 April–13 May 2010 (5 weeks) with the sample of 47 post-graduate learners from $n = 65$ post-graduate students who has filled the pre attitude scale, but the real number of $n = 47$ only, who have participated regularly untill the end of the experiment.

Concerning Fig. 4.5, learners were fragmented into two main groups, one was learning online and the second was learning offline. Both groups were treated by the same CBPM learning model as mentioned before. Students were assigned to one of the learning groups randomly. All participants were asked to answer a questionnaire once before starting the learning project and a second time after finishing the learning project for both groups. During 5 weeks, the online-based group used the system of PHD-LAB to learn and share knowledge,

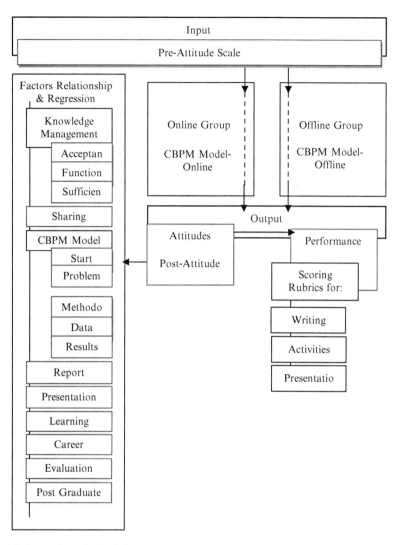

Fig. 4.5 Research method's design

in order to finish writing their reports and presentations. However, the offline group was learning offline concerning the same CBPM learning model. The questionnaire included demographic data; IT, Web 2.0 and e-Learning students background skills; attitude scales towards CBPM learning model; and PHD-LAB web-based system. Students were asked kindly to fill the questionnaire in a peaceful atmosphere without any stress. The total of 47 responses pre and post-project were collected. In order to assess cognitive performance for both groups, the researcher used the study's scoring rubrics: writing rubric, activities rubric and presenting rubric.

Table 4.1 Reliability of rubrics

No. items	Mean/item	Variance/item	St.div/scale	No. stu	Cronbach's Alpha
Reliability of writing report					
39	3.477	1.194	22.31	47	0.930
	Mean/scale	Variance/scale			
	135.58	497.98			
Reliability of presentation					
30	3.357	0.517	16.47	47	0.887
	Mean/scale	Variance/scale			
	100.695	271.55			

7.2   Data Collection

Scoring rubrics (grading rubrics) are used frequently by teachers to provide students with a guideline for completing papers or projects and can serve to communicate what is required or expected. Businesses may also use scoring rubrics for employee evaluations (wiseGEEK 2010). Four scales (instruments) have been conducted to collect the data. In order to determine the outcomes of performance and learners' attitudes toward PHD-LAB online system four scoring rubrics have been conducted: (a) a writing rubric for measuring the final research's report; (b) an activities rubric for evaluating the project's social activities; (c) a presentation rubric for assessing the final research presentation; and (d) an attitude scale.

7.3   Reliability of Rubrics

One method of further describing a scoring rubric is during the use of anchor papers. Anchor papers are a set of scoring responses that illustrate the nuances of the scoring rubric. A given rater may refer to the anchor papers throughout the scoring process to illuminate the differences between the score levels (Moskal 2000). After every effort has been made to clarify the scoring categories, other evaluator may be asked to use the rubric and the anchor papers to evaluate a sample set of responses. Any discrepancies between the scores that are assigned by the evaluators will suggest which components of the scoring rubric require more clarification. Any differences in interpretation should be discussed and right adjustments to the scoring rubric should be negotiated. Although this negotiation process can be time consuming, it can also greatly enhance reliability (Yancey 1999). Table 4.1 illustrates the reliability of our study's main rubrics.

Table 4.2 Reliability of attitude scale

No. items	Mean	Variance	St. div	No. stu	Alpha Coron
97	2.358	0.105		47	0.985

7.4   Attitude Scale

The study's attitude scale includes $n = 21$ negative items versus $n = 79$ positive items, total numbers are $n = 100$ items. The items were categorized into 9 main factors fragmented into 16 sub-categories, in order to determine learners' attitudes toward the CBPM (PHD-LAB) web-based social system. The effects of CBPM learning model were assessed by a retrospective pre-test. In the retrospective pre-test, the learners ($n = 20$) were asked to state how much they would have agreed with each item in the scale before and after the running of their project. Responses were given on a three-point Likert scale ($1 = $ Disagree, $2 = $ not decided, $3 = $ Agree). Seven potential outcomes of the CBPM learning model were assessed.

7.5   Reliability of Attitude Scale

Concerning Table 4.2 the internal consistency coefficient of original form of Cronbach Alpha is calculated as 0.985. The attitude scale includes $n = 79$ positive and $n = 21$ negative, a total of $n = 100$ items and $n = 9$ factors.

8   Results and Discussion

8.1   Hypothesis 1: Learner Performance Between Groups

The results presented in Tables 4.3 and 4.4 indicated that the p-value of the total students' performance is 0.659 and, therefore, the difference between the two groups' means it is not significantly different from zero at the 5% level of significance. There is an estimated change of 24.74% ($SE = 12.28\%$). However, there is insufficient evidence ($p = 0.659$) to suggest that PHD-LAB web-based social project management system does not change the mean of learners' performance. Therefore, this hypothesis is rejected. Accordingly, the difference between the two groups' means it is not significantly different from zero at the 5% level of significance concerning to sub-performance factors: writing the report, social activities/tasks and presentation's students. Therefore, no significant difference was found between groups relating performance in writing the report ($SE = 6.7\%$; $P = 0.913$), as well as there is no significant was found between groups relating performance in social activities/tasks ($SE = 3.5\%$; $P = 0.583$). Finally, this study found also no significant

Table 4.3 Hypothesis 1 group statistics-performance

	Group	N	Mean	Std. deviation	Std. error mean
Report	Online group	22	140.1364	22.05468	4.70207
	Offline group	25	126.5200	23.90802	4.78160
Activities	Online group	22	68.4545	12.24639	2.61094
	Offline group	25	58.7600	11.67362	2.33472
Presentations	Online group	22	106.5909	19.50985	4.15951
	Offline group	25	102.7200	14.19072	2.83814
Sum of performance	Online group	22	313.1818	41.80868	8.91364
	Offline group	25	288.4400	42.29764	8.45953

Table 4.4 Independent samples test-hypothesis 1 performance

		F	Sig.	t	df	Sig. (2-tailed)	Mean difference
Report	Equal variances assumed	0.012	0.913	2.020	45	0.049	13.61636
	Equal variances not assumed			2.030	44.888	0.048	13.61636
Activities	Equal variances assumed	0.385	0.538	2.777	45	0.008	9.69455
	Equal variances not assumed			2.768	43.612	0.008	9.69455
Presentations	Equal variances assumed	4.011	0.051	0.784	45	0.437	3.87091
	Equal variances not assumed			0.769	37.915	0.447	3.87091
Sum	Equal variances assumed	0.197	0.659	2.012	45	0.050	24.74182
	Equal variances not assumed			2.013	44.370	0.050	24.74182

difference between groups relating performance in making presentation (SE=4.9%; P=0.051).

The Result of sub hypothesis 1 indicates that Web 2.0 technologies have no influences on the development and enhancement of learners' performance that was represented in: (a) writing skills; (b) social activities skills; and (c) presenting skills.

This result may be inconsistent with many studies which are researching in the direction of technology enhancing and developing research's generic skills. Lai and Ng (2010) reported that wikis can develop IT, collaboration and organization skills. In the same context Cheng et al. (2011) believe that online discussion forums can improve student's performance via reading and posting. Some studies were focusing on special skills mainly writing and how it can be promoted via Web 2.0 technologies. Sorapure (2010) defends the importance of Web 2.0 for develop writing skills and critical thinking for learners, coming to the same results as many other studies: that Web 2.0 tools play an important role for providing opportunities to help students to think deeply through social networking (Meyer, 2010a), to enhance group work for academics (Chong 2010), to increase supporting for long life learning and informal learning (Ebner et al. 2010), to gain experiences (Hammond 2000) and to encourage reflection and dialog between learners (Makoul et al. 2010).

Nonetheless, this study's results can be discussed in light of studies with the same context and direction, mainly the study of Maranto and Barton (2010) who

Table 4.5 Group statistics-hypothesis 2 concerning learners' attitude

	Group	N	Mean	Std. deviation	Std. error mean
Totalpost	Offline group	25	200.2000	38.95724	7.79145
	Online group	22	276.0000	9.96183	2.12387

Table 4.6 Independent samples test-hypothesis 2 concerning learners' attitude

	F	Sig	t	df	Sig	Mean diff.
Variance assumed	21.870	0.000	8.864	45	0.000	75.8000
Variance not assumed			9.386	27.52	0.000	75.8000

reported a fraught paradox of using social networking in writing for learners. They reported that this technology undercut concepts of more conventional rhetorical spaces. The writing of Fred Turner (2006), concerning from Cyberculture to Counterculture, reports how the history of computer networking is full with paradox, for example since 1960, DARPAnet emerged from the military industry as complex networking for training – the wave of group work and collaborative-based computer has been flourished, but, by 1990, the system has been changed of the sort of personal integrity and individualism, and collaboration waves in that time were avoided. Also, since the last few years until now the wave of social working and learning has been flourishing due to social media and Web 2.0 technologies.

The other view for interpretation of our results is the model of Blinded learning which is now fraught of acceptance by many current studies and researches. Koese (2010) believes that the blended learning model can be supported witheb2.0 technologies. Also it enables students and teachers to perform effective educational activities that cannot be experienced with popular applications or systems on the market. He concluded that the students think that the online learning activities are performed easily in the realized model. In our case we have provided the same conditions for both Online and Offline groups. What has happened in this study's case is that the offline learners' group was connected for daily workshop – project-based learning methods – with the researcher, like the online group, which was giving both the same opportunities of connecting and communicating. This sets the conditions to expect that there will be no differences between them in terms of performance.

8.2 Hypothesis 2: Learners' Attitude Between Groups

The results are presented in Tables 4.5 and 4.6 and indicate that the p-value of the total students' performance is 0.000 and, therefore, the difference between the two groups' means is significantly different from zero at the 5% level of significance. There is an estimated change of −75.8% (SE=8.55%). However, there is insufficient evidence (p=0.000) to suggest that PHD-LAB web-based social project management system does change the mean of learners' attitude. Therefore, this hypothesis is accepted. According to Amin (2007) the group which has the higher

Table 4.7 Attitude towards CBPM learning model

| Sig (p-value) | Means | | df | t |
	Online	Offline		
1 CBPM model: start project				
0.003	16.0455	11.2400	45	5.545
2 CPBM model: problem design				
0.000	11.8182	7.3200	45	7.323
3 CPBM model: methodology				
0.000	11.8182	7.4000	45	6.755
4 CPBM model: data analysis				
0.000	10.6364	6.9200	45	4.966
5 CPBM model: results discussion				
0.000	11.9545	7.4800	45	7.066

value of the mean, is the group to which the differences relate to. Accordingly, the online group has a more positive attitude towards web-based learning and research practices than offline the group.

The Result of the sub hypothesis 2 concerning Web 2.0 technologies (PHD-LAB web-based system) has influences on the promotion and enhancement of learners' attitude towards web-based academic research practices and informal learning.

This result is consistent with many researches and studies that argue that Web 2.0 technologies enhance learners' attitude towards learning through: (a) create, share, visualize and evaluate knowledge with others; (b) using Web 2.0 in academia; (c) proposals of academic research activities and practices; (d) communication and collaboration; (e) managing projects and tasks which is predicted in future usages; (f) improve and promote the feeling and sense of community; (g) collaboration, sharing and acceptance (ease of use, usefulness); (h) knowledge management; (i) promoting academic work and scholarly research practices; (j) design research activities; (k) social interaction; (l) effectual thinking and behavioral; and (m) development of intention of participation (Uzunboylu et al. 2010; Augustsson 2010; Usluel and Mazman 2009; Kear et al. 2010; Yang et al. 2007; Halic et al. 2010; Fischer and Reuber 2011; Kirschner and Karpinski 2010; Carmichael and Burchmore 2010; Liaw et al. 2008). In the following part in this study we discuss in detail the sub-factors of the attitude scale.

8.2.1 Attitude Towards CBPM Learning Model

Table 4.7 presents statistically significant differences between the means of both online and offline groups of learners' attitude towards the CBPM learning model. Therefore, the online group have a more positively attitude towards CBPM than the offline group. What we mean with CBPM tested phases are the steps which have been followed by learners to accomplish their tasks. Start project, design the problem, method, analysis and discuss are the mainstay of study's learning model. This result point into the same direction as many other studies, which in detail focus on the importance of Web 2.0 technologies on learners' performance in collaborative and project-based learning environment. It takes an important place on the value of individual cognitive gain and collaboration interaction. It may also enhance team performance by increasing the quality of the team outcome. Students can learn to formulate ideas and opinions more effectively through group discussion. Based on social constructivist and activity theory, web-based learning systems can enrich collaborative learning activities for knowledge management (Liaw et al. 2008; Uzunboylu et al. 2010). Social interaction is assimilated by Web 2.0 technologies as an important output and typical characteristic of Web 2.0 tools. In this context this study has emphasized, along with others researches, the importance of this point. Fischer and Reuber (2011) emphasized that social interaction plays a central role in effectuation processes, they added that Twitter as a microblogging platform can facilitate a marked increase in interaction. Interaction can enhance and increase reflection and sense of community (Halic et al. 2010; Kear et al. 2010; Augustsson 2010). Furthermore, utilitarian reflection and peer pressure positively influences the understanding and intention of participating in Web 2.0 tools (Yang et al. 2007).

Some other researches deal with the development of certain purposes of web-based systems for managing knowledge and projects and their effectiveness on learning outcomes. Learning management system (LMSs) and Content Management system (CMS) have considerable relevance on effective learning, Rubin et al. (2010), and Cavus and Kanbul (2010) concluded that LMS can support or hinder active engagement, meaningful connections, easy communication and formative feedback (Bianco and Michelino 2010; Laleci et al. 2010). Other researchers developed proposal system congruence with project-based learning, Koese (2010) reported that student's academic achievement can be improved greatly if they are provided with an advanced web environment where they have effective learning experiences. Web 2.0 technology is not only about technological artifacts. It is more important to see them as contexts or environments of coexistence, interaction, as well as a guide for personality development and construction of identities (Hernandez-Serrano et al. 2009; Ardaiz-Villanueva et al. 2010).

The project in this study related to academic research activities and projects' tasks. Therefore, this study developed a web-based social community-based project management system, the PHD-LAB system, in order to deal with all of those fraught activities and tasks individually and socially. Result indicate that learners' attitude towards the system is significantly positive. Academic research project, mainly master and doctoral work has higher comprehensive tasks and activities needed to be accomplished. Web 2.0 via PHD-LAB system proposes specific technology for academic research and plays an important role for providing many tiers of facilities and services for novice researchers to deal deeply with their research and learning informally. Our system provides different kinds of services concerning to the tier of computer-mediated-communication (asynchronous/synchronous) mainly forum, blog, micro blogging, social network, whiteboard, shout box, chatting, comments system, in order to provide a sense of community and socialization. The tier of project management deals with tasks' management and organization as well as the

Table 4.8 Outcomes of learning: writing of the final report

	Means			
Sig (p-value)	Online	Offline	df	t
Writing/presenting of the final report				
0.000	11.9091	7.2800	45	8.175
Presentation				
0.000	11.9545	6.8800	45	8.005

future of project management functions. The last tier is the knowledge management tier, which provides facilities for creating, sharing, visualizing and evaluating knowledge with peers and experts. In sum, the more system deals with specific activities and academic interactions the more it is accepted by learners and experts.

8.2.2   Outcomes of Learning: Writing of the Final Report

According to Table 4.8 there are statistically significant differences between online and offline groups' attitude in project performance (writing and presentation skills). Learners who were learning online via PHD-LAB system have a better? Attitude (mean = 11.9) towards learning by writing and presenting their projects than learners who were learning offline (mean = 11.95).

In Web 2.0, writing and research activities are increasingly integrated both spatially and conceptually, and presents how research and writing together participate in knowledge production. The writing teacher has shifted with blogs and wikis in particular because these kinds of projects stimulate writing for real and responsive audiences. Web 2.0 tools know how to create content, how to share content and how to converse about content. According to Sorapure (2010) the use of computer could be supported, interactive and have visual representations of abstract data to amplify cognition. Data with writing process is converted to information in order to yield insight. The researches in Infovis (the way to present and visualize text via computer supportive software) allow student users to visualize text written by themselves or others. In this discussion, this study focuses on the affordance of how specific Web 2.0 technologies have been developed to model the integration of research and writing (Purdy 2010). The educational impacts and influences of wikis have become apparent, and their use in first and second language learning has quickly increased. Mak and Coniam (2008) highlighted the facilities and futures of wikis as collaborative writing platforms. Wikis can be used for a variety of purposes to aid language and writing research projects. Wikis allow learners to easily create HTML document, graphical pages and links to external resources. With wikis learners work towards the final document, all intermediate copies are retained. This provides invaluable learning for learners whereby they can see what errors they initially made. Writing is as well implemented by many other kinds of Web 2.0 tools, mainly forums and blogs, but forums and blogs were invented to give sense of discussion and daily events rather than writing processes themselves (Miyazoe and Anderson 2010).

Table 4.9 Future opportunities of PHD-LAB system

| Sig (p-value) | Means | | df | t |
	Online	Offline		
Web 2.0 and learners' characteristics				
0.003	21.7273	18.4000	45	4.610
Web 2.0 and research career				
0.000	–	–	45	3.048
Web 2.0 and evaluation				
0.009	28.2727	19.6800	45	8.716
Web 2.0 and adopt it by post-graduate program				
0.969	18.0909	16.3200	45	2.616

PHD-LAB system in this research provides various kinds of writing and reflective tools, mainly forums, blogging, comments system and wikis. Each learner has opportunities to create his/her own article and he/she has the choice to give his/her peers permission to share his/her writing for the purposes of review and collaborative work. Learners in this research did not feel comfortable to assess each other with wikis, but they fetl more comfortable when the experts and supervisors took place within the assessment process of the wikis for the purpose of correcting writing and reshaping ideas. Learners' prefer not to interfere directly into others' work, and they found the comment's system an optimal tool, to comment and share with their peers. On the other hand, students find the idea of article/wiki at the same time, is more usefulness and easy to use, than to use a separated wikis' system, which still has more complex graphical user's interface than forums or blogs. These conclusions were supported by what Miyazoe and Anderson (2010) reported.

8.2.3 Attitude Towards Future Work of PHD-LAB System

In this section this study investigated learners attitudes towards some future facilities and opportunities which can be assimilated as extended work and future objectives of our system for researchers and academics who can be either experts or novices. The result indicates that there are significant differences between online and offline groups in learners' attitude towards the future of PHD-LAB system which includes: system and learners individuals; academic research career; evaluation; and reuse the system officially with post-graduate education in the same faculty where learners study.

Web 2.0 tools and technologies support and enhance long life and informal learning, and are presented as a solution to solve many problems and dilemmas in research activities and academic work. Students reported that our system took advantage of Web 2.0 technology, mainly social communication and collaboration between peers and experts whenever formal and informal style of learning in the same faculty or remote places. The system helps learners plagiarize less from source text. While the web is open and responsible for increased incidents of plagiarism, that gives learners an opportunity to produce as well as to consume the text (Purdy 2010). Concerning the reuse of our system for future official education of post-graduate students, this study found no significant differences between the two groups. The means of the two groups were almost close. Accordingly, the online and offline groups would like more practicing and adopting of such technologies in their programs in the future (Table 4.9).

9   Conclusion

The CBPM learning model may benefit the overall individual and social learners' performance and learning activities especially with scholarly research activities for postgraduate learners. Learning via communities of practice, body of tasks and knowledge management system occur the understanding and knowledge transfer. Puntambekar (2006) suggested learners gain a better understanding of their learning processes when provided with opportunities to reflect on their collaborative learning outcomes, such as notes, conversations, drafts, group management skills, and so on. One of the suposed? Benefits of project-based learning is a deeper and more flexible knowledge base relevant to the problem (Hmelo-Silver 2004). This study has assessed the impacts of CBPM learning model on learning outcomes. The outcomes of scholarly research activities learning process has been evaluated via three main instruments: (a) scoring rubric of writing, in order to evaluate final report and writing's skills, (b) scoring rubric of presenting, in order to evaluate learners' presentations' skills, and (c) scoring rubric of tasks' activities, in order to evaluate learners' social activities and contributions. These instruments have been measured for eligibility (reliability and validity).

The study was conducted with the offline version of CBPM learning model, as well as with the online version which was assimilated as PHD-LAB web-based system. The researcher conducted the PHD-LAB system by adopting JOOMLA open-source content management system CMS. The system provided three main services for learners which are: knowledge management system, communities of practice and project management. Academic research activities have been developed into five main tasks' modules (starting project, design the problem, method, analysis, and discussion), with four additional modules which are: writing references, active presentations, writing reports, and instructional design. Each task's module has been supplied with tasks' loop learning strategies, which includes four main processes: reading, practicing/training, sharing with others and production. Tasks have been accomplished by the both of online learners groups' and offline's one.

The results indicated that no significant differences exist between online and offline learners' group in terms of project performance (writing, presenting, and social activities). Nonetheless, there are significant differences between online and offline learners' groups in terms of learning attitudes towards academic research projects and activities online.

References

Amin, U. (2007). Statistical analysis by using SPSS, Academic Bookshop, 2nd print, Cairo.

Ardaiz-Villanueva, O., et al. (2010). Evaluation of computer tools for idea generation and team formation in project-based learning, Computers & Education, 1–12.

Augustsson, G. (2010). Web2.0 pedagogical support for reflexive and emotional social interaction among Swedish students, Internet and Higher Education.

Bakker, R.M., et al. (2010). Managing the project learning paradox: A set-theoretic approach toward project knowledge transfer, *International Journal of Project Management*.

Bevarly, D. (2009). Maslow 2.0 – A New Hierarchy of Needs for Collaboration. Retrieved 21.01.2011 from Weblog: (http://www.aheadofideas.com/?p=156).

Bianco, F. & Michelino, F. (2010). The role of content management systems in publishing firms, International Journal of Information Management 30, 117–124.

Carmichael, P. & Burchmore, H. (2010). Social software and academic practice: Postgraduate students as co-designers of web2.0 tools, *Internet and Higher Education* 13, 233–241.

Cavus, N. & Kanbul, S. (2010). Designation of web2.0 tools expected by the students on technology-based learning environment, Procedia Social and Behavioral Sciences 2, 5824–5829.

Cheng, C.K., Paré, D. E., Collimore, L-M., Joordens, S., & Serious Games (2011). Assessing the effectiveness of a voluntary online discussion forum on improving students' course performance, Computers & Education 56, 253–261.

Chong, E.K.M. (2010). Using blogging to enhance the initiation of students into academic research, Computer & Education 55, 798–807.

Ebner, M., Lienhardt, C., Rohs, M., & Meyer, I. (2010). Microblogs in higher education- A chance to facilitate informal and process-oriented learning, *Computers & Education* 55, 92–100.

Fischer, E. & Reuber, A.R. (2011). Social interaction via new social media: How can interactions on Twitter affect effectual thinking and behavior, *Journal of Business Venturing* 26, 1–18.

Halic, O., Lee, D., Paulus, T., & Spence, M. (2010). The blog or not to blog: student perceptions of blog effectiveness for learning in a college-level course, *Internet and Higher Education* 13, 206–213.

Hammond, M. (2000). Communication within on-line forums: the opportunities, the constraints and the value of a communicative approach, *Computers & Education* 35, 251–262.

Han, S. H., Kim, D. Y., Kim, H., & Jang, W-S. (2008). A web-based integrated system for international project risk management, *Automation in Construction* 17, 342–356.

Hernandez-Serrano, M.J., González-Sánchez, M. & Muñoz-Rodríguez, J. (2009). Designing learning environments improving social interaction: essential variables for a virtual training space, *Procedia Social and Behavioral Sciences* 1, 2411–2415.

Hmelo-Silver, C. E. (2004). Problem-based learning: What and how do students learn? *Educational Psychology Review*, 235–266.

Kear, K., Woodthorpe, J., Robertson, S. & Hutchison, M. (2010). From forum to wikis: Perspectives on tools for collaboration, *Internet and Higher Education* 13, 218–225.

Kirschner, P.A., Karpinski, A.C. (2010). Facebook and academic performance, *Computers in Human Behavior* 26, 1237–1245.

Koese, U. (2010). A web-based system for project-based learning activities in "web-design and programming" course, *Procedia Social and Behavioral Sciences* 2, 1174–1184.

Lai, Y.C. & Ng, E.M.W. (2010). Using wikis to develop student teachers' learning, teaching, and assessment capabilities, *Internet and Higher Education*, 2010.

Laleci, G.B., Aluc, G., Dogac, A., Sinaci, A., Kilic, O. & Tuncer, F. (2010). A semantic backend for content management systems, *Knowledge-based systems* 23, 832–843.

Learning Approaches & Technologies: The CALT Perspective. The Center for Advanced Learning Technologies, *Web Site*, retrieved on February 27, 2010, from http://www.insead.fr/CALT/Publication/CALTReport/calt-perspective.pdf.

Liaw, S.S., Chen, G.D., Huang, H.M. (2008). Users' attitudes towards web-based collaborative learning systems for knowledge management, *Computers & Education* 50, 950–961.

Mak, B. & Coniam, D. (2008). Using wikis to enhance and develop writing skills among secondary school students in Hong Kong, *System* 36, 437–455.

Makoul, G., et al. (2010). using an online forum to encourage reflection about difficult conversations in medicine, *Patient Education and Counseling* 79, 83–86.

Maranto, G., Barton, M. (2010). Paradox and Promise: MySpace, facebook, and the sociopolitics of social networking in the writing classroom, *Computer and Composition* 27, 36–47.

Meyer, K.A. (2010a). Web2.0 research: Introduction to the special issue, *Internet and Higher Education* 13, 177–178.

Meyer, K.A. (2010b). A comparison of web 2.0 tools in a doctoral course, Internet and Higher Education, 2010.

Milentijevic, I. et al. (2008). Version control in Project-based Learning, Computer & Education 50, 1331–1338.

Miyazoe, T. & Anderson, T. (2010). Learning outcomes and students' perceptions of online writing: Simultaneous implementation of a forum, blog, and wiki in an EFL blended learning sitting, *System* 38, 185–199.

Mohamed, B, Köhler, T.(2009). Learning management systems as tool for community-based project management. In: Meißner, K. & Engelien, M.: Virtuelle Organisation und Neue Medien (2009).

Moskal, Barbara M. (2000). Scoring rubrics: what, when and how?. Practical Assessment, Research & Evaluation, 7(3). Retrieved September 25, 2011 from http://PAREonline.net/getvn.asp?v=7&n=3 . This paper has been viewed 295,859 times since 3/29/2000.

Puntambekar, S. (2006). Analyzing collaborative interactions: Divergence, shared understanding and construction of knowledge. *Computers & Education*, 47, 332–351.

Purdy, J.P. (2010). The changing space of research: Web2.0 and the integration of research and writing environments, *Computers and Composition* 27, 48–58.

Rinner, C., et al. (2008). The use of web2.0 concepts to support deliberation in spatial decision-making, *Computers Environment and Urban System* 32, 386–395.

Rodriguez, K. & Al-Ashaab, A. (2005). Knowledge web-based system architecture for collaborative product development, *Computers in Industry* 56, 125–140.

Rubin, B., Fernandes, R., Avgerinou, M. D., Moore, J. (2010). The effect of learning management systems on student and faculty outcomes, *Internet and Higher Education* 13, 82–83.

Schindler, M. & Eppler, M. (2003). Harvesting project knowledge: a review of project learning methods and success factors, *International Journal of Project Management* 21, 219–228.

Sorapure, M. (2010). Information visualization, web2.0, and the teaching of writing, *Computers and Composition* 27, 59–70.

Tuncay, N., & Ekizoglu, N. (2010). Bridging achievement gaps by "free" project based learning, *Procedia Social and Behavioral Sciences* 2, 5664–5669.

Turner, Fred. (2006). From counterculture to cyber culture: Steward Brand, the Whole Earth Network, and the rise of digital utopianism. Chicago and London: The University of Chicago Press.

UNESCO (2007). Report on the implementation of the Promotion and Use of Multilingualism and Universal Access to Cyberspace. Retrieved 16.01.11 from http://portal.unesco.org/ci/en/files/26047/12041267483EGYPTE.pdf/EGYPTE.pdf.

Usluel, Y.K. & Mazman, S.G. (2009). Adoption of web2.0 tools in distance education, *Procedia Social and Behavioral Sciences* 1, 818–823.

Uzunboylu, H., Bicen, H. & Cavus, N. (2010). The efficient virtual learning environment: A case study of web2.0 tools and windows live spaces, *Computers & Education*.

Wertenbroch, A. & Nabeth, T. (2000). Advanced Learning Approaches & Technologies: The CALT Perspective. The Center for Advanced Learning Technologies, *Web Site*, retrieved on February 27, 2010, from http://www.insead.fr/CALT/Publication/CALTReport/calt-perspective.pdf.

WiseGEEK (2010). what is a scoring rubric, *Web Site*, retrieved on June 13, 2010, from http://www.wisegeek.com/what-is-a-scoring-rubric.htm.

Yancey, K.B. (1999). Looking back as we look forward: Historicizing writing assessment. *College Composition and Communication*, 50, 483–503.

Yang, X., Li, Y., Tan, C. H. & Teo, H.H. (2007). Students' participation intention in an online discussion forum: Why is computer-mediated interaction attractive? *Information and Management* 44, 456–466.

Yoo, S.B. & Kim, Y. (2002). Web-based knowledge management for sharing product data in virtual enterprises, *Int. J. Production Economics* 75, 173–183.

Part II
Collaborative Learning

Chapter 5
Collaborative Language Learning Game as a Device Independent Application

Razia Sultana, Markus Feisst, and Andreas Christ

1 Introduction

The need for more and more people to learn different languages has never been higher. Since globalization increases, the old boundaries like geographical position, technological difficulties regarding communication etc that separated language groups are becoming increasingly blurred by the relative ease of travel, the advances in technology, the seek of higher studies and the internationally focused economic systems. As a result, foreign language benefits have never been more valuable.

Natural acquisition of language after puberty is blocked by a loss of "cerebral plasticity" supposedly caused by the completion of the development of cerebral dominance, or lateralization of the language function. It is this biologically based critical period, according to Lenneberg´s opinion, that is responsible for the fact that *"automatic acquisition from mere exposure to a given language seems to disappear after this age (puberty)"* and *"foreign accents cannot be overcome easily after puberty"* (Lenneberg 1967). Well known example of this hypothesis is "Genie (Curtiss 1977; Nova 1997), Chelsea (Newport 1991), and Victor (Shattuck 1980)." All of them were adult, victims of language deprivation and underwent intensive and long term language training. They all were able to gain some mastery but none of them became a fluent speaker. Another report on an earlier case of language deprivation involving a girl called Isabelle, who had been isolated from language from a very early age. Unlike Genie and Chelsea, Isabelle's circumstance was discovered when she was only six, and within 2 years she was a normal speaker (Davis 1949). Even though none of those adult language learners ever became as fluent as

R. Sultana (✉) • A. Christ
University of Applied Sciences Offenburg, Badstrasse 24, 77652 Offenburg, Germany
e-mail: razia.sultana@hs-offenburg.de; christ@hs-offenburg.de

M. Feisst
University of Nottingham, Wollaton Road, Nottingham, NG8 1BB, UK
e-mail: Markus.Feisst@nottingham.ac.uk

P. Isaias et al. (eds.), *Towards Learning and Instruction in Web 3.0: Advances in Cognitive and Educational Psychology*, DOI 10.1007/978-1-4614-1539-8_5,
© Springer Science+Business Media, LLC 2012

Table 5.1 Available language learning tool in the market

Name of the tool	Properties	URL
Rosetta stone	Supports 31 languages	www.rosettastone.com
Talk now	Supports 110 languages	http://www.esl.net/talk_now.html
Byki by transparent language	Supports over 70 languages	http://www.byki.com
Tell me more	Supports 9 languages	http://www.tellmemore.com
eLanguage learn to speak etc	Supports 4 languages	http://www.elanguage.com

a native speaker, their slow and steady progress also implies that adult achievement in learning second language should not be pre-judged (Krashen 2006).

Adult learners need an easy and interesting process or a tool to serve a useful purpose for learning a new language. The proposed language learning game is such a tool. There are plenty of other helping tools available in the market. Table 5.1 summarises the most popular of them. None of those helping tools are device independent and they are not emphasizing on the interactions with other people for practicing the language or facilitating collaborative learning. To learn a new language an adult learner needs his helping tool always available with him that he may learn and interact with others any time anywhere he wants. Nobody is carrying a high-end device like a laptop all the time and will not be motivated to open it somewhere for learning purpose just for couple of minutes. The only device that appears to be a potential solution to these problems is a small mobile device like a mobile phone, which is always switched-on and everybody is carrying it everywhere with him/her. The Language Learning Game (LLG) is the helping tool which is providing the user with an easy and efficient way to improve their knowledge level of a desired language by using exclusively their mobile phone.

LLG is a very suitable and useful example of a device independent mobile learning system as well because of the large amount of varying devices with significantly different features and functionalities that will be used by the end users. This is true not only to support different learners, e.g., all learners within one learning community, but also to support the same learner using different equipment parallel and/or at different times. This application may significantly be enhanced by including virtual reality content presentation in near future (Christ et al. 2009). Whatever the purpose is, it is impossible to develop and adapt content for all mobile devices individually due to different capabilities of the devices, cost issues and author's requirement (Feisst et al. 2005; Omari 2006; Tiong et al. 2010). A solution should be found to enable the automation of the content adaptation process (Gaedke et al. 1998; Hyungshin et al. 2010). In order to realize such a system three major requirements have to be fulfilled: (1) Identification of the connected device (2) Generation, structuring and storage of generalized content and (3) Transformation process from general content to optimized and device dependent content (Caballe et al. 2010).

In the proposed game a flashcard system is used to exchange dynamically generated flashcards among a group of people who are anonymous, where it is not predictable who will use what kind of device and what kind of data format will be used as a content of a flashcard (Meawad et al. 2008). The goal of the game is to improve language learning by creating a story within a group. The language learning game group work has an advantage over traditional group work, where some people does not want to participate because they are afraid of making mistakes (Imai 2010). The anonymity of the participants during this game appears to be a solution to this problem.

At this moment, a simplified prototype is used to evaluate the functionality and behaviour of the client as well as the server software. In this way it is relatively easy to modify the software in order to integrate or modify functionality proposed by the test groups.

1.1 Pedagogical Concept

To learn a foreign language interactivity with others that facilitates practice of the desired language is very important because learners acquire fluency by actually using whatever skills they have. They should be presented with activity-based approaches that engage them in interactive experiences and support the development of intrapersonal and interpersonal skills. As the learners develop their ability to understand, appreciate, and relate positively to others using the target language, they learn to demonstrate constructive attitudes and values through participation in challenging real-life situations.

The collaborative learning theory has exerted great influence on language teaching and learning. Through their participation in collaborative activities students socially construct knowledge (Schoenfeld 1992). They can elaborate on their existing knowledge and build new knowledge when they articulate their reasoning (Ploetzner et al. 1999), integrate other group members' reasoning (Stahl 2000), reflect on misconceptions, and work toward a shared understanding (Van den Bossche et al. 2006). However, in order to collaborate effectively during these processes, the students need to display positive collaborative behaviors (Johnson et al. 1990), and it has been observed that they generally do not do so without assistance (Lou et al. 2001). Small-group collaboration can be supported in several ways: through the use of human facilitation to guide the interaction (Hmelo-Silver 2004), precollaboration training (Prichard et al. 2006), or scripting of the collaborative interaction by giving students designated roles and activities to follow (Fischer et al. 2007; Kollar et al. 2006). Especially for writing, previous studies show that all the participants in a collaborative learning process obtain satisfactory results but the students with lower writing ability make more progress than those with higher ability. But higher ability students will also benefit from the experience of tutoring (Ge 2011).

Previous studies and analysis also show that in the area of collaborative learning cultural differences of the participants in a group do have an impact on participant´s satisfaction, interest and motivation. It was also reported that the lack of peer engagement and intercultural communication has happened because of religion, political views or for personal feeling (Hannon et al. 2007). For example: people tend to avoid finding fault with each other so as to save face. Moreover, a lot of people do not participate in a team work actively because of the fear of making mistakes (Carducci et al. 2009). They feel shy and confused about their level of knowledge. This is a great barrier for knowledge sharing in collaborative learning. In learning process emotions and comfortable environment plays very important role because emotions do not merely facilitate, filter, or hinder an individual's inner cognitive functioning; rather, they can in any forms mediate development, especially when learning is embedded in an interpersonal transaction (Imai 2010)

Errors are a natural part of language learning. This is observed from the development of a child's first language as well as of second language learning by both children and adults. A very common phenomenon for a learner is that he learns more from his mistakes (Helbig et al. 2001). Formerly a child's speech was seen as just a faulty version of the adult's. Instead of this idea now it is recognized as having its own underlying system which can be described in its own terms, and later the system develops towards that of adults (Littlewood 1998). Researchers have realized the importance of focusing on learners' errors especially for adult learners´ process of language learning. According to error analysis usually the errors made by learners are systematic rather than random. Many researchers began to realize that *"learners' errors need not be seen as signs of failure. On the contrary they are the clearest evidence for the learner's developing systems"* (Zha et al. 2007).

Availability of the supportive tool (example: LLG), collaborative corrections, digital resources (example: mobile phone) and peer assistance could become important resources in formulating a space for learners' creative engagement (Cekaite 2009).

2   Description of the Game

There are some prerequisites to get benefit out of LLG. This is not useful for a beginner but for such a person who has basic knowledge of the desired foreign language. The game requires a supervisor who has very good knowledge of the foreign language to perform overall check at the very end. If a new device or technology is required to provide a service; it is never possible to reach a lot of people within a short time. The game neither requires a new technology nor a new device, it requires only a device which supports Java application and can access Internet. The reason behind focusing on mobile phone is to reach a huge number of people any time anywhere. Nowadays the mobile phone as a device became almost a part of human body because most of the time everybody is carrying his mobile phone with him. New language learning needs a lot of interaction with other people. LLG can meet this entire requirement by implementing a flashcard system on a mobile phone without asking for a physical presence on a certain place and without keeping the participant waiting for an action actively (Newport 1991).

The instructor or supervisor will create the game; decide about the total number of group members in each group and the game end condition. Group members will be collected randomly. Each group should contain not more than 3–5 members. Slavin showed that groups with two or three members usually would do better than groups with four or more members (Slavin 1987). They will be writing sentences and the aim is to build a short story in the desired language. When a group member writes and sends a sentence the other members of the group will have a chance to dispute by proposing another version of the sentence or they can simply agree with it. They are only allowed to change spelling or grammatical mistakes in their proposed version. Afterwards all group members will receive a flashcard with the proposed sentence and possible corrected versions on the other side of the card. At this stage every group member has to decide at which version s/he agrees and vote for that one. The sentence with the most votes gets elected. In case of equal votes the first submitted one wins. Every group member has to create one sentence in one cycle. Generally the game is finished after 3–4 cycles. For example if the group contains five members and the story ends after four cycles then the total number of sentences of that story will be 20. The final short story is sent to all group members as well as to a supervisor who will perform an overall correction. After that all the participants will receive a flashcard with all the mistakes done by them while playing the Game along with the correction made by the supervisor. This overall correction is necessary because there might be a situation when the majority of members of a group agree with a wrong sentence. At the end the received flashcard, which will show the correction made by the supervisor will help them to learn correctly. This process could be depicted as a flowchart (Fig. 5.1).

2.1 Description of the Game States

From a pedagogical point of view and various research results it is established that competition fosters a win-lose situation where superior students reap all the rewards and draw all the recognition and mediocre or low-achieving students reap none. In contrast everyone benefits from a Collaborative Learning environment. Students help each other and in doing so build a supportive community which raises the performance level of each member. Their critical thinking skills increase and their retention of information and interest in the subject matter improves. This in turn leads to a higher self esteem of all the participants, which is the ultimate goal of LLG. It is designed in such a way that all the participants need to communicate with each other frequently. The reason behind this communication is their improvement will be depending up on knowledge sharing among the group members and at the end among all the participants including the teacher. So the game requires some activities from the participants and it has different states (Fig. 5.3). First of all participants need to log-in to the system (Fig. 5.2). The first screen that is displayed to the player is log-in, where the users can write their corresponding credentials (User ID and password provided by the university saved in LDAP server). Log-in is one of the most important parts of this total procedure because of data security, access right over the system and more specifically to assign a participant in a group. The server is in charge of connecting to the LDAP server and retrieve the information of the user and to verify that the user exists as well as the password introduced is the correct one. Some of the information of the user needs to be stored in a local table in order to have quick access to this

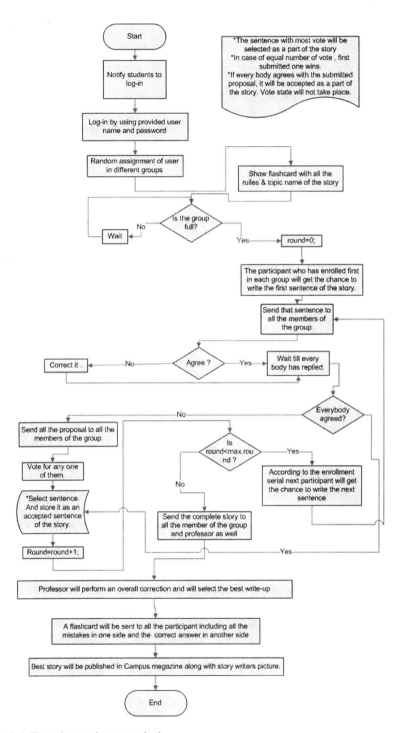

Fig. 5.1 Flow-chart to show game logic

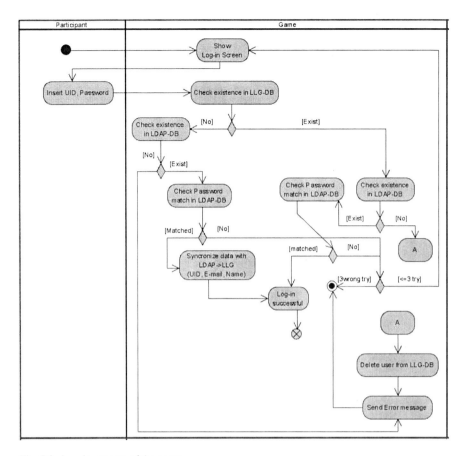

Fig. 5.2 Log-in process of the game

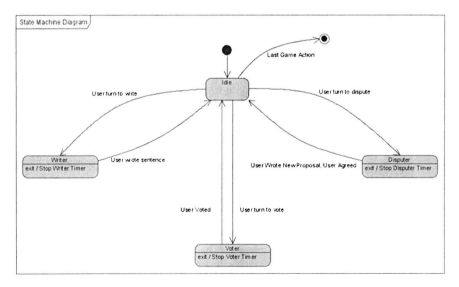

Fig. 5.3 State machine diagram to show different states of the game and the participants

data such as email, mobile number. After a successful log-in, a selection procedure of the courses will take place if it is the first time log-in. After the user has selected the game (course) to play, his state information and the state of the selected game are retrieved.

By using that information the server can decide which actions the user is allowed to do and how the game should behave. The use of timers is important in order to control that the game is not blocked by a player. The only state that does not start a timer is when the user is waiting for an action that should be done by a team member. For the other states a timer should run each time when the player obtains a new action to do. It is also important sending a message notifying that the state for a user has changed and an action from him is needed. The state machine diagram (Fig. 5.3) will depict different states of the game which is applicable for all the participants as well.

2.1.1 Wait/Idle State

After a successful log-in procedure all the participants will be in wait state until the group has required number of participants. This is also considered as a default state of this system. Whenever either the game or any one of the participants is waiting for the next required activity, their current state will be wait/idle. This is the only state where there is no time out period.

2.1.2 Write State

When the group is full, immediately afterwards writer timer will be started, the game and the participant who enrolled himself in to the game first will be in write state. He will be notified for his action and have the chance to write the first sentence of the story. Apart from the game itself and that particular participant all the others are still in wait state until a written sentence has been submitted. After submission writer timer will be stopped, disputer timer will be started; the game will go to dispute state; the writer of that submitted sentence will go to wait state; all the other participants of the group will go to dispute state along with the game and will receive notification about their state and action. In write state the writer is creating a flashcard.

2.1.3 Dispute State

In this stage of the game submitted sentence by the writer will be presented to all participants who are in dispute state. They will check for all sort of grammatical mistakes along with spelling mistake. After checking an individual participant may agree if he thinks the written sentence is correct. If he found any mistake he has the chance to make another proposal. By making another proposal participants are adding another

Fig. 5.4 Prototype of future outlook of the multidimensional flashcard on a mobile device (Feisst et al. 2009)

side to the created flashcard by the writer. The possible outlook of a multidimensional flashcard could be as Fig. 5.4. After disputing the timer will be stopped.

2.1.4   Vote State

Apart from the written sentence if in dispute state any new proposal was made then all the participants of the group and the game will go to the vote state. Voter timer will be started and everybody will receive notification. All the proposals will be presented in front of the participants to select the best one. Here they not only will check for the mistakes but also the suitability of a sentence for a story. The sentence with most votes will be accepted as a part of the story. In case of equal vote first submitted one will be accepted. Afterward voter timer will be stopped. Then the next member of the group will get write state for the next sentence and writer timer will be restarted. This is how the game will be continuing until it reaches the game end condition which was decided by the supervisor at the very beginning while creating the game.

2.1.5   End of the Game and Rewarding Procedure

The system will show a Game over page containing the complete story to all the participants when the game reaches the ending condition. Ending condition will be provided by the supervisor while creating the game at the very beginning. After completion of the story it will be sent to the corresponding supervisor for overall correction. He will evaluate individual performance along with group performance. Then all the participants will receive a flashcard with all the mistakes they made while building the story on one side and the correction on the other side of the card. From this card a participant will be able to know if he has made any common mistake together with all the other members of the group. Here everybody will be evaluated individually and as a group. Individual rewarding is important because individual performance could be better than group performance. Sometimes it is possible that a correctly written sentence was not selected because of lack of knowledge of the group members but for the effort the writer of that sentence should be appreciated. At the end best writer and best group will be rewarded.

2.2   Framework of the Game

The structure (Fig. 5.6) was created to extend the use of this application in any mobile device and to have a framework that can support multiple multimedia elements such as images, videos, sounds or simple text. It was decided to use Servlets to achieve the goals. In this project the only task of Servlet is to filter all the requests. It is in charge to receive the requests from a browser or a mobile phone, is responsible of calling the appropriate methods of the logic and is also responsible to submit the response to the client. The logic is in charge of the business logic that means connecting to the database server, connecting to the LDAP server for log-in purposes and transforming the response into the client's output. The following use cases will explain how the framework is working to recognize the device, to create a generalized version of content which is XML because *"XML has been proven to be adequate and a powerful technology to store content in a presentation independent manner. By defining an additional attribute inside the XML tags, it is possible to classify the content. At the same time, this will help the author generate learning material for different devices in an efficient and structured way. Also, the content can be used in different formats (XHTML, PDF, etc.) as well as with different technologies (browser, applet, MIDlet, Ajax, etc.)"* (Feisst et al. 2005) and to translate this generalized content in a device dependent manner: The following structure (Fig. 5.5) is showing that the idea is reusable and future proof because it is always possible to enhance the existing structure by adding new Games or elements without having a major change in the existing part. For example FlashCardSystem.xml and folder.xml is added without requiring any change in the existing part of LanguageLearningGame.xml.

Use case 1. The user is using his browser to connect to the game: The user goes to the website address of the game and a log-in window appears in the browser. The

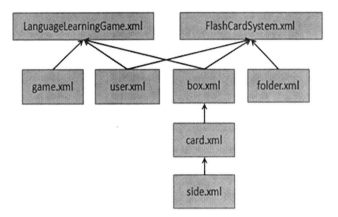

Fig. 5.5   General XML document structure

user writes his credentials and presses submit button. The browser sends the request to the server. The request of log-in is taken by the Servlet, it recognizes that it is a browser version because in the request parameters there is no specification of the device. Then, the Servlet sends the log-in request to the Logic. As no parameters defining the device are set, the Logic will recognize that the client is using the browser version of the game. The Logic verifies if the credentials are correct (Fig. 5.2) and in case that the log-in is "not successful" an Error XML response (created by the Logic) is translated into HTML; which is later passed to the Servlet as a response to the client's browser. In case that the log-in is "successful" a Success XML response is translated into HTML and sent to the client.

Use case 2. The user is using his mobile phone to connect to the game: The user first should install the corresponding MIDlet that will be responsible to translate all the responses made by the server. The user starts the application and a log-in window appears. The user writes his credentials and submits the request. The MIDlet is in charge of sending the log-in request adding a special parameter called "device = mobile." The request is sent to the Servlet that recognizes the log-in request; when this request is sent to the Logic it will recognize that the client is a mobile device. As in the previous use case the Logic verifies the credentials but sends the corresponding "Error XML" or "Success XML" response without translation to the client device. In this case the device is the responsible one for transforming the XML in an understandable user interface. LDAP server is used for log-in purpose, taking the advantage that each student and professor information is already available in the university server.

How the logic works with the translation from XML to a device dependent output? Once the request arrives, the business logic (Fig. 5.6) will use all the parameters received in the game actions. Once the game actions are finished a response is built as XML. At this point the Logic already knows, whether the client is using a browser or a mobile device. So if the user is playing with browser, OutputHTML is instantiated as it contains methods that will transform the XML into a proper HTML. If the

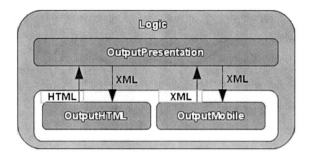

Fig. 5.6 Logic structure for presentation

user is playing with a mobile device, the XML will be sent to the client without making any change. As explained before, the responsible application to create the user interface in the mobile version is running on the client side and the procedure will give output based on the client device´s own capabilities.

In the XML response the state and the expected action by the participant are encoded. Depending on < state > -tag and < action > -tag further data is added. The example below shows the defined structure of the response built as XML

Courses List Selection
```
<game>
<state>success</state>
<action>course_selection</action>
<courselist>
<option id='[id of the course]'>[course name]</option>
<option id='...'>...</option>
</courselist>
</game>
```

3 Analysis of the Test Result

Three prototype-tests, for two different languages having 13 groups with three members on an average in each group, are already done. Participants' opinion along with corresponding language courses' professors has been collected by providing a questionnaire which included open questions as well. With the help of prototype all the important functions and features were tested. Findings based on the overall statistics of the game are very positive (Fig. 5.7). Not only the participants but also the corresponding teachers are also very interested to accept this game as a part of their course. They asked if it is possible to implement this game as a part of Modular Object-Oriented Dynamic Learning Environment (Moodle).

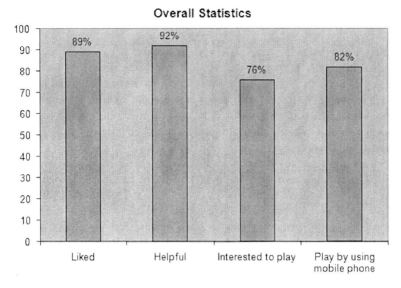

Fig. 5.7 A chart to show different percentage of the participants in three different tests based on their opinion

Sample output of a collaboratively built story by a group of three members before correction (by the supervisor): "*I would prefer to travel by plane because you can travel much faster by plane then by train. I think travelling by train is cheaper then travelling by plane. In some case travelling by plane isn't much more expensive then travelling by train but for the environment flying isn't good at all! In my opinion travelling by plane is saver then travelling by train because there are more safety checks before a plane is allowed to start but if there is happening something during the flight there is just a little chance to survive.*"

After the third prototype test according to participants' opinion all the requested and required improvements were implemented in the system. At this moment a fourth field test is running, where all the participants have complete freedom to choose high-end and/or low end device according to their convenience where ever they want and whenever they want. Since it is not predictable who is using what kind of device, what kind of communication medium, what is participants personal context or situation for example is he in a class room, meeting room or in supermarket and when is he going to use the system (LLG), all sort of notification and alert is sent as *Short Message Service (SMS)* and *Electronic mail (e-mail)*. Due to the deadline of this book chapter submission it is not possible to show analysis of the recent test result because the field test is still running.

4   Conclusion

Learning a new language takes time and dedication. After childhood, picking up additional languages becomes more academic and less organic. That is why it is necessary to make the language learning process interesting, easy and less stressful for adult learners. The goal of this project is to provide a Language Learning tool as a game where all the participants will be able to improve their language level by knowledge sharing (Omari 2006), by using a mobile device, for example a mobile phone that we all are carrying everywhere along with us all the time. It facilitates the participants to access the system as per his convenience without time and place constrains. The collaborative story building process of LLG makes each participant bound to interact with his team members every now and then to deal with a real-life situation which is not predictable. For example it is not possible to guess what sentence is going to be written by another team member, among couple of proposals which one is going to be accepted as a part of the story. Even though LLG requires very active participation and as a result none of the participant has to wait or feel stressed because for all sort of required activities participants will be notified. LLG is providing a comfortable environment and taking good care of participants´ emotion to ensure participants´ maximum level of benefit. Since the game is played anonymously there is no possibility of occurring problems regarding cultural differences or knowledge level differences or personal feeling. Various research results show that learners learn from their mistakes too. It is a way of analysing personal improvement. Even if a proposal made by a participant was not accepted as a part of the story, it will remain saved in the database. Any time a participant can see and compare his proposal with accepted sentence and at the end with supervisor's correction.

From the statistics shown above (Sect. 4: Analysis of the test results) the most positive and important side is, among all the participants almost everybody thought and felt this game will be a helpful tool to learn a new language. From the given answers of the provided questionnaire we know that they think it is a creative way to learn a new language because

- They can practice the grammar and learn new vocabulary.
- Everybody can evaluate himself by comparing with the other group members.
- This game is highly interactive which is very important to learn a new language.
- At the same time everybody is a teacher and a student.
- They can write without fear of making mistake and nobody was feeling shy because they were playing anonymously.
- In the vote state everybody can compare and then select the correct sentence.

This evaluation shows that participants were provided with a comforting learning environment where their affective state was taken into account, LLG was a supportive tool, this tool did not require any new or unknown digital device assistance because the students were able to use either their own mobile phone or own computer or PDA, anonymity was a factor that gave them the freedom to give their best effort which enhanced peer assistance and as a result collaborative performance.

References

Christ, A., Feisst, M., & Curticapean, D. (2009). "Mobile Learning a new Paradigm of e-Learning in Optics and Photonics," in *Education and Training in Optics and Photonics*, Retrieved from http://www.opticsinfobase.org/abstract.cfm?URI=ETOP-2009-ETC4.

Caballe, S., Xhafa, F., Daradoumis, T., & Juan, A. A. (2010). *Architectures for Distributed and Complex M-Learning Systems: Applying Intelligent Technologies*, (Ed.). USA: IGI Global.

Cekaite, A. (2009). Collaborative corrections with spelling control: Digital resources and peer assistance. *International Journal of Computer-Supported Collaborative Learning, Vol. 4, No. 3* pp. 319–341.

Carducci, Bernardo, J. (2009). *The Psychology of Personality.* (2nd ed.). Malden, MA: Wiley-Blackwell.

Curtiss, S. (1977). Genie: A Psycholinguistic Study of a Modern-Day "Wild Child". New York: Academic Press. Retrieved from http://www.jstor.org/pss/1746947.

Davis, K. (1949). *Human Society.* New York: Macmillan.

Feisst, M., Santos, D. R., Mitic, J., Christ, A. (2005). Adaptive Heterogeneous Learning System, *mLearn2005 Book of Abstracts*, Cape Town, South Africa.

Feisst, M., Christ, A. (2009). Designing a 3D User Interface for a Flashcard System with Android , *mLearn2009 8th World Conference on Mobile and Contextual Learning Proceedings*, Florida, USA.

Fischer, F., Mandl, H., Haake, J., & Kollar, I. (2007). *Scripting computer-supported collaborative learning cognitive, computational, and educational perspectives. Computer-supported collaborative learning series.* New York: Springer.

Gaedke, M., Beigl M., Gellersen H., Segor C. (1998). Web Content Delivery to Heterogeneous Mobile Platforms, *Workshops on Data Warehousing and Data Mining: Advances in Database Technologies*, vol 1552, 205–217.

Ge, Z. (2011). *Exploring* e-learners' perceptions of net-based peer-reviewed English writing, *Computer Supported Collaborative Learning, Vol 6*, 75–91 doi.org/10.1007/s11412-010-9103-7.

Hannon, J., D'Netto, B. (2007). Cultural diversity online: student engagement with learning technologies, *International Journal of Educational Management, Vol. 21* Iss: 5, 418–432.

Helbig, G., Götze, L., Henrici, G., Krumm, H. G. (2001). *Deutsch als Fremdsprache, Germany,* WB-Druck, Rieden/Allgäu.

Hmelo-Silver, C. E. (2004). Problem-based learning: What and how do students learn? Educational *Psychology Review*, 16(3), 235–266.

Hyungshin, C., Myunghee, K. (2010). Applying an activity system to online collaborative group work analysis. *British Journal of Educational Technology,Vol. 41 No. 5*, 776–795.

Imai, Y. (2010). Emotions in SLA: New Insights From Collaborative Learning for an EFL Classroom. *The Modern Language Journal, Vol. 94, No. 2.* 278–292.

Johnson, D. W., & Johnson, R. T. (1990). Cooperative learning and achievement. In S. Sharan (Ed.),*Cooperative learning: Theory and Research* (pp. 23–37). NY: Praeger.

Kollar, I., Fischer, F., & Hesse, F. W. (2006). Collaboration scripts—A conceptual analysis. *Educational Psychology Review*, 18(2), 159–185.

Lenneberg, E. H. (1967). *Biological Foundations of Language.* New York:Wiley.

Littlewood, W. (1998). *Foreign and Second Language Learning[M].* Cambridge: Cambridge University Press.

Lou, Y., Abrami, P. C., & d'Apollonia, S. (2001). Small group and individual learning with technology: A meta-analysis. *Review of Educational Research*, 71(3), 449–521.

Meawad, F. & Stubbs, G. (2008). A framework for enabling on-demand personalized mobile larning. *Int. J. Mobile Learning and Organisation, Vol. 2, No. 2*, 133–148.

Newport, E. (1991). Contrasting concepts of the critical period for language. In S. Carey, and R. Gelman, (Eds.), *The Epigenesis of Mind: Essays on Biology and Cognition.* Hillsdale: Lawrence Erlbaum Associates.

Nova. (1997). Secrets of the Wild Child (Video program). March 1997. Boston: WGBH. Retrieved from: http://www.pbs.org/wgbh/nova/transcripts/2112gchild.html.

Omari, R. (2006). A SW Module for Mobile Device Dependent Content Delivery, (Unpublished Master Thesis), University of Applied Sciences Offenburg, Germany.

Ploetzner, R., Dillenbourg, P., Preier, M., & Traum, D. (1999). Learning by explaining to oneself and to others. In P. Dillenbourg (Ed.), *Collaborative Learning: Cognitive and Computational Approaches(pp 103–121),* UK, Elsevier Science Publishers.

Prichard, J. S., Stratford, R. J., & Bizo, L. A. (2006). Team-skills training enhances collaborative learning. *Learning and Instruction, 16(3),* 256–265.

Schoenfeld, A. H. (1992). Learning to think mathematically: Problem-solving, metacognition, and sense making in mathematics. *In D. Grouws (Ed.), Handbook for research on mathematics teaching and learning,* New York: Macmillan.

Shattuck, R. (1980). *The Forbidden Experiment: The Story of the Wild Boy of Aveyron.* New York: Kodansha International.

Slavin, R. E. (1987). Ability grouping and student achievement in elementary schools: A best-evidence synthesis. *Review of Educational Research,* 57(3), 293–336.

Stahl, G. (2000). A model of collaborative knowledge building. In B. Fishman & S. O'Connor-Divelbiss (Eds.), *Fourth international conference of the learning science (pp 70–77)* Mahwah, Erlbaum.

Stephen, D., Krashen. (2006). Lateralization, Language Learning and the Critical Period: Some New Evidence, Language Learning, Vol 23 no 1 pp 63–74 Retrieved from http://onlinelibrary.wiley.com/doi/10.1111/j.1467-1770.1973.tb00097.x/pdf.

Tiong. T. (2010). *Multiplatform E-Learning Systems and Technologies: Mobile Devices for Ubiquitous ICT-Based Education,* USA Information Science Reference.

Van den Bossche, P., Gijselaers, W., Segers, M., & Kirschner, P. (2006). Social and cognitive factors driving teamwork in collaborative learning environments. *Small Group Research,* 37, 490–521.

Zha, Y., & Hong, Y. (2007). Errors in Language Learning, *Sino-US English Teaching, Vol 4,* No.2, 34–38.

Chapter 6
Collaborative Learning Tools in Higher Education and Life-Long Learning

Cosmin Porumb, Sanda Porumb, Bogdan Orza, and Aurel Vlaicu

1 Introduction

A lot of research has been done in the field of learning processes and learning activities. This has resulted in various theories such as cognitive learning theories, constructivist theories, and social-historic theories. Shaozi et al. (2003) illustrated that each of these theories is associated with a number of specific design principles and prescriptions. In parallel to the development of theories there was also an explosion of network-based technologies, mainly Internet and Web-based, enabling traditional and non-traditional distance learning approaches. Most of the developments have been learner and teacher centered. Group centered designs consider that learning is achieved through constructivism and collaboration.

According to Tan and Chan (2008), the changing nature of work and study under knowledge-based economy of this century constrains the teachers and students to adopt new methods of dealing with complex issues that require new types of knowledge. They need to work, collaborate and learn new things from a variety of resources and people, to investigate questions and bring their learning back to their dynamic learning communities. The number of learning communities grows up but just some of them have the expected success. Often new collaboration tools focus on a specific solution or collaboration task only, without considering the integration of this process into a large but easy to use and very suggestive environment. Moreover, new collaboration technologies require a change in human interaction. Thus the uptake is mainly driven by the benefit. If users do not experience an immediate personal benefit new applications are not applied even if the new tools are properly introduced.

Led by social and technological problems in the third generation of e-learning systems the authors propose the design and the implementation of a low cost

C. Porumb (✉) • S. Porumb • B. Orza • A. Vlaicu
Technical University of Cluj-Napoca, Cluj-Napoca, Romania
e-mail: cosmin.porumb@com.utcluj.ro; sanda.porumb@com.utcluj.ro;
bogdan.orza@com.utcluj.ro; aurel.vlaicu@com.utcluj.ro

P. Isaias et al. (eds.), *Towards Learning and Instruction in Web 3.0: Advances in Cognitive and Educational Psychology*, DOI 10.1007/978-1-4614-1539-8_6,
© Springer Science+Business Media, LLC 2012

prototype based on a Web 2.0 Collaboration Architecture that with advanced educational services in different domains such as mathematics, physics, engineering, social sciences or foreign languages. The authors review common groupware problems and reflect the changes in both higher education and life-long learning. The book chapter highlights the Web 2.0 approach in the e-service environments, especially e-learning area. It describes the open architecture adapted to the requirements of a generic collaborative learning framework and the manner it can be easily customized for different domains. The chapter also illustrates how Computer-Supported Collaborative Learning (CSCL) tools improve the knowledge building process and what kind of solutions should be adopted in order to avoid the CSCL weaknesses.

2   Low-Cost Architecture

A large number of web-sites are built using PHP and MySQL on the Linux platform with Apache as the web server. This combination is known as the LAMP architecture. Apache, PHP and MySQL are also available on the Windows platform giving rise to combinations like WAMP (Windows, Apache, MySQL and PHP) and WIMP (where the IIS web server is used instead of Apache). Even though LAMP is a very popular architecture there has been little work to characterize and benchmark the architecture, especially at an application level.

In reality LAMP describes any architecture that relies on an open source operating system, open source web server, open source database, and open source programming language for its implementation. In fact, an open architecture means cost effectiveness but also high performance. We built a complex e-learning framework based on an extended LAMP architecture. Its block diagram is illustrated in Fig. 6.1.

The implementation started from the classic LAMP architecture including Apache and MySQL database servers and had been focused on integrating new components in order to improve the collaborative learning capabilities: virtual library and media server. The MySQL database stores the entire information regarding the subscribers in the knowledge community (students, teachers, and tutors), courses, educational content, even affiliates to the education programme. The Apache web server hosts the web components that implement the knowledge community approach, learning management features and access control to the functional components and resources. The OSFlash Red5 media server should provide with audio/video communication capabilities, media streaming and recording features and video capture functionalities as well as remote shared objects support. The virtual library is a distributed component that provides with file management (conversion block) and multimedia capabilities (media library). The educational content uploaded by the lecturers is converted to slideshow format using the conversion block and stored into the media library (SCORM compliant). The media content recorded during the interactive assessment, online courses, webminars, tutorials, or resulted as video-assisted multimedia presentations will be stored into the media library and delivered to the end-users using the media streaming component.

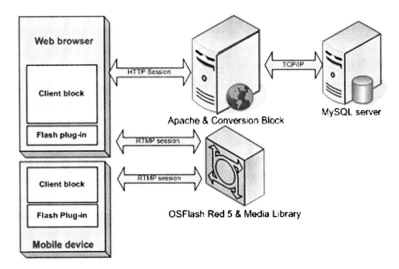

Fig. 6.1 System architecture

The extended LAMP architecture preserves the most classic LAMP advantages such as cost effectiveness, flexibility, and scalability, as well as cost-effectiveness. Since each layer in the stack is based on an open source solution, the entire stack can be implemented for the cost of development plus the cost of hardware. No piece of the stack requires software licenses. The LAMP stack is arguably easier to maintain and expand, and quicker to adjust to business requirements. If mobility is required, the end-user accesses the e-learning services using the mobile device (min-laptop, tablet PC, even smartphone). The LAMP architecture is horizontally scalable, meaning it grows as adding hardware to it. No single piece of the architecture is a bottleneck because each piece of the stack grows on its own, and is loosely coupled to the other pieces in the stack. In that case, the system specifications highlighted the importance of the multimedia capabilities such as: video communication, media recording/streaming, virtual shared space, knowledge and application sharing. The system architect easily introduced the open source OSFlash Red5 media server and Java-based file format conversion block and increased the storage capabilities in order to support the needed functionalities.

3 CSCL Prototype for Improving the Educational Act

We assessed some of the most popular e-learning platforms such as Moodle or Dokeos that comply with the traditional blended learning requirements. They provide: flexible individual study (time and space independence in the learning act), well-defined course structure, statistics and reports related to teachers and students tasks, as well as classroom-based activity support. Many specialists consider blended learning as more complex. Manseur and Manseur (2009) presented the synchronous distance

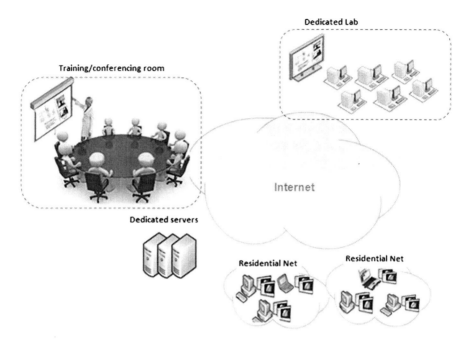

Fig. 6.2 Hybrid classware

learning concept (SDL) and its applications to Electric and Computer Engineering
and Mathematics. Students follow lectures live via videoconferencing but they attend
laboratory sessions taught by on-site faculty. The video conferencing system has been
used for linking the local and the remote classrooms: the tutor teaching in one location
is videotaped and can be seen on a TV screen in the other classroom live.

Our approach highlights the "hybrid classware" concept and the manner it can be
implemented within an integrated e-learning platform (details in the Fig. 6.2). The
hybrid classware should enable the teachers and students to blend the traditional
face-to-face educational act with the advanced technology in order to improve the
teaching/learning features and make the education more effective. Such a hybrid
classware implementation consists of the control panel, video communication component, virtual shared space, annotation tools, resource management component,
quick quiz, class statistics, and asynchronous text messaging tool. It should provide
educational equipment integration: the video projector/TV will be used for projecting the educational content in the real classroom, the PC/laptop/tablet with broadband connection facilitates the educational session control, and webcam, microphone,
speakers, mouse/graphical tablet will be increase the interaction with the class.
A simple student that remotely accesses the blended learning session needs the following equipment: PC/laptop/tablet with broadband connection, webcam, headset,
mouse / graphical tablet in order to actively participate to the course/webminar/tuto-
rial session. If there are students that remotely access the blended learning session
from the same location (dedicated lab or conferencing room), they also need video

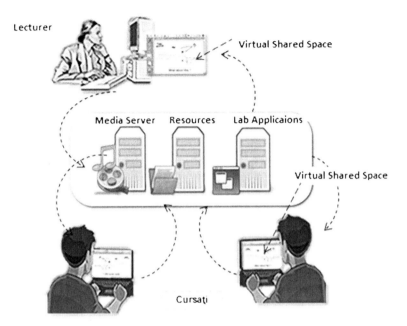

Fig. 6.3 Synchronous collaborative learning approach

projector/TV, speakers and microphone. The prototype also enables the tutors and students to integrate smartboard components in the virtual educational environment (simpler content projection and class interaction).

The hybrid classware concept is based on the synchronous collaborative learning approach (illustrated in Fig. 6.3). The virtual shared space is used for displaying the educational resources and the tutor's annotations over the educational materials in a real-time manner. Both tutor and active student will be able to interact with the educational resources and share it among the class by scrolling the resource page by page or slide by slide, add new explanations and annotations (text and graphics). The virtual shared space implements the shared object approach, so, each event on the tutor's/active student's space will be automatically illustrated to the other students. These features make the virtual learning space much closer to the real environment and the educational act occurs as in the real classroom where the teacher uses the video projector for displaying the educational content and marker for annotations.

Individual study and asynchronous collaborative learning provides students with flexible study, time and space independence, and allows teachers to create and manage interactive educational content (SCORM compliant). The most important asynchronous collaborative learning components are: virtual library, multimedia messaging, forum, course authoring tools, media streaming component, project- and problem-based learning tool (illustrated in Fig. 6.4). The virtual library implements the educational content management features, multimedia

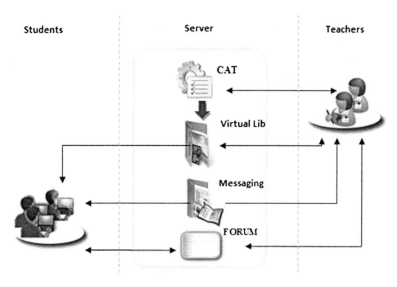

Fig. 6.4 Asynchronous collaborative learning tools

messaging and forum enables students and tutors to share concepts and opinions about the teaching/learning themes/subjects, course authoring tool allows the teachers to create the educational content as video assisted-multimedia presentations and media streaming component delivers the educational content. Project- and problem-based learning approach is used for improving the students' knowledge and soft skills (communication skills and team work).

If customizing the prototype for *non-formal education*, especially learning during the working life, the following aspects should be taken into consideration: the subjects can learn informally through the use of instructional media, mostly from their occupations, workplaces, colleagues, touring, mass media, information technologies, environment or even nature. In other words adults learn from experiences, problem solving or good practices can be easily included in the *learning during the working life scenario*.

The individual study components and asynchronous learning tools will be used in order to create and deliver interactive materials related to good practices and working successes, especially problem solutions and working experiences. The important subjects should be discussed during hybrid classware sessions that enable the employees to share ideas and concepts or resources in a synchronous manner.

The assessment methods in lifelong learning vary from company to company. Most of them are focused on technical skills and they can be considered as similar with students' knowledge evaluation in higher education. The others regard the soft skills, mental behavior and management capabilities. They are based on group meetings, social and technical solutions adopted during project situations, or colleagues' feedback.

4   Fixing Problems in CSCL Environments

Williams and Roberts (2002) illustrated strengths and weaknesses of the computer-supported collaborative work such as effects on academic stuff, repositioning of the responsibility of learning, educational content, interaction time management, communication application of workplace skills, computer competency, or class geography and size. The prototype allows the e-learning service providers to fix a list of problems related to the computer-supported collaborative learning area. It can be easily adapted to the requirements in the fields of primary and secondary education but it is focused on challenges of virtual universities, MSc and PhD programmes and life-long learning.

4.1   Issues Regarding the Academic Staff

The educational process is conducted by lecturers without experience with many of the CSCL techniques, neither blended learning capabilities, they did not have any training in delivering collaborative classes via a computer, smartboard, or tablet PC and they do not realize that sometime they have been collaborating between themselves by the use of the emails and phone conversations (during the lectures and tutoring/mentoring sessions).

The proposal highlights both user- and group-centered learning concepts that allow the lecturers to prepare the educational content to be shared among the class and conduct virtual classroom sessions and students to actively participate to the educational process, by interacting with the lecturers and educational resources (educational materials, lab applications and equipment). The prototype is designed using the Web 2.0 principles, so, the application should be easy-to-use, the graphic components are simple but very suggestive and comprehensive and the server-side components are powerful, affordable and stable.

There are four main features that characterize the Web 2.0 applications and the authors focused on these when proposing the low-cost architecture: decentralization, openness, dynamic and user orientation. These features match with social software application problems: Decentralization – as a consequence of being a real network, every node has the ability to act as emitter and receptor of information; Openness – using standards in communication, free licenses on content, promotes collaboration; Dynamic – applications are developed and deployed quickly. User suggestions are attended and supported; User orientation – easier and better user interfaces facilitates participation.

The system architect included other important aspects that help the lecturers within the educational process. The lecturer always prefers to present to the class the own materials such as scanned copies of notes, Word/RTF/PDF documents, PPT presentations, even web resources they already used in the traditional classroom. The lecturers are able to schedule collaborative sessions (hybrid classware sessions), prepare the materials for the online classes by updating the media library, control the class and interact with the educational resources and students attending session. Usually, the

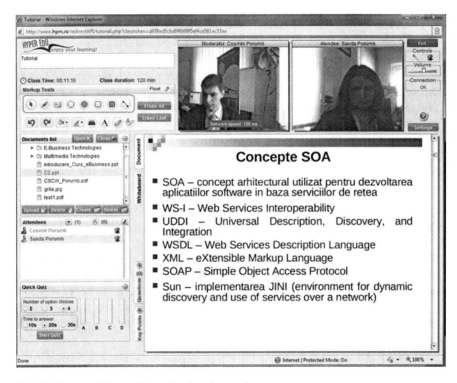

Fig. 6.5 Tutor module – collaborative learning session

lecturer must interact with the class in order to add more explanations related to the presented materials. The virtual shared space consists of two different tabs, document and whiteboard. The first one allows the lecturer to share the educational resources with the students by presenting it slide by slide/page by page and make graphics (handwriting, lines, circles, rectangles) and text annotations on the document surface. The whiteboard looks like an empty white page used by the lecturer when adding more explanations to the presented educational material. The whiteboard can be also used in a collaborative session if the lecturer decides to lively assess the knowledge of the class by enabling one of the students to have the whiteboard control for a short exercise. The teacher module and its components (video components, annotations tools, list of educational resources, control panel, quick quiz, class statistics, attendee list and virtual shared space) are illustrated in Fig. 6.5.

4.2   Responsibilities of Learning

According to Williams and Roberts (2002) the traditional education system encourages competition and individual responsibility between students and discourages any interaction, whereas the collaborative learning environments redefine the relationship between students and lecturers by creating a supporting environment versus a competitive one. In the traditional system the lecturer presents the educational materials to the class but the asynchronous collaboration transfers the lecturer's role to that of facilitator and resource guide as CSCL requires that the student takes a more active role in his/her own learning.

The proposed technology supports both traditional and collaborative learning and combines those two concepts in order to allow the teacher to make face-to-face presentations of the educational materials (video communication link and annotation tools), to have full control of the class, monitor students, control project activities (project teams monitoring), etc. The framework also allows the student to actively participate to the course presentation, communicate to the teacher in a real-time manner and collaborate with his/her colleagues for achieving the project goals. At the end of the educational session, the lecturer should enable the quiz component and all the students are able to assess their knowledge.

In traditional engineering education, knowledge assessment consists of complex procedures such as periodical evaluation, project evaluation and the final knowledge assessment and it involves the teachers and students. The assessment model in the third generation of e-learning is learner-centered and it consists of questions with one or more correct answers, as well as open answers. So, the students should complete the online assessment tests and the teacher will receive notifications about students' tests and centralizes the results before closing the educational act. We propose a blending assessment method that preserves the traditional assessment methods and the flexibility the online assessment tools grant.

The prototype allows the teachers to assign team or individual projects and collaborate with the teams using the (a)synchronous collaborative learning tools such as Project-based Learning (PBL) Tool, Online Focus Group (OFG) component, Multimedia Messaging and Project Forum. The PBL tool implements the Scrum methodology, so, the teacher is able to remotely manage each project by defining the sprints and scheduling the periodical meetings, live demo sessions included. The students work as a team, that way they develop not just the knowledge but also the soft skills. SGM tool enables the students to continue their team work remotely and improves the team work and communication skills.

There are many collaborative tools that implements similar functionality. What is new in such a system regards the intelligent component that dynamically controls the system configuration, elaborates the statistics and analytical reports, assures adaptive quality of service based on bandwidth conditions and implements a resource pooling mechanism that complies with the server overloading and media library access. The statistics and reports will be used for evaluating the quality of learning act and predicting effectiveness of these new e-learning methodologies.

4.3   Educational Content

Williams and Roberts (2002) point out that many of the current handbooks and textbooks are not designed to promote group activities and provide minimal suggestions on how to promote these activities, although a few publishers are now tailoring their books to cater at least partially for collaborative learning. CSCL techniques still require the formulation of handouts but these handouts are designed more to create a relationship among the students and provide a basis for them to work together. Since there is very little supporting information, the lecturers themselves may often have to develop this information in the forms of worksheets and any other appropriate materials.

The prototype architect considers the lecturer's effort and designs a complementary tool that allows the lecturer to dynamically handle the educational content. Two types of educational content are stored into the e-learning platform: public and private content. If the lecturer considers one of his/her materials as really important for the public interest, that material will be uploaded on the server, convert to slideshow format (SCORM compliant) and stored into the media library as a public material. If the material is private or the lecturer has no rights to make it public, it will be converted to the slideshow format and then stored into the media library as private. The tutor is able to browse the media library, load public/private materials on the shared space (document tab) and share it among the hybrid classware. The educational resource is presented within the document surface as in the original editor (see Fig. 6.5) and both lecturer and active student can interact with, at will. Each interaction automatically generates updates of the remote shared objects, so, each local event (scroll, annotate, video, audio) is automatically presented on the document surface of each virtual shared space instance, so, it can be observed by all the participants to the collaborative session.

Asynchronous collaborative learning is also a need. The tutor should be able to create and store interactive learning content. The prototype contains the *Course authoring tool* that allows the teacher to build educational resources as video-assisted multimedia presentations and store them into the virtual library. The student accesses the virtual library, browses the content and manages the own schedule. The course authoring tool, illustrated in Fig. 6.6, implements the educational resource management in the individual study approach: lecturer creates video assisted multimedia presentations review the content and store it into the media library. The student browse the course support or live class records, find the interesting material and uses the media player, for interactively review it. The video assisted multimedia presentations can be easily used in the hybrid classware sessions during the periodical discussions or interactive tutorials.

Even if video-assisted multimedia presentation creation means lecture's extra-work and it is usually a laborious process that format highlights important advantages. It is obvious that blended learning activities are very complex and require a lot of effort from the lectures but when putting the individual study and hybrid classware together, the average retention factor will be more than 80% after completing the individual study tasks and it will increase during the hybrid classware session. Moreover, the degree of satisfaction most of the students cherish when using such a system will be very high.

Fig. 6.6 Course authoring tool

4.4   Interaction

Williams and Roberts (2002) highlights the interaction that takes place between students as one of the major components of the CSCL environment. Teamwork is vital to a successful CSCL environment. The interactivity that takes place such as the giving and receiving of help and feedback, the exchanging of resources and information and being able to challenge and encourage other students is materialized in many research studies elaborated in the last years. There are four main types of interaction the presented with: interaction with resources, interaction with teachers, interaction with peers and interaction with both teacher and learner through an interface.

The collaborative learning framework presented in that book chapter supports the interactive learning concept and highlights the aspects related to the web presence, "face-to-face" interaction, real-time collaboration, knowledge sharing and multi-modal interactivity. Technically, the web presence is illustrated in the "list of attendees" where the lectures and all the students registered to the hybrid classware appear, each one with his/her status (off/online), "face-to-face" interaction happens when the student and lecturer share opinions using the hybrid classware tools, real-time collaboration and knowledge sharing means that lecturer and students simultaneously use the virtual shared space component in order to load, and scroll educational materials, or make text and graphics annotations over the material pages. The collaborative session is recorded and stored in a compact format and the course attendees will be able to review the live class using the media player component.

According to Ambikairajah et al. (2007) teaching signal processing courses at any level (higher education or life-long learning) presents challenges in conveying complex mathematical concepts, retaining the students' attention, and addressing individual student needs in a large classroom, so, only a small percentage of students are able to grasp the key concepts at the time of the live lecture delivery. The other students have to understand the topics presented in their own time and with whatever assistance is available. That way, the recording of rich multimedia information combining video and lecture or dynamically annotated tutorial slides can be used to improve self-directed student learning and offer new possibilities for course delivery. In practice, most annotations serve as attention marks, providing critical linkage between the slide content and spoken context.

Engineering consist of lecture attendance, project development, hands-on laboratory-based activities and computer simulation work. That way the educational act can be considered as learner-centered. The prototype presented in the first part of the book chapter also implements learning management capabilities and allows the students to schedule online laboratory activities. The resource pooling mechanism dynamically allocates one virtual machine for each student that scheduled a virtual laboratory session. Just the simulation software package needed for completing the lab tasks will be loaded in the virtual machine. The activity starts with an interactive tutorial when the tutor describes the tasks and gives some suggestive examples related to the practice. At the end of the practice, the student saves the own work then the tutor can verify it. If the tasks are not properly done, the tutor notifies the student to repeat the work or attend a collaborative session in order to fix the problems together.

Interacting with the resources is an important feature when talking about collaborative learning in foreign language. Here, the learners need dictionary or text-to-speech capabilities. Other innovative components integrated in such a collaborative learning framework are the five languages dictionaries (English, French, Italian, Portuguese and German) and TTS module, illustrated in Fig. 6.7. That way, learners can easily translate words from a language to another one and then render the correct pronunciation in the speakers. These features help the learner to improve the pronunciation and the communication skills. Drawing and handwriting functionalities make the virtual tool closer to the real teaching process, they allow the lecturer to present the educational content like in the traditional way.

An intelligent module allows the end-users to involve special equipment and applications in the educational/training process. For example, in the medicine domain, with today's unstoppable rise in technological progression, everybody is aware of benefits lifelong learning provides with. Teachers and experienced specialists should be able to schedule training sessions, present special cases, from diagnosis to treatment schemas, and assist their students and young physicians to improve their skills during a real medical act. A real-time tutorial among physicians using echographs or other special medical equipments can occur just using the virtual classroom component that allows resource and application sharing as well as video streaming.

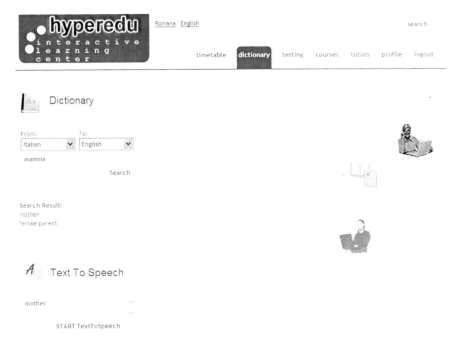

Fig. 6.7 Student module – dictionary and TTS components

5   Deployment and Customization

The real testing of learning cloud includes the students enrolled in applied electronics and telecommunications, Faculty of Electronics, Telecommunications and Information Technology, at the Technical University of Cluj-Napoca. We considered the students in third and fourth years of studies, as well as the MSc and PhD students, and proposed a learning cloud environment built around Citrix XenServer. XenServer is an enterprise-ready, cloud-proven virtualization platform that contains all the capabilities required to create and manage a virtual infrastructure and provides an efficient management of Windows and Linux virtual servers and delivers cost-effective server consolidation. The initial setup, illustrated in Fig. 6.8, must support the teaching/learning activities and practice.

   The setup is built as an elastic learning cloud infrastructure that initially runs eight virtual machines at the initial point: two allocated for web hosting, two for the data warehouse, two for media hosting and two for the virtual library. The learning management system allows the students to schedule online laboratory activities. The resource pooling mechanism dynamically allocates 20 virtual machines when the first student scheduled a virtual laboratory session. When 15 of these virtual machines are allocated, the resource pooling mechanism allocates other 20. Each virtual machine allocated for virtual lab work runs just the simulation software package needed for completing the current tasks.

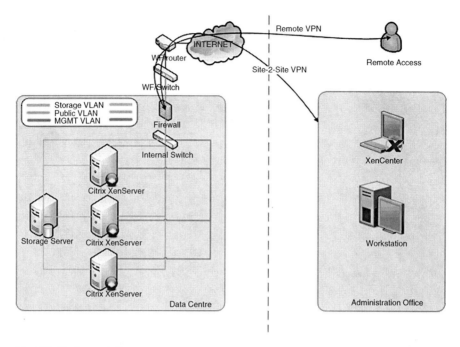

Fig. 6.8 Deployment diagram

CSCL solutions must be affordable, available, scalable, supportable, and manageable.

Affordable: Real-time collaboration total cost ownership (TCO) tends to exceed projections due to the high costs of maintaining a globally accessible real-time communications infrastructure. Linux offers a really high uptime and the system components work properly on a Linux server machine. In conclusion, the framework can be considered affordable.

Available: The TCO of real-time collaboration must include the cost of downtime. As virtual collaboration becomes more strategic to the educational process, the cost of downtime increases. A cost effective collaboration solution must therefore be highly available, so, the system architect proposed an elastic cloud computing setup that starts with eight virtual machines and dynamically instantiates one virtual machine for each student that schedule a virtual lab session.

Scalable and high-performance: The end-users increasingly demand sophisticated real-time learning collaboration functions such as rich multimedia. These video/voice/data requirements, coupled with performance and reliability challenges posed by the variability of Internet access (including dial-up links, ISDN, Wi-Fi, satellite, and other bottlenecks) and the need to support large numbers of attendees, place stringent architectural requirements on collaboration solutions.

In order to demonstrate the framework capabilities we propose three different assessment cases. The first case includes a reliable Internet connection. The testing report highlights the following communication parameters: video resolution – 320×240 pixels, video frame rate – 10 fps / key frame interval – 30, H.264 video compression standard; audio sample rate – 22.1 kHz, 8 bits/sample, equipment/ application sharing resolution – 1024×768 pixels, frame rate – 5 fps, response time varies between 15 and 100 ms. The second assessment case is based on a poor Internet connection. The testing report includes the parameter values: video resolution – 160×120 pixels, video frame rate – 5 fps, / key frame interval – 30, H.264 video compression standard; audio sample rate = 22.1 kHz, 8 bits/sample, equipment/ application sharing resolution – 800×600 pixels, frame rate = 2–4 fps, response time is between 100 and 250 ms. The third case underlines the possibility of extending the e-learning services in the mobile area. We used two Android tablet connected to a 3G network and a PC. The set of values has been similar to the second case, excepting the Internet connection bottlenecks or the situation when the response time raises over the acceptance limit (300 ms) when the video transmission will be stopped until it will be become acceptable (less than 100 ms for more than 5 s).

The novel educational methods and concepts discussed in the book chapter have gained excellent acceptance from experienced students in master programmes and life-long learning and have shown potential for increasing their understanding beyond the level provided by traditional methods. Our testing continued in higher education with the "Multimedia Technologies" course, English line of study. The results have been more than satisfied. The team work was correctly percept by all the students, they work together in order to complete the projects in timeline, the class interaction has been gradually improved due to the hybrid classware implementation and the periodical evaluation had good results, as well as the final test. Finally, the students involved in Erasmus grants remotely attend the lectures without any constrains from the teachers' part.

6 Conclusions

The book chapter illustrates a reliable and easy-to-use Internet Supported Collaborative Learning prototype that complies with the extended LAMP architecture. The system is developed in order to fix a set of issues met in the CSCL area such as: problems with the academic staff, time management, responsibilities during the educational process, interaction or educational content. The goals for real-time collaboration technologies are straightforward, for that reason, we must add some other important aspects to the ones already enumerated.

The prototype illustrated in the book chapter integrates advanced teaching technologies such as smart boards, tablet PCs, digital tablet pens, or video projectors, within a stable and powerful educational environment that supports blended learning services. The lecturer is able to manage the educational process using two main educational components integrated in a "hybrid classware" implementation. The virtual classroom component enables the lecturer to remotely conduct the class and the virtual shared space component allows him/her to present the educational content in a traditional way. The students can opt for both learning services in the classroom, so lively attend the teacher's exposure, or to virtually participate to the learning process, using the web browser. Both attendance modes supported by the hybrid classware implementation enable the student to interact with the class and educational resources but the virtual educational act might be more effective than classroom-based. The students involved in the higher and postgraduate education belong to the "Net Generation," they have a strong IT background and consider the advanced technology as very useful in the teaching/learning act. In conclusion, the success of the hybrid classware implementation and blended learning approach depends on the IT background of the academic staff involved in the educational act.

Project- and *problem-based learning* approaches are also implemented in the collaborative learning framework. The tutor is able to define projects with different degrees of difficulties and plans tasks and milestones. The students select a project, review the requirements and subscribe, work as a team and complete the tasks according to the project plan. The team members communicate each other using the project messaging or remotely collaborate using the *online focus group* tool. OFG tool allows the students to schedule project meetings work as a team, correct/help each other, even invite the tutor in order to clarify important aspects or lively demonstrate the results they achieved.

Software simulation and hands-on experiments mean remote access to lab applications and equipment. The students are able to complete their tasks in the lab, from home or campus and the teachers can monitor their activities and evaluate the tasks, centralize the results and analyze the statistics and reports. The elastic learning environment dynamically allocates one virtual machine for each student that remotely accesses the lab infrastructure. Sometimes lab activities involve application and equipment sharing. The functionality is also included in the prototype. Its role is to enable teachers to collaborate with the students during the virtual laboratory sessions.

Based on the cloud computing paradigms, Software as a Service (SaaS), Platform as a Service (SaaS) and Infrastructure as a Service (SaaS), the proposed framework permits the e-learning service providers to extend their legacy e-learning systems in order to support blended learning capabilities in higher and postgraduate education.

Acknowledgement This paper was supported by the project "Development and support of multidisciplinary postdoctoral programmes in major technical areas of national strategy of Research – Development – Innovation" 4D-POSTDOC, contract no. POSDRU/89/1.5/S/52603, project co-funded by the "European Social Fund through Sectoral Operational Programme Human Resources Development 2007–2013."

References

Ambikairajah, E., Epps, J., Sheng, M., Celler B., 2007. *Tablet PC and Electronic Whiteboard Use in Signal Processing Education In IEEE SIGNAL PROCESSING MAGAZINE.* pp. 130–133.
Manseur, R. and Manseur, Z., 2009. A Synchronous Distance Learning Program Implementation in Engineering and Mathematics. *Proceedings of the 39th ASEE/IEEE Frontiers in Education Conference,* San Antonio, TX.

Shaozi, L., Zhongpan, Q., Tangqui, L. & Huowang, C., 2003. Architecture of computer supported collaborative learning based on EJB middleware and its implementation. *Proceedings of the 8th International Conference on Computer Supported Cooperative Work in Design.* pp. 142–148, Vol.1.

Tan, C. and Chan Y. Y., 2008. Knowledge Community: A Knowledge-Building System for Global Collaborative Project Learning. Proceedings of the IEEE, Volume 96, Issue 6. pp. 1049–1061.

Williams, S. and Roberts, T.S., 2002. Computer-Supported Collaborative Learning: Strengths and weaknesses. *Proceedings of the International Conference on Computers in Education.* pp. 328–331.

Xiaoyan M., Walter, D., Berry, C., 2008. Work in progress - a study of the effect of instructional media in an undergraduate electrical circuits course. *Proceedings of the Frontiers in Education Conference.* pp. 1–2.

Part III
Technology, Learning and Expertise

Chapter 7
Technologies and the Assessment of Higher Order Outcomes

A Snapshot of Academic Practice in Curriculum Alignment

Margot McNeill, Maree Gosper, and John Hedberg

1 Introduction

Higher order learning such as evaluation, problem solving and creative thinking are espoused as fundamentals of university learning. Advocates of these skills, such as Bradshaw et al. (2002), promote their potential to increase the degree to which students can apply their learning to new situations without the need for explicit prompting (Boud and Falchikov 2006; Bransford et al. 1999). This application can be improved if students become aware of themselves as learners at a metacognitive level and are supported in learning how to monitor and assess their own strategies and resources (Bransford et al. 1999). Yet, although they appear in many graduate attribute statements and descriptions of unit outlines, little is known about how well academics understand how to devise the curriculum and assessment methods to elicit these higher order outcomes. Understanding these links between higher order outcomes, curriculum design and the potential of new technologies affordances takes time, a scarce commodity for today's time poor academics.

In revising Bloom's (1956) original taxonomy, Anderson et al (2001) added an additional knowledge dimension to form a matrix which highlights the array of possible objectives and the relationship between them. Of particular interest in this study were the lower right hand categories, denoted by the diagonal pattern in Table 7.1, skills and knowledge associated with critical thinking, creativity and self-assessment.

As they have been introduced into education, many new technologies have been heralded as having the potential to spark re-examination of assessment strategies (Jonassen and Reeves 1996; Philips and and Lowe 2003). The opportunities offered by technologies to support the design, delivery and administration of diagnostic, formative and summative assessment have been well documented in the literature

M. McNeill (✉) • M. Gosper • J. Hedberg
Macquarie University, Sydney, Australia
e-mail: margot.mcneill@mq.edu.au; maree.gosper@mq.edu.au; john.hedberg@mq.edu.au

P. Isaias et al. (eds.), *Towards Learning and Instruction in Web 3.0: Advances in Cognitive and Educational Psychology*, DOI 10.1007/978-1-4614-1539-8_7,
© Springer Science+Business Media, LLC 2012

Table 7.1 The revised Bloom's taxonomy

Knowledge dimension	The cognitive process dimension					
	Remember	Understand	Apply	Analyze	Evaluate	Create
Factual						
Conceptual						
Procedural						
Meta-cognitive						

(Crisp 2007). Social networking tools such as blogs and wikis have been explored for their potential to capture both the processes of student learning and the final artifacts to be submitted, in either collaborative or individual contexts (Boulos et al. 2006; Bower et al. 2009; Churchill 2007; Hewitt and and Peters 2006). Shepherd raises the possibility that the use of these technologies could enable higher education to "better assess aspects of learning that have proved difficult to assess using more conventional means" (2009, p. 386).

While the technologies themselves may have potential for enhancing assessment practices in higher education, Gray et al (2010) warn that while including students' use of social networking tools seems to make sense for university learning, the substantial differences from traditional forms of assessable student work need to be acknowledged: "The interactivity and social interaction that it encourages cannot be assigned or marked to full effect by using assessment strategies that academics may have used previously, for written reports, essays, examinations or class presentations, for example" (p. 105) The academics' ability to integrate the tools into an aligned curriculum is essential (Böttger and and Röll 2004; Burns 2005; Ma 2009). The assessment practices themselves need to change in order to achieve an effective match between assessment processes and technologies.

A study by Samuelowicz and Bain (2002) suggested that, whatever the outcomes they intend for their students, academic perspectives about the role of assessment in teaching and learning might be more influential in determining whether their units are designed to address higher order learning outcomes. In exploring academic attitudes toward assessment and feedback, they found orientations ranging from "reproduction of important bits of knowledge, procedure and skill" to "transforming conceptions of the discipline and/or world". Depending on the level of these understandings, appropriate assessment tasks could range from multiple choice questions testing understanding of facts to open-ended questions testing the ability to apply principles to a given, familiar situation. Conversely, if academics perceived assessment as part of the learning required to challenge existing knowledge, then they were more likely to design assessment requiring higher order tasks such as evaluation and creation of new solutions (Samuelowicz and and Bain 2002).

Gosper (2011) advocates a three-phased approach for using technologies to scaffold students' development of higher order intellectual skills. The MAPLET framework can be used to guide the integration of technologies to make more explicit the learning processes underpinning the curriculum. Yet, while much of the literature advocates this alignment between learning outcomes, teaching and learning activities, assessment tasks and technology uses, how much does academic practice in curriculum design reflect the theory? This paper reports on research conducted in an Australian University which aimed to explore this question.

2 Method

The research being reported is part of a larger study into academic practice in using technologies to support the assessment of higher order learning. Conducted over 4 years at an Australian university, the study explored how academics understand:

- The learning processes underpinning the assessment of higher order learning;
- The affordances of social networking tools for capturing learning processes and interactions; and
- The links between assessment strategies and technology affordances – lecturers' ability to develop strategies for use in their own assessment practice.

Due to space limitations, the scope of this chapter is limited to the third aim.

Participants in the study were the convenors of online units using the University's Learning Management System (LMS). These academics were chosen because they were already working in an online environment and have an understanding of the limitations and strengths of the online environment.

In the previous phase of the study, a series of in-depth interviews was conducted with a selective sample of unit convenors from across the University. Although space does not allow for a detailed description of the interview results, more information is available about this qualitative phase of the study in McNeill, Gosper and Hedberg, (2010a). In order to explore whether the broad themes emerging from this previous qualitative phase of the study related to a larger sample from across the University, an online survey was developed. The survey used Anderson et al. (2001)*Taxonomy for Learning, Teaching and Assessing* and Samuelowicz and Bain's (2002) *Orientations Toward Assessment* as frameworks, to explore:

- The types of learning technologies the convenors used and for what type of learning;
- The focus of learning outcomes, teaching and learning activities and assessment tasks; and
- The convenors' attitudes toward the role of assessment in learning and teaching.

The design of the survey drew heavily on the results of previous phases of the study, including the technologies chosen for inclusion (McNeill 2010). Although the intention of the study was to explore practical rather than statistical significance, questions requiring rating on five point likert scales were included in order to facilitate more efficient data analysis. The survey development software 'SurveyMonkey' was used to deliver the survey. While this paper addresses the questions relating to curriculum design overall, the results pertaining to the uses of technologies to support assessment are relevant to the discussion and have been included in summary form.

3   Results

Of the 734 academics invited to participate, 180 responded to the survey (24.5%) although some respondents did not answer all questions. The first part of the survey asked about the context of the chosen units. Respondents represented a wide range of discipline areas and all faculties although there was large representation from Humanities. Post-graduate units were most commonly represented with 31.8% respondents, which when combined with (17.9%) final year units, accounted for 49.7% of the units represented. Middle years of undergraduate programs were reported by 29.1% of respondents, followed by 21.2% from first year. The highest representation was from units with a mixture of internal and external enrolment modes, (51.1%) followed by internal only (41.6%) and external only (7.3%) modes.

The second part of the survey asked participants to indicate (using a five point scale) which technologies they used to support assessment and the types of learning outcomes these were used to target. The results are summarised in Table 7.2, with the types of learning outcomes listed in the first column and the technologies used in relation to each of these in the remaining columns. Responses indicating uses to a large or moderate extent were included in the tallies. The total number of respondents using each type of technology is included at the bottom of each column.

Table 7.2 Technologies as targeting specific learning outcomes

Answer options	Quiz	Discussion forum	Wikis	Blogs	Online portfolios	Virtual worlds
Recognise or recall information, concepts or procedures	**80.7%** **(46)**	28.8% (33)	22.2% (2)	37.5% (6)	44.4% (4)	33.3% (2)
Understand, explain, categorise or summarise information	58.2% (32)	45.4% (54)	66.6% (6)	55.6% (10)	40.0% (4)	33.3% (2)
Apply information, concepts or procedures in a range of situations	45.5% (20)	**63.5%** **(52)**	66.6% (6)	55.6% (10)	60.0% (6)	33.3% (2)
Analyse, organise or deconstruct concepts, procedures or scenarios	29.7% (16)	45.3% (53)	**66.7%** **(6)**	44.5% (8)	50.0% (5)	33.3% (2)
Evaluate or make judgments about concepts, situations, procedures or hypotheses	33.9% (18)	52.1% (62)	60.0% (6)	55.6% (10)	60.0% (6)	**60.0%** **(3)**
Create, design or construct hypotheses ideas, products, procedures or scenarios	7.6% (4)	28.0% (32)	**80.0%** **(8)**	47.0% (8)	60.0% (6)	33.3% (2)
Critique or evaluate their own knowledge or performance	35.8% (19)	39.1% (45)	44.4% (4)	**72.2%** **(13)**	70.0% **(7)**	33.3% (2)
Total responses	**57**	**121**	**10**	**18**	**10**	**6**

The highest percentage of use for each tool in relation to the cognitive processes is highlighted in bold. The two most commonly used tools, discussion forums and online quizzes had the highest response rate for the categories of application and recall respectively. Of the 57 respondents using quizzes, 46 indicated that they used them to assess whether students could recognize or recall information, concepts or procedures. Students' ability to understand or apply information also featured highly. Overall, discussion forums were the most widely used technology, with 129 of the total 176 respondents (73.3%) indicating they used them.

The data on how technologies were used suggested that there is a continued focus on lower order outcomes by the majority of respondents, with a small number exploring emerging tools and targeting the higher order outcomes. There were examples of respondents using wikis, blogs, online portfolios and virtual worlds for higher order outcomes, but relatively low numbers. Of the ten respondents using wikis, eight indicated that they targeted creativity as a higher order learning outcome. Metacognitive knowledge, where students were assessed on their ability to critique or evaluate their own performance, featured most highly in the use of blogs and online portfolios, followed by understanding and evaluation. Evaluation was the target with the highest rating for virtual worlds, although it is difficult to draw conclusions from such small numbers of respondents. Creation tasks featured strongly for wikis and online portfolios although numbers were small.

The next series of questions in the survey explored perceptions about curriculum alignment between intended learning outcomes, teaching and learning activities, assessment strategies and technologies.

3.1 Respondents' Curriculum Design

Participants were asked about the types of learning intended as outcomes for the students in a unit selected by the respondents. Results are reported in Table 7.3.

In regard to learning outcomes the most common was application, with 94.4% of respondents agreeing that this was targeted to a large or moderate extent. Evaluation and analysis were also highly rated, with 90% and 88.1% of respondents agreeing that they were targeted to a large or moderate extent. Outcomes associated with recalling information and creativity were more likely to be targeted to a small extent, not at all or viewed as not applicable. Participants were also able to comment on their intended learning outcomes in a free text question. Their comments reiterated the options above, such as a focus on student understanding or application. For example, *apply unit concepts to their own work situation*. Graduate capabilities such as collaboration, decision-making, capacity to work in a team or project management also featured in some of the comments, such as *learn how to work in a team and manage a project – time and self management*.

Table 7.3 Types of intended learning outcomes targeted in the unit

The INTENDED LEARNING OUTCOMES target the students' ability to:

Answer options	To a large extent	To a mod extent	To a small extent	Not at all	N/A	Rating average	Response count
Recognise or recall information, concepts or procedures	19.8% (32)	**40.7%** **(66)**	32.7% (53)	6.2% (10)	0.6% (1)	2.27	162
Understand, explain, categorise or summarise information	33.5% (54)	**50.9%** **(82)**	13.7% (22)	1.9% (3)	0	1.84	161
Apply information, concepts or procedures in a range of situations	**67.1%** **(108)**	27.3% (44)	5% (8)	0.6% (1)	0	1.39	161
Analyse, organise or deconstruct concepts, procedures or scenarios	**57.9%** **(92)**	30.2% (48)	8.2% (13)	2.5% (4)	1.3% (2)	1.59	159
Evaluate or make judgments about concepts, situations, procedures or hypotheses	**62.5%** **(100)**	27.5% (44)	7.5% (12)	0.6% (1)	1.9% (3)	1.52	160
Create, designs or construct hypotheses ideas, products, procedures or scenarios	**35%** **(56)**	33.1% (53)	22.5% (36)	5% (8)	4.4% (7)	2.11	160
Critique or evaluate their own knowledge or performance	**41%** **(66)**	31.1% (50)	22.4% (36)	3.7% (6)	1.9% (3)	1.94	161
Other (please specify)							8
Answered question							162

3.2 Teaching Activities

The next set of questions related to the learning activities. Participants were asked about the extent to which the teaching activities facilitated the development of the specified outcomes.

Results from these questions are presented in Table 7.4. Respondents indicated that application, evaluation and analysis were most likely to be targeted to a large extent. Of the respondents 94.2% and 89.4% indicated that application and evaluation, respectively, were targeted to a large or moderate extent. Creativity and recall were least prevalent.

Table 7.4 Types of learning targeted by teaching and learning activities

The current LEARNING & TEACHING ACTIVITIES are designed to support students to:

Answer Options	To a large extent	To a mod extent	To a small extent	Not at all	Not applicable	Rating average	Response count
Recognise or recall information, concepts or procedures	18.8% (30)	**47.5%** (76)	28.1% (45)	5.6% (9)	0	2.21	160
Understand, explain, categorise or summarise information	36.6% (59)	**50.3%** (81)	11.2% (18)	1.9% (3)	0	1.78	161
Apply information, concepts or procedures in a range of situations	**65.4%** (104)	28.8% (46)	5% (8)	0.6% (1)	0	1.41	159
Analyse, organise or deconstruct concepts, procedures or scenarios	**48.8%** (78)	38.8% (62)	9.4% (15)	2.5% (4)	0.6% (1)	1.68	160
Evaluate or make judgments about concepts, situations, procedures or hypotheses	**57.5%** (92)	31.9% (51)	8.8% (14)	1.3% (2)	0.6% (1)	1.56	160
Create, designs or construct hypotheses ideas, products, procedures or scenarios	35.2% (56)	29.6% (47)	25.8% (41)	5.7% (9)	3.8% (6)	2.13	159
Critique or evaluate their own knowledge or performance	35.8% (57)	**36.5%** (58)	20.8% (33)	6.3% (10)	0.6% (1)	1.99	159
Answered question							161

3.3   Assessment Tasks

The final set of questions focused on the extent to which assessment tasks addressed the specified outcomes.

As shown in Table 7.5, the type of assessment tasks most frequently focused on application, with 93.8% of respondents agreeing that this was targeted to a large or moderate extent. Evaluation and analysis followed with 88.7% and 88.8% respectively. Almost one third of respondents to this question (49) indicated that they assessment tasks targeted creativity to a small extent or not at all. Similarly, meta-cognition was rated as not at all or to a small extent by 50 respondents.

4   Analysis

The survey was designed to explore academic perspectives on curriculum design, with questions targeting the learning outcomes, teaching activities, assessment tasks and technologies.

In order to establish a clearer picture about the respondents' curriculum designs, the results for the types of learning targeted to a large or moderate extent for intended learning outcomes (ILOs), teaching and learning activities (TLAs) and assessment tasks (ATs) were summarised in Table 7.6. Rating averages for each category were also included, based on the five point likert scale with 1 being to a large extent and 5 being not applicable.

The cognitive processes rated most highly are bolded. Almost 95% of respondents indicated that application of knowledge or concepts was important or very important. Evaluation and analysis were also important or very important to around 90% of respondents. While it is heartening that relatively fewer designs focus on the recall of concepts or procedures, the higher order targets of creativity and metacognition are also less frequently represented.

In keeping with the findings of the first two phases of the study, many convenors have intentions of higher order outcomes but don't necessarily design all elements in the curriculum accordingly. Over two thirds of survey respondents indicated that they targeted higher order outcomes such as creativity and metacognition, however designing the curriculum to elicit these outcomes seems challenging for many. They were less likely to target these in their teaching activities and their assessment tasks. For example, in analyzing the responses to the items about meta-cognition, 116 of the 161 respondents to this question (72.1%) indicated that their learning outcomes targeted students' ability to critique or evaluate their own performance. Of the respondents, 66.4% indicated that their assessment tasks targeted meta-cognition to a large or moderate extent and 10% indicated they were not targeted at all or were not applicable. Results of an earlier survey in the study established that the most frequently used assessment tasks were the more traditional options of essays and assignments along with exams. There was a strong focus on the end product of learning with little use of technology options to capture the learning processes (McNeill, et al 2008).

Table 7.5 Types of learning targeted by assessment tasks

The current ASSESSMENT TASKS are designed to assess whether students can:

Answer options	To a large extent	To a mod extent	To a small extent	Not at all	Not applicable	Rating average	Response count
Recognise or recall information, concepts or procedures	25% (40)	**39.4%** (63)	28.8% (46)	6.3% (10)	0.6% (1)	2.18	160
Understand, explain, categorise or summarise information	38.9% (63)	**45.1%** (73)	14.8% (24)	0.6% (1)	0.6% (1)	1.79	162
Apply information, concepts or procedures in a range of situations	**62.5%** (100)	31.3% (50)	4.4% (7)	0.6% (1)	1.3% (2)	1.47	160
Analyse, organise or deconstruct concepts, procedures or scenarios	**55.9%** (90)	32.9% (53)	8.1% (13)	1.2% (2)	1.9% (3)	1.60	161
Evaluate or make judgments about concepts, situations, procedures or hypotheses	**56.6%** (90)	32.1% (51)	8.2% (13)	1.3% (2)	1.9% (3)	1.60	159
Create, designs or construct hypotheses ideas, products, procedures or scenarios	35.4% (57)	30.4% (49)	23.6% (38)	6.8% (11)	3.7% (6)	2.13	161
Critique or evaluate their own knowledge or performance	29.8% (48)	**36.6%** (59)	23.6% (38)	8.1% (13)	1.9% (3)	2.16	161
Answered question							162

Table 7.6 Types of learning targeted for the Anderson et al categories to a large or moderate extent

Answer options	Intended learning outcomes	ILO rating average	Teaching & learning activities	TLA rating average	Assessment tasks	AT rating average
Recognise or recall information,	60.5%	2.27	66.3%	2.21	64.4%	2.18
	(98)		(106)		(103)	
Understand, explain, categorise	84.4%	1.84	86.9%	1.78	84%	1.79
	(136)		(140)		(136)	
Apply info, concepts or procedures	**94.4%**	1.39	**94.2%**	1.41	**93.8%**	1.47
	(152)		**(150)**		**(150)**	
Analyse, organise or deconstruct concepts,	**88.1%**	1.59	87.6%	1.68	**88.8%**	1.60
	(140)		(140)		**(143)**	
Evaluate or make judgments	90%	1.52	89.4%	1.56	**88.7%**	1.60
	(144)		(143)		**(141)**	
Create, designs or construct	68.1%	2.11	64.8%	2.13	65.8%	2.13
	(109)		(103)		(106)	
Critique or evaluate their own knowledge or performance	72.1%	1.94	72.3%	1.99	66.4%	2.16
	(116)		(115)		(107)	
Response count	162		161		162	

Despite the promise of the new social technologies, this study concludes that change is slow and that advances in assessment strategies, particularly when technologies are used, have not been dramatic. While the study indicates that many unit convenors are well intentioned about the outcomes they intended for their students and show alignment in how they conceptualise their units, higher order learning as the target of curriculum design seems elusive. Application of concepts and procedures is most prevalent and the higher order outcomes of creativity and metacognition seem most problematic. The most widely used tools remain quizzes and discussion forums, associated with the University LMS and are most likely to target student ability to apply concepts and/or procedures. Despite the prevalence of a range of technologies with affordances to support more innovative assessment processes, practices seem to perpetuate traditional models. Those who indicated that they explore emerging tools were more likely to target higher order cognitive processes, however numbers in these categories were considerably smaller than the lower order processes. For example, while only small numbers used wikis, blogs or e-portfolios, these respondents were more likely to use them to support the assessment of higher order outcomes such as creativity and metacognition and to recognize the affordances offered such as encouraging student reflection.

In the earlier phases of the study, assessment processes in capstone units were found to be more likely to be designed to elicit higher order outcomes (McNeill, 2010). To explore this issue in the survey data, the results were filtered to compare the responses about assessment tasks from convenors of first year and final year units. Comparing the results from first year and final year undergraduates revealed that the curriculum designs for the units are not dissimilar. Application is more likely to be targeted to a large or moderate extent in undergraduate units, but only by a small margin. Of the 33 respondents teaching first year units, 90.9% targeted application to a large or moderate extent, as compared with 85.7% of respondents convening final year units (n = 28). Evaluation is more likely to be targeted to a large or moderate extent in final year units than first year, with 92.6% and 87.1% respectively. According to the MAPLET framework (Gosper 2011), the curriculum focus of final year students should be substantially different from that of first year units; targeting the refinement and extension of "robust interconnected knowledge networks that form problem solving schemas with embedded principles, procedures and heuristics; and the development of metacognitive skills" (p. 27).

The results provide a timely reminder that training and support initiatives need to focus on supporting teaching staff in making appropriate use of the basic tools available in the centralized LMS system. While the newer social networking tools may offer potential to expand the repertoire available to academics in how they assess student learning, these tools require a greater understanding of both the technology and pedagogy implications. What is required next is a sustained effort for professional development initiatives to support unit convenors in making clear links between the elements of their curriculum, including technologies, to elicit the types of outcomes they intend.

5 Conclusion

This survey was limited to exploring the perspectives of those convenors of online units at one Australian university who used the centrally supported LMS. While there may be other views from those using different platforms, the results provide a snapshot of current uses of technologies and perspectives about curriculum alignment overall, including intended learning outcomes, teaching and learning activities and assessment strategies.

The results suggest that while many academics intend higher order outcomes, they are less likely to design their teaching activities or assessment tasks accordingly, especially if technologies are used to support the assessment process. The results provide a realistic baseline when considering the rhetoric around the heralded affordances of new technologies and reinforce the findings from previous phases of the study that the predominant focus of technologies is on assessing lower order outcomes, indicative of a focus on perpetuating rather than transforming assessment. They present a reminder that professional development initiatives need to focus on developing academics' capacity to design their curricula to elicit higher order outcomes, selecting and integrating technologies as part of this holistic approach.

Analysis of the survey data will continue to explore these themes of alignment and transformation in more detail, to inform professional development initiatives which, rather than promoting tools out of context, target support for academics in using tools to refine their strategies for assessing higher order learning.

References

Anderson, L., Krathwohl, D., Airsasian, P., Cruikshank, K., Mayer, R., Pintrich, P., et al. (Eds.). (2001). *A taxonomy for learning, teaching and assessing: A revision of Bloom's taxonomy of educational objectives*. New York: Longman.

Biggs, J., & Tang, C. (2007). *Teaching for quality learning at university* (3 rd ed.). Berkshire: Open University Press.

Bloom, B. S. (Ed.). (1956). *Taxonomy of Educational Objectives: The Classification of Educational Goals*. New York: McKay.

Böttger, M., & Röll, M. (2004). *Weblog Publishing as Support for Exploratory Learning on the World Wide Web*. Paper presented at the Cognition and Exploratory Learning in the Digital Age (CELDA) 2004.

Boulos, M. K., and, Maramba, I., & Wheeler, S. (2006). Wikis, blogs and podcasts: a new generation of Web-based tools for virtual collaborative clinical practice and education. *BMC Medical Education, 6*(41).

Boud, D., & Falchikov, N. (2006). Aligning assessment with long-term learning. *Assessment & Evaluation in Higher Education, 31*(4), 399–413.

Bower, M., Hedberg, J., & Kuswara, A. (2009). *Conceptualising Web 2.0 enabled learning designs*. In Australasian Society for Computers in Learning in Tertiary Education (ASCILITE), Auckland, (pp. 1153–1162).

Bradshaw, A. C., Bishop, J. L., Gens, L. S., Miller, S. L., & Rogers, M. A. (2002). The relationship of the World Wide Web to thinking skills. *Educational Media International, 39*, 275–284.

Bransford, J. D., Brown, A. L., & Cocking, R. R. (1999). *How People Learn: Brain, Mind, Experience, and School*. Washington, D.C.: National Academy Press.

Burns, M. (2005). Tools for the mind. *Educational Leadership, 63*(4), 49–53.

Churchill, D. (2007). *Blogs, other Web 2.0 technologies and possibilities for educational applications*. Paper presented at the 4th international conference on informatics, educational technology and new media, Sombor, Serbia.

Crisp, G. (2007). *The e-assessment handbook*. New York: Continuum International Publishing.

Gosper, M. (2011). A Framework for Matching Aims, Processes, Learner Expertise and Technologies. In Ifenthaler, D., Isaias, P., Spector, J.M., Kinshuk, Sampson, D. (Eds.) *Multiple Perspectives on Problem Solving and Learning in the Digital Age*. New York: Springer.

Gray, K., Thompson, C., Sheard, J., Clerehan, R., & Hamilton, M. (2010). Students as Web 2.0 authors: Implications for assessment design and conduct. *Australasian Journal of Educational Technology, 26*(1), 105–122.

Hewitt, J., & Peters, V. (2006). *Using Wikis to Support Knowledge Building in a Graduate Education Course*. Paper presented at the World Conference on Educational Multimedia, Hypermedia and Telecommunications (EDMEDIA), Chesapeake, VA.

Jonassen, D. H., & Reeves, T. (1996). Learning with technology: using computers as cognitive tools. In D. H. Jonassen (Ed.), *Handbook of research for educational communications and technology* (pp. 693–719). New York: Macmillan.

Ma, A. W. (2009). Computer Supported Collaborative Learning and Higher Order Thinking Skills: A Case Study of Textile Studies *Interdisciplinary Journal of E-Learning and Learning Objects, 5*, 145–167.

McNeill, M., Gosper, M., & Hedberg, J. (2008). Engaging students with higher order learning (or not): insights into academic practice. A paper presented at the ATN Assessment Conference, November 2008.

McNeill, M. (2010). Technologies to support the assessment of complex learning in capstone units: Two case studies. In Ifenthaler, D., Isaias, P., Spector, J.M., Kinshuk, Sampson, D. (Eds.) *Multiple Perspectives on Problem Solving and Learning in the Digital Age*. New York: Springer.

McNeill, M., Gosper, M. & Hedberg, J. (2010a). Academic practice in aligning learning outcomes, assessment strategies and technologies: Joining the dots (or not). In M. B. Nunes & M. McPherson (Eds.), *Proceedings of the IADIS International Conference e-Learning* (Vol. 1, pp. 129–138). Freiburg, Germany: IADIS.

Philips, R., & Lowe, K. (2003). *Issues associated with the equivalence of traditional and online assessment*. Paper presented at the 20th Annual Conference of ACSILITE: Interact, Integrate, Impact.

Samuelowicz, K., & Bain, J. (2002). Identifying academics' orientations to assessment practice. *Higher Education Research and Development, 43*, 173–201.

Shephard, K. (2009). E is for exploration: Assessing hard-to-measure learning outcomes *British Journal of Educational Technology, 40*(2), 386–398.

Chapter 8
Visual Algorithm Simulation Exercises with Authentic Data Sets

Ville Karavirta and Ari Korhonen

1 Introduction

Motivation has an important role in education, and many approaches have been tried to motivate students. Engaging visualizations and meaningful teaching materials are one approach. Koike et al. (2005) developed an adaptive e-learning system, and argued that adaptive, appropriate teaching materials motivate students. Ahoniemi et al. (2007) note that humor and real life examples in computer science (CS) assignments increase student motivation. We believe that, in general, the use of materials that involve practical use of authentic data sets has a role to play to motivate students because they see the activity to be relevant to the learning needs. That is, examples and exercises that are derived from authentic sources, reflecting real-world data sets, should engage students and stimulate their imagination so that they will be more motivated to learn. And, no doubt, better motivation enhances the learning.

Algorithm Visualization (AV) has been used to improve students' understanding of the many abstract concepts occurring in CS. AVs aid learning difficult concepts and make learning more interesting. Lately, making the visualization more interactive has been argued to increase the learning benefits (Hundhausen et al. 2002; Naps et al. 2003a). Naps et al. (2003a) specified Engagement Taxonomy where they hypothesize that the learning benefits increase as the interactivity increases. For learning graph algorithms, there already exist numerous engaging algorithm visualization systems and topic-specific visualizations such as ALVIE (Crescenzi and Nocentini 2007), Animal (Rößling and Freisleben 2002), IAPPGA (Wu 2005), and Leonardo Web (Bonifaci et al. 2005). All of the existing systems use abstract data, typically simple textbook examples in which letters denote nodes, and numbers denote the weighted edges to represent a graph. While this is beneficial for learning graph algorithms, it does not reflect any real-world application of the algorithms.

V. Karavirta (✉) • A. Korhonen
Department of Computer Science and Engineering, Aalto University, P.O.Box 15400,
FI-00076 Aalto, Finland
e-mail: ville.karavirta@aalto.fi; ari.korhonen@aalto.fi

P. Isaias et al. (eds.), *Towards Learning and Instruction in Web 3.0: Advances in Cognitive and Educational Psychology*, DOI 10.1007/978-1-4614-1539-8_8,
© Springer Science+Business Media, LLC 2012

In this paper, we will demonstrate the use of authentic data, in contrast to abstract data, to provide interactive exercises based on AV. We introduce a framework for algorithm visualizations to capture the students' interest by making them to construct their own animations using real-world data sets as suggested by the Engagement Taxonomy (Naps et al. 2003a) and Ahoniemi et al. (2007). Using authentic data has become easier in the recent years thanks to the rapid increase in the amount of (semantic) data available. The research question we are trying to answer is *can we utilize semantic data to provide students with assignments on graph algorithms with authentic data?*

To answer this, we create a mashup on top of Google Maps (http://maps.google.com/) to visualize location data fetched from DBPedia (Auer et al. 2008). A mashup is "a Web page or Web site that combines information and services from multiple sources on the Web" (Murugesan 2007). Mashups have gained more and more popularity on the Internet, and there exist several programmable APIs (see, for example, http://www.programmableweb.com). Moreover, many businesses base their whole existence on building applications on top of third-party APIs. There are, for example, numerous applications built on top of Twitter and Facebook.

The open data sets enable building of innovative web services and mashups. In educational context, online data sources have been used in programming assignments to make them more interesting (DePasquale 2006; Thornton and Edwards 2008). In our case, the end product is a visualization of a graph on a map, where the nodes are real locations, such as Bridges in New York. The interaction comes from students simulating graph algorithms by clicking nodes or edged on the graphs. Our preliminary results show that this novel approach is a motivating way to provide interactive AV to learners, and thus improve the learning experience as well as enhance the learning outcome.

The rest of the paper is organized as follows. Section 2 introduces the concept of semantic web, DBPedia, and the field of algorithm visualization with the vast number of existing systems for learning graph algorithms. Section 3, in turn, shows our solution to the research question. Section 4 discusses the anecdotal evidence from our first experiences with students using the exercise. Finally, Section 5 discusses the suitability of our approach to education and concludes the paper.

2 Background

2.1 Semantic Web and Web Mashups

The vision of the semantic web introduced by Berners-Lee et al. (2001) is a web where meaning (semantics) is defined for information. This allows machines to use this meaning to understand the information better, thus allowing more intelligent and automated services to be built. Although Ding and Finin (2006) concluded that the amount of semantic data is increasing, the data is sparse. Thus, there is a need for gathering the data from several sources. Not only to collect reasonable amount of data, but also for making it more reliable. Fortunately, a more recent study by Halpin (2009) showed that there is useful data available on semantic web.

As the main reason for the increased usefulness of data on semantic web, Halpin mentions the release of services like DBPedia. DBPedia is *"a community effort to extract structured information from Wikipedia"* (Auer et al. 2008). In addition, it links Wikipedia data with other open data sets on the web. Like a lot of data on semantic web, DBPedia stores the information as RDF (Resource Description Framework, a W3C Recommendation). Humans and machines can query the RDF data with SPARQL using the SPARQL endpoint DBPedia provides.

The increase in usable semantic data has seen a surge in web mashups, services combining data from various sources on the web (Murugesan 2007). For the end user of the mashup, the service appears as one integrated service. Zang et al. (2008) mention map synthesis, enterprise information integration, and web service tracking as some of the use-cases for mashups. They also note that the most popular API used in building mashups is Google Maps.

2.2   Learning Graph Algorithms

Student engagement is an important part of algorithm visualization. Previous research on educational algorithm visualization suggests that the more engaging the visualizations the better the learning results (Hundhausen et al. 2002; Naps et al. 2003b). This has been hypothesized in the Engagement Taxonomy introduced by Naps et al. (2003b), which defined six levels of engagement. These engagement levels are *no viewing* (no visualization is used), *viewing* (students are passively watching a visualization, possibly controlling the execution by, for example, moving backward and forward and changing the speed), *responding* (adds interaction in the form of questions related to the content of the visualization), *changing* (students are allowed to change the visualization, for example, by providing the input data to an algorithm), *constructing* (students themselves are required to construct an algorithm visualization), and *presenting* (expects students to explain an algorithm using a visualization, which can be created by the student herself or by someone else).

For all of the engagement levels, there are several existing systems for teaching graph algorithms. For the constructing level, which is of interest for us, there are three systems available: PILOT (Bridgeman et al. 2000), PathFinder (Sánchez-Torrubia et al. 2009), and TRAKLA2 (Malmi et al. 2004).

PILOT is targeted to tracing exercises in which the learner solves problems related to graph algorithms. The system provides the learner a graphical illustration of the correctness of the solution along with the score and an explanation of the possible errors made. The current tool, however, is limited to graph algorithms, and especially the minimum spanning tree problem. Thus, there is no underlying general-purpose application framework that can be extended to other concepts and problem types without creating a new interface. PathFinder is a similar system targeted to learning Dijkstra's shortest-path algorithm. TRAKLA2, however, incorporates a

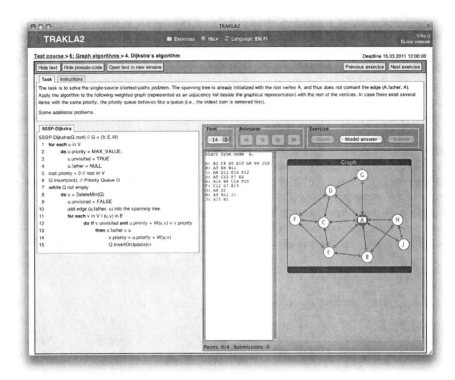

Fig. 8.1 A graph algorithm exercise in TRAKLA2 (Malmi et al. 2004)

general-purpose application framework for illustrating other concepts than graphs as well. TRAKLA2 can be utilized to provide exercises for basic data structures (stack, queue), sorting algorithms, priority queues, hashing, search trees, and graph algorithms.

A common approach in all of the existing systems is the use of abstract data, typically a random graph with letters or numbers (see Fig. 8.1 for an example of an exercise in TRAKLA2). While this is suitable for learning the algorithm, it gives no idea of the many applications of the algorithm. This is the issue we will tackle in our system presented in the next section.

3   Visual Algorithm Simulation Exercises with Authentic Data

In this section, we will describe our solution to use authentic location data in visual graph algorithm simulation exercises. The developed application is a special purpose software client in a spatial data infrastructure (SDI). We will start by describing the exercises from a student perspective and proceed to introducing the technology used.

3.1 Visual Algorithm Simulation

In *visual algorithm simulation*, the learner is performing similar mental processes than in desk checking of an algorithm, but in an interaction with a visual computerized environment (Korhonen 2003). In typical desk checking, the programmer is trying to follow the logic of an algorithm by ensuring there are no bugs. This is done manually line by line. Many teachers use similar approach while assigning exercises to their students. Students are supposed to show how an algorithm computes its result by using pen and paper. However, in contrast to desk checking, *visual algorithm simulation exercises* provide computer support for the process. In addition, the algorithm involved is correct, thus the learner is not expected to find a bug, but supposed to confirm the logic instead. This is done by simulating the execution of the code lines of the algorithm in a visually appealing environment.

Typically algorithm simulation exercises comprise abstract data only. In many graph algorithms, however, it would be more natural to execute the algorithm with authentic data. Thus, in location data algorithm simulations, graph algorithms are learned and simulated by clicking nodes and edges on a real map. Compared with the Engagement Taxonomy, students are working on the constructing level. That is, students are required to construct an algorithm visualization by performing the correct simulation operations. This makes the exercises similar to those in TRAKLA2 (Malmi et al. 2004), where students simulate (graph) algorithms with random nodes composed of alphabetic keys. However, we believe that working with authentic data makes the simulations more attracting and motivating as the performance highlights an actual application for the algorithm. Our example is related to Dijkstra's algorithm, but we believe the idea can be extended to other visual algorithm simulation exercises as well.

3.2 Location Data Algorithm Simulation Exercises

The main parts of our location data simulation exercise are shown in Fig. 8.2. The numbered parts are briefly explained below.

1. Drop-down boxes for selecting the data in the exercise.
2. Visualization of the graph on top of Google Maps.
3. The same graph as an adjacency list.
4. Buttons to undo/redo operations as well as to submit the solution.
5. Information about the node the mouse pointer was last hovering over.

Next, we will describe the different features available to the student.

Task and instructions The task is as a real-world application of the algorithm. For example, in the Dijkstra's algorithm, the task is to find the shortest route from one of the locations to all other locations on the map. Furthermore, instructions on simulating the algorithm as well as the pseudo code of the algorithm are also given.

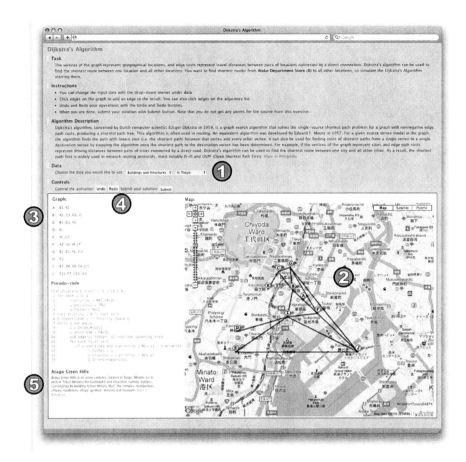

Fig. 8.2 An exercise with Buildings and Structures of Tokyo as the data

Selecting the data Students can choose the data using the drop-down boxes. Many categories are available to choose from, for example Buildings, City districts, Sports Stadiums, and Capital cities. Every category includes subcategories specifying the data for a smaller geographical area, for example, Buildings in Tokyo, City districts of Prague, or Football stadiums used in UEFA European Championships.

Viewing the data The data is visualized on a map. In addition, the graph is shown as an adjacency matrix.

Data about the node Whenever the mouse pointer hovers over a node in the map, information for that location is shown on the lower left side of the page. This is information about the location and it includes essentially the abstract of the Wikipedia article. This can lead to students learning about the different locations instead of the graph algorithm. In addition, when hovering over a node, the name of the location is shown as a tooltip.

Simulating the algorithm   Depending on the algorithm in question, the simulation is performed by clicking either nodes or edges. Clicking the nodes or edges in the textual adjacency matrix on the left has the same effect. This hopefully enables a better accessibility of the exercises. Each operation creates a new step in the simulation sequence, which is the answer students submit at the end. Students can undo the simulation steps and thus move backward in the generated animation. Also, redoing the undone steps (moving forward) is possible.

Immediate feedback and grading   Once the student has completed the simulation of the algorithm, he/she can ask for feedback. Feedback is asked by submitting the solution to the server, where the answer is checked. Student gets immediate feedback as the number of correct steps in his/her sequence as well as the correct sequence.

3.3   Technology

The main functionality is implemented in JavaScript (JS) running in the student's browser. JavaScript has come a long way from the days of it being used to show annoying blinking components and image rollovers on otherwise static web pages. It has evolved into a language for building complex web applications, and is thus suitable for our use. Another major reason was that we are using the dynamic Google Maps, which offers a JS code library. All web browsers support JavaScript, and we have tested our solution with Chrome, Safari, Internet Explorer, and Firefox.

Since the client is in JavaScript, a server-client model was required. To be able to trust the grading, it cannot be done in the client side where all source code of JS is visible to students. Furthermore, making queries to DBPedia is easier on the server to avoid having to work around same origin policy restrictions of browsers. Moreover, caching of query results on the server can avoid making same requests for all users, thus ending up with fewer requests to DBPedia. On the server-side, we have a simple Django (http://djangoproject.com/) application with a database mainly to cache the results of DBPedia queries as well as to store student submissions. The randomization of the initial graph and grading of the student solutions are on the server side as well.

DBPedia offers a SPARQL endpoint, allowing us to query for data using SPARQL. To help make the queries, we are using the Python sparql-wrapper (http://sparql-wrapper.sourceforge.net/). The wrapper handles the communication after given the SPARQL query to execute. The results of the query can be either JSON or RDF, but the wrapper handles both of these, and makes the result available as a Python dictionary.

The queries we make are fetching locations for a single category in the DBPedia (for example, Airports in Italy). In addition to the items geolocations, we also fetch information *about* the location. This additional information is essentially the abstract of the Wikipedia article as well as the URL of the article.

Once we have the data, we select a random set from the locations to be used by a single instance of the exercise. This way, the exercise data is slightly different each time. Among the locations, we randomly add edges from the set of possible edges generated by running Delaunay triangulation (Delaunay 1934). This ensures there are no crossing edges in any exercise instance.

3.4 Teacher's Point of View

New data sets can be added by introducing new query categories from DBPedia. For this, there are administrator pages to ease the process even further. The most time consuming part of adding new data is the search for suitable categories from DBPedia. In the current version, this needs to be done by manually browsing the collection.

Adding more algorithms is fairly straightforward. In order to simulate an algorithm, a server-side implementation of the algorithm is needed. This needs to be written in Python and must give the number of correct steps in a simulation sequence. If the algorithm requires other data structures and/or visual components, however, the implementation will be much more complicated. At the moment, the code assumes that all algorithms work on graphs.

Another issue is how to integrate the exercises with existing learning management systems (LMS). We have integrated it with our TRAKLA2 environment to be used in a Data Structures and Algorithms course. The TRAKLA2 environment embeds links to the exercises passing the student identification as a parameter. Once the student submits the exercise, the results are passed on to TRAKLA2 through its API. If the LMS makes it possible to add links to the exercise that identify the user as well as offers an API for submitting results, the exercises can be integrated by writing a simple extension that takes care of submitting the results to the LMS. It should also be noted that the exercises could be used without any LMS.

4   First Experiences with Students

The system has been tested with students twice in a Data Structures and Algorithms course for CS majors. This is quite a large course with some 100 enrolled students a year. TRAKLA2 has been used in this course for a long time to deliver visual algorithm simulation exercises as a part of course home assignments. Other activities in this course include lectures, closed lab exercises, and a final examination. Students are expected to solve some 25–30 exercises in TRAKLA2. From each correctly solved exercise, they can gain a number of points, and the sum of all points determines a partial course grade in scale 0–5. This is a compulsory part of the course, and 50% of all points is requires to pass this part with grade 1, and 90% is required to get the highest grade 5. TRAKLA2 exercises, however, contribute only 30% to their final grade. In addition, closed lab exercises and final examination contributes 30% and 40% to the final grade, respectively. In our experiment, one of the TRAKLA2 exercises was replaced with a location data simulation exercise covering Dijkstra's algorithm.

In the first time, an exercise on Dijkstra's algorithm was used as an optional exercise (Karavirta 2010) in Spring 2010. There was a link to the exercise among compulsory TRAKLA2 exercises. Not surprisingly, the voluntary exercise did not attract many students. In total, only $N_{2010} = 29$ students tried the exercise with various data, resulting in 62 exercise initializations. However, since there were no points to be gained, only six students actually submitted their solution for grading. Thus, we did not get a lot of data to analyze.

In Spring 2011, the same exercise was offered in a way that the students got points from it. This time, $N_{2011} = 47$ students (out of the 126 on the course) did 437 initializations and 187 submissions of the exercise. After submission, we asked them to fill a feedback questionnaire and we got feedback responses from 31 students. Our interest was on students' attitudes towards the new kind of exercises, thus the questionnaire included the following statements, choices, and a question:

Statement 1: This was more interesting than the TRAKLA2 exercises

- Fully agree, Agree, Disagree, Fully disagree

Statement 2: This was more difficult than the TRAKLA2 exercises

- Fully agree, Agree, Disagree, Fully disagree

Question 1: Free response (comments, ideas, bugs, etc)

Statistics from the data used by students is presented in Table A.1 in Appendix A. The most popular data set ("Districts of Helsinki" in 2010, "Buildings and Structures in Helsinki" in 2011) was the default set used every time a student opened the exercises. Not surprisingly, the second most popular data set in 2010 was the Buildings and Structures of Helsinki. These numbers indicate that the data should be something relevant for the student, such as familiar places from their environment. However, also unusual places attracted students to some extent. Maybe because of these were known for these students for some reason or the other. It should also be noted, that all data sets were initialized at least by one student in 2011.

4.1 Feedback Questionnaire

The results of the responses to the two statements are reported in Tables 8.1 and 8.2. Most of the students (31) answered the two statements, both in four-option scale ranging from "fully disagree" to "fully agree". In addition to the number of students selecting each option, we have reported the percentage of students that received full points of the exercise, i.e., managed to complete all steps of the simulation correctly. Moreover, we have calculated how many submissions the students did in overall, how many submissions they did on average, and what was the average of the maximum points they received (only the best submission among all the possible submissions a single student did is taken into account).

Table 8.1 Results from Statement 1 (This exercise is more difficult than TRAKLA2 exercises)

Choice	Students	Full points (%)	Subs	Avg subs	Inits	Avg. # of inits	Avg Max points
Fully disagree	2	50	3	1.5	10	5	66.5
Disagree	9	78	28	3.1	73	8.1	56.8
Agree	6	100	16	2.7	52	8.7	70
Fully agree	14	57	82	5.9	194	13.9	53.3

We have reported on the number of students selecting each option, how many percentage of those received full points from the exercise, how many initializations/submissions they did, what was the average number of initializations/submissions, and the average maximum points of the best submissions, respectively. The maximum points from the exercise were 70

Table 8.2 Results from Statement 2 (This exercise is more interesting than TRAKLA2 exercises)

Choice	Students	Full points (%)	Subs	Avg subs	Inits	Avg. # of inits	Avg Max points
Fully disagree	1	0	2	2	5	5	63
Disagree	7	86	26	3.7	62	8.9	64
Agree	12	67	60	5	143	11.9	58.7
Fully agree	11	73	41	3.7	119	10.8	54.1

We have reported the same columns as in Table 8.1

In Table 8.1, all the six students who responded "agree" to the statement, got finally full 70 points from the exercise. To achieve this, they were required to submit the exercise in average of 2.7 times. However, most of the students fully agree with the statements, and from those students, only 8/14 managed to fully complete the exercise even though they tried 5.9 times in average. This observation suggests that the subjective opinion of the difficulty of the exercise depends on how much effort they needed to invest in it.

Although this more applied exercise was considered to be more difficult, it was also considered to be more interesting than other TRAKLA2 exercises. This is shown in Table 8.2, in which more than 2/3 of the students agree or fully agree (23/31) with the statement. In addition, the more initializations (tried it with different data) the students did on average, the more they agree with the statement.

In the following, we have divided the open feedback responses into three sets. We got two very positive comments, four critical comments, and one mixed comment. Some of them are translated from Finnish. In addition, the names are fictional.

Positive Comments

Alice: *Nice one. I liked the Google map presentation. I didn't have to guess what TRAKLA wants me to do next. I just used the algorithm.*

Bob: *[The exercise] demonstrates well how the algorithm works. It is also easier [than TRAKLA2 exercises] to apply, as the exercise is not that abstract. Although, finding the shortest route is not that hard, in case of letters connected with arcs, the shortest path is more inconvenient to perceive.*

Negative Comments

Cecily: *No way to do this without pencil&paper unless you can remember tons of numbers at the same time*

Don: *Too difficult to visualize the lengths of the edges. Hovering over the edge should show the length on the map.*

Fatima: *Keeping track of the actual distance to already reached nodes is harder, as it isn't shown unlike in TRAKLA. I found the correct routes but not in correct order, so have to try again with paper. Also it seems like you can't select edges "backwards" (e.g. I selected I-G, when correct is G-I), I thought that it wouldn't make a difference by looking at the map.*

Errol: *Why the exercise is started from letter B, and not from A? No doubt it was told in the exercise, but I missed it, thus I needed to solve the exercise again "in vain".*

A Mixed Comment

Greg: *Very nice practical exercise, although some sort of a model answer or at least a guide would have been nice.*

Although, there are more negative than positive comments, the negative comments are more related to the functionality of the exercise, not the learning experience. That is, positive comments emphasize the fact that the exercise is more concrete than the corresponding TRAKLA2 exercise. Thus, at least some students seem to value applied use of visualizations.

We should not neglect the negative comments, however. The current implementation could be improved by providing more tools to keep track of the state of the algorithm as Cecily and Don both suggested. In addition, some details need to be changed, for example, to make it more obvious where to start as Errol pointed out. These are more or less usability issues that we can fix for the next time. However, it is important to collect the feedback also in the future as new issues can arise.

Moreover, some of the issues can be taken into a broader consideration while trying to develop the concept further. For example, Greg's comment about the model solution is related to the fact that most of the TRAKLA2 exercises have a model solution available. This feature could be a nice addition also for location data algorithm simulation exercises.

5   Conclusions

Motivation has an important role to play in learning. In this paper, we have introduced a novel approach to motivate students in Data Structures and Algorithms course by providing visual algorithm simulation exercises based on real-world data. While there are an increasing number of visualization systems available that try to motivate and engage students, we are not aware of any similar approaches to use authentic data to teach graph algorithms. The use of real-world examples was one of the motivation approaches suggested by Ahoniemi et al. (2007). We believe that, together with student-selectable data sets, authentic data can stimulate students' imagination and better capture their interest so that they will be more motivated to learn.

There seem to be other factors too, however. As our first year's experiment indicated, points gained from the exercises are an even stronger motivational factor here. The exercises need to be compulsory (i.e., a certain amount of points are needed to be collected to pass the course) in order to attract students' attention. Only very few students actually solved the exercises in the first year even though quite many initialized it.

In the second year, the exercise was compulsory. Our data shows that although the students felt that the exercise was more difficult than similar TRAKLA2 exercises, they found it more interesting. This supports our view that authentic data sets motivate at least some students.

From a pedagogical point of view, one of the disadvantages in our approach is that there might be distractions drawing students' focus away from the actual algorithm. The authentic location data might encourage students to read about the places, and end up reading articles on Wikipedia instead of solving the exercise.

From the technological point of view, the constructive part of this work is a proof-of-concept that general services such as semantic data and maps can be successfully used as building blocks in educational systems. Using such components is easy and makes development of new tools much faster than by implementing everything from scratch. Obviously, implementing a map service that is as comprehensive as Google Maps, and collecting data set as vast as DBPedia (or Wikipedia) would be completely out of reach for projects such as this one. Thus, educational mashups are a viable approach that we feel should be researched more in the future.

Mashups may cause some technical problems that come with the usage of third party APIs and data. The main issue is that if Google Maps or DBPedia servers are not responding, the exercises cannot be initialized or shown. For DBPedia, this problem can be avoided by caching the query results, as is done in our solution. However, this issue is not as serious as one would initially think; it is more probable that servers used in education administered by faculty staff are down than those of Google. A bigger issue is the reliability of the data from DBPedia, which comes from Wikipedia. The data can be modified by anyone on the Internet, so there might be incomplete or incorrect data as well. This happened during the implementation of the system, for example, as one building in Tokyo appearing in the middle of the Atlantic Ocean and a district of Helsinki near Stockholm, Sweden.

5.1   Future Directions

Our future plan is to evaluate the pedagogical effectiveness of the exercises and answer the question: Are the learning results equally good or even better than, say, the results with TRAKLA2? Our initial findings and the student comments seem to indicate the approach is useful, but more conclusive data needs to be gathered to verify this.

From the technical point of view, an interesting future direction (which we have already implemented in the development version) is to use the student's current location as the base for the data. Using the Geolocation API available in modern browsers, we can find out the students current location. By querying DBPedia for data around that location, we can contextualize the exercises for the specific location. This enables location-aware learning that adapts to the student's current context. This has obvious privacy-related issues, and we have not used it on a course yet. However, the plan is to use it next year with the location-aware data being one choice of data among the other fixed-location data sets.

A pedagogical issue with the current version is that coming up with stories behind the assignment is difficult. While, for example, for Dijkstra's algorithm there is a natural application for location data, not all algorithms make sense on such data. Why would you want to run a DFS on a random graph between Capitals in Africa? This is the reason we only used Dijkstra's algorithm in our initial student experiments. Thus, we look into broadening the scope of our framework to support spatial algorithms where our map-based approach would be highly suitable. Previous work on algorithm visualization in teaching spatial algorithms has been promising (Nikander et al. 2008). However, as the simulation mechanisms in the spatial algorithms implemented by Nikander et al. are quite complex, we will start with creating animations of such algorithms on location-based data. In such approach, we can still engage the students using, for example, pop-up questions that require prediction of next steps of the algorithm.

One of the important features of TRAKLA2 system is the model solution. That is an algorithm animation visualizing how the exercise should have been solved. Another feature in TRAKLA2 is the opportunity to reset the exercise with a new input data, if the student's solution was incorrect. This way he or she can try out the exercise as long as it is solved correctly. These features should be incorporated also into the visual algorithm simulation exercises with authentic data, as we believe they can significantly improve the learning results. That is to say, one of the interesting phenomena with TRAKLA2 exercises is the fact that very large portion (typically some 10%-30%) of all students receive full points of all the exercises (100%) even though 90% is required to the best mark (5/5). This phenomenon together with the authentic data in general will be one of our main research questions in the future.

Appendix A Data-sets used by students

Table A.1 Data sets used by students in years 2010 and 2011. The columns show the number of initializations and submissions for both years

Data set	Inits in 2010	Subs in 2010	Inits in 2011	Subs in 2011
Buildings and structures in Helsinki	7	–	274	141
Districts of Helsinki	35	4	–	–
Countries Arab league members	–	–	23	5
Countries states of the holy Roman empire	–	–	20	4
Buildings and structures in Amsterdam	1	–	18	6
Buildings and structures in leeds	–	–	14	2
Buildings and structures in Melbourne	–	–	14	2
Countries states of Mexico	–	–	11	3
Airports in Germany	1	–	9	5
Airports in England	1	–	8	2
Buildings and structures in Vienna	–	–	7	2
Buildings and structures in Oslo	–	–	6	3
Towns in Cheshire	2	–	4	2
Airports in Italy	1	–	5	–
Buildings and structures in Edinburgh	1	–	4	2
Districts of Prague	1	1	4	2
Buildings and structures in Croydon	–	–	4	2
Buildings and structures in Budapest	1	–	3	1
Towns in Vilnius county	1	–	3	2
Buildings and structures in Copenhagen	–	–	3	–
Districts of Manchester	1	–	2	1
Airports in Japan	2	1	–	–
Bridges in Washington	2	–	–	–
Presidential palaces	2	–	–	–
Towns in Cameroon	2	–	–	–
Buildings and structures in Madrid	–	–	1	–
UEFA European championship stadiums	1	–	–	–

References

Ahoniemi, T., E. Lahtinen, and K. Valaskala, 2007. Why Should We Bore Students When Teaching CS? *Lister, R. and Simon, editors, Seventh Baltic Sea Conference on Computing Education Research (Koli Calling 2007)*, volume 88 of CRPIT, pp. 227–228.

Auer, S., C. Bizer, G. Kobilarov, J. Lehmann, R. Cyganiak, and Z. Ives, 2008. DBPedia: A Nucleus for a Web of Open Data. *Proceedings of 6th International Semantic Web Conference, 2nd Asian Semantic Web Conference (ISWC + ASWC 2007)*, pp. 722–735.

Berners-Lee, T., J. Hendler, and O. Lassila, 2001. The semantic web. *Scientific American*, 5.

Bonifaci, V., C. Demetrescu, I. Finocchi, G. F. Italiano, and L. Laura, 2005. Portraying algorithms with leonardo web. *Web Information Systems Engineering - WISE 2005 Workshops*, volume 3807 of Lecture Notes in Computer Science, pp. 73–83.

Bridgeman, S., M. T. Goodrich, S. G. Kobourov, and R. Tamassia, 2000. PILOT: An interactive tool for learning and grading. *Proceedings of the 31st SIGCSE Technical Symposium on Computer Science Education*, pp. 139–143.

Crescenzi, P. and C. Nocentini, 2007. Fully integrating algorithm visualization into a CS2 course.: a two-year experience. *ITiCSE '07: Proceedings of the 12th annual SIGCSE conference on Innovation and technology in computer science education*, pp. 296–300.

Delaunay, B., 1934. Sur la sphère vide. Izvestia Akademii Nauk SSSR, Otdelenie Matematicheskikh i Estestvennykh Nauk, Vol. 7, pp. 793–800.

DePasquale, P., 2006. Exploiting on-line data sources as the basis of programming projects. *SIGCSE '06: Proceedings of the 37th SIGCSE technical symposium on Computer science education*, pp. 283–287.

Ding, L. and T. Finin, 2006. Characterizing the Semantic Web on the Web. *Proceedings of the 5th International Semantic Web Conference*.

Halpin, H., 2009. Is there anything worth finding on the semantic web? *WWW '09: Proceedings of the 18th international conference on World wide web*, pp. 1065–1066.

Hundhausen, C. D., S. A. Douglas, and J. T. Stasko, 2002. A meta-study of algorithm visualization effectiveness. *Journal of Visual Languages and Computing*, Vol. 13, No. 3, pp. 259–290.

Karavirta, V., 2010. Real-World, Student Selectable Data for Education – Learning graph Algorithms. Proceedings of the IADIS International Conference Cognition and Exploratory Learning in Digital Age, pp. 129–136.

Koike, H., T. Ishikawa, K. Akama, M. Chiba, and K. Miura, 2005. Developing an e-learning system which enhances students' academic motivation. *SIGUCCS '05: Proceedings of the 33 rd annual ACM SIGUCCS conference on User services*, pp. 147–150.

Korhonen, A., 2003. Visual Algorithm Simulation. *Doctoral Dissertation (Tech Rep. No. TKO-A40/03)*. Helsinki University of Technology.

Malmi, L., V. Karavirta, A. Korhonen, J. Nikander, O. Seppälä, and P. Silvasti, 2004. Visual algorithm simulation exercise system with automatic assessment: TRAKLA2. *Informatics in Education*, Vol. 3, No. 2, pp. 267–288.

Murugesan, S., 2007. Understanding Web 2.0. IT Professional, Vol. 9, No. 4, pp. 34–41.

Naps, T. L., G. Rößling, V. Almstrum, W. Dann, R. Fleischer, C. Hundhausen, A. Korhonen, L. Malmi, M. McNally, S. Rodger, and Ángel J. Velázquez-Iturbide, 2003a. Exploring the role of visualization and engagement in computer science education. *SIGCSE Bulletin*, Vol. 35, No. 2, pp. 131–152.

Naps, T. L., G. Rößling, J. Anderson, S. Cooper, W. Dann, R. Fleischer, B. Koldehofe, A. Korhonen, M. Kuittinen, C. Leska, L. Malmi, M. McNally, J. Rantakokko, and R. J. Ross, 2003b. Evaluating the educational impact of visualization. *SIGCSE Bulletin*, Vol. 35, No. 4, pp. 124–136.

Nikander, J., J. Helminen, and A. Korhonen, 2008. Experiences on using TRAKLA2 to teach spatial data algorithms. *Proceedings of the Fifth Program Visualization Workshop (PVW 2008)*.

Rößling, G. and B. Freisleben, 2002. ANIMAL: A system for supporting multiple roles in algorithm animation. *Journal of Visual Languages and Computing*, Vol. 13, No. 3, pp. 341–354.

Sánchez-Torrubia, M. G., C. Torres-Blanc, and M. A. López-Martínez, 2009. PathFinder: A visualization eMathTeacher for actively learning Dijkstra's algorithm. *Electronic Notes in Theoretical Computer Science*, 224:151–158. Proceedings of the Fifth Program Visualization Workshop (PVW 2008).

Thornton, M. and S. H. Edwards, 2008. A data type to exploit online data sources. *SIGCSE Bulletin*, Vol. 40, No. 3, pp. 114–118.

Wu, M., 2005. Teaching graph algorithms using online Java package IAPPGA. *SIGCSE Bulletin*, Vol. 37, No. 4, pp. 64–68.

Zang, N., M. B. Rosson, and V. Nasser, 2008. Mashups: Who? What? Why? *CHI '08 extended abstracts on Human factors in computing systems*, pp. 3171–3176.

Chapter 9
E-Mentoring in Vocational Teacher Education

David Lord and Nele Coninx

1 Introduction

Europe-wide, mentoring is often seen as an ideal "solution" to lifelong learning issues where work-based learners do not have access to traditional teaching environments. Significant elements of teacher training courses are 'delivered' in the work place, and this has resulted in a great demand for mentors and coaches. However, the standards for mentor training, the effectiveness of the mentoring techniques, and the availability of suitable mentors are all issues which have caused widespread concern. In the UK, a number of government reports have highlighted the essential nature of mentoring in the delivery and learning of subject specialist skills (Dixon et al. 2010), and there has been a call for the professionalisation of the mentoring role. In Hungary recent legislation has made mentoring a compulsory element of initial teacher training. The situation in many countries is that mentoring systems are in urgent need of development, and that the establishment of e-mentoring systems, to effectively address the "distributed" nature of work-based learning, is an extremely important aspect of that development.

This paper stresses the importance of, and investigates possibilities for, e-mentoring and e-coaching in vocational teacher education, by considering the considerable impact of three recently completed projects on the field. It reports their results in the light of current research and makes recommendations for the further development of the e-mentoring systems discussed.

The first project examined is "Motivate" (Masters level opportunities and technological innovation in vocational teacher education). This EC-funded project was conducted by a consortium of seven higher education institutions from Finland,

D. Lord (✉)
University of Huddersfield, Huddersfield, UK
e-mail: d.lord@hud.ac.uk

N. Coninx
Fontys University of Applied Sciences, Eindhoven, The Netherlands
e-mail: ns.coninx@fontys.nl

P. Isaias et al. (eds.), *Towards Learning and Instruction in Web 3.0: Advances in Cognitive and Educational Psychology*, DOI 10.1007/978-1-4614-1539-8_9,
© Springer Science+Business Media, LLC 2012

Greece, Holland, Hungary, Portugal and the UK, and concerned the design and implementation of Masters level modules for the teacher training curriculum. The modules involved e-mentoring, with work – based learning facilitated by "technological innovation".

The second project used in the investigation is the "ASSOCiate Online" (Achieving Subject Specialist Online Communities) initiative, involving the development and operation of an on-line learning resource and network of teachers in the UK. This "specialist on-line community" facility provides e-mentors for teacher trainees in a wide range of subject specialist areas.

The third project under review concerns "synchronous coaching", a technique resulting from research in the Netherlands on coaching and mentoring effectiveness, which highlighted the importance of timely feedback, preferably given during the performance rather than after it. The technology in the project enabling immediate feedback is the WIME (Whisper In My Ear) device, but other mobile learning technologies may be equally appropriate. In addition to this research into technology, the project also conducts an investigation into the vocabulary and terminology used in these situations, to improve the criticality of the feedback.

Finally, in the concluding section of the paper, results from all three projects are collectively considered, and directions for extended work in the area are identified. The "Implement" (Improving lifelong learning through e-mentoring) project is proposed, which will develop international standards and networks for e-mentors, and promote innovative use of technology in e-mentoring systems.

2   E-Mentoring and Teacher Education

E-mentoring systems in the teacher education sphere can be classified according to the timeliness of feedback provided by the mentor. The first two projects described and analysed in this section involve "asynchronous" feedback, where all communications between mentor and mentee take place before or after the event. The third project utilizes "just in time" techniques, where the mentoring or coaching intervention occurs at the same time as the learning experience, in this case a teaching performance. The role and responsibilities of the e-mentor also suggest a method of categorization, and these factors dictate the level of mentor training required. In the Motivate project, a peer-mentoring system was developed, with e-mentors and their mentees holding 'equal status' in the learning process, whereas in the "ASSOCiate Online" and "Synchronous Coaching" projects, the mentors or coaches held supervisory and assessment roles in the learning, and adopted an advisory role in the process.

2.1   The Motivate Project

The aim of the Motivate project was twofold: to develop modules for the teacher education curriculum at Masters level, and to incorporate new and emerging technologies into the delivery of the curriculum (Lord and Pentelenyi 2009).

The innovatory practices were designed to directly benefit the two Hungarian higher education institutions in the partnership, although the result of the module development was to harmonize the teacher training curriculum in all participating countries. A variety of Web 2.0 technologies (such as social networking systems, blogs, wikis, and the virtual world environment, Second Life) were utilised to facilitate the curriculum developments

The "Teaching a Specialist Subject" module, developed in the Motivate project, is of particular interest here, since it involved a form of e-mentoring by the student teachers' peers in the learning process. Unlike other 'common modules' in the project, delivered in English, it was decided that, for this particular module, delivery would take place in the native language of the partner country, and the two participating institutions in Hungary created a collaborative network using the Moodle virtual learning environment as the delivery platform. This enabled the Hungarian teacher trainees to easily share pedagogical methods and resources, initiate discussions on teaching issues related to the specialist area, and engage in troubleshooting of problem areas of the specialist teaching. The 72 students involved were geographically dispersed, mainly from Budapest and Dunaujvaros (where the Hungarian partner institutions were located), but also from other parts of Hungary, and therefore only on-line communication was possible via the Moodle platform.

Toth (2009) conducted a case study on "Teaching Specialist Subjects" with these students, and performed a qualitative evaluation of their interactions on the discussion forums. She reported the effect on the quality of interaction and the motivation to engage with debate, of various factors relating to the participants: the past experience of teaching, the familiarity with ICT and technology, evidence of extrovert qualities/shyness, age and gender. The case study resulted in some interesting observations being made, which informed analysis of the performance of peers in an e-mentoring role.

It was quickly apparent that the participants on the collaborative platform may have been "equal" in terms of their status as students of the module, but they were not equal in their contributions to discussion and debate, with certain students stepping up to the role of e-mentor and adviser to others. Toth recounted the experiences of a student who overcame shyness, and a poor level of ICT skills, to become an inspirational guide to others in subject specialist matters. Another young student teacher, with effective study skills using internet technologies, adopted the role of e-mentor to a very full extent, helping more experienced, yet less technologically adept, teachers with the pedagogical use of ICT.

Some students, in the early stages of the Motivate project, were unwilling to participate fully in the learning communities, and lacked the necessary motivation to take on the e-mentor role to support their peers. They argued that there was no assessment credit available for participation, and that helping others did not directly address module outcomes. These issues were addressed, as discussed in the conclusion to this paper, in the later phases of the project.

In the UK students were supported in the collaborative networking tasks of Motivate by having access to on-line subject specialist communities (Lord 2008) via the ASSOCiate Online platform, described in the next section of the paper.

2.2   The ASSOCiate Online Project

The ASSOCiate Online project was developed in response to UK government policy related to the teaching of subject specialist skills, promoting the "essential" nature of mentoring in that teaching process. The ASSOCiate Online initiative created a national collaborative platform for subject specialists in the vocational teacher education field, and has continued to grow and develop since its inception in 2004. The platform facilitates the development of on-line subject specialist communities, allowing cooperation and collaboration between geographically dispersed vocational teachers working in similar fields to their own.

The potential of ASSOCiate Online to support e-mentoring has been appreciated and exploited since the initial design of the platform. Lord (2004) suggested that participation in the on-line community should be a compulsory element of mentor training, with experts in particular specialist fields, who are fulfilling the role of mentor to initial teacher trainees, providing online support and contributing their expertise to online discussion. However, it soon became apparent that peer interaction on the platform was just as valuable to teacher trainees as the availability of 'experts'. "Find a buddy" and "Find a Professional Twin" facilities were incorporated into the provision. After registering onto the system, and entering teaching interests and a profile, the database was automatically searched for a "buddy", someone with similar interests, and a "professional twin", someone who shares a similar profile and teaches the same courses.

User evaluations revealed issues of mismatched expectations between students and their "peer mentors", with some appearing "needy", and making unreasonable demands on the buddy or twin. To alleviate this problem, in later versions of ASSOCiate Online, experienced teachers have been employed as e-mentors on the system, with a well-defined job role and scope of operation. The current situation is that ASSOCiate Online is a community of trainee teachers with electronic access to experienced subject mentors and moderated learning materials. The scale of the membership of the community, across the whole of the UK, ensures that trainees have access to peers and experts, no matter how diverse or specialized their teaching context (Lord et al. 2010).

2.3   The Synchronous Coaching Project

Synchronous coaching is a specialized aspect of e-mentoring, and the project described here is essentially different to and distinct from the foregoing projects. It is, in fact, feasible that synchronous coaching could be usefully implemented in addition to the type of e-mentoring in Motivate or ASSOCiate Online, because its operation occurs at the time of teaching practice, not before, as part of preparation, or after, as a reflective and evaluative exercise. The synchronous coaching project has examined feedback given to the student teacher during class performance, using a technology enabling "immediate" feedback, the WIME (Whisper In My Ear) device.

The traditional way of coaching consists of a student teacher who is teaching and a mentor who observes the behaviour of the student teacher in the actual classroom setting. If the student teacher experiences some difficulties, the student teacher and the mentor discuss the problems which occurred afterwards. In circumstances most beneficial for the student teacher they can discuss this immediately after the lesson. However, in practice, there is some time between the given lesson by the student teacher and the feedback obtained from the mentor (and sometimes a student teacher has to wait more than a week for feedback).

A body of literature provides scientific evidence that immediate or synchronous coaching is more helpful to student teachers (Hunt 1980; Goodman et al. 2008; Fry and Hin 2006; Farrell and Chandler 2008; Scheeler et al. 2006, 2008; Rock et al. 2009; Scheeler and Lee 2002). There are different ways to give immediate performance feedback. One way is that a coach can interrupt or even stop the lesson and gives the specific performance feedback. This method has disadvantages such as a decrease of concentration and self esteem of the pre-service teacher. Also, because of the disruption, there is valuable lesson time lost (Scheeler et al. 2006).

Another method is synchronous coaching. Synchronous coaching provides pre-service teachers with immediate, on-the-spot feedback while these pre-service teachers are engaging in classroom instruction (Giebelhaus 1994). Although researchers have used various forms of technology to provide immediate feedback, the Whisper-in-my-ear (WIME) is widely the most used device. Researchers have variously referred to this technology as a "Bug-in-Ear (BIE)," "wireless earphone," a "mechanical third ear device," or an "electronic audio-cueing system" (Rock et al. 2009). Many are already familiar with WIME technology in the form of the earpiece that a person wears to allow 'hands-free' operation of a cell phone. In the current context, WIME technology refers to a small ear bud receiver that transmits verbal communication from a transmitter to a receiver. In general, WIME technology has been used effectively in a number of disciplines to improve practices in the field. WIME technology has evolved from its initial use in psychotherapy (Korner and Brown 1952) to many other professions including dentistry, special education, retail, mass media, security, sports, and the general public (Goodman 2005; Scheeler and Lee 2002). Despite the knowledge base of synchronous coaching, it is not yet commonly used in the field of secondary education (Scheeler et al. 2006).

When using WIME technology in a teacher education situation, the coach delivers prompts and feedback to the trainee teacher wearing the ear piece to provide messages or cues for behavior. Synchronous coaching using WIME technology, provides immediate, specific performance feedback during instruction that does not interfere with teaching, except to cue the pre-service teacher to use effective teaching behavior (Goodman et al. 2008). The trainee is the only one to hear the prompts and can then decide what to say or do next (Goodman and Duffy 2007). Research on the delivery of this feedback that is not disruptive to the learning process of pre-service teachers is critical (Scheeler et al. 2004).

The implications for the use of synchronous coaching given by these researchers are implemented in the synchronous coaching mode as used in the Netherlands experiment. Fontys University of Applied Science (the Netherlands) has a tradition in synchronous coaching, and during recent years, this type of e-mentoring has undergone an accelerated development: the Netherlands have already reached the fourth generation of synchronous coaching.

The first generation of synchronous coaching was especially aimed at trying out equipment and possibilities for its use. The Fontys Pedagogically Technical University of Applied Science (Fontys PTH) experimented with student teachers by whispering short messages, using different types of equipment. In a national SURF-project called Active Audience synchronous coaching was widely tested. Several educational settings pilots were carried out, using a variety of techniques. In some specific settings (intervision, supervision or coaching) direct feedback was given by using an ear piece. This method can also be used for practicing conversation techniques, such as interview skills, and the implementation of application conversations. Professors, who acted as coaches, considered the synchronous coaching technique as a valuable additional technique. The profit is especially present in the immediateness of the feedback: the student teacher can process observations immediately and apply suggested improvements. The interventions which appeared to work best were short: approximately four words. However, it was frequently difficult to find the right moment for the intervention. The quality and the usability of equipment proved to be of large importance in educational settings. For problems such as noise, the use of a sound communication set for synchronous coaching was recommended for student teachers.

Hooreman et al. (2008) initiated the second generation of synchronous coaching at the Fontys Vocational Teacher Education faculty (Fontys FLOS). The behaviour of a group of 40 student teachers was examined by means of video recordings of teaching situations where required behaviour was stipulated in advance. Comparison of a research group undertaking synchronous coaching, and a control group coached in a traditional manner, showed that by synchronous coaching the quality of didactic behaviour increases more rapidly, and the time to show the required teacher behaviour more rapidly decreases. Also the research indicated that not all performance feedback is suitable for synchronous coaching. For example specific profession content information can hardly be whispered without causing cognitive overload by student teachers. Recommendations were formulated. Coaches who are newcomers to synchronous coaching need to follow a training programme. An important component of the process must be to reduce cognitive overload. By standardizing the messages the coach can reduce the cognitive overload on the trainee. However, a student teacher also needs a training programme where the possible messages can be discussed in advance of the teaching session. When a student teacher shows less competent behaviour, a specific description of ideal observable teacher behaviour must be whispered. During a training programme the student teacher must learn these behaviour indicators (with corresponding performance feedback), and additionally receive general information concerning the synchronous coaching technique.

The third generation of synchronous coaching started in 2008 with a second PhD project on synchronous coaching organized by Nele Coninx. The main aim of this research project is to test the data of Hooreman (Hooreman et al. 2008) in vivo (in actual class room practice). Firstly, the expected observable teacher behaviour indicators were established for the ideal interpersonal, pedagogical and organizational performance behaviour for student teachers. A competent interpersonal student teacher is a teacher who can keep order in the classroom. For this interpersonal behaviour 16 ideal observable behaviour indicators have been established. A pedagogically competent teacher can differentiate in attention to several students. Twelve ideal observable behaviour indicators have been established for this aspect of the teaching process. Finally, an organisationally competent teacher can arrange lessons and instruction in such a manner so that students most effectively learn. For this 30 ideal observable behaviour indicators have been determined. In a computer programme CONPAS (Coaching Or Newcomers' Practical Assistant System) the indicators have been incorporated as 'buttons'. Each indicator has been recorded and then added as a small audio file into the computer programme. By pressing a button the audio file corresponding to a certain behaviour indicator is played. This way a coach can whisper during a lesson (by pushing buttons) without the students in the class knowing something is whispered at the trainee teacher. The equipment used consists of a lap top, from which the coach sends the whispered messages, and a receiving set for the student teacher. This research confirms that the usability of the equipment is still a significant determinant of the success of the system. The setting up of the equipment was an onerous task for the coach in this phase of the project. Easily transportable and installed equipment is necessary for the perceived success of synchronous coaching.

The fourth generation of synchronous coaching addresses some of the concerns regarding the usability of equipment. The use of an iPad instead of a lap top was the first improvement. Secondly, the original version of the computer programme CONPAS was adapted to the needs of users and re-written to enable the programme to run also on MAC (iPad). Thirdly, a new WIME technology is introduced. The earlier WIME devices had ear pieces which 'closed' one ear off. A student teacher had sometimes difficulties to hear every pupil in the class room. The new WIME devices use the boon structure of the skull to communicate to a student teacher and he/she can now hear the whole class.

Thus the Dutch researchers and teacher educators have taken the WIME technology, and developed a tool kit with a web-based application which makes it possible for the coach/mentor to unobtrusively whisper keywords to the student teacher.

In the construction of the keywords, attention was given to the syntax, as well as to the semantic features of the keywords. It was necessary to take into account the "cognitive load" and the ambiguity/uncertainty of messages. A high cognitive load in student teachers leads to mental strains, because the student teacher simultaneously has to pay attention to the given whispered keywords while teaching and listening to the demands of the children in the class. This phenomenon is referred to by Chandler and Sweller (1992) as the split attention effect. The effect is related to two competing but equally important information sources. Firstly, the message to the student teacher should not display any ambiguity and uncertainty. Uncertainty is caused by a lack of information; and, therefore, adding more information will resolve this issue, but the process will result in longer messages. Ambiguity is the existence of multiple, possibly conflicting, interpretations of the message. Ambiguity is not easy to resolve, but it can certainly be alleviated by the provision of more information. Finding the balance between not making a message too long, so that the chance for producing cognitive overload will be greater for student teachers on the one hand, and resolving ambiguity and uncertainty on the other hand, was a key issue in the research. Secondly, related to semantic issues, the interpretation of the message by the student teachers was crucial. The interpretation of the keywords needed to be evaluated by the student teachers as "good" feedback. Shute (2008) defines good feedback in terms of messages that are specific and goal oriented, with some clues for the student teacher to learn how to teach (Hattie and Timperley 2007).

The keywords, therefore, are hints or clues for the trainee teachers to know what they might change in their teaching behaviour, without suffering from 'cognitive overload' in the process of receiving the instruction while simultaneously dealing with the classroom situation. The keywords were constructed on the implications of the literature and provide specific feedback to address the main problems student teachers face (achieving effective classroom management, giving clear instructions to pupils, and catering for the individual needs of pupils). In finalizing the technology used, the researchers compared the different technologies used in synchronous coaching from the literature, and assembled an appropriate system. They also developed a training program for the use of synchronous coaching in the class room.

Preliminary results are positive, with student teachers and coaches evaluating this coaching mode as effective. The consensus is that feedback given was more specific, useful and goal oriented than feedback which may have been provided in a traditional coaching mode. Looking closer at the evaluations and the degree of success achieved Coninx et al. (2010b) identified some prerequisites for synchronous coaching to be effective: there must be a training programme devised to fully prepare coaches and trainees; pupils in the classroom must receive an explanation of the synchronous coaching taking place; the student teachers need to be eager and receptive towards the concept of synchronous coaching.

The synchronous coaching project is currently being extended in a longitudinal study over a longer time period, with an increased sample size, a larger vocabulary of whispered keywords (designed to be more specific and goal-orientated), and consideration being taken of other factors affecting and indicating the student teachers' development. The researchers are interested in the changes in behaviour patterns of the student teachers, as observed and perceived by the student teachers themselves, the coaches (mentors) providing the feedback, and the pupils from the actual classroom. Preliminary results show that student teachers change in interpersonal behavior in only two lessons perceived by student teachers and coaches, but what is more special is that it is also perceived by the pupils of the classroom (Coninx et al. 2010a)

Evaluation of the synchronous coaching is planned on the four levels of reaction, learning, behaviour and results (Kirkpatrick and Kirkpatrick 2006), specifically: (1) determining the reaction towards synchronous coaching by student teachers and coaches (for example, do student teachers find this coaching mode useful?); (2) assessing the learning of student teachers (for example, do student teachers learn new knowledge of class room management?); (3) behaviour of student teachers (for example: do student teachers change their behaviour patterns?) and (4) results of student teachers (for example: do pupils who receives lessons from student teachers who received synchronous coaching get better grades?)

3   Conclusion

With the widespread adoption of the practice of learning in the work-place, vocational teacher training and development is based predominantly in the schools, colleges, universities and training organizations where the vocational education is delivered. It is clear from examination of the three projects that e-mentoring, in a variety of forms, is providing an important new approach to learning in these circumstances.

Findings from the Motivate and ASSOCiate Online project indicate that the role of the potential e-mentor needs to be well-defined, and that, particularly in a peer mentoring situation, there should be specific incentive provided to adopt that role. Toth (2009) reports a great deal of satisfaction experienced, from what is in effect an e-mentoring role, by the students of the Motivate module. To ensure more engagement with the on-line interaction, it was concluded in the Motivate project that the process of supporting peers' learning should be credited within the assessment of the course being taken.

The best way to achieve credit for e-mentoring activities, and to standardize ('professionalize') the mentoring support role is to incorporate a module on mentoring into the teacher education curriculum. (It was mentioned in the introduction section of this paper, that mentoring is now a compulsory element of the Hungarian initial teacher training curriculum, for example.)

Although the results of the synchronous coaching study are positive, they have to be interpreted within the limitations of the study. Student teacher learning was not assessed. In teacher training research, there are effects to consider in addition to changes in student teachers' behaviour. Future research on providing synchronous coaching to student teachers will also need to include assessment of student teacher learning, to determine if changes in student teacher behaviour is caused.

From all three projects considered, it is clear that effective communication is crucial to the successful development of the interaction and relationship between mentor and mentee. Careful consideration also needs to be given to the nature of that relationship, whether the mentoring role is purely advisory and supportive, or whether the mentor is required to make judgments or assessment decisions based on the observed performance.

There are also issues common to all three projects regarding the use of new and emerging technologies. Firstly, there needs to be information provided to the designer of the e-mentoring system regarding availability of technologies that are appropriate for use in the particular circumstance. Secondly, information is needed as to the scope of the technologies adopted, and whether they are being used to their full potential. Thirdly, all participants in the e-mentoring process need adequate exposure to the systems, and sufficient training in their use, to feel comfortable with the involvement with the technologies. Further research into the many facets of innovative use of new technologies is required, including an investigation into the possibilities of e-mentor training in virtual world teaching scenarios, as Lord (2009) considered in the Motivate project.

Many of the issues mentioned in conclusion here are addressed in a new project proposed by a European consortium of higher education institutions, with which the authors of this paper are involved. European Community funding under the Lifelong Learning Programme is to be requested for the IMPLEMENT project (IMProving Lifelong learning through E-MENToring). The overall aim of the project is to investigate and exploit the potential of mentoring systems in a lifelong learning context, given advances in technology, and the availability of electronic delivery methods.

More specifically, the Implement project will contribute to the knowledge base in the e-mentoring field in the following ways:

- Initial research will be undertaken into mentoring methods and techniques, and electronic support systems, in order to better understand the nature of the mentoring role and the underpinning educational theory. Research papers and reports into e-mentoring and associated fields will be produced, with topics of research including specifications and standards for mentors, (teaching and learning methods for) work-based learning, mobile learning, observation and communication technologies, communications protocols for mentors/ coaches. It is intended that the wider research community will benefit from the research outputs of the project, particularly the collection of research papers on e-mentoring, the case studies, the seminar papers and the final conference proceedings planned.
- National initiatives in mentoring practices will be examined, and recommendations made for Europe-wide standards in mentor training. A set of mentoring standards will be produced, aiming to professionalize the e-mentoring role in vocational teacher education. An e-mentoring research compendium will provide a collection of partner reports of the current institutional, regional and national situation on e-mentoring, presented as responses to a series of questions on a pro-forma. In addition to a description of the current situation, the report of each partner will contain a 'needs analysis' to inform the development and uptake of mentoring systems in later stages of the project.
- Masters level certification to professionalize the role of mentoring in teacher education contexts will be developed and implemented, and this will take the form of a module on e-mentoring at Masters level, which addresses the mentoring standards. The module will have accompanying documentation and teaching materials.
- Synchronous coaching training, delivered initially by the Dutch partners and 'cascaded' to the partner countries, will be further developed, and will include a 'synchronous coaching' training pack, with the necessary hardware and training materials (the CONPAS toolkit mentioned earlier). The Implement project will provide the opportunities to further investigate synchronous coaching opportunities in vocational education, by identifying common characteristics of critical professional situations for student teachers, where synchronous coaching can be

used. This will provide a context for the development of training materials, and enable the improved design and delivery of the trainers' workshop. Further exploration will be made of the communication skills required and the appropriateness of the vocabulary used, when engaging in synchronous coaching.

- The availability of mentors will be increased by the establishment of on-line mentor databases and professional networks at the regional, national and international levels, using the model of ASSOCiate Online. Networks of e-mentoring practice and on-line databases of subject specialist mentors in the vocational teacher education field will be created.

- The e-mentoring developments will make significant impact on both the research and teaching communities. Partner institutions need to implement lifelong learning strategies, and the application of innovative e-mentoring methods (exemplified by the synchronous coaching techniques) to work-based learning situations, satisfies this need very effectively. There are immense benefits of e-mentor network creation at regional and national levels, and the common standards and network specifications, put in place by the project, will ensure that networking and collaboration extends to the international level. The development of the e-mentoring professional standards in the project leads to improved quality of mentor-mentee relationships, in the consortium and in the wider vocational education community. Within the dissemination process of the Implement project it will be possible to ensure mentor availability and quality through adherence to protocols for the networks of e-mentors. The skills of providing critical feedback, and listening skills, with empathic responses to issues, will be embedded within the developed materials and standards, and will be available to all concerned with the development of e-mentoring in vocational teacher education after the end of the project.

References

Chandler, P., & Sweller, J. (1992). The split-attention effect as a factor in the design of instruction. *British Journal of Educational Psychology, 62,* 233–246.

Coninx, N.S, Kreijns, C.J., Jochems, W.M.G. (2010a). *Changes in interpersonal behavior of student teachers due to immediate coaching with WIME (Whisper in My Ear) device.* Poster presented at ICIRE conference, Boulder, United States of America. (dd. 28/04/2010).

Coninx, N.S, Kreijns, C.J., Jochems, W.M.G. (2010b). *Perceived success of immediate coaching of student teachers with WIME (Whisper In My Ear) device.* Paper presented at SITE conference, San Diego, United States of America. (dd. 01/04/2010).

Dixon,L, Bailey,W, Blamires,C, & Robinson,D (2010) Mentoring in Teacher Education. In: *Teaching in Lifelong Learning.* Open University Press, Milton Keynes, pp. 198–205. ISBN 9780335234684.

Farrell, A.C., Chandler, D. (2008). Cooperating teachers` impressions of the whisper-in-my-ear (WIME) and traditional communication feedback methods for physical education in preservice teachers. *Education and Human development, 2*(1), 1–9.

Fry, J.M., Hin, M.K.T. (2006). Peer coaching with interactive wireless technology between student teachers: satisfaction with role and communication. *Interactive learning environments, 14*(3), 193–204.

Giebelhaus, C.R. (1994). The bug-in-the-ear Device: An anlternative Student Teaching Supervision Strategy, paper presented at the association of teacher educators `annual conference, Atlanta, GA.

Goodman, J. I. (2005). Increasing Learn Units by special education teachers: Supervision via bug-in-ear technology. (Doctoral dissertation, Florida Atlantic University, 2005) . *Dissertation Abstracts International-A 66/01, 144.*

Goodman, J.I., Duffy, M.L. (2007). Using BUGS to increase student participation. *Teaching exceptional clildren plus, 3* (4), retrieved from: http://scholarship.bc.edu/education/tecplus/vol3/iss4/art3.

Goodman, J.I., Brady, M.P., Duffy, M.L., Scott, J., Pollard, N.E. (2008). The effects of `bug-in-ear` supervision on special education teachers` delivery of learn units. *Focus on autism and other developmental disabilities. 23* (4), 207–216.

Hattie, J. & Timperley, H. (2007). The power of feedback. *Review of educational research, 77*(1),81–112.

Hooreman, R. W, Kommers, P. A. M., & Jochems, W. M. G. (2008). Synchronous coaching of the trainee teacher: an experimental approach. Unpublished doctoral dissertation, Eindhoven, Technical University of Eindhoven press, The Netherlands.

Kirkpatrick, D. L., & Kirkpatrick, J. D. (2006). Evaluating Training Programs: The Four Levels. Berrett-Koehler Publishers, Inc: San Fransisco.

Korner, I., & Brown, W. (1952). The mechanical third ear. *Journal of Consulting Psychology, 16*(1), 81–84.

Hunt, D.D. (1980). Bug-in-the-ear technique for teaching interview skills. *Journal of medical education, 55,* 964–966.

Lord, D, Burton,S, Fisher,R, & Webb,K (2010) Subject specialist pedagogy. In: *Teaching in Lifelong Learning.* Open University Press, Milton Keynes, pp. 181–187. ISBN 9780335234684.

Lord, D&Pentelenyi,P (2009) Review of the project Motivate - Masters level opportunities and technological innovation in vocational teacher education. In: *Motivate: Masters Level Opportunities and Technological Innovation in Vocational Teacher Education.* Ligatura, Hungary, pp. 9–16. ISBN 9789638611345.

Lord, D (2009), "Technological Innovation in MOTIVATE: Lessons in Second Life", *MOTIVATE conference (Published proceedings: ISBN 963 661 503 9),* Heraklion, Greece.

Lord, D (2008), "Learning to Teach a Specialist Subject: Using New Technologies and Achieving Masters Level Criteria", *MOTIVATE conference,* Budapest, Hungary.

Lord, D (2004), "Specialist On-line Communities in Initial Teacher Training", *Budapest Polytechnic Jubilee Conference,* Budapest, Hungary. Published proceedings: ISBN 963 7154 31 0.

Rock, M.L., Gregg, M., Thead, B.K., Acker, S.E., Gable, R.A., Zigmond, N.P. (2009). Can You Hear Me Now? Evaluation of an online wireless technology to provide real-time feedback to special education teachers-in-training. *Teacher Education and Special Education, 32*(1), 64–82.

Scheeler, M.C., Lee, D.L. (2002). Using technology to deliver immediate corrective feedback to preservice teachers. *Journal of behavioral education, 11* (4). 231–241.

Scheeler, M.C., McAfee, J.K., Ruhl, K.L., Lee, D.L. (2006). Effects of corrective feedback delivered via wireless technology on preservice teacher performance and student behavior. *Teacher education and special education, 29* (1), 12–25.

Scheeler, M.C., Macluckie, M., Albright, K. (2008). Effects of immediate feedback delivered by peer tutors on the oral presentation skills of adolescents with learning disabilities. *Remedial and special education, 11,* 1–10.

Scheeler, M.C., Ruhl, K.L., McAfee, J.K. (2004). Providing performance feedback to teachers: a review *Teacher education and special education, 27*(3), 396–407.

Shute, V. (2008). Focus on formative feedback. *Review of educational research, 78*(1), 153–189.

Toth,A (2009) Case Study on Teaching Specialist Subjects. In: *Motivate: Masters Level Opportunities and Technological Innovation in Vocational Teacher Education.* Ligatura, Hungary, pp. 139–145. ISBN 9789638611345.

Chapter 10
The IPTEACES E-Learning Framework: Success Indicators, the Impact on Student Social Demographic Characteristics and the Assessment of Effectiveness

Nuno Pena and Pedro Isaias

1 Introduction

With the publication of Regulatory Rule 17/2006-R, specifically with regard to qualification courses for Insurance Intermediaries – (resulting from an implementation of the EU directive on insurance mediation), it became mandatory for all new insurance intermediaries to attend a certification course. This certification targets a diverse social-demography and geographically dispersed range of attendees. This demanded a new approach to e-learning instructional design. To develop this training and certification solution in an e-learning format (having as a formal requirement a final face-to-face examination), it was considered vital to design a specific and proprietary e-Learning "framework" which could contain in itself the "learning principles" and that it would fit, as far as possible, the diversity and heterogeneity in terms of different ages, gender, educational background, previous knowledge in the area, literacy, computer proficiency, organizational culture, motivations, values and experience/inexperience in e-Learning, etc.

This framework, was primarily inspired through a pedagogical benchmark (mainly Gagné's Nine Events of instruction (Gagne 1985; Gagne et al. 1992), Merrill's Principles of Learning (2002, 2007), Keller's ARCS's model (2008) and van Merrienboer's Ten Steps to Complex Learning (2007)), as well as in a close observation of award winning ecourses (e.g., Brandon Hall Excellence in Learning Awards, International e-Learning Association Awards) and corporate e-Learning best practices (e.g., Bersin and Associates reports). With this framework in mind, we've conceived and designed an instructional design framework that could materialize, largely on a single approach, an appropriate learning strategy for different learners in order to fit the different learning preferences and also to respect other specific differences.

N. Pena (✉) • P. Isaias
Universidade Aberta (Portuguese Open University), Lisbon, Portugal
e-mail: nuno.raposo.pena@gmail.com; pisaias@univ-ab.pt

P. Isaias et al. (eds.), *Towards Learning and Instruction in Web 3.0: Advances in Cognitive and Educational Psychology*, DOI 10.1007/978-1-4614-1539-8_10,
© Springer Science+Business Media, LLC 2012

2 Overview of IPTEACES Framework

Front-End Procedures – In order to transform technological prerequisites (often causing entropy to the end user) in transparent and intuitive information to the learner, this phase is divided in two areas: "Browser Check" and "Help Desk" which intends to demystify any technological complexity and minimize eventual lack of micro-informatics proficiency (Fig. 10.1). In order for a student to attend an e-Learning course it is necessary that he possesses the necessary technical requirements and the majority of the potential students don't understand exactly what these requirements mean and/or if their computer has these requirements. In order to overcome this restrain that can be decisive in terms of potential drop-out, "Browser Check" functionality was developed which automatically diagnoses the student's browser as well as it indicates the need or not for an installation. However, if students feel any difficulty or complication, they are invited to contact directly the Helpdesk by phone or by email. From our experience, Help Desk is especially helpful and fruitful when student's need to access the eCourse from a home computer. Our metrics show that it is mainly at night that student's study more hours and more continuously. In this case, helpdesk has a key role in solving technical and usability problems.

Student E-Learning Kit – Manuals, Quick Reference Guides and FAQ's: Different manuals are provided to the students and these are considered to be significant and relevant and sometimes are a pre-requisite to the adequate attendance

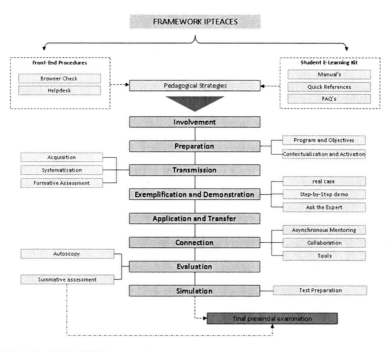

Fig. 10.1 The IPTEACES Framework

of the course. However, experience tells us that the students don't always read these materials before accessing the course. In order to overcome this constraint, a mechanism was developed, in the form of an animated step by step demonstration, to see how the student observes how to access the course, how to navigate in the course as well as an overview of the course's main functionalities (Quick Reference Guide). In other words, it is given to the students, in a quick and clear format, the minimal and essential steps. Similarly, the traditional Frequently Asked Questions (html, pdf) was transformed in animated (flash movie) responses to the students. The *reading* paradigm/approach was complemented with an easier and quicker form: the "animation/observation" mode.

Pedagogical Strategies (Detail of the IPTEACES Framework):

- **Involvement** – This strategy aims to *immerse* the student in the context of a real business or corporate scenario, where he is confronted with a problem (Merrill 2002, 2007) or with a particular working situation. The student will play a role (e.g., of a new employee of a department or a company; has a need for a training program and to obtain a new certification to gain a new promotion or progression). This character dialogues and interacts, along the course, with others that will appear several times throughout the course and sets up a short narrative in the form of dialogue. From a pedagogical point of view, it seeks to *gain the attention* of the student (Cf. – Gagné's first event "Gaining Attention"; Keller's first principle of ARCS -"Motivation to learn is promoted when a learner's curiosity is aroused due to a perceived gap in current knowledge"), surrounding and projecting him in a situation that simulates reality, thus enhancing motivation and making a connection with everyday workplace problems.
- **Preparation** – This strategy is divided into two complementary stages: Presentation of "Program and Objectives" and "Contextualization and Activation":

   (a) *Program and Objectives* – Presentation of the program, objectives and what is expected of the student (Cf. – Gagné's second event *"Informing the learner of the Obj*ective"; Keller's second principle: "Motivation to learn is promoted when the knowledge to be learned is perceived to be meaningfully related to one's goals"). It is necessary to inform and make sure that the learner understands, in detail, the relevance, the suitability and applicability of the course as well as what is expected of him. This approach details the generic objectives and goals into small chunks that are objective and measurable, that is, into specific objectives (in *stricto sensu*). The achievement, by the student, of a certain specific objective can be accessed through a specific set of questions directly linked with this objective and therefore it can be determine if the student has achieved that specific goal. If a specific goal is not achieved, the feedback from the assessment will lead the student directly (the student is guided) to the content related to this specific training gap. There is an intimate connection between specific objectives, the contents related to this specific objective and a set of questions that can assesses if this specific objective is achieved by the learner.

(b) *Contextualization and Activation* – Before starting the *"Transmission"* phase (learning content), this strategy seeks to make an introduction, a contextualization or a reminder of the subject (or related / prerequisites) so the student can activate prior existing knowledge (Cf. – Gagné's third event *Stimulating Recall of Prerequisite Learned Capabilities*; Merrill's *Activation principle – Learning is promoted when learners activate relevant cognitive structures by being directed to recall, describe, or demonstrate relevant prior knowledge or experience*). Activation is enhanced when learners recall or acquire a structure for organizing new knowledge. In other words, it seeks to establish relationships between new concepts or new information and concepts and existing knowledge or with some prior experience. As students begin to learn new information, instruction should involve the recall of prior learning to establish a common foundation of understanding. It intends the interaction of new material or information with pre-existing cognitive structure on the individual.

- **Transmission** – This phase is divided in three complementary moments: Acquisition (learning content), Systematization and Formative Assessment.

    Acquisition is the central strategy for presenting the learning content of the course. This strategy (Gagné's fourth event *Present the Stimulus Material*) is where the new content is actually presented to the learner. Content should be chunked and organized meaningfully and in order to appeal to different learning modalities, and therefore a variety of media should be used if possible, including text, graphics, audio narration, and video – however respecting the main recommendations from Cognitive Load Theory (Clark et al. 2006). After partially presenting new learning content which are typically related to one specific objective, it is advisable to carry out a *systematization* through a recapitulation of concepts and ideas taught. It is also advisable, at the end, to create a graphical representation of the relationship between the concepts and ideas (new learning material) through the use, for instance, *"concept maps"* (showing the relationships among concepts) or *"dynamic diagrams"*. In order to inform the learner if he has understood and has achieved the objective, he should be presented with an exercise or a set of questions in a *formative assessment* before he can proceed through the course.

- **Exemplification and Demonstration** – This phase is mainly based on Merrill's (2002, 2007) "demonstration principle" and it was divided into three complementary sub-strategies: *Real Case, Step-by-Step Demo* and *Ask the Expert.*

(a) *Real Case* is an exemplification based on real situations, real problems and seeks to confront learners with authentic real-life situations, while it tries to illustrate the relevance of the content. It also intends to demonstrate concepts learned. It is advisable to have more than one real case in order to diversify the illustration and to maximize the comprehension of a problem/situation. Through the use of several examples (from simple to more complex) this strategy tries to promote the comprehension of the lowest common denominator, what is common in all the examples showed ("the essence").

(b) *Step by step demo* is a type of guided exemplification (Cf. Gagné's fifth event *Providing learning guidance*) that seeks to illustrate the decomposition of a problem into phases and components and demands and a detailed and commented analysis of the parts that compose the complexity of a situation, of a problem.

(c) *Ask the expert* is a more complex situation in which the student, who is faced with a problem is given a more structured example. The student may ask, in predetermined areas of the course, advice from the expert (through the internal e-course email functionality) on how the problem could be resolved and supported by the hand of a specialist.

In synthesis, this phase follows Merrill's principle that learning is promoted when learners observe a demonstration of the skills to be learned that is consistent with the type of content being taught. Demonstrations are enhanced when learners receive guidance that relates instances to generalities, and when learners observe media relevant to the content. Merrill summarizes this "third principle" as "Show me". Show me involves both demonstration and guidance. Effective guidance involves steering learners to relevant information and helping them to compare a variety of demonstrations.

- **Application and Transfer** – This phase focus on the effort to maximize the *transfer of learning*, for the promotion of the ability to flexibly apply what has been learned in new situations (Cf. Gagnés fifth and sixth event – *Eliciting learning guidance* and *Providing feedback*; Keller´s third principle *Confidence* and Merrill's *Application principle*). As referred by van Merriënboer and Kirschner (2007), the fundamental problem facing instructional designers is education and training's apparent inability to achieve the transfer of learning. This phase is an opportunity for the learner to apply the learned knowledge or skill, first with guidance and gradually without guidance and receiving sustainable feedback and support. This phase is mainly based in Merrill's *Application principle – Learning is promoted when learners engage in the application of their newly acquired knowledge or skill that is consistent with the type of content being taught*. Application is effective only when learners receive intrinsic or corrective feedback, and when learners are coached and when this coaching is gradually withdrawn for each subsequent task. This is also complementary to what Keller considers in his third principle, "*Motivation to learn is promoted when learners believe they can succeed in mastering the learning task*". Confidence, the third ARCS category, incorporates variables related to student's feelings of personal control and expectancy for success.

- **Connection** – This phase focuses on mentoring, collaboration and tools.

(a) *Asynchronous Mentoring* – Along the frequency of the course, students may face some specific questions that are needed to be clarified. In this sense, an integrated e-mail functionality was developed inside the course in order for the student to question their tutor –asynchronous mentoring through direct email. Each screen in the course has an individual identification, a specific code. Within each screen, there is a box that can be activated by the student that allows him to ask questions to his tutor. Each question is specific (directly concerned with the contents of each screen) and therefore there is no propensity for generic questions, only specific, anchored ones. For the tutor it is much easier and quicker to respond to the student as well as for understanding the exact problem.

(b) *Collaboration*: there are two kinds of discussion forums available: *Supervised discussion Forums'* and *Peer discussion forums'*. In each learning module, there is always a Supervised Discussion Forum. In this Forum all the posts are visible to everyone in the e-Learning class, which is divided by small groups, and connected with their associated Tutor. Here are mainly discussed items concerning the course or procedures connected with the learning process or certification program. Peer discussion forums are also available without direct supervision of the tutor. Here students can exchange ideas, doubts, materials and get connected and feel as part as an e-Learning class.

(c) *Tools*: This feature complements the contents of the course and gives the student access to a glossary of terms, job aids, documentation, worksheets, templates, articles, legislation and other pragmatic materials.

- **Evaluation: Autoscopy and Summative evaluation**
  Throughout the e-Learning course, several moments of formative assessment occur with great regularity which provide guidance, feedback and inform the student how he is achieving the learning objectives. At the end of each learning module the system proposes that the student submits to do an Autoscopy (self evaluation). The intention is to analyze whether, strictly from the student's point of view, if he feels that he has achieved the learning objectives, in other words, the degree of fulfillment that each student thinks he has reached. This feature is optional and allows those who take this questionnaire a later confrontation with the results obtained from the summative evaluation. The output confronts the level of self awareness that the student has of himself and specifically of his learning achievement.

  Upon completing modules, students are required to perform a final assessment. This test, a summative evaluation, is intended to assess objectively if the student has achieved the specific objectives of each of the learning modules. The score of the test, on the scale, varies from 0% to 100%, where success is considered to have been achieved with a score equal to or greater than 70%. Only those students who achieve at least 70% pass to the next learning module. There is always a detailed feedback from the results of the summative assessment. Students can see their classification (score), which of the questions are correct and incorrect, they can compare their answers with the correct answer and, in the end, the application creates a learning path directly connected with the contents related to the learning gap.

  This strategy is based directly with Gagné's eight event, *Assess performance*, as well as to Keller's fourth principle *"Motivation to learn is promoted when learners anticipate and experience satisfying outcomes to a learning task"* – which is represented in the ARCS model by *Satisfaction*. It is necessary for learners to have positive feelings about their learning experiences and to develop continuing motivation to learn.

- **Simulation**

  A common definition of a simulation is a reproduction of an item or event. A true simulation has a specific goal in mind – to mimic, or simulate, a real system so that we can explore it, perform experiments on it, and understand it before implementing it in the real world. It provides an immersive learning experience. In this particular certification course, a simulation exam was built, similar to the one that the candidates need to pass on face-to-face examination after completing with success all the e-Learning modules. This application is composed of a test with 50 questions, chosen randomly from the database (of more than 900 questions), to which the trainee will have to answer in a maximum time of 1 h. Each time the student generates a new test, new questions are again randomly selected as well as the order of the choices in each of the questions. This allows students real practice for the final exam and anticipates what is expected of them in terms of the necessary knowledge. This assessment/simulation, like the real one, is completed without the ability to receive additional coaching, feedback, or hints. The student knows his classification and which questions are correct and which are incorrect.

  This strategy takes into account Gagne's ninth event (*Enhance retention and transfer to the Job*) and especially Merrill's *Integration Principle*, – *Learning is promoted when learners integrate their new knowledge into their everyday life by being directed to reflect on, discuss, or defend their new knowledge or skill.* Also, Keller contends that motivation to learn is promoted and maintained when learners employ volitional (self-regulatory) strategies to protect their intentions – after becoming motivated to achieve a goal, it is necessary to persist in one's efforts to achieve it, which is the focus of this principle.

3 Overview of Student's Demographic Characteristics and Success Indicators

3.1 Brief Characterization of Student's Demographic Indicators

A brief description of the universe of students who attended the courses in the period under review is presented (Table 10.1). We will then highlight the most representative of each category:

3.2 Brief Characterization of Success Indicators: Approvals, Failures, Drop-outs and Evaluation of Satisfaction

Among the 3,726 learners who attended the intermediaries' certification course, 3,542 passed the course (approbation rate of 95.0%), and 184 failed (failure rate of 4.9%). More precisely, concerning the three exam session, 3,100 learners (83.2%)

Table 10.1 Brief characterization of student's demographic indicators

Industry	From a total of 3,726 learners, 1,614 learners (43.3%) come from the insurance industry and 2,112 learners (56.7%) belong to the banking industry
Gender	There was a very similar distribution of the learners of both genders although male learners have a slightly higher representation, totaling 1,953 learners (52.4%), in comparison with 1,773 (47.6%) of female learners
Age groups	The learners represent an average age of 34 years old, and a standard deviation of 8.8 years. The data show a high variability in the age characteristics of the learners because they are between 18 and 71 years old. The distribution of the learners in the different age groups has a higher number of learners in the age category between 24 and 34 years old
Academic qualifications	Data show a high variability due to the existence of learners with different education levels. In first place, the secondary education is the level which includes more individuals, with a total of 1,607 learners (43.1%). Secondly, 1,447 learners have an undergraduate degree, reaching a representation of 38.8% and 522 learners with Primary Education (14.0%)
Residency	Residence of the learners also shows a high variability, because the learners come from different parts of the Portuguese territory, so that we analyzed the distribution of the learners in the 18 regions

were approved the first time they took the exam, 382 learners were approved on the second exam session (10.2%), and finally 60 learners on the third exam session (1.6%). The global average score of the learners is 82.5%, with a standard deviation of 11.0, which shows a high variability of the results of the learners. Concerning the dropouts, 25 learners (0.7%) did not conclude the educational process. Among the 3,526 learners, 1,770 learners answered the survey of evaluation of satisfaction, obtaining a response rate of 50.2%. The analysis of the answers showed that, generally, the learners were satisfied or very satisfied with the course, ranking their answers over three on a four point Likert scale. The majority (76.9%) of the students didn't had a previous e-Learning experience in a professional context.

4   Analysis of the Final Scores Through the Use of Regression Trees

As stated previously, our main goal was to design an efficient instructional design framework that could materialize, largely on a single approach, an appropriate learning strategy for different learners in order to fit the different learning preferences and also to respect other specific differences. In order to analyze the rate of accomplishment of our goal, and especially to improve quality assurance in future e-Learning projects using this framework, it was felt necessary to further deepen the understanding as to which group or groups was this framework most appropriate. In this sense, we intended to determine the impact that this framework had among the socio demographic characteristics previously identified (Industry, Gender, Age groups, Academic Qualifications and Residency), and to see if this framework was more appropriate for a specific group (or groups).

We wanted to estimate the existence of significant statistical differences in the average score obtained by the learners (82.5%), according to the demographic data. We considered relevant to analyze in more detail the success indicators of the insurance intermediaries' certification course (score) and distinguish the relevancy of the variables analyzed previously, through the development of statistical predictive methods. In this case we used decision tree, more specifically regression tree via exhaustive CHAID algorithm.[1]

The literature defines a decision tree (DT) as a tree-like structure used for classification, decision theory, clustering, and prediction functions. It depicts rules for dividing training data into groups based on the regularities in the data. A DT can be used for categorical and continuous response variables. When the response variables are continuous, the DT is often referred to as a regression tree. If the response variables are categorical, it is called a classification tree.

A decision tree model consists of two parts: creating the tree and applying the tree to the database. To achieve this, decision trees use several different algorithms. In our case we choose Exhaustive CHAID, a modification to the basic CHAID algorithm, which performs a more thorough merging and testing of predictor variables. Exhaustive search CHAID was proposed by Biggs et al. (1991). Exhaustive CHAID does not check the p-value against a predetermined threshold value but performs a more thorough merging and testing of predictor variables. This technique requires more computing and analysis time. The merges of classes continues (without reference to any threshold value) until only two categories remain for each predictor. The algorithm then selects from among the predictors the one that yields the most significant split (Nisbet et al. 2009: 247) (Chart 10.1).

The top level, also known as the root of the tree, denotes all data. The second level is the first partition of the data according to the most important splitting factor suggested by the algorithms. The further down the level, the less important is the factor. In this case, firstly and somehow unforeseen (we expected academic background and/or age group to be the main differentiation factors – due to traditional characteristics of successful online learners described in the literature – e.g., Boyd 2004; Schrum and Hong 2002a, b), Industry emerges as the primary variable differentiating the final grades obtained by students (it appears that industry-specific mind set or culture somehow may have a significant role and that is a topic for future research). In this analysis, gender and residency did not reveal any significant effects.

Objectively, this procedure has identified that the trainees from the insurance industry and banking industry, have, on average, different final ratings ($p < 0.0001$, $F = 202.5$), more specifically, the trainees from the insurance industry have an

---

[1] We used "IBM SPSS Statistics 18".

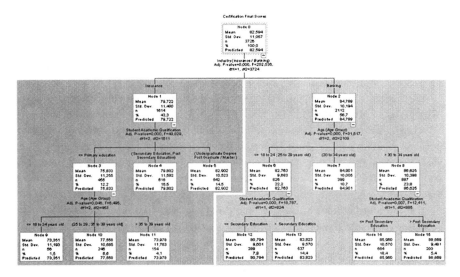

Chart 10.1 Overall regression tree: overview segmentation graphic of the final grades of students, according to demographics

averaged final score of 79.7% compared to the trainees of the banking industry whose average in the final classifications is 84.7%. In this sense, the importance of demographic characteristics of trainees is observed as predictive of their final performance in the final examination for certification, exerting different influences in this context according to industry of activity of learners.

Given the relevance of these results, we analyzed the existence of predictive relations, specifically in each Industry.

4.1 Insurance Industry

This section has, as its specific objective, testing groups of trainees within the insurance sector based on their demographic characteristics. The results testify to the differentiating role of the academic qualifications due to the existence of statistically significant differences in final grades obtained by students (p < 0.0001, F = 49.8). The results thus demonstrate the existence of three groups of trainees according to their different academic qualifications: firstly, a group of students with qualifications at the level of higher education, post graduation or master degree, that obtained an average of 82.9% on their final grades; secondly a group of graduates with qualifications at the level of secondary education and post secondary education who had an average score of 79.8% and finally a group of graduates with qualifications at the level of Primary education, whose average rated 75.8% (close to the minimum passing score of 70%).

The results also showed that the groups of trainees with educational level of higher education, post graduation or master degree, and secondary education have a greater homogeneity in comparison with the group of graduates with Primary education. The regression tree also showed the existence of significant differences in mean scores obtained by graduates with qualifications at the level of primary education, depending on their age ($p=0.046$, $F=6.4$), namely the group of learners aged between 18 and 24 years who had the lowest average score of 73.3%, the group of learners aged between 25 and 39 years attained higher rankings with an average of 77.5% and finally the group of students aged 35 years and above who obtained an average of 73.9%.

4.2   Banking Industry

Considering the students from the banking industry, we also evaluated the existence of groups of trainees with different final scores. The results show, firstly, that the age of the trainees is the first differentiating variable, resulting in the existence of three groups of trainees with different average scores ($p=0.000$; $F=31.6$): the group of learners aged between 18 and 24 years who had the lowest average score of 82.7%, the group of learners aged between 30 and 34 years old attained higher rankings with an average of 84.9% and finally the group of students aged from 35 years and above who obtained an average of 86.6%.

On the above level, the regression tree shows also that academic qualification influences the performance of learners. The group of trainees aged between 30 and 34 years is the most internally homogeneous, showing no differences according to educational attainment, contrary there is a greater heterogeneity of the other two groups. In the group of learners aged between 18 and 29 years witnessed the existence of two groups with different educational attainments ($p=0,000$; $F=18,7$), including a group with qualifications at the level of Primary education who reach the lowest average ratings of 80.7% and a group of graduates with qualifications at the level higher education, post graduation or masters degree, reaching a higher average rating of 83.8%.

Thus, among the group of trainees aged between 18 and 29 years there is the existence of two groups with different educational attainments ($p=0,000$; $F=18.7$), specifically a group having qualifications of Primary education and secondary education achieved the lowest average ratings of 80.7% and a group of graduates with qualifications at the level of high school, higher education, post graduation or master degree reaching a higher average rating of 83.8%. Within the group of trainees aged over 35 years, there is the existence of two groups of students with different qualifications, including a group of graduates with qualifications at the level of primary education, secondary and post secondary with a lower average ratings of 85.9% and a group of graduates with qualifications higher education, post graduation or masters degree that have a higher average ratings of 88.8%.

5 Measuring the Effectiveness of EPTEACES E-Learning Framework: The Case Study of Insurance Intermediaries Certification Course

In the context of the assessment of e-Learning Systems effectiveness, Levy (2006, 2009) developed an investigation by querying students concerning the characteristics of e-learning systems that they value and consider important during their learning experience and in the attempt to understand the relationship between the value learners attribute to e-learning systems and the satisfaction learners experience with e-learning systems. This author states that it is not the number of satisfied students or the level of satisfaction that suggest the system's effectiveness. Rather, it is the extent to which students are more satisfied by the system performance with what they perceive as important.

Information System literature defines satisfaction as the perceived performance level students find at a post-experience point of time with e-learning systems (Doll and Torkzadeh 1991), whereas following Value Theory, value is defined as an enduring core belief about the level of importance students attribute to the e-learning system (Rokeach 1969: 160).

Levy (2006, 2009) proposes measures of learners' perceived value and learners 'perceived satisfaction, for assessment of the true effectiveness of an e-learning system – here defined as the "entire technological, organizational, and management system that facilitates and enables students learning via the Internet" (Levy and Murphy 2002). E-learning systems are considered effective when learners value its characteristics as highly important and are highly satisfied by those same characteristics.

Levy (2006, 2009) proposed a set of characteristics that learners found important, or value, when using e-Learning systems. The list of e-Learning systems characteristics was built primarily from an exhaustive review of literature and subsequently through exploratory focus groups, as well as in a qualitative questionnaire. Levy (2006) developed an assessment of such characteristics using a survey instrument. This survey was based upon prior validated measures from education and Information System literature included satisfaction and value items for each of the 48 e-learning system's characteristic, as well as learners' overall value measure, overall satisfaction measure with e-learning system, and an overall perceived learning measure. Due to the heterogeneity nature of the e-Learning system characteristics proposed – 48 e-Learning System characteristics, Levy grouped them according to the four dimensions proposed by Webster and Hackley's (1997): technology and support (14 characteristics), course (12 characteristics), professor (7 characteristics), and learner's dimension (15 characteristics).

In order to determine the level of effectiveness of our e-Learning project, we applied Levy's proposed methodology. However, due to the specificity of this e-Learning course (asynchronous e-Learning with strong component of self-learning) we've decided to withdraw the Professor dimension and therefore extract the seven e-Learning system characteristics directly linked with this dimension. Our online questionnaire was then composed by the other three Dimensions covering a total of 41 e-Learning System characteristics: technology and support dimension (14 characteristics), Course dimension (12 characteristics) and learner's dimension (15 characteristics) – (Cf. Appendix I). This decision was based on our interpretation that the Professor dimension and the correspondent seven characteristics were more pertinent to a different nature of e-Learning courses, as for example synchronous e-Learning courses (videoconference) or in blended e-Learning courses.

5.1   "Value-Satisfaction Grid" and "Learners' Value Index of Satisfaction" (LeVIS index)

Levy (2006, 2009) proposed two benchmark tools based on the outputs of the questionnaire that can be complemented: "the Value-Satisfaction grid" and "LeVIS index".

The objective of "Value-Satisfaction grid" is to provide an indication for action and improvement priorities for the e-Learning system dimension and the e-Learning systems characteristics. The "Value-Satisfaction grid" was developed in a similar manner to the S.W.O.T. (acronym for Strengths, Weaknesses, Opportunities, and Threats) used by many marketing scholars. In the adaptation to the e-Learning context, the "Value-Satisfaction grid" was based on aggregated student perceived satisfaction as well as aggregated student-perceived value of e-Learning system characteristics. This grid was constructed by positioning the e-Learning system characteristics of each dimension, where the mean characteristics satisfaction scores are positioned on the horizontal axis and the mean characteristics value scores are positioned on the vertical axis. The dimension grid was developed for each of the three dimensions. Similarly, "Value-Satisfaction grid" for the overall system was constructed. In this study the measures scale ranges from 1 to 6, while no scores were noted below 3 in satisfaction and below 3 in value, resulting in the use of 4.5 as the cut-off point between low and high on both axes of the grid (Fig. 10.2).

The "Value-Satisfaction grid" does not provide however a measure of the magnitude of e-Learning system effectiveness and therefore should be complemented with other tool. "LeVIS index" is proposed by Levy as a benchmarking tool combining the learners' perceived value and satisfaction in order to indicate learners' perceived e-Learning systems effectiveness. The "LeVIS index" was proposed as the multiplication of the overall satisfaction (S) by the overall value (V). "LeVIS index" provides a score of the overall magnitude of the effectiveness of the e-Learning system under study. The two items (S and V) are measured on a scale of 1 to 6, and the "LeVIS index" is calculated as:

$$\mathrm{LeVIS} = \left(\frac{1}{36}\right) \cdot \mathrm{V_o} \times \mathrm{S_o}$$

Fig. 10.2 The value-
satisfaction grid (Adapted from
Levy (2006))

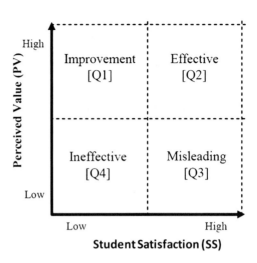

The results provide assessment of magnitude of learners' perceived effectiveness integrating all learner' dimension value measures and dimensions satisfaction measures with e-Learning system under study. The magnitude of LeVIS provides that when LeVIS is near 0, this indicates very low learners' perceived e-Learning systems effectiveness. When LeVIS is near 1, this indicates very high learners' perceived high learners' perceived e-Learning systems effectiveness. This measure provides that if only one of the two measures (S or V) is high, the overall system measure (LeVIS) score is not high. As noted by Levy, an observed limitation of LeVIS is due to the equal importance given for value and satisfaction.

6 Assessing the Effectiveness of IPTEACES E-learning Framework (N = 1317)

The application of the adapted version of the online questionnaire took place during the period from May 2009 to June 2009, targeting 2,531 students distributed by Insurance Industry and Banking Industry. The response rate was 52.03%, i.e., 1,317 trainees. More specifically, 59.6% of respondents were from banking industry and 39.9% were from insurance industry.

6.1 Overall LeVIS index: The Effectiveness of EPTEALAS e-Learning Framework

Levy (2006, 2009) proposed the following categorization for LeVIS index overall scores. If LeVIS overall score:

- ≥ 0.9375 – Very high effectiveness;
- ≥ 0.75 and < 0.9375 – High effectiveness;

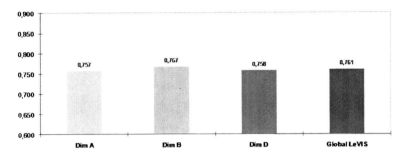

Fig. 10.3 Overview of LeVIS index of EPTEALAS e-Learning framework

- ≥ 0.5625 and < 0.75 – Good effectiveness;
- ≥ 0.3750 and < 0.5625 – Moderate effectiveness;
- ≥ 0.1875 and < 0.3750 – Low effectiveness and
- < 0.1875 – Very low effectiveness.

Results from the Global LeVIS index indicate that the overall e-Learning system under study reached a global score of 0.781 and therefore should be classified as "High Effectiveness" (Fig. 10.3). All the Dimensions are above 0.75 global score and therefore can be considered as having High effectiveness, (Dimension A – 0.757; Dimension B – 0.767, Dimension D – 0.758), with a particular emphasis on Dimension B – Course which had the highest score of all Dimensions.

7   Overall Value-Satisfaction Grid of the 41 E-Learning System Characteristics' (All Dimensions)

As we can see in the Figure above, all the 41 e-Learning system characteristics are situated in the Q2 quadrant of the Value-Satisfaction Grid, i.e., in the Effective Quadrant (Fig. 10.4). All the characteristics and dimensions are considered effective. However, as stated before, having "excellence" as a reference, as it can be seen in this overall grid, there are seven e-Learning System Characteristics that are somehow separate from the other 34 (less effective) and therefore should need to have a quality improvement plan.

These seven e-Learning system characteristics positioned on the lowest corner of the Q2 quadrant somehow represent that there are two groups (or sub-categories) that should be consider to have priority in terms of quality improvement: HelpDesk (A1, A2 and A3) originally corresponding to Dimension A – Technology and Support and Class (D3, D2, D4 and D5) originally corresponding to Dimension D – Learner.

The first priority for quality intervention should concern sub-category which we designate as HelpDesk (A1, A2, and A3).We can observe that the importance scores of these tree items are higher than the ones corresponding to satisfaction scores. In this case it should be implemented a strategy in order to gain a superior level of

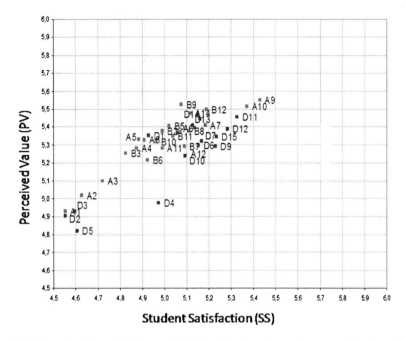

Fig. 10.4 Overall value-satisfaction grid of the 41 e-Learning system: zoom-in view of Q2 quadrant

satisfaction from the students concerning HelpDesk services by increasing, for example, the helpdesk SLA's (service level agreements).

The second priority should concern sub-category, which we designate as Class (D3, D2, D4 and D5), and that originally corresponds to Dimension D – Learner. More specifically, D2, D3, D4 and D5 were e-Learning system characteristics that were considered by the students as been valuable and that there is the need to increase their level of satisfaction.

It is our believe that, in both cases, "helpdesk" and "class", the e-Learning system characteristics corresponding to each sub-category have intrinsic similitude's and are intimately connected. Therefore increasing the satisfaction level on A1 or A2 will have a positive impact on A3; increasing the satisfaction level on D2 and D3 will impact D4 and D5.

8 Conclusions

Our main goal was to design an efficient instructional design framework that could materialize, largely on a single approach, an appropriate learning strategy for different learners in order to fit the different learning preferences and also to respect other specific differences. From the results achieved, it has been accomplished the creation of a pragmatic and straightforward instructional design framework, based on pedagogical benchmarks as well as in e-Learning best practices, that can be an applied in many e-Learning projects that face significant diversity in their attendees.

Unlike the ideal profile of successful online learners characteristics, so often identified in the projects need to train heterogeneous populations efficiently, rapidly, with limited investment (it is not possible to develop several versions of a course) and having a very low dropout rate. Although there are evident and significant differences in the final scores between student groups, this framework has achieved the main objective and has transformed those who do not have "the ideal profile of a successful online learner" into successful e-Learning candidates.

Having a diverse range of attendees, this framework has produced results that are considered to fulfill the typical main objectives of an e-Learning project: high approval rate, low dropout rate and high level of satisfaction from the students, as well as from a management point a view has achieved a high level effectiveness based on international benchmark tools.

This e-Learning project achieved the category of "High effectiveness" (score = 0.757) based on the assessment from 1,317 students on satisfaction and importance of 41 e-Learning system characteristics. However, having excellence as reference, the output of the "Overall Value-Satisfaction Grid" showed witch system characteristics and dimensions should have a priority improvement plan. These tools combined together give Managers the correct and adequate information for action improvement in the context of e-Learning quality.

The most significant limitation of this study is that, so far, this framework only had an implementation in one particular project (although the size of the sample was significant). In this sense, it should be applied in the future to other populations, other industries and to other subjects.

Appendix I

Techcnology and support dimension	
A1	Quick answer from technical support via phone
A2	Quick answer from technical support after-hours via e-mail
A3	Quality of technical support
A4	System operation time (up-time)
A5	Reduced system errors
A6	System security (discourage hacking, secure access, etc.)
A7	Access to courses from anywhere in the world (via the Internet)
A8	High Network availability & Low network congestion
A9	Learning at anytime of the day (schedule flexibility)
A10	Submit assignments from anywhere (via the Internet)
A11	Different system tools (chat, bulletin-board or discussion forums, etc.)
A12	Access of all courses from one area (My LMS)
A13	Taking quizzes remotely (off-campus)
A14	Review course materials

(continued)

(continued)

Techcnology and support dimension

Course dimension	
B1	Availability of course content
B2	Quality content of courses
B3	Amount of material in courses
B4	Interesting subject matter
B5	Difficulty of subject matter
B6	Availability of other content (syllabus, objectives, assignments, schedule)
B7	Enjoyment from the courses/lessons
B8	Ease-of-use (with course content, navigation, interface, etc.)
B9	Similar of interface across all online courses
B10	Gathering information quickly
B11	Organization of courses (content of courses, organization of assignments, etc. across all course modules)
B12	Taking practice tests prior to graded test
Learner dimension	
D1	Learning a lot in these classes
D2	Amount of interaction with classmates
D3	Quality of interaction with classmates
D4	Classmates' attitude (across all courses)
D5	Being part of a 'class' although it was online
D6	Your comfort with online learning and technology
D7	Your Internet and computer skills
D8	Self-discipline and time management
D9	Cost of courses
D10	Cost of ISP and Internet access
D11	Reduced travel cost/time (to and from campus)
D12	Ability to travel while taking online courses (for business or other)
D13	Employer support and your ability to work while learning
D14	Attendance to family responsibilities
D15	Family support

References

Biggs, D., DeVille, B. & Suen, E. (1991). A Method of Choosing Multiway Partitions for Classification and Decision Trees. Journal of Applied Statistics18(1):49–62.

Boyd, D. (2004). The characteristics of successful online students. New Horizons in Adult Education, 18(2), 31–39.

Clark, R., Nguyen, F., & Sweller, J. (2006). Efficiency in Learning: Evidence-Based Guidelines to Manage Cognitive Load. San Francisco: Pfeiffer.

Doll, W. J., & Torkzadeh, G. (1991). The measurement of end-user computing satisfaction: Theoretical and methodological issues. MIS Quarterly, 15(1), 5–9.

Gagne, R. M. (1985). The Conditions of Learning and Theory of Instruction , 4th ed. New York: Holt, Rinehart and Winston.

Gagne, R., Briggs, L. & Wager, W. (1992). Principles of instructional design (4th ed.). Englewood Cliffs, NJ: Prentice-Hall. Instructional message design: principles from the behavioral and cognitive sciences (Englewood).

Keller, J. (2008). 'First principles of motivation to learn and e3-learning' Distance Education Vol. 29, No. 2, pp. 175–185.

Levy, Y., & Murphy, K. (2002). Toward a value framework for online learning system. In Proceedings for the Hawaii International Conference on System Sciences (HICSS – 35), 1–9.

Levy, Y. (2006). Assessing the value of e-learning systems. Hershey, PA: Information Science Publishing.

Levy, Y. (2009). Murph, K. & Zanakisy, S. ,A Value-Satisfaction Taxonomy of IS Effectiveness (VSTISE): A Case Study of User Satisfaction with IS and User-Perceived Value of IS, International Journal of Information Systems in the Service Sector, 1(1), 93–118.

Merrill, D. (2002). First principles of instruction. Educ. Technol. Res. Dev., 50(3), 43–59.

Merrill, D. (2007). First principles of instruction: a synthesis. In R. A. Reiser & J. V. Dempsey (Eds.), Trends and Issues in Instructional Design and Technology, 2nd Edition (Vol. 2, pp. 62–71). Upper Saddle River, NJ: Merrill/Prentice Hall.

Nisbet, R., Elder, J. & Miner, G. (2009). Handbook of statistical analysis and data mining applications. London: Academic Press.

Rokeach, M. (1969). Beliefs, attitudes, and values. San Francisco, CA: Jossey-Bass Inc. Publishers.

Schrum, L., & Hong, S. (2002a). Dimensions and strategies for online success : Voices from experienced educators. Journal of Asynchronous Learning Networks, 6(1).

Schrum, L., & Hong, S. (2002b). From the Field: Characteristics of Successful Tertiary Online Students and Strategies of Experienced Online Educators. Education and Information Technologies, 7(1), 5–16.

van Merriënboer, J. G., & Kirschner, P. (2007). Ten Steps to Complex Learning. Mahwah, NJ: Lawrence Erlbaum Associates.

Webster, J. & Hackley, P., "Teaching effectiveness in technology-mediated distance learning." Academy of Management Journal, 1997, Issue 6, Vol. 40, pp. 1282–1309.

Part IV
Toward Web 3.0 in Education

Chapter 11
Key-Roles in VLEs: A Metric Based on Social Network Analysis

Paola Pasqualino, Maria Assunta Barchiesi, Elisa Battistoni, and Gianluca Murgia

1 Introduction

The process of knowledge development in a community is strongly influenced by the level of collaboration among its members, which is principally obtained through their interpersonal communication (Wenger et al. 2002). This fact has pointed in evidence the role played by organizational informal networks in the development of effective Knowledge Management (KM) practices (Cross et al. 2001), and has strengthened the social constructivist view of learning (Vygotskij 1978).

This latter perspective considers learning as an active process of knowledge construction made by the learners' community with the support of the teacher, rather than the acquisition of knowledge communicated by the teacher (Duffy and Cunningham 1996). Besides, the highlight of the learning process is the comparison, produced by social interaction, among the learners' meanings, which generates a more shared, rich and realistic interpretation of data (Hewitt and Scardamalia 1998). First of all, social interaction leads learners to organize their knowledge, in order to better explain their own points of view. Secondly, it gives learners the possibility to increase their wealth of knowledge, through the acquisition of knowledge and experiences owned by others. Finally, social interaction supports the development of several meta-cognitive and social skills, such as leadership, negotiation, and workgroup.

This collaborative approach requires some specific metrics in order to map the role played by each learner in the learning process. These metrics could be developed

P. Pasqualino (✉) • M.A. Barchiesi • E. Battistoni
Department of Enterprise Engineering, "Tor Vergata" University of Rome, Rome, Italy
e-mail: paola.pasqualino@uniroma2.it; barchiesi@dii.uniroma2.it; battistoni@dii.uniroma2.it

G. Murgia
Department of Information Engineering, University of Siena, Siena, Italy
e-mail: murgia@unisi.it

P. Isaias et al. (eds.), *Towards Learning and Instruction in Web 3.0: Advances in Cognitive and Educational Psychology*, DOI 10.1007/978-1-4614-1539-8_11,
© Springer Science+Business Media, LLC 2012

by using different methodologies, such as questionnaires and content analysis, but their high level of subjectivity could affect the correct detection of the roles within the learning community. These roles could be related both to the social activities made by the learner (i.e., the impact of cooperation inside a group, or among the different groups that compose the class) and, specifically, to the learner's contribution to the knowledge development process. As specific metrics make it possible to identify experts within a community, metrics could also be useful to the resolution of one of the most urgent problems of Web 3.0 – that is the need to find the most credible sources of information in a particular field (Jensen 2007). These metrics could help the teacher in managing the development of knowledge flows inside the learners' community, giving also some insights for the creation and the evaluation of the teams in the class (Ounnas 2008).

Thanks to the fact that Virtual Learning Environments (VLEs) make it possible to keep track of communications among members, we can develop metrics to identify credible and reliable sources by analyzing communication using Social Network Analysis (SNA) (Cross et al. 2002). Using SNA in virtual communities most authoritative researchers (Everett and Borgatti 1999) consider only a very limited set of indicators, such as the degree centrality, while a few others develop a deeper analysis, which provides a more useful framework for understanding the characteristics of knowledge flows inside communities and the roles played by members. Among them, Cross and Prusak's framework (2002), which is based on four key-roles that generally are critical in the development of knowledge flows in organizations, represents one of the most cited SNA frameworks in the research literature. Nevertheless, it seems more focused on the Knowledge Management field and fails to provide an operational elaboration of the key-roles in terms of metrics. This deficiency is the motivating problem addressed in our work. After elaboration of Cross and Prusak's key roles (2002), we consider the problem of knowledge flow representation. That discussion is followed by a description of the development of appropriate metrics and their application in an actual case.

2   Cross and Prusak's Key-Roles in VLEs

Nie et al. (2010) assert the importance of informal networks in organizations, due to their impact on information and knowledge sharing. Moreover, in organizational contexts, Cross and Prusak (2002) argue that the effectiveness of informal networks can be improved if managers focus on some key-roles, whose presence is critical for the performance of any organization: Central Connectors (CCs), Boundary Spanners (BSs), Information Brokers (IBs), and Peripheral Specialists (PSs). These key-roles, which will be described below, are identified thanks to SNA, and we suggest that they could be recognized also in VLEs. Therefore, in our work we propose a transposition of the four key-roles already defined by Cross and Prusak from an organizational context to a learning one, providing some metrics to detect them and applying these metrics to a real e-learning course. Indeed, it is our opinion that being able to identify key-roles in a VLE can help in understanding if there is someone who might impede or facilitate collaboration among learners. This awareness can be of paramount importance, mostly for the teacher, who can understand how communication flows can be managed and redirected to improve the learning experience.

2.1   Central Connectors (CCs)

In an organization, CCs have more direct relationships with other colleagues and are the central points around which other nodes are organized. Often, they are not the formal leaders within a unit or a department, but they know who can provide critical information or expertise. CCs help the company, linking colleagues and increasing organizational performance: they handle most technical questions by themselves or guide their colleagues to someone else who has the relevant expertise in the informal network.

In VLEs, there are often small groups of active people responsible for most of the communication. They are important members that are connected to the group and who often call for new streams of knowledge. The effective functioning of the network can be assured by a small group of individuals or by a single participant. In both cases, this small group or individual becomes the pivot around which the learning process develops. Very often, this role is just played by the teacher: indeed, he/she takes the role of moderator and facilitator, so leaning toward the stimulation of new ideas generation or speaking in moments in which the development of the community keeps track of slowdowns.

2.2   Boundary Spanners (BSs)

In an organization, BSs have relationships with people outside their own informal network. For instance, they communicate with people in other departments, or even in other organizations. BSs assume a strategic role in exchanges of information and experiences.

In VLEs it is easy to find subgroups of people in which the communication is more intense. BSs within a course are those participants who facilitate communication flows between different subgroups, thus coordinating the communication between several subgroups in the network (Wenger 1998). A key part of this role is to handle information flows and to build social bonds, thereby creating the conditions for trust and interdependency and making all players aware of the knowledge flows that occur in different communication threads. Also in this case, it is possible that the teacher be a BS: indeed, his/her interventions in the forums can create links between different subgroups of students.

2.3   Information Brokers (IBs)

In the informal network of an organization, IBs keep different subgroups together. IBs hold the power of CCs without necessarily possessing the same number of direct links. Indeed, they can exploit indirect connections. If they do not communicate across subgroups the network as a whole will split into smaller, less-effective segments.

In VLEs communication between participants integrates a vertical "teacher–student" communication with a horizontal communication among peers. To enable the latter communication level it is important that the connectivity of the network be preserved. IBs are people in the network of relationships who keep connected several subgroups. Differently from BSs, removing an IB would split the network in two or more parts. Therefore, in a VLE IBs make knowledge accessible to everybody.

2.4   Peripheral Specialists (PSs)

In an organization, PSs act on the border of the network, offering expertise to members of the group as it is needed, but not necessarily connecting frequently with many other colleagues. They possess specific kinds of information or technical knowledge that they provide to other members of the group whenever it is needed.

In a VLE, PSs are experts on a specific topic of the course. Therefore, PSs do not intervene frequently, but only on certain topics. Nonetheless, with their interventions they tend to solve problems, adding new knowledge and sharing learning experiences.

Having provided a brief description of the four key-roles, we are going to develop some metrics for their identification making use of SNA, and highlighting the importance of representation methods of knowledge flows inside the community.

3   Comparing Two Different Representation Methods of Knowledge Flows in VLEs

SNA is a very powerful technique to analyze the relationships between members of social systems because of its wide sphere of application (from sociology to organizational studies) and the different scales of investigation (from interpersonal relationships to international ones).

This kind of analysis represents the social relationships in terms of nodes and ties of a graph and allows a limitless number of maps of relationships depending on the researchers' needs and on the kind of analysis.

We propose two different maps of ties because the comparison between them may help us to confirm or contextualize conclusions and interpretations about participants' key-roles in the VLE, and also to ask further questions about the relationship between the shape of the interaction patterns in the two networks and the knowledge development in the VLEs.

Since in an information network an incoming arrow points out that someone is being sought out for information or advice and an outgoing arrow that someone is seeking information or advice (Cross and Prusak 2002), we propose an initial map with connections built according to the following rules:

- There is an arrow from *a* to *b* if *b* posts a message in answer to *a*.
- If *t* is the teacher and he/she answers to a message which is a reply to other posts there is an arrow to him/her from all his/her predecessors in the forum, until the beginning of the forum has been reached or until another post of the teacher is found.
- In order to avoid loops we exclude the arrows from a node to itself, because we aim at identifying the role played by each node with respect to the others in the network. A loop could represent an action of self-assessment, or self-regulation, or self-reflection, etc. These kinds of actions are very important for individual learning but do not provide any information about the connections with the others and, then, about the role played in the network.

This representation is similar to that proposed by Aviv et al. (2003), except for the orientation of the arrows, which is inverted, and for the particular role of the teacher (who interacts to systematize previous interventions). We propose to invert the orientation of the arrows because we aim to represent only the actual knowledge flows between participants in the forums.

Indeed, as Aviv et al. (2003) suggested, participants in asynchronous discussion forums can be represented as sending response messages among themselves and these exchanges define the *responsiveness relations* between them. It is possible to build the response matrix by labeling its rows and columns with numbers representing the students, the tutors and the teachers. The entry (a,b) – that is row a, column b – of that matrix is the number of messages sent by agent a as responses to previous messages sent by b during the life of the asynchronous learning network (a new thread may be started by posting a message that is not technically a reply to an earlier message in a forum).

Contrary to Aviv et al. (2003), we consider answers as feedbacks to sent messages. Indeed, in order to examine the effective knowledge flows in a learning community, we should consider that:

1. When an individual posts a message in a discussion forum he/she addresses it to all the members of the forum.
2. Anyone can read everything.
3. Anyone can read nothing (an individual can voluntarily ignore messages or entire forums).

Thus if a node a replies to a message of node b (sends a feedback) we can state that node a was certainly reached by the message of node b, and there is a knowledge flow from b to a. If the node b, in turn, does not reply to a's answer we can state nothing about the flow from a to b, because node b might have ignored a's post.

Our first connection map preserves the direction of the relationship, and it is consistent with the information network. In addition, this representation allows us to evaluate the effectiveness of a message and its ability to create knowledge flows. This network represents only the real knowledge flows and, therefore, we name it Actual Knowledge Network (AKN).

Nevertheless, this representation fails to depict one of the principal characteristics of forums, which is that in such virtual arenas each individual contributes to the development of knowledge available to all the participants through an incremental process (Iovanella et al. 2006). Thus, we also propose a second representation, aiming to make visible the interaction dynamics hidden in the threads.

In this second representation:

- There is an arc from b to a if b posts a message in answer to a.
- If b answers to a and c answers to b, in addition to the arc from b to a, there are the arcs from c to b and from c to a.
- We exclude only the arcs from a node to itself, in order to avoid loops.

This connection map assumes that all previous posts affect those that follow because of their primacy in the discussion, influencing the thinking of the others and setting knowledge flows. Indeed, individuals in VLEs are generally asked by the facilitator (teacher or tutor) to open new threads when they wish to introduce novel topics of discussion, and to reply to previous posts when they wish to contribute to already existing debates: these simple rules allow a better rationalization of the posts and an easier reading of the topic threads. Nevertheless, even if the first post arranges the topics of the discussion, each following message brings incremental knowledge. This is the reason why the orientation of the ties is inverted compared to the AKN representation: in a specific thread each answer to a message is not considered as a feedback, but as a contribution to the knowledge development that involves each poster and all previous ones.

Thus our second representation, which we name Incremental Knowledge Network (IKN), shows potential knowledge flows among participants who posted in the VLE (indeed, we can infer nothing about knowledge flows among participants who did not post, because we cannot obtain for each post the number of readings and the identity of the readers).

In Table 11.1 we show an example of data related to a discussion forum. Starting from these data, Fig. 11.1 shows the differences between AKN and IKN. AKN is made up only by four arcs, while in IKN there are seven arcs. Besides, the node characterized by the highest *outdegree*[1] in AKN (i.e. a) is that with the highest *indegree*[2] in IKN; this is due to the fact that this node represents the actor who started the discussion, providing information to other actors and obtaining several feedbacks from them.

---

[1] The outegree of a node a is the number of arcs originating with node a (Wasserman and Faust 1999).

[2] The indegree of a node a is the number of arcs terminating at node a (Wasserman and Faust 1999).

Table 11.1 Example data of
a discussion forum

Author	Message	Date
a	Help	02/03/07 15:45
b	Re: help	02/03/07 15:46
t (teacher)	Re: help	02/03/07 15:47
c	Re: help	02/03/07 15:48
c	Re: help	02/03/07 15:55
t (teacher)	Re: help	02/03/07 15:57

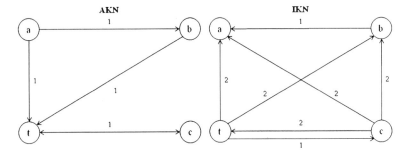

Fig. 11.1   AKN and IKN representations of the forum in Table 11.1

4   A Metric for Key-Roles Identification in VLEs

In this paper we want to develop metrics for the four Cross and Prusak's key-roles, which we think could be strategic for knowledge development and sharing in a VLE. To this aim we use hub and authority indexes, and we also investigate the presence of cut vertices for brokerage positions. These indices were selected according to the specific representation method of knowledge flows.

Moreover, since identification metrics are based on SNA, different methods to build the network of interactions can provide different results for the key-roles: in other words, it is possible that using a representation a learner is detected as playing a specific role (say, as an example, CC), while using a different representation the same learner plays a different role or does not play any role at all. Therefore, we are also interested in analyzing how different representation methods of knowledge flows in a VLE can provide the teacher with different results; we also want to determine whether and to what extent these results are consistent and can be used to improve learning and instruction. To this aim we propose two different methodologies to build the network of interactions and we apply them to the same e-learning course, in order to compare the results coming from the analysis of key-roles.

Since each lesson focuses on a single topic of the course, in order to determine the key-roles and, in particular, those people able to spread knowledge across different topics of the course, we choose as unit of analysis the set of discussion forums related to a single lesson (for the sake of brevity we simply name it "lesson"). In this way we can detect knowledge exchanges both within a topic and across different topics. Key-roles can play an important part for each topic of the course. Moreover, students could change their roles passing from the forums of one lesson to those of another one.

In AKN representation, nodes have an outgoing arc if they get an answer to some posts of a lesson. Therefore, having many incoming arcs means both being more central in the network and giving a lot of information. If we were interested only in the number of answers posted by an individual in the network a degree measure would be sufficient to identify a CC. Nonetheless, in our perspective a CC is not only a source of information, but also an authoritative source of information: therefore, a simple degree measure is not sufficient for our purposes. If a person is an authoritative source of information on a topic and provides many reliable answers[3], that person will spread good quality information throughout the network and will increase his/her *indegree* value. Moreover, if a node receives much information from an authoritative source it will have a higher number of outgoing arcs towards that source, so increasing its own hub value and the authority value of the source. From these considerations we can say that an authoritative source of information will have a high authority value.

Therefore, we propose to consider the authority of the node as a proxy for the central connector. Indeed, according to Cross and Prusak (2002), CCs serve the network in a positive way, linking others, and increasing, in our case, the knowledge. Therefore, by answering (incoming arc), a learner adds elements of knowledge to the network. CCs will be people in the network with high authority values for most lessons of the course. From now on, by saying "high index value" we mean that the value of the index must be in the higher 25% of the distribution of its values; by saying "low index value" we mean that the value of the index must be in the lower 25% of the distribution of its values; finally, by saying "most lessons" we mean at least 2/3 of the lessons. The limit of 25% can be reviewed. Indeed, the analyst should define the particular threshold value as a trade-off between two different needs: on the one hand, the threshold should not be too high, because in that case it could become impossible to find out any key-roles to address to in order to improve the learning process. On the other hand, the threshold should not be too low, otherwise many people would assume a key-role in the VLE, so making the analysis worthless.

From the same considerations made for CCs it follows that a node which receives much information from authoritative sources in the network will have a high hub value. Moreover, if it spreads this information in subgroups in the network – so acting as a BS – it will also have a high authority value. Therefore, we propose to check boundary spanners by measuring both hub and authority. In particular, in our work we say a person is a BS between lessons i and j, and we name it $BS_{i,j}$, if that person has a high hub value in lesson i and a high authority value in lesson j.

Peripheral specialists offer their expertise to others rather than receive it; moreover their experience is very specific to a field. For this reason we seek PSs through

---

[3] Since we are analyzing an educational environment, we suppose that students have no incentive in consciously providing wrong information. Moreover, even if a student should provide a wrong information, the teacher can cut in on the discussion forum to rectify it.

the comparison between their centrality in one lesson and in the whole course. To us, a person is a PS if that person has a high authority value in one lesson and a low authority value in all the others.

In IKN representation, nodes have outgoing arcs if they answer to some posts: for us who answers may be an expert in the field, so giving authoritative answers. Moreover, providing many answers increases the node *outdegree*, which is linked to the hub position of the node, making it more central in the network.

Besides, people who get many answers are more likely to have much information. Moreover, if answers come from those who have experiences in the field we can suppose that the quality of the information they provide is high. Since receiving an answer corresponds to have an incoming arc this will increase the authority value of the receiving node and the hub value of the sender. Starting from these considerations, we propose to seek central connectors on the basis of hub values. Indeed, by answering (outgoing arc) a learner adds elements of knowledge to the network. Therefore, CCs will be people in the network with high hub values for most lessons of the course.

For the same reasons, we seek boundary spanners through the combination of authority and hub indexes. Indeed, a BS is a person who serves as a "roving ambassador" (Cross and Prusak 2002) of informal networks (he receives information from its network and spreads them to others), and "through his relationship with CCs in other informal networks, he serves as an efficient conduit of information" (Cross and Prusak 2002). Therefore, in our work we say a person is a BS between lessons i and j, and we name it BS$_{i,j}$, if that person has a high authority value in lesson i and a high hub value in lesson j.

A PS is a person who is an expert on a specific topic (that of one lesson), while he/ she is at the margin of the network for all the other topics. Therefore, we propose that a PS should have a high hub value in one lesson and a low hub value in the others.

Finally, in both representations the information broker is checked by the presence of cut vertices: indeed, a cut vertex is a node whose deletion increases the number of components in the network.

For the identification of this last role we have taken as unit of analysis the whole set of forums in the course: indeed, IBs have the power of totally impeding knowledge sharing between individuals, by disconnecting the network. If IBs would have been checked on the single lesson, they would have disconnected people in that lesson. Anyway, we are interested in that the knowledge of a specific lesson can flow in the whole course and in that it can reach each individual, directly in that lesson or passing through linkages with other lessons.

5   Case Study

We have examined the asynchronous discussion forums of the "Leadership" course in the Master in Business Engineering program at the Business School of the Faculty of Engineering at Tor Vergata University of Rome. This course has been provided completely online: the teacher used an open source e-learning platform (Moodle) to share learning objects and to communicate with the learners. The teacher of this course considers discussion forums as a very powerful tool that enriches the contents of each lesson through debating and sharing knowledge and experiences. Participation in the forums has been completely free and voluntary. Many lesson topics were deepened in forums: for each lesson the teacher opened at least two threads and encouraged learners to participate in them and to add other threads based on their own interests, experiences, and curiosities on the topics of the course. This style of forum management allowed him to create an active learning process involving both learners and the teacher.

Due to the fact that participation in the forums was not mandatory it becomes interesting to find out if there is some key-role in the course. Therefore, we have applied our framework and analysis to forums of three different classes (from 2006–2007 to 2008–2009).

5.1 Data

Starting from the discussion forums, we have built a learning network for the topics of each lesson, considering each post as a contribution to the discussion and, therefore, to the creation and sharing of new knowledge. We have also built a learning network for the course as a whole. Since the courses for 2006–2007 and 2007–2008 were made up of three lessons, and that for 2008–2009 of six lessons, under each of the two representations (AKN and IKN) we have four networks for the first two courses and seven networks for the last one. Indeed for both representations we have:

- For 2006–2007: one network for the forums of each of the three lessons and one network for the forums of the whole course (four networks).
- For 2007–2008: one network for the forums of each of the three lessons and one network for the forums of the whole course (four networks).
- For 2008–2009: one network for the forums of each of the six lessons and one network for the forums of the whole course (seven networks).

For each representation, once the networks of each lesson and of the entire course had been built, we have first of all removed isolated nodes (respectively nine, six, and two for the three classes), obtaining a total amount of 77 learners and one teacher. Then we have determined hub and authority values for each node and for each network. On the basis of these values we are able to identify CCs, BSs and PSs for the course. It is worth noting that the teacher has not been removed from the network in order not to alter the distribution of links among the students. Anyway, the teacher has not been included in the search for the key-roles, because otherwise he/she could have played some roles. Indeed, the teacher has many incoming/outgoing arrows (depending on the particular representation method of knowledge flow), as he/she intervenes in the forums to stimulate the conversation, to correct faults, and so on. To exclude the teacher from the analysis the distribution of hub and authority indexes has been determined without his values.

Tables 11.2–11.4 show the distributions of hub and authority values for the three classes under both representations.

Table 11.2 Hub and authority value distributions for 2006–2007 under both representations

2006–2007		Course		Lesson 1		Lesson 2		Lesson 3	
43 nodes	Representation	Hub	Authority	Hub	Authority	Hub	Authority	Hub	Authority
Max	IKN	0.2751	0.2843	0.3320	0.2663	0.3156	0.3332	0.2595	0.2619
	AKN	0.3043	0.2183	0.3698	0.1477	0.1967	0.2429	0.3369	0.2331
Min	IKN	0.0085	0.0123	0.0000	0.0000	0.0000	0.0000	0.0411	0.0023
	AKN	0.0000	0.0129	0.0000	0.0000	0.0000	0.0000	0.0000	0.0139
Average	IKN	0.1248	0.1295	0.0991	0.1252	0.1131	0.1183	0.1362	0.1330
	AKN	0.0980	0.0964	0.1100	0.0463	0.0485	0.1212	0.1078	0.0970
Std. Dev.	IKN	0.0545	0.0768	0.0788	0.0856	0.0592	0.0936	0.0574	0.0723
	AKN	0.0706	0.0524	0.0988	0.0378	0.0531	0.0769	0.0670	0.0496

Table 11.3 Hub and authority value distributions for 2007–2008 under both representations

2007–2008		Course		Lesson 1		Lesson 2		Lesson 3	
15 nodes	Representation	Hub	Authority	Hub	Authority	Hub	Authority	Hub	Authority
Max	IKN	0.3484	0.4217	0.4856	0.4184	0.3169	0.3754	0.6124	0.3694
	AKN	0.4575	0.1491	0.4899	0.2353	0.4937	0.0654	0.4165	0.3081
Min	IKN	0.0654	0.0797	0.0000	0.0000	0.0000	0.0000	0.0113	0.0000
	AKN	0.1422	0.0448	0.0000	0.0000	0.0000	0.0000	0.0000	0.0532
Average	IKN	0.1932	0.2373	0.1740	0.2104	0.1764	0.2396	0.1692	0.2364
	AKN	0.2408	0.0905	0.2043	0.0893	0.2504	0.0141	0.2276	0.1169
Std. Dev.	IKN	0.0701	0.1025	0.1318	0.1483	0.1062	0.1038	0.1477	0.1172
	AKN	0.1010	0.0317	0.1724	0.0735	0.0971	0.0278	0.1165	0.0670

Table 11.4 Hub and authority value distributions for 2008–2009 under both representations

2008–2009		Course		Lesson 1		Lesson 2		Lesson 3		Lesson 4		Lesson 5		Lesson 6	
22 nodes	Representation	Hub	Authority	Hub	Authority	Hub	Authority	Hub	Authority	Hub	Authority	Hub	Authority	Hub	Authority
Max	IKN	0.3254	0.3994	0.2940	0.4160	0.4573	0.4448	0.4514	0.4785	0.4577	0.4580	0.3021	0.4520	0.6059	0.5201
	AKN	0.3471	0.2866	0.4515	0.2885	0.0000	0.3780	0.0434	0.6112	0.4322	0.1426	0.6435	0.0309	0.0000	0.5774
Min	IKN	0.0254	0.0128	0.0000	0.0000	0.0000	0.0000	0.0000	0.0000	0.0000	0.0000	0.0000	0.0000	0.0000	0.0000
	AKN	0.0000	0.0021	0.0000	0.0000	0.0000	0.0000	0.0000	0.0000	0.0000	0.0000	0.0000	0.0000	0.0000	0.0000
Average	IKN	0.1552	0.1654	0.1308	0.1556	0.1318	0.1101	0.1280	0.1324	0.1486	0.1294	0.1325	0.1668	0.1151	0.0867
	AKN	0.1432	0.1159	0.1346	0.1083	0.0000	0.1260	0.0021	0.1169	0.1424	0.0398	0.1558	0.0151	0.0000	0.0825
Std. Dev.	IKN	0.1045	0.1133	0.1043	0.1457	0.1782	0.1638	0.1471	0.1582	0.1389	0.1569	0.1053	0.1320	0.1900	0.1664
	AKN	0.1052	0.0881	0.1273	0.0842	0.0000	0.1826	0.0095	0.1888	0.1675	0.0455	0.1566	0.0136	0.0000	0.2070

Table 11.5 Key-roles under IKN representation

| | Academic year | | | | | | | | | | | |
| | 2006–2007 | | | | 2007–2008 | | | | 2008–2009 | | | |
IKN repr. ID	CCs	BSs	PSs	IBs	CCs	BSs	PSs	IBs	CCs	BSs	PSs	IBs
2										$BS_{1,2}$ $BS_{3,1}$ $BS_{3,2}$ $BS_{4,1}$ $BS_{4,2}$		
4											PS	
8										$BS_{4,1}$ $BS_{4,3}$ $BS_{5,1}$ $BS_{5,3}$		
10										$BS_{6,2}$		
11						$BS_{1,3}$						
12										$BS_{2,1}$		
15					CC	$BS_{3,1}$ $BS_{3,2}$						
16									CC	$BS_{1,4}$ $BS_{1,5}$ $BS_{1,6}$ $BS_{2,1}$ $BS_{2,4}$ $BS_{2,5}$ $BS_{2,6}$		
17											PS	
19										$BS_{3,2}$ $BS_{3,4}$		
24										$BS_{2,1}$		
26		$BS_{2,3}$										
32	CC											
34		$BS_{2,1}$ $BS_{3,1}$										
40	CC											
Total	2	2	0	0	1	2	0	0	1	7	2	0

5.2 Results

The application of the metrics described in Sect. 4 to the data described in Sect. 5 clearly points out that there is a relation between the identified key-roles and the specific representation method of knowledge flows adopted for the analysis.

IKN representation provides the key-roles synthesized in Table 11.5.

As we can see, we have 2 CCs for 2006–2007 (identified by ID 32 and 40), 1 CC for 2007–2008 (ID 15) and 1 CC for 2008–2009 (ID 16). Moreover, we find 2 BSs for 2006–2007 (ID 26 and 34) and 2007–2008 (ID 11 and 15) and 7 BSs for 2008–2009 (ID 2, 8, 10, 12, 16, 19, and 24).

It must be noted that the number of BSs for each academic year is small with respect to the total number of students in the course, in line with Cross, Prusak and Parker's requirements (2002): indeed, according to these authors the number of BSs in a network should be limited.

Also, we find no PS in 2006–2007 and 2007–2008 and 2 PSs in 2008–2009 (ID 4 and 17).

None of the 3 academic years show cut-vertices in IKN representation: therefore, we have no IBs.

Finally, there are respectively four, two and nine students who play a key-role for the 3 academic years: as an example, node 15 is both CC and BS ($BS_{3,1}$ and $BS_{3,2}$) for the 2007–2008.

The search for key-roles has then been carried out over AKN representation. We show the results in Table 11.6.

Summing up, for the sake of reading, the results shown in the Table, we can note that for 2006–2007 we have 3 CCs (ID 17, 26 and 34), 4 BSs (ID 17, 26, 34 and 52), 1 PS (ID 24), and 3 IBs (ID 9, 31 and 40); in 2007–2008 there is only 1 CC (ID 10) and 1 IB (ID 8), while there are 2 BSs (ID 10 and 11) and 4 PSs (ID 5, 6, 11 and 17); finally, for 2008–2009 we have no CCs, but 8 BSs (ID 2, 8, 10, 16, 18, 19, 20 and 24), 3 PSs (ID 4, 17 and 23) and 3 IBs (ID 8, 20 and 24).

Finally, there are respectively 8, 6 and 11 students who play a key-role for the 3 academic years.

Comparing the results from the two representations, we can note that in most cases there are less students playing a specific key-role in IKN representation than in AKN: this can be explained with the fact that AKN representation produces less dense networks, due to its building rules.

By comparing Tables 11.5 and 11.6, we can note that the nodes which play a key-role can differ in the two representations, having adopted different rules to map knowledge flows. In particular, it is worth recalling that AKN represents only certain knowledge flows, while IKN maps also some potential knowledge flows: indeed, an answering node throws an arc not only toward the enquiring node, but also toward all the predecessors in the discussion. This means that the answering node adds a piece of knowledge which is at the disposal of everyone in the forum, but it can still remain unpicked. Therefore, the arc is thrown independently on the fact that it is actually received or not by other people.

On the basis of these considerations, the key-roles should be read in different ways. In AKN representation a CC is such only with respect of actual knowledge flows, while in IKN representation it is such also with respect of potential knowledge flows. Analogous considerations can be made for all the other roles.

Table 11.6 Key-roles under AKN representation

| AKN repr | Academic year | | | | | | | | | | | |
| | 2006–2007 | | | | 2007–2008 | | | | 2008–2009 | | | |
ID	CCs	BSs	PSs	IBs	CCs	BSs	PSs	IBs	CCs	BSs	PSs	IBs
2										$BS_{1,2}$ $BS_{4,1}$ $BS_{4,2}$		
4											PS	
5							PS					
6							PS					
8								IB		$BS_{3,4}$ $BS_{3,5}$ $BS_{4,5}$ $BS_{5,4}$		IB
9				IB								
10					CC	$BS_{3,2}$				$BS_{6,2}$ $BS_{6,5}$		
11						$BS_{3,1}$	PS					
16										$BS_{5,1}$ $BS_{5,2}$		
17	CC	$BS_{1,2}$					PS				PS	
18										$BS_{2,6}$		
19										$BS_{6,2}$ $BS_{6,3}$		
20										$BS_{6,5}$		IB
23											PS	
24			PS							$BS_{2,4}$ $BS_{2,5}$ $BS_{4,2}$ $BS_{4,5}$ $BS_{6,2}$ $BS_{6,4}$ $BS_{6,5}$		IB
26	CC	$BS_{2,3}$										
31				IB								
34	CC	$BS_{1,2}$ $BS_{2,1}$ $BS_{3,1}$ $BS_{3,2}$										
40				IB								
52		$BS_{1,2}$										
Total	3	4	1	3	1	2	4	1	0	8	3	3

Anyway, it is worth noting that some nodes in each academic year play the same key-role in both representations. Specifically, there are some shared BSs for 2006–2007 (ID 26 and 34), for 2007–2008 (ID 11) and for 2008–2009 (ID 2, 8, 10, 16, 19, and 24). Moreover, for the latter academic year we find also two shared PSs (ID 4 and 17).

5.3   Educational Hints for the Teaching Strategy

Having identified the four key-roles in each representation provides the teacher with some educational hints.

Indeed, in both representations CCs are people who give lots of information to others in the network: so, they are probably spreading their knowledge. Therefore, their presence is an enrichment for the network and the teacher should address these people to facilitate the diffusion of new knowledge across the network. Moreover, the teacher should try to keep CCs' active answering in the discussion forums. Indeed, if a CC stops playing his role the educational potential of the network will decrease.

Moreover, in both representations BSs represent persons who receive information from very active people in one subgroup and diffuse it toward other subgroups: therefore, identifying BSs in the learning network can show the teacher which is the sharing path of information and knowledge. The teacher should pay his attention not to lose the interactivity of BSs: therefore, if a BS should decrease its participation in the discussion forums, the teacher should stimulate and involve him again.

In both representations PSs are people who have a specific kind of knowledge and share it with others. Nonetheless, for learning purposes it is important that these people be more involved in the discussion forums, so as to acquire new information and new pieces of knowledge. Therefore, the teacher should particularly address PSs, both to improve the sharing of their specific knowledge and to better integrate them in the network to increase their set of knowledge.

Finally, in both representations IBs are the only way for two or more subgroups of the learning network to communicate. If they should stop participating in the discussion forums, the subgroups could not share their information anymore. From this point of view, therefore, IBs play a highly strategic role and are a critical resource, because they can impede the transfer of information in the network. The teacher should try to limit as much as possible the number of IBs in the network, by stimulating people to create new direct connections.

6   Conclusions and Future Developments

In this paper we have proposed two different representation methods of interactions among students in a VLE, which account for actual and potential knowledge flows. Starting from these representations and making use of SNA we have proposed some metrics to identify Cross and Prusak's key-roles in a VLE. Then, we have applied these metrics to test for the presence of the four key-roles in a managerial e-learning course over 3 academic years. Being aware that there are students in the course that can play a specific role can provide the teacher with useful hints to improve knowledge acquisition and sharing among participants in the course.

In order to strengthen our metrics, we intend to integrate them with other tools based on content analysis, so as to classify the messages in accordance with their content. By doing so, we will better evaluate the actual contribution of each message to the knowledge development in the community. Our final purpose may be the creation of an integrated and reliable tool that supports the teacher in the management of students' interactions in the VLE.

Using such a tool it will be interesting to analyze if there is some influence between the specific role held by a student and his learning performance in the course. Indeed, according to the SN perspective, some individuals may outperform their peers because they occupy structurally advantageous positions than others in the network (Brass 1984; Burt 1992; Ibarra 1993; Cho et al. 2007).

References

Aviv, R. Erlich, Z., Ravid, G., & Geva, A. (2003). Network analysis of knowledge construction in asynchronous learning networks. *Journal of Asynchronous Learning Networks, 7*(3), 1–23.

Brass, D. J. (1984). Being in the right place: a structural analysis of individual influence in an organization. *Administrative Science Quarterly, 29*(4), 518–539.

Burt, R. S. (1992). *Structural holes: the social structure of competition.* Cambridge, MA: Harvard University Press.

Cho, H., Gay, G., Davidson, B., & Ingraffea A. (2007). Social networks, communication styles, and learning performance in a CSCL community. *Computers & Education, 49*(2), 309–329.

Cross, R., Borgatti, S. P., & Parker, A. (2002). Making invisible work visible: Using social network analysis to support strategic collaboration. *California Management Review, 44*(2), 25–46.

Cross, R., Parker, A., & Prusak, L. (2001). Knowing what we know: Supporting knowledge creation and sharing in social networks. *Organizational Dynamics, 3*(2), 100–120.

Cross, R., & Prusak, L. (2002). The people who make organizations go – or stop. *Harvard Business Review, 80*(6), 104–112.

Cross, R., Prusak, L, & Parker, A. (2002). Where work happens: the care and feeding of informal networks in organizations. *Iko: IBM Institute for Knowledge Based Organizations.*

Duffy, T. M., & Cunningham, D. J. (1996). Constructivism: Implications for the design and delivery of instruction. In Jonassen, D. H. (Ed.), *Handbook of research for educational communications and technology* (pp. 170–198). New York: Simon & Schuster Macmillan.

Everett, M. G., & Borgatti, S. P. (1999). The centrality of groups and classes. *Journal of Mathematical Sociology, 23*(3), 181–201.

Hewitt, J., & Scardamalia, M., (1998). Design principles for distributed knowledge building processes. *Educational Psychology Review, 10*(1), 75–96.

Ibarra, H. (1993). Personal networks of women and minorities in management: a conceptual framework. *Academy of Management Review, 18*(1), 56–87.

Iovanella, A., Armenia, S., Italiano, G. F., & Murgia G. (2006). Using social network analysis for the study of asynchronous interaction in e-learning. *Proceedings of the 1st International Conference on e-Learning, Montreal, Canada, 22–23 June 2006* (pp. 207–216). Reading: Academic Conferences Limited.

Jensen, M. B. (2007). The new metrics of scholarly authority. *Chronicle of Higher Education,* *53*(41), B6.

Nie, K., Lin, S., Ma, T., & Nakamori, Y. (2010). Connecting informal networks to management of tacit knowledge. *Journal of Systems Science and Systems Engineering, 19*(2), 237–253.

Ounnas, A. (2008). Semantic Web-based Group Formation for E-learning. *PhD Symposium in the 5th European Semantic Web Conference 2008, Tenerife, Spain, 1–5 June 2008* (pp. 51–55).

Vygotskij, L. S., (1978). *Mind in society: The development of higher psychological processes.* Cambridge, USA: Harvard University Press.

Wasserman, S., & Faust, K. (1999). *Social Network Analysis.* Cambridge, UK: Cambridge University Press.

Wenger, E., McDermott R., & Snyder, W. M., (2002). *Cultivating communities of practice: A guide to managing knowledge.* Boston, USA: Harvard Business School Press.

Wenger, E. (1998). *Communities of practice: Learning, meaning, and identity.* Cambridge, UK: Cambridge University Press.

Chapter 12
First on the List: Search Engine Optimization Contests as Authentic Learning

Mark Frydenberg and John S. Miko

1 Introduction

The process of promoting a Website so that it becomes easily discoverable by search engines is known as Search Engine Optimization (SEO). Because a higher placement within search results is more likely to drive traffic to a Website, companies, bloggers, and individuals go to great lengths to have their names or products found within the first page of a search engine's results. Two popular techniques for improving a site's ranking among search engines include modifying its HTML code to contain relevant keywords, and promoting the site on other Websites via external links known as backlinks. As the amount of content on the Web grows, it becomes increasingly important to include appropriate metadata that will enable search engines to find it.

This paper describes a competitive learning exercise in which students create a Website to promote a fictitious product online, and vie for top positions within search results on three popular search engines. Their goal is to implement a variety of SEO techniques in order to determine those which are the most effective. Students at two universities in the United States participated in this exercise during the spring 2010 semester.

One group of students was enrolled in CS 299, an experimental, multi-disciplinary elective course entitled Web 2.0: Technology, Strategy, Community, offered at Bentley University, a business university in Massachusetts. CS 299 introduces students to Web 2.0 technologies, concepts, and applications, and their impact on business and society. The second group of students was enrolled in MIS 342, an

M. Frydenberg (✉)
Bentley University, Waltham, MA, USA
e-mail: mfrydenberg@bentley.edu

J.S. Miko
Saint Francis University, Loretto, PA, USA
e-mail: jmiko@francis.edu

P. Isaias et al. (eds.), *Towards Learning and Instruction in Web 3.0: Advances in Cognitive and Educational Psychology*, DOI 10.1007/978-1-4614-1539-8_12,
© Springer Science+Business Media, LLC 2012

e-commerce and e-marketing elective course offered at Saint Francis University, a small, private liberal-arts university in Pennsylvania. MIS 342 introduces students to the technological infrastructures, corporate strategies, and use of computer networks for Internet retailing. Because SEO is increasingly becoming a necessary skill in the workplace, understanding search engine optimization methods and techniques will benefit students' future careers in advertising, Web development, multimedia, marketing, and business. (Spradling et al. 2008; Middleton 2009) Connolly describes the value for students to have skills in SEO techniques:

> Search engines in general (and Google in particular) act now as the main portal into most public Websites. As such, it is increasingly important that students learn how search engines work, how to design Websites for optimal search engine results, and how sponsored links systems such as Google's AdSense work (Connolly 2009, p. 76).

SEO has found its place in college courses in computing and IT (Sabin et al. 2005; McCown 2010), e-commerce, marketing, and business (Charlesworth 2009; Xing and Zhangxi 2006), new media (Spradling et al 2008), and library science (Atwater-Singer 2006). Across the disciplines, "critical examinations of ... search results are imperative for understanding how information is organized and retrieved. By introducing ideas of relevance, proximity and ranking, students can transfer learned skills to other information resources" (Atwater-Singer 2006, p. 3).

While the literature points to several courses that include SEO in their content, little has been written about teaching methods and ways to engage students in actively learning about SEO techniques. Sabin et al. (2005) describe an exercise in which students must refine search queries to find an effective combination of search terms that will result in a particular site rising to the top of the Google search results. Given the importance of SEO as a valuable future career skill, and the need to learn about and analyze the effectiveness of techniques that one might try in order to improve a site's ranking, these research questions emerged:

- How is participating in an SEO Contest an authentic learning experience?
- Does a competitive assignment provide an added incentive for learning about SEO?
- How does participating in an SEO contest impact student learning about SEO?

2 Search Engines and Search Engine Optimization

As the World Wide Web has matured, the role of search engines has become more prominent. "Search engines have gained an increasingly powerful position by channeling the attention of millions of users" (Evans 2007, p. 21). At its simplest, a search engine is "comprised of three main components: a database of web pages (called an index), a method for finding web pages and indexing them, and a way to search the database" (Malaga 2010, p. 69). Search engines display results based on a page's relevance to the desired search terms. In addition to content on the page itself, Google's PageRank algorithm considers hyperlinks from one page to another serve as "a sort of endorsement of the 'authority' of the page being linked to" (Hendler et al. 2008, p. 64). SEO requires an understanding of how search engines work in order to find information. Search engines rely on applications called *spiders* or *bots* that *crawl* the Web looking for new pages to index. Spiders often examine the structure of a Web page in order determine relevance of its content. For example, some spiders give certain elements of a Web page, such as its title and its major heading, special emphasis (Morochove 2008, p. 47). Manually submitting a Web page's URL to a search engine may cause its content to be indexed as well.

3   SEO Contests as an Authentic Learning

An SEO contest is a competitive online event in which participants must create and promote a Website over a period of time such that their site achieves the highest position or ranking in search results for a specified search query at a designated future date and time. The winners generally receive a cash prize. (Evans 2007) Marketing organizations often hold SEO contests in order to gain data on the effectiveness of various SEO techniques. In order to provide a level playing field, contest organizers usually provide guidelines regarding what techniques are or are not permissible for participants to implement, and describe the exact criteria for winning. This section describes the implementation of an SEO contest as a project given to students in two sections of CS 299 and one section of MIS 342 to engage them in learning about SEO techniques.

Herrington et al. (2003) describes authentic learning environments as modeling real life problems. Their activities have real world relevance; are not well-defined; require investigation of a task over a period of time, and from different perspectives. They encourage collaboration and reflection, and can be integrated across different subject areas. Authentic activities are integrated such that they reflect real world assessment, and allow competing solutions with a diversity of outcomes. They "engage learners in the work of professionals" (Elliott 2007, p. 34). Authentic learning extends to online activity "through careful design of Web-based learning environments" (Herrington et al. 2004). The instructors fashioned an SEO contest as a Web-based authentic learning environment for their students to learn about SEO. The adaptation of such an industry-standard contest as a classroom exercise provides a new way to engage students in authentic learning through its hands-on, competitive nature.

Students in the two sections of CS 299 promoted fictitious iPhone applications for Norwegian Tourism or Burmese recipes, while students in MIS 342 promoted an iPhone application for Tuvaluan recipes. These topics were chosen because they contained words and phrases that were commonly searched on Google individually, and in some combination, but a check on Google prior to the start of the project showed no search results for pages containing all of the relevant keywords.

Students were permitted to choose any Web technology or application with which they were familiar in order to create their Websites. Each site had to have at least two pages: the home or landing page, which contained sample content about the fictitious product, and a second page, which contained a description and log of the steps that students completed in order to optimize the site. Each Website also had to display a disclaimer informing the reader that this site was created for an academic exercise, and that the product represented was not a real product. Because this was a learning exercise, students were permitted to use any SEO techniques with which they are familiar or wanted to try throughout the contest.

While real-world SEO contests may last for several months, in this exercise, students had 4 weeks to take steps to bring their sites to the top of the search results. Students were asked to record the date and the position/ranking of their site within search results on Google, Bing, and Yahoo! every day for the duration of the project in order to try to determine those actions which produced higher positions in search results. . This gave students "a more authentic learning experience based on experimentation and action" (Lombardi 2007, p. 2). There were some small differences in implementation of the contest between the CS 299 and MIS 342 classes. Due to class sizes, CS 299 students worked in groups of three or four; while MIS 342 students completed the project individually. CS 299 students whose pages appeared on first page of search results for the key phrase received 5% extra credit on the final exam. The two MIS 342 students whose pages made the top of the search results received gift cards to a regional convenience store.

All MIS 342 students had previously purchased their own domain names and hosted their Websites on the college server, while CS 299 students were not required to purchase a domain name. Most MIS 342 students coded the HTML for their sites manually, while most CS 299 students used free Web applications such as WordPress, Yola, Blogger, or Google Sites to create their Websites.

The instructors provided a similar lecture and reading materials to their respective students regarding Search Engine Optimization prior to the start of this exercise, including the techniques mentioned in Table 12.1 above. Students in both courses were surveyed anonymously at the end of the exercise regarding their learning

Table 12.1 Popular SEO techniques

Techniques for ensuring a site is indexed by a search engine
- Manually submit a site to search engines
- Create an XML Site Map

SEO techniques for modifying the site itself
- Place key words in the title tag
- Place key words in meta-tags
- Include key words in HTML file names
- Place key words in headings and content
- Provide frequently updated content

Techniques for drawing traffic to a site
- Encourage backlinks (links from other sites to yours)
- Promote a site using social media tools such as Facebook or Twitter
- Select a relevant domain name

Fig. 12.1 Google search results for "norwegian tourism iphone application"

experience during and as a result of the SEO contest, their understanding of SEO techniques and concepts prior to starting and after completing it, and the techniques that they found to be most effective.

Figure 12.1 shows Google's search results for the phrase "Norwegian tourism iPhone application." Note that the highest ranking result is from a purchased domain name, norwegianiphoneapp.net, and another from norwegiantourism.net trails it slightly. One group created a page for its site on Facebook, and another student used digg.com to vote or endorse his group's site. Both of these activities, which mentioned and contained backlinks to their respective sites, appeared closer to the top

Fig. 12.2 The Norwegian tourism iPhone application home page. This site holds the top position in Google's search results

of the Google search results. Tweets from students who promoted their site on Twitter also appeared in the first page of Google's search results. Two other Websites, created and hosted with Yola and WordPress, also appear lower in the first page of the Google search rankings.

Figure 12.2 shows the home page for the top-ranking site on Google, norwegianiphoneapp.com. It is a blog created with WordPress, which students updated regularly during the contest. The blog's sidebar also contains a Twitter Feed for the application.

Figure 12.3 shows some of the steps taken by the winning team. They purchased domain names and immediately installed Google Analytics, a software tool for pro-

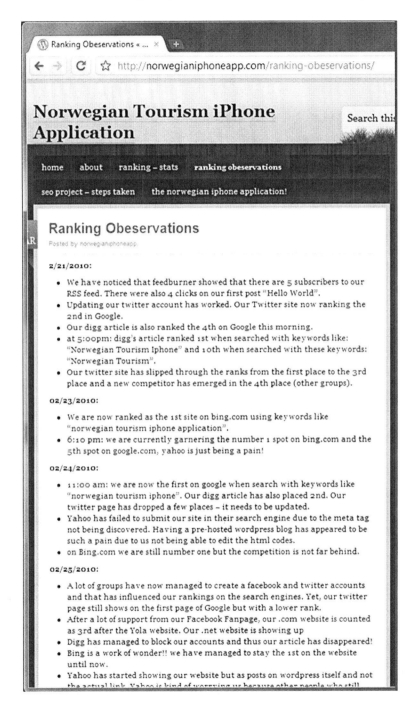

Fig. 12.3 Students discover which techniques result in higher search placement

viding statistics on site usage, at the start of the project, to track the visitors to their site and determine which other sites had linked to theirs. They discovered that updating their Twitter stream caused it to appear higher in the search rankings.

4   Assessment of SEO Contest as Authentic Learning

Sixteen MIS 342 students and 38 CS 299 students participated in this exercise during the spring 2010 semester. Prior to the start of the project 40 of the 54 students (74.1%), indicated that they either "strongly disagreed" or "disagreed" with the statement that they were familiar with SEO techniques prior to the project. This suggested that while they may have been familiar with the importance or objectives of SEO, most students have not taken the steps to actually optimize a site. Also shown in Fig. 12.4, 49 of the 54 students (90.7%) reported having a better understanding of SEO techniques after the completion of the project.

In addition to completing self-evaluations after the contest ended, students were required to provide a report analyzing the techniques and SEO strategy their team implemented and their impact on the SEO rankings they observed. The instructors

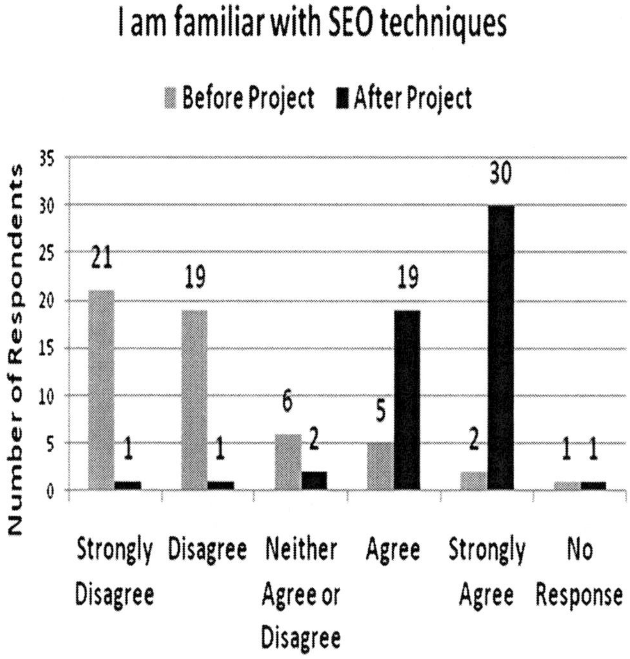

Fig. 12.4 Familiarity with SEO before and after the contest

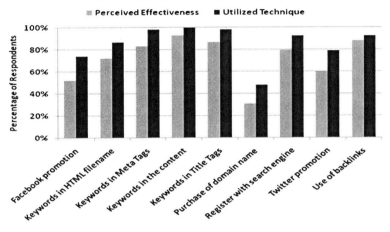

Fig. 12.5 SEO Techniques used and their perceived effectiveness

evaluated these reports as a measure of student learning about SEO concepts and students' ability to convey that knowledge. Figure 12.3 shows an example strategy that one team implemented, and the learning that accompanied it.

Authentic learning requires students to reflect on their experiences and draw conclusions from their findings (Herrington et al. 2003). Students who completed this project commented that they had an increased understanding and familiarity with SEO techniques. The exercise provided just-in-time authentic learning about SEO through experimentation and hands-on experience. One student remarked:

> We learned many different techniques that the marketing team needs to employ in order for their company to have a web presence. No matter how good the product may be, if you cannot find it on the first couple pages of Google or any other search engine, then it probably will not be found and adopted by consumers.

The problem itself encouraged students to select the SEO techniques that they wished to investigate. Figure 12.5 shows the most popular techniques that students used to promote their sites. The students perceived the following techniques to be most effective: placing keywords in the content of their web pages (93%), the creation of backlinks to their Web page (88%), the placement of keywords in the title tag of their web page (87%), the placement of keywords in the meta tags of their web pages (83%), and registering their web page with the various search engines (80%). These results align closely with an experimental research study conducted by Evans (2007) that concluded that high quality content (p. 27) and the number of backlinks into a web page (p. 30) are two of the primary factors in determining a web page's placement among search results. Further, all of these techniques are among those highly recommended by leading search engine practitioners (Jones 2008).

"Students involved in authentic learning are motivated to persevere despite initial disorientation or frustration" (Lombardi 2007, pg. 4). Students realized that it takes dedication to achieve results, as shown by this student's remark:

> I learned that it's not easy to optimize your website. It takes a lot of time along with patience for it to work. You need to constantly be up-to-date with it, so that your website shows up on search engines. One minute it may be there, while the other it may lose its (higher) ranking.

Only a few CS 299 students purchased relevant domain names for their Websites, while all MIS 342 students made use of the personal domain names that they had previously purchased as part of their course. Several CS 299 students commented on the fact that purchasing a relevant domain name gave some groups an unfair advantage. One student said:

> I learned that if you actually spent money, you won the competition. I think the assignment should have excluded ways in which you pay to get to the top. We all know that if you pay enough for something, you can be on top. Using alternative resources and capabilities that we were supplied with should have been enough.

Another student said "Those who purchased domain names seemed to have better results than those who used 'free' website domains," referring to names chosen as subdomains of popular online Website creation tools, such as norwegiantourism. wordpress.com . Future iterations of this contest in a classroom setting may prohibit students from using part of the key phrase appears in a site's domain or subdomain. This is a restriction placed on many real-world contests.

One group discovered that a dynamic website with blog capabilities gets recognized by the search engines more readily than a static website. Others commented on the perceived need to frequently update their sites in order to maintain their search rankings. Said one student: "I learned that in order to achieve a good result your page must be continuously updated. Also, even if you buy a domain name which includes the keywords of the search, you may not come first in the search results. SEO is not always a precise science."

Figure 12.6 conveys that 31 of the 54 students (57.4%) "agreed" or "strongly agreed" that the competitive nature of the project was a motivating factor for them to work more regularly at completing this project.

By the end of the project, over 88% of students, 47 of 53, noted that they had a better understanding of the importance of SEO in an overall online marketing strategy, as shown in Fig. 12.7. Students commented on the competitive nature of the project, and the "real world" feel that the project had as a result. One said, "I loved this assignment. I really enjoyed competing against my classmates. It was almost like we were organizations competing against one another."

Table 12.2 summarizes ten characteristics of authentic learning environments (Herrington et al. 2003), and describes how each is manifest in the SEO contest exercise.

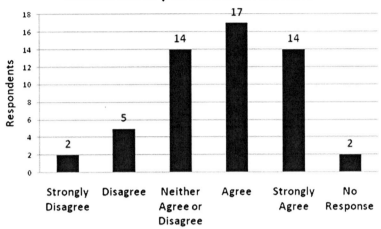

Fig. 12.6 Impact of competition on student effort

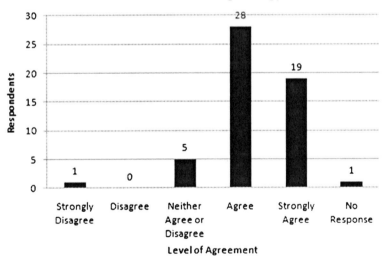

Fig. 12.7 Measure of student understanding of SEO

Table 12.2 SEO contests and Authentic Learning Characteristics

Authentic learning characteristic	Manifest in the SEO contest project
Problem has real-world relevance	Students create a website for a hypothetical product, and promote it online. Students see the relevance of achieving a first-page position in search results from their own daily interactions on the web. Placing the exercise as a competitive contest for students creates novelty. The exercise mirrors the requirements of a real-world activity
Problem is open-ended	Students have the flexibility to use the tools they know in order to create their websites, and must choose from among a variety of SEO techniques to experiment and implement in order to promote their sites. Some of these techniques are based on classroom learning, others by applying lessons learned from individual reading or research. Students must ascertain the effectiveness of their choices through a process of discovery and evaluation over time
Task to be investigated over a sustained period of time	The SEO contest by nature runs over a fixed interval of time, and requires students to give it regular attention in order to achieve desired results, and recognize the steps taken in order to do so
	This exercise was held over a 4-week period. To document their learning, students were required to regularly analyze the effectiveness of the steps they took to promote their websites. Their reports include observations such as "Well I think we figured it out today. After changing our homepage from a static page to a dynamic page made up of the latest posts and adding tags we made it on yahoo and bing! We added 25 tags based on variations of 'Tuvaluan recipes iPhone application' and such. We posted two posts to our main page. We think the key to moving one's site up on Google is by having lots of posts that are posted regularly with lots of tags"
Allow for exploring a task from different perspectives	The students in the classes participating in this exercise were from diverse backgrounds and majors, all enrolled in an elective course. Each brought the perspective of his or her own major or minor (marketing, information technology, media arts, accounting, for example) to this project when considering the techniques to use. More technical students relied on modifying the site's HTML and internal structure in order to improve its rankings; less-technically oriented students tended to make use of off-site techniques to drive traffic to their sites and therefore try to improve their rankings
Provide for collaboration	CS 299 students worked together in groups of four to complete the project, and needed to learn to divide the tasks necessary for creating and promoting the site, and selecting, analyzing, and evaluating SEO techniques. Because collaborative learning may take place both in person or online, students used appropriate online collaboration tools (i.e., wiki, video/audio conferencing) to communicate with each other, and share their results with their classmates

(continued)

Table 12.2 (continued)

Authentic learning characteristic	Manifest in the SEO contest project
Provide an opportunity to reflect on the experience	The goal of the exercise was to learn about SEO techniques in an experiential way, and how to determine which ones are effective. This requires students to both gather and analyze their own data, in order to create and test their hypotheses on which techniques that they tried worked the best. Students used a page of their Websites to reflect on their process, and identify the successes and shortcomings of the strategies they employed
Seamlessly integrate with assessment	The activity is competitive, with real world assessment, as the winners were determined not by the instructors, the students, or their peers, but rather by their groups' position in search results from Google, Yahoo!, and Bing. Different groups were able to experiment with similar techniques and strategies. Students were graded based on their documentation of the steps they took, their explanations of the techniques that did or did not work, their interpretation of their results, and their position within search results. Many groups simply provided a list of steps taken with little or no analysis
Create polished products in their own right	Students created a simple, but complete Website, which required them to apply, enhance, or develop new web skills. The real product of this exercise, however, is the experience students had of continuously promoting the site, and the stories that students are able to tell as a result of having completed it. Their "tangible product" is a report describing their road to the top, and the rationale behind the steps taken to get there. They have a better understanding of SEO strategies having gone through the process
Allow competing solutions and a diversity of outcomes	Because only one group's site could achieve top ranking on each search engine, similar steps taken by different groups produced a variety of outcomes. Students learned that they could influence their sites' search ranking results by applying a variety of techniques

5   Lessons Learned

It is important to note that the generalizability of these research findings may be limited since they mainly rely on student self-evaluations after completing the SEO contest project. Student accounts of their teams' progress and achieved search results were evaluated by their instructors. These provide an independent measure of understanding of SEO concepts. While the data and discussion presented in this paper thus far describes the results after the initial offering of this assignment by two instructors teaching similar courses at their respective universities, the assignment has evolved and changed during subsequent semesters to reflect lessons learned from prior student experiences.

This section describes variations in project requirements based on student patterns and behaviors while completing the assignment.

During the first iteration of the project, some students purchased a domain name, and others thought this provided an unfair advantage. The assignment has since been changed to require that students use only free online tools and services. They could not purchase domain names or spend money on advertising or other services that might impact their position in search results.

The technical aspect of the assignment expanded to require students to use industry-standard content and traffic analysis tools such as Website Grader (websitegrader.com) and Google Analytics (google.com/analytics) to identify ways that they might improve their sites for SEO and identify site usage patterns. Website Grader is an SEO tool that provides a report of structural changes to make to a page's content and underlying HTML code in order to improve its rankings. Google Analytics provides information about traffic that Web pages receive, and the locations of visitors who browse them. Using these tools allowed students to explore SEO techniques based on objective feedback, and required additional critical thinking and analysis to make changes based on their findings, and see whether or not these changes impacted search result rankings. Since by its very nature an SEO contest occurs over weeks and months and is somewhat iterative, students adapted their SEO strategies throughout the contest focusing on techniques that they found most effective as they went along.

Rather than having the instructors provide the hypothetical business, product, or entity to promote, later iterations of the assignment saw students brainstorm that entity. As a result, students created Websites to promote fictitious rock bands, tablet computers, and gadgets. This added to the level of ownership of the project, as students could determine those key words and phrases to promote for these items. This enabled them to better understand criteria for which SEO is appropriate. They learned that the terms taken in combination should have few, if any, previous search results. They also learned that some key words were more competitive than others, and that the term or combination of terms for which they were optimizing their sites needed to be common enough to show up, but obscure enough that they wouldn't be eclipsed by so many other search results. For example, during one semester students promoted a fictitious "Bedrock Tablets" manufacturer of tablet computers. Searches for the terms "bedrock tablets" prior to the start of the SEO contest showed results mostly related to geological formations, not high-tech devices. By the end of the project, top Google search results for those terms were exclusively for the fictitious gadgets that students were promoting, as shown in Fig. 12.8.

The instructors helped students create opportunities to do empirical testing that might lead to opportunities for discovery. For example, when a student hypothesized that Google gave significant weight to backlinks to his site, students considered ways that they might be able to investigate this claim. As a result, students began requesting reciprocal links from other classmate competitors in the SEO contest. Students also learned unexpectedly that social media sites impact search result rankings, as they noticed that content and multimedia that they posted to Twitter, YouTube, and Yahoo! Answers often ranked higher than the sites they were trying to promote. This suggests that a site's popularity impacts ranking as much as the content it contains. In the search for "bedrock tablets" in Fig. 12.8 above, YouTube

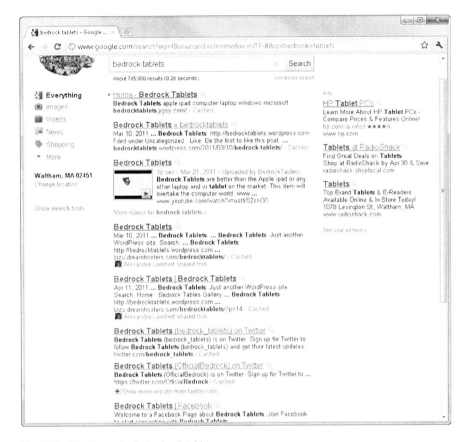

Fig. 12.8 Search results for bedrock tablets

videos, Twitter posts, and Facebook pages comprise four of the top ten search results. Said one student:

> I learned that it takes time for your site to move up on search engine rankings and that continuous publishing of content has a lot to do with how you are ranked by search engines like Google and Bing. Using keywords and also tying in social media help establish your site as an authoritative source of information. To my surprise, Google seemed to place a lot of value on the use of Twitter, as I noticed that the leading project in our class for a Google search was greatly due to their large following on Twitter. However, this group was not number one on Bing and Yahoo. I thought that was very interesting.

6 Conclusion

Search Engine Optimization is a relevant topic to introduce to students of computing, marketing, business, health education, and other disciplines. Students see the practical value for companies, bloggers, and individuals to appear in the top position of search engine results in order to promote their products, services, or brands.

The SEO contest described here exhibits many of the characteristics of authentic learning environments. It mimics a real-world, ongoing scenario that allows for a variety of outcomes. In the process students learn by exploring and reflecting on the outcomes of various SEO techniques that effective SEO is part art, part science, and part luck. This exercise enables students to gain valuable skills in SEO techniques that will be helpful in their future careers.

References

Atwater-Singer, M. (2006). Google whacking: Exploiting Google in an instructional classroom. Indiana Libraries, 25(4). Retrieved from https://scholarworks.iupui.edu/handle/1805/1499.

Charlesworth, A. (2009). Internet Marketing: A practical approach. Oxford, UK: Butterworth-Heinemann.

Connolly, R. W. (2009). No longer partying like its 1999: Designing a modern web stream using the IT2008 curriculum guidelines. Proceedings from The 10th ACM conference on SIG-information technology education. York: Association of Computing Machinery, 74–79. Retrieved May 15, 2010 from http://doi.acm.org/10.1145/1631728.1631752.

Elliott, C. (2007). Action Research: Authentic Learning Transforms Student and Teacher Success. Journal of Authentic Learning 4(1), pp. 34–42. June 2007. Retrieved June 1, 2010, from http://www.oswego.edu/academics/colleges_and_departments/education/jal/vol4no1/4%20Elliot%20Action%20Research%20p%2034-42.pdf.

Evans, M. P. (2007). Analyzing Google rankings through search engine optimization data. Internet Research, 17(1), 21–37.

Hendler, J., Shadbolt, N., Hall, W., Berners-Lee, T. &l Weitzner, D. (2008). Web science: an interdisciplinary approach to understanding the web. Communications of the ACM, 51 (7), 60–69. Retrieved May 20, 2010 from http://doi.acm.org/10.1145/1364782.1364798.

Herrington, J., Oliver R., & Reeves, T. C. (2003). Patterns of engagement in authentic online learning environments. Australian Journal of Educational Technology, 19(1), 59–71. Retrieved May 19, 2010, from http://www.ascilite.org.au/ajet/ajet19/herrington.html.

Herrington, J., Reeves, T., Oliver, R. and Woo, Y. (2004). Designing authentic activities in web-based courses. Journal of Computing in Higher Education 16, no. 1, (September 1): 3–29. http://www.proquest.com/ (accessed May 28, 2010).

Jones, K. B. (2008). Search Engine Optimization. Indianapolis, IN: Wiley Publishing.

Lombardi, M. (2007). Authentic Learning for the 21st Century: An Overview. EduCause Learning Initiative, Retrieved May 24, 2010 from http://net.educause.edu/ir/library/pdf/ELI3009.pdf.

Malaga, R. A. (2010). Search engine optimization - black and white hat approaches. Advances in Computers, 78, 2–41.

McCown, F. (2010). Teaching web information retrieval to undergraduates. Proceedings from The 41st ACM technical symposium on computer science education. Retrieved May 15, 2010 from http://doi.acm.org/10.1145/1734263.1734294.

Middleton, D. (2009, December 28). Landing a job of the future takes a two track mind, Wall Street Journal. Retrieved May 20, 2010 from http://online.wsj.com/article/SB10001424052748703278604574624392641425278.html.

Morochove, R. (2008). Search engine optimization: Advertising 101. PC World, 26(7), 47.

Sabin, M., Higgs, B., Riabov, V, & Mereira, A. (2005). Designing and running a pre-college computing course. Journal of Computing Sciences in College, 20(5), 176–187.

Spradling, C., Strauch, J., & Warner, C. (2008). An interdisciplinary major emphasizing multimedia. Proceedings of the 39th SIGCSE Technical Symposium on Computer Science Education

(SIGCSE '08). ACM, New York, NY, 388–391. Retrieved May 14, 2010 from http://doi.acm. org/10.1145/1352135.1352270.

Xing, B. & Zhangxi, L. (2006).The impact of search engine optimization on online advertising marketing. Proceedings from The 8th International Conference on Electronic Commerce. ACM, New York, NY, 519–529. Retrieved May 14, 2010 from http://doi.acm.org/10.1145/ 1151454.1151531.

Chapter 13
Teachers' Training in Exploiting 3D Virtual Worlds for Teaching and Learning

Demetrios G. Sampson and Pavlos Kallonis

1 Introduction

Today, the emergence of technologies, such as 3D Virtual Worlds (VWs), which provide realistic three-dimensional environments and offer engaging, interactive and immersive experiences, creates new opportunities for teaching and learning. These opportunities are related to the faithfulness of the educational activities representation within 3D VWs and also to the enhanced aspects of interaction provided within them (Dalgarno and Lee 2010). During recent years, several researchers have recognized the educational and training potential of 3D VWs (Molka-danielsen and Deutschmann 2009; Wankel and Kingsley 2009) due to their unique features, such as the recreation of the sense of presence (Hodge et al. 2009), their immediateness (Lucia et al. 2008), the real world simulations provided (Oktay and Folmer 2010), and the new experiences that may not be possible, non cost-effective and even dangerous to represent in the real world (Wiecha et al. 2010).

Furthermore, there are a number of studies that are investigating the educational affordances of 3D VWs and examine the potential of using them in teaching and learning (Bignell and Parson 2010; de Freitas and Neumann 2009; Dickey 2005; Jarmon et al. 2008, 2009; Kalyuga 2007; Konstantinidis et al. 2010). On the other hand, researchers argue that 3D Virtual Worlds are *empty spaces* (Bartle 2003; Livingstone and Bloomfield 2010; Wahlstedt et al. 2008). The term *empty spaces,* is used in order to depict that 3D Virtual Worlds, at first offer unstructured virtual land, which can be populated with 3d virtual objects and various activities that can be supported by these 3d virtual objects. As *empty spaces* they could become valuable for

D.G. Sampson (✉) • P. Kallonis
Department of Digital Systems, University of Piraeus, Piraeus, Greece

Centre for Research and Technology Hellas (CERTH),
Informatics and Telematics Institute (ITI), Thessaloniki, Greece
e-mail: sampson@unipi.gr; pkalloni@iti.gr

P. Isaias et al. (eds.), *Towards Learning and Instruction in Web 3.0: Advances in Cognitive and Educational Psychology*, DOI 10.1007/978-1-4614-1539-8_13,
© Springer Science+Business Media, LLC 2012

education under the condition that they are designed in such a way so as to support the implementation of specially designed educational activities, rather than just providing access to digital educational content within a 3D virtual environment. To this end, the increased interest of exploiting 3D Virtual Worlds in education and training, has led to the development of educational tools and applications which aim to integrate existing learning technologies (such as Course Management Systems) in 3D Virtual Worlds infrastructure (such as Second Life). The development of such tools shows the potential of transforming 3D Virtual Worlds into valuable tools within formal educational settings, as they provide the opportunities to create *spaces* that can support enhanced *out-of-the-classroom* educational activities (Livingstone and Bloomfield 2010).

On the other hand, school teachers must be encouraged to model effective use of technology in their own educational practices, taking into account the possible educational benefits that digital technologies such as 3D VWs offer (UNESCO 2009). Nevertheless, in order to achieve that, teachers and trainers should not only be aware of 3D VWs technical capabilities but also understand how to exploit 3D VWs functionalities to support their students' learning. Within this context, there are research studies that focus specifically on teachers' experiences either through using 3D VW in their teaching activities (Esteves et al. 2009; Jarmon et al. 2009; Konstantinidis et al. 2010) or through their participation in 3D VW supported Continuing Professional Development (CPD) (Girvan and Savage 2010; Vasileiou and Paraskeva 2010). These studies have raised issues, such as, (1) the extra pressure applied to teachers who teach within 3D Virtual Worlds, and (2) the lack of understanding of the new possibilities offered by 3D Virtual Worlds in teaching and learning.

Thus, pedagogically meaningful use of 3D VWs remains a major challenge for teachers and trainers, since 3D VWs introduce new concepts and possibilities that even teachers who are experienced and keen on using digital technologies are not familiar with. To this end, Bignell and Parson (2010), considering only the technical aspect of 3D VWs, have presented a set of skills that a teacher has to acquire to teach within Second Life.

In our work, we acknowledge the need (a) for identifying solid competence descriptions for teachers and trainers being capable of teaching within 3D VW and (b) for building appropriate modules for Continuing Professional Development programmes that can support the acquisition of these competences (Kallonis and Sampson 2010a, b).

To this end, we have investigated a number of initiatives (Sampson and Kallonis in press) that aim to:

- **Identify the competences that a teacher should have in order to teach effectively within a 3D Virtual World**. Bignell & Parson have proposed a list of skills that a teacher should acquire in order to be effective in teaching within Second Life (Bignell and Parson 2010).
- **Design and organize training activities** for teachers' education on the exploitation of 3D Virtual Worlds for teaching and learning. A typical example has been

reported on how the Role Playing Teaching Model can be used within Second Life (Vasileiou and Paraskeva 2010).

- **Design and develop applications** which integrate well-known and already widely used tools (such as Course Management Systems) with the currently established infrastructure of 3D Virtual Worlds (such as Second Life). An example is the SLOODLE Project that aims to integrate Moodle with Second Life (Livingstone 2009).
- **Develop specially-designed 3D Virtual Learning Environments** within general-purpose 3D Virtual Worlds mainly for supporting online learning communities related to the exploitation of 3D Virtual Worlds for teaching and learning. Typical examples of such *spaces* are the SLOODLE Island (Livingstone and Kemp 2010), the EdTech Island (Smith and Berge 2009) and the MUVEnation Island (Oliver and Carr 2009).

Based on this review of the relevant literature, we have concluded that (a) 3D Virtual Worlds are becoming important for formal education as they provide realistic three-dimensional environments, offer engaging, interactive and immersive experiences, and create new opportunities related to learning and teaching, and (b) it is useful for teachers and trainers to understand these environments and explore their possibilities in enhancing their daily educational practices.

To this end, teachers and trainers should acquire relevant competences, as part of their Continuing Professional Development that would enable them to model effective use of 3D VWs in their educational practices (Kallonis and Sampson 2010a, b).

In this book chapter, we present a module for continuing professional development which is based on the Synectics "Making the strange familiar" instructional strategy (Joyce et al. 2000, p. 232); aiming towards acquiring appropriate competences for teaching within 3D Virtual Worlds and for modeling the effective use of 3D VWs in their educational practices.

This is part of our work in this field, which is based on the following steps (Kallonis and Sampson 2010a, b)

- **Step 1** – Identify the **key concepts** related to using 3D Virtual Worlds for teaching and learning.
- **Step 2** – Formulate a **competence description proposal** (novice level) for teachers being capable of teaching in 3D Virtual Worlds.
- **Step 3** – Design a module for Teachers CPD Programmes that supports the acquisition of these competences based on **Synectics** "Making the strange familiar" instructional strategy.
- **Step 4** – Implement a **3D Virtual Classroom Simulation** to support the module.
- **Step 5** – Validate the proposed module with School Teachers.

Figure 13.1 presents our contribution in relation to the previously mentioned initiatives for Teachers' and Trainers' CPD in 3D VWs.

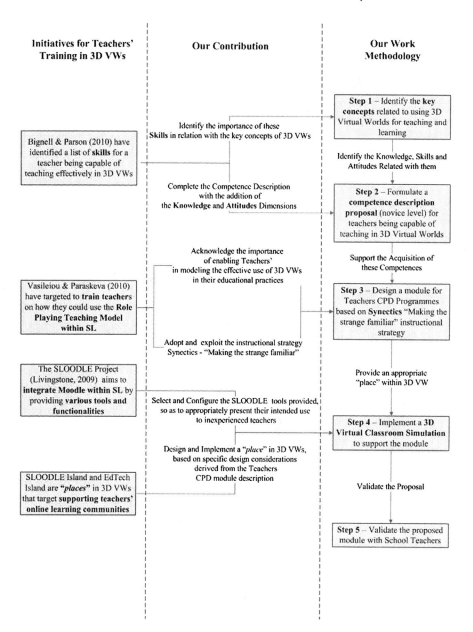

Fig. 13.1 Overview of our work in teachers' and trainers' training on exploiting 3D virtual worlds in teaching and learning

2   3D Virtual Worlds Key Concepts for Teaching and Learning

Eshenbenner and colleagues (2008) and Dalgarno and Lee (2010) have acknowledged the potential educational benefits of 3D VWs. They state that 3D Virtual Worlds offer unique learning and teaching opportunities, as they constitute rich, engaging, immersive, motivating and highly interactive environments. This is due to the fact that 3D VWs: (1) recreate the sense of presence, (2) are immediate, (3) are adaptable, (4) offer the possibility to simulate the real world, (5) offer the possibility to create new experiences that may not be possible or may be difficult to represent in the real world, (6) could be offered for experimentation and (7) allow for synchronous and asynchronous communication and collaboration.

Thus, these characteristics can be considered as the **key concepts** that would be important to be understood by school teachers who want to exploit 3D Virtual Worlds in their educational practices. This claim can be made through the examination of their definitions given in contemporary research studies:

- **Recreate the sense of presence:** This is made possible by the use of Avatars, which enable users to take an identity either similar to or different from theirs. This allows them to explore and interact with environments, which can be designed and developed in such a way so as to simulate either real-life or imaginary settings (Petrackou 2009). The sense of presence in 3D VWs could be divided in three different types (Hodge et al. 2009). Those are: *the cognitive presence*, which enables students to understand and acquire the knowledge presented in 3D Virtual Worlds; *the affective presence*, which enables students to feel emotionally engaged with the educational activities presented in 3D Virtual Worlds; and *the social presence*, which enables students to interact and communicate using their Avatars in a similar way as they do in real life.
- **Immediateness:** The immediateness offered by 3D VWs is related to the outcomes of the interactions that the students perform within them by using their Avatars. Those outcomes are presented immediately in the 3D VWs and are visible to the students. Moreover, the immediateness of 3D VWs is also implemented within communication and interaction tools, allowing student-to-student and teacher-to-students real time interactions to take place (Lucia et al. 2008). Finally, the best practices of implementing the immediateness offered by 3D VWs suggest the development of systems that facilitate the exploration and the interactions with the educational content and the educational activities presented in the 3D VWs. Those systems achieve that by helping students acquire meaningful contextual information that is derived from the virtual objects presented in a 3D VW (Oktay and Folmer 2010).
- **Adaptability:** 3D VWs offer many opportunities to capture students' activity, to develop user profiles and to use this information in order to present them with personalized content according to their needs (Chittaro and Ranon 2008). Moreover, by combining the immediateness presented in 3D Virtual Worlds with their potential to be adapted according to the students' preferences, it is possible to design and develop platforms that feature real time tracking of the students

actions. This may result to the development of a dynamic environment that is reconfigured accordingly, in order to present the students with educational content and educational activities related to their preferences (Bonis et al. 2008).

- **Real world simulations:** It is possible to simulate places, environments and activities in 3D VWs. Those simulations may facilitate teaching and learning as they could be used either as substitutes to real world situations that are difficult to be recreated and/or as supplements to real world activities allowing different types of interactions to take place (Yamamoto et al. 2010). Moreover, by combining the ability of 3D VWs to integrate with external systems, it might be possible to implement pedagogical agents with behaviors that simulate those of an actual teacher (Garrido et al. 2010).

- **New experiences:** 3D VWs can be used as a means of providing with settings and situations that may be very difficult and/or non cost-effective and/or dangerous to represent in the real world (Wiecha et al. 2010). Moreover, it is possible to present students with experiences that it is impossible to recreate in the real world giving them the opportunity to explore environments and interact with situations that may never be able to find in the real world (Trewin et al. 2008).

- **Experimentation:** 3D VWs offer the possibility to support experiments that present different outcomes according to the data that students insert using different tools (in the forms of virtual objects) presented in 3D VWs (Vrellis et al. 2010). Moreover, through the provision of tools for the creation of virtual objects, it is possible to design and develop models of different devices and/or other artifacts, presenting multiple layers of representational degree with which students can interact and experiment (Callaghan et al. 2009).

- **Synchronous communication and collaboration:** 3D VWs allow students to collaborate and communicate in real time (Prasolova-Forland and Chang 2007). Moreover, using specific software students can manipulate and reconfigure virtual objects simultaneously like in real life (Syamsuddin and Kwon 2009).

3 Proposed Module for Teachers' CPD

In this section we present our proposed module for Teachers' Continuing Professional Development designed and described following the principles of constructive alignment, which was devised by Professor John B. Biggs and defined as "a principle used for devising teaching and learning activities, and assessment tasks, that directly address the learning outcomes intended in a way not typically achieved in traditional lectures, tutorial classes and examinations" (Biggs and Tang 2007, p. 7). The proposed module is provided through a 3D Virtual Classroom Simulation (presented in Fig. 13.2) that supports its training and assessment activities, which is presented extensively in Sampson & Kallonis (in press).

Based on the constructive alignment principle we have followed the next steps, in order to design the proposed module:

- **Step 1** – Develop a **Competence Description (novice level)** of teachers capable of teaching in 3D Virtual Worlds.

Fig. 13.2 The 3D virtual classroom simulation that supports the teachers CPD module (Sampson and Kallonis in press)

- **Step 2** – Describe the **educational objectives** of the proposed module using **Blooms' Revised Taxonomy** (Anderson and Krathwohl 2001).
- **Step 3** – Design and Describe the **Educational Activities** to be presented in the module for Teachers' Continuing Professional Development.
- **Step 4** – Design and Describe the **Assessment Activities** to be presented in the module for Teachers' Continuing Professional Development.
- **Step 5** – Present the **module for Teachers' Continuing Professional Development** in a concise and consistent way.

3.1   Competence Description (Novice Level) of Teachers Capable of Teaching in 3D Virtual Worlds

UNESCO (2009) states that "educational systems around the world are under increasing pressure to use the new information and communication technologies (ICTs) to teach students the knowledge and skills they need in the twenty-first century" (p. 6). Thus, teachers should transform their educational practices by modelling effective use of technology in order to provide their students with innovative and engaging educational activities. To this end, UNESCO (2009) identified competences that teachers should have in order to effectively integrate ICT in their educational practices. Nevertheless, there is not a consistent competence description for teachers capable of effectively integrating 3D Virtual Words in their educational practices available in the current literature.

Acknowledging this limitation and taking into consideration the statement made by UNESCO (2009), "in order to use ICT effectively, teachers must be capable of not only know how they work but also understand how to use their functionalities to support their students learning" (p. 1), we have devised a competence description for teachers capable of teaching in Second Life (SL).

More precisely, our competence profile is an extension to the list of skills proposed by Bignell and Parson's (2010) with the addition of the missing competences related with the **knowledge** and **attitudes** dimensions that teachers should also be equipped with, in order (a) to understand how to use those skills in their educational practice, and (b) to believe that if they use them it would be helpful for their students learning.

It should be also mentioned that as there is no other similar list and/or module for Teachers' Continuing Professional Development in literature, we have defined the novice level of those competences in accordance to the proficiency levels (Novice, Advanced and Proficient) that were proposed as an extension to IEEE LOM in Sampson (2009).

More specifically, Bignell and Parson (2010) divide their list in three different levels of skills, namely elementary, basic and advanced. Those levels present the skills that a teacher should be equipped with in order to teach effectively within Second Life by:

- *Performing simple teaching tasks*, such as moving their Avatar closer to their students and talk to them (elementary level),
- *Performing more complex tasks*, such as giving items to their students (basic level), and
- *Being able to model effective use of the tools presented within Second Life in their educational practices*, such as to combine the functionalities of the available 3D VW supported educational tools (e.g. virtual whiteboard, virtual laptop etc.) without any help from an expert (advanced level).

Bignell and Parson (2010), in their proposed list of skills, mainly considered technical aspect of Second Life, such as, skills that are related to the navigation using Avatars, the organization of personal inventories and the communication opportunities presented within Second Life. Although, these are skills that are useful in order to function effectively within a 3D VW such as Second Life, we claim that they are not enough to enable teachers modeling effective use of Second Life in their educational practices.

Thus, we have developed a competence description (at novice level) for teachers capable of using SL effectively to support their teaching, by extending Bignell & Parson's list with the addition of Knowledge Competence Dimension and Attitudes Competence Dimension. Furthermore, as it was previously mentioned the module for Teachers' CPD is presented through a 3D Virtual Classroom Simulation. Thus, the competences in every dimension, namely, knowledge, skills and attitudes, were enhanced with competences descriptions related to using a specifically designed *place* (which, in our study is a 3D Virtual Classroom Simulation) within 3D VWs. Table 13.1 presents our proposed competence profile described using the three different dimensions of competences (knowledge, skills and attitudes).

Table 13.1 Competence description (Novice level) for teachers and trainers capable of teaching within 3D virtual worlds

Competences description	
Knowledge (K)	K1. Understand the key concepts of 3D Virtual Worlds
	K2. Understand the similarities between a 3D Virtual Classroom and a traditional classroom in order to identify the key concepts as affordances of 3D Virtual Worlds for education
	K3. Understand the differences between a 3D Virtual Classroom and a traditional classroom in order to identify the key concepts as affordances of 3D Virtual Worlds for education.
	K4. Understand the potential of 3D Virtual Worlds to support teaching and learning
Skills (S)	S1. Know how to use the basic functionalities of SL for navigation, control and communication according to Bignell and Parson's list (elementary and basic level) (2010)
	S2. Know how to use the tools presented in a 3D Virtual Classroom Simulation
	S3. Be able to transfer their own simple Educational Activities in a 3D Virtual Classroom Simulation using the tools presented in it
	S4. Be able to organise and present new simple Educational Activities using a 3D Virtual Classroom as an environment for teaching
Attitudes (A)	A1. Be interested in exploiting 3D Virtual Worlds in Real Education
	A2. Be motivated in participating in more Teachers' CPD programs related to the exploitation of 3D Virtual Worlds in Education

3.2 Educational Objectives Related to the Proposed Competence Description

As it was previously mentioned 3D Virtual Worlds recreate the sense of presence. Hodge et al. (2009) have acknowledged that there are three different types of presence within 3D VWs, namely, cognitive presence, affective presence and social presence. Each one of them dictates different types of interactions within a 3D VW.

Our aim is to match the above mentioned competences with the possible interactions that the teachers' will perform while they participate in our proposed module, namely cognitive interactions, affective interactions and social interactions respectively (John et al. 2010). Thus, we propose the exploitation of the revised Bloom's Taxonomy devised by Anderson and Krathwohl (2001) in order to depict the intended teachers' cognitive, affective and social interactions through a representation of educational objectives.

The educational objectives of our module are presented using the Conceptual Knowledge Dimension for Cognitive Interactions, the Procedural Knowledge Dimension for Affective Interactions and the Meta-cognitive Knowledge Dimension for Social Interactions.

- **Conceptual knowledge (related to the knowledge competence description):** The teachers should **understand** the concepts presented in 3D Virtual Worlds. Then, **analyze** their possible exploitation in teaching and learning by **matching** the similarities between a 3D Virtual Classroom Simulation in Second Life and a traditional classroom in the real world. This can be achieved if they **recall** their previous experiences in a traditional classroom and **explain** the similarities and the differences with a 3D Virtual Classroom Simulation in Second Life. Finally, the teachers should **identify** and **interpret** those concepts as affordances that 3D Virtual Worlds offer that can be used by teachers to model effective use of 3D VWs in their educational practices.

- **Procedural knowledge (related to the skills competence description):** The teachers should **understand** and **apply** the different functionalities presented in Second Life. This will help them to **explore** the potential of the 3D Virtual Classroom Simulation. Moreover, teachers should **evaluate** and **apply** those functionalities in order to **design** and **organize** educational activities in the 3D Virtual Classroom Simulation. Finally, the teachers by **combining** their understanding about the key concepts and their skills in using the tools presented with their previous experiences should be able to **model** effective use of 3D VWs in their educational practices.
- **Meta-cognitive knowledge (related to the attitudes competence description):** The teachers should **recall** and **evaluate** the training activities in which they have participated and **judge** whether the 3D Virtual Worlds present educational benefits that can eventually lead to an evolution of their educational practices.

3.3 Instructional Strategy of the proposed Module for Teachers' CPD Programmes

The proposed module had been designed and developed for selected teachers and trainers, who are experienced in using digital technologies both in their life and in their educational practices. It is also anticipated that they present high motivation and interest in the continuing professional development and appreciate the potential value of innovative digital technologies for education.

In Sect. 3.1, we have presented the Competence Description that targets the above mentioned group of teachers. The next step is to select an appropriate instructional strategy which presents design considerations for the development of our training activities that could foster the acquisition of the described competences.

To this end, we have selected to use the instructional strategy of Synectics "Making the Strange Familiar" which is defined as "a strategy for making the students understand and internalize new or difficult concepts and ideas, through the use of analogies between concepts or ideas which are familiar to the students to the new concepts or ideas presented" (Joyce et al. 2000, p. 232; Talawar and Sheela 2004, p. 14). This instructional strategy is considered as appropriate for (1) exploring and understanding social problems by relating them to familiar situations through the use of metaphors, (2) problem solving, as this instructional strategy offers the opportunity to understand a problem by relating it to previous experiences and apply solutions based on them, (3) creating a design or a product based on the combination of previous experiences and ideas with the new concepts and/or possibilities presented and (4) understanding unfamiliar and/or abstract concepts through the identification of their similarities and differences to familiar concepts, ideas and/or objects (Joyce et al. 2000; Keyes 2008; Talawar and Sheela 2004).

Moreover, the problem which is targeted by our proposed Continuing Professional Development module is (a) to help teachers and trainers understand the concepts related to 3D Virtual Worlds, (b) explore the new possibilities that 3D Virtual Worlds present for teaching and learning and (c) acquire basic competences for teaching within them. Based on this analysis we consider (1) as thestrange part of the analogy, the concepts and the competences related with teaching within 3D Virtual Worlds and (2) as the familiar part of the analogy the teachers' experiences in a traditional classroom.

Thus, we claim that the use of this strategy can (a) facilitate teachers and trainers to understand the unfamiliar concepts presented in 3D Virtual Worlds by exploring the similarities and differences between a "traditional" classroom and a 3D Virtual Classroom, and (b) enable teachers and trainers to design simple educational activities by transferring their previous experiences and ideas using the tools presented in a 3D Virtual Classroom Simulation.

3.4   Design of the Assessment Activities

Before, presenting the design of the proposed module of Teachers' Continuing Professional Development we should consider also the design and the development of assessment activities that are aligned with the educational objectives of the proposed module.

In order to design the assessment activities of our proposed module, we consider using some of the ideas presented in the proposal made by Ibanez et al. (2010) on how to assess knowledge and skills within 3D Virtual Worlds combined with the types of assessment activities proposed in the Dialog Plus Taxonomy (LADiE 2006). Thus, we present the design considerations that are derived from the above studies according to three different aspects: *assessment of knowledge, assessment of skills and assessment of attitudes*.

Ibanez et al. (2010) state that the traditional assessment of knowledge features prompts that present questions to students which they should answer. However, they propose that the assessment of knowledge within a 3D VW should be directly related to the use of specifically designed and developed virtual objects that assess students through their interactions with them. Taking that into consideration, we choose to follow a blended approach using both traditional means and virtual world objects for the assessment of knowledge. Thus, we have designed and implemented:

- **Oral assessment activities** which will be presented through a virtual object that allows chatting and recording of conversations,
- **Written exercises** that guide the teachers to justify their opinions and

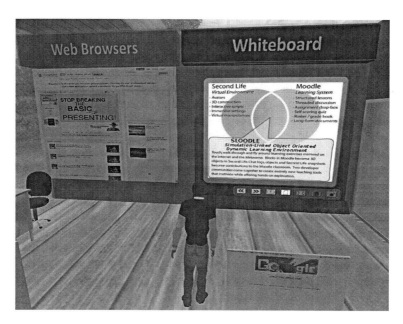

Fig. 13.3 Virtual web browsers and virtual whiteboards facilitate the presentations assessment activities

- **A presentation assessment** using specifically selected virtual objects that allow the presentation of slides, multimedia, web sites and/or textures (presented in Fig. 13.3).

Ibanez and colleagues (2010) also propose that the assessment of skills should feature activities that identify whether students could use their knowledge effectively to support their actions. This leads them to claim that 3D Virtual Worlds can offer simulation activities in order to support the assessment of skills. To this end, we present several different simulations of "traditional" classroom tools to teachers and trainers, which they can use in order to combine the new knowledge and skills that they have received with their previous experiences so as to create simple educational activities within Second Life. These assessment activities feature:

- The modeling of effective use of Second Life in educational activities that can be represented as **artifacts** in the 3D Virtual Classroom Simulation, and
- A **self-assessment activity** in which there are several criteria related to the exploration of the 3D Virtual Classroom Simulation that teachers and trainers should meet according to their interactions with the virtual objects presented (presented in Fig. 13.4).

Finally, Ibanez and colleagues (2010) propose that we should also assess if the students could acquire, evaluate, communicate and handle the knowledge and skills

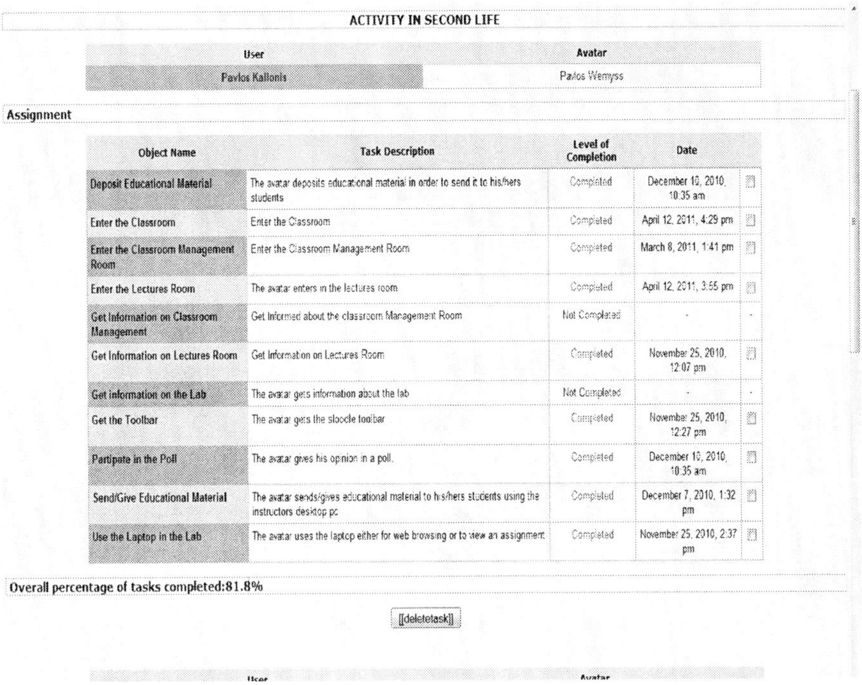
ACTIVITY IN SECOND LIFE

User	Avatar
Pavlos Kallonis	Pavlos Wemyss

Assignment

Object Name	Task Description	Level of Completion	Date
Deposit Educational Material	The avatar deposits educational material in order to send it to his/hers students	Completed	December 10, 2010, 10:35 am
Enter the Classroom	Enter the Classroom	Completed	April 12, 2011, 4:29 pm
Enter the Classroom Management Room	Enter the Classroom Management Room	Completed	March 8, 2011, 1:41 pm
Enter the Lectures Room	The avatar enters in the lectures room	Completed	April 12, 2011, 3:55 pm
Get Information on Classroom Management	Get Informed about the classroom Management Room	Not Completed	-
Get Information on Lectures Room	Get Information on Lectures Room	Completed	November 25, 2010, 12:07 pm
Get information on the Lab	The avatar gets information about the lab	Not Completed	-
Get the Toolbar	The avatar gets the sloodle toolbar	Completed	November 25, 2010, 12:27 pm
Partipate in the Poll	The avatar gives his opinion in a poll.	Completed	December 10, 2010, 10:35 am
Send/Give Educational Material	The avatar sends/gives educational material to his/hers students using the instructors desktop pc	Completed	December 7, 2010, 1:32 pm
Use the Laptop in the Lab	The avatar uses the laptop either for web browsing or to view an assignment	Completed	November 25, 2010, 2:37 pm

Overall percentage of tasks completed:81.8%

[[deletetask]]

Fig. 13.4 The proposed list of interactions for the self-assessment activity through the SLOODLE tracker system

presented to them during their participation in the module, but also if they believe that these would lead them to be more effective in their work and/or activities. Thus, we have designed and implemented assessment activities that:

- Allow teachers to make a **summary** related to their overall experience as participants to the proposed module, and
- Also share their notes about the **practical application** of what they have learned with the other participants through their personal blogs (presented in Fig. 13.5).

The above mentioned types of assessment activities were implemented seamlessly in the module as simple educational activities in which teachers and trainers will participate and the appropriate data for assessment will be collected.

3.5 Overview of the Proposed Module

The proposed module consists of seven phases that feature different educational and assessment activities as presented in Table 13.2.

Fig. 13.5 Making a blog entry using an avatar from within second life through the SLOODLE toolbar

4 Conclusions

3D Virtual Worlds provide potential educational benefits due to the fact that they allow high representation fidelity of both educational activities and educational content. Thus, through 3D VWs teachers and trainers can offer immersive and interactive learning experiences to their students. However, most studies focus on the students' perspectives of functioning and learning within 3D VWs. To this end, there is a lack of studies that are related to teachers' and trainers' perspectives on exploiting 3D VWs for their educational practices. Moreover, the contributions of existing such studies focus mainly on the technical skills that teachers' and trainers' need to acquire in order to function properly within 3D VWs. On the other hand, the pedagogically meaningful use of 3D VWs remains a major challenge for teachers and trainers since it presupposes the understanding of key concepts for teaching and learning within 3DVWs. As a result, there is a need for identifying solid competence descriptions for teachers and trainers being capable of teaching within 3D VW and for building appropriate modules for Continuing Professional Development programmes that can support the acquisition of these competences.

Within, this context, in this book chapter we present part of our work in the field of teachers' training in exploiting 3D VWs for teaching and learning. More specifically, we have (a) discussed the key concepts of 3D VWs in teaching and learning, (b) presented a competence description (at novice level) for teachers and trainers capable of teaching in 3D VWs, (c) described a module for teachers'

Table 13.2 Overview of the proposed module

First phase: Substantive input	**Presentation of the new concepts:** The educator presents the main concepts related to 3D Virtual Worlds as they were defined previously in this book chapter
	Discussion on the new concepts (Knowledge assessment activity): The educator triggers a short discussion aiming to identify the first impression that the new concepts presented made to the teachers and their first understanding on what was presented to them
Second phase: Direct analogy	**Presentation of the analogy:** The educator presents the analogy of a traditional classroom to a 3D Virtual Classroom Simulation and triggers a discussion on finding the parts where the analogy connects
Third phase: Personal analogy	**Reinforce the analogy:** The teachers express how it would have been if they were teaching in a 3D Virtual Classroom Simulation and use these expressions to further reinforce the analogy
Fourth phase: Comparing analogies	**Brainstorming on the analogy similarities:** Through brainstorming the teachers find and describe the similarities between the two parts of the analogy
	Describe and justify the similarities (Knowledge assessment activity): The teachers participate collaboratively in a written exercise in which they should write down the similarities of the analogy that were derived from the brainstorming session and use proper justification to support them
Fifth phase: Explaining differences	**Brainstorming on the analogy differences:** Through brainstorming the teachers find and describe the differences between the two parts of the analogy
	Describe and justify the differences (Knowledge assessment activity): The teachers participate collaboratively in a written exercise in which they should write down the differences of the analogy that were derived from the brainstorming session and use proper justification to support them
Sixth phase: Exploration	**Learn the basics:** The teachers with the help of the educator create their own Moodle Accounts and Second Life Accounts, select and/or create their Avatars and then enter the 3D Virtual Classroom Simulation. There the educator presents some of the basic skills for teaching in Second Life as described in Bignell and Parson (2010). The teachers try to use the basic functionalities and the educator provides them with immediate and constant feedback
	Explore the 3D virtual classroom simulation: With the help of the educator the teachers explore the 3D Virtual Classroom Simulation in order to understand how they can (1) use the tools that are presented in the 3D Virtual Classroom, (2) manipulate and reconfigure the tools as they like (individually and collaboratively) and (3) use the communication facilities presented in the 3D Virtual Classroom. The educator provides teachers with immediate and constant feedback
	Self-assessment on the exploration (Skills Assessment Activity): The teachers are presented with a list of specific tasks related to the exploration of the 3D Virtual Classroom Simulation which indicates what actions have the teachers completed and which are the tasks that have not been completed yet

(continued)

Table 13.2 (continued)

Seventh phase: Generating analogy	**Divide into groups:** The educator divides the teachers in groups and makes some proposals for activities that could be supported by the 3D Virtual Classroom Simulation
	Organize simple educational activities (Skills assessment activity): The teacher groups use the tools presented in the 3D Virtual Classroom Simulation in order to organize simple educational activities. Moreover, the teachers can always get support from the educator if they face any problems with the use of the functionalities presented in the 3D Virtual Classroom Simulation. In this way the teachers generate their own analogies (educational activities in a "traditional" classroom to educational activities in a 3D Virtual Classroom Simulation)
	Presentation of the simple activities (Skills assessment activity): When, the teacher groups finish the organization of their activities, they present them to their colleagues, so as to stimulate discussion amongst them
	Comment on the activities (Attitudes assessment activity): After completing the previous activity the teachers use the Chat Logger and discuss again the analogy that was previously presented to them, revisiting the similarities and the differences of a "traditional" classroom to a 3D Virtual Classroom Simulation
	Comment on the module (Attitudes assessment activity): Finally, the teachers are given the opportunity to comment on the module expressing their opinions about the educational activities that were conducted and about the 3D Virtual Classroom Simulation that they have used in the two last phases of the module. The comments will be published in their Moodle Blogs using the SLOODLE Toolbar. The educator should help the teachers if they face any problems in setting up the SLOODLE Toolbar

training for acquiring these competences based on the instructional strategy of Synectics "Making the strange familiar". Our aim is to set the starting point for designing and developing full teachers' and trainers' Continuing Professional Development programmes that target (1) to enable teachers' and trainers' model the effective use of 3D VWs in their educational practices and (2) along with specifically designed *places* developed and presented within 3D VWs (such as 3D Virtual Classroom Simulations) to provide teachers' and trainers' with experiences that can be applied in real life teaching and learning (such as classroom management activities).

Acknowledgement The work presented herein has partly been supported by the "Exploiting 3D Virtual Worlds in Lifelong Learning" project funded by the Greek General Secretariat of Research and Technology (Project Code: 3SMEs2009). It reflects the views only of the authors and the GSRT cannot be held responsible for any use which may be made of the information contained therein.

References

Anderson, L. W., & Krathwohl, D. R. (Eds.). (2001). *A taxonomy for learning, teaching and assessing: a revision of Bloom's taxonomy of educational objectives: complete edition.* New York : Longman.

Bartle, A. R. (2004). *Designing virtual worlds.* USA: New Riders Publishing.

Biggs, J & Tang, C. (2007). *Teaching for quality learning at university.* Maidenhead : McGraw-Hill and Open University Press.

Bignell, S. & Parson, V. (2010). Best practice in virtual worlds teaching version 2.1. Retrieved February 26, 2011, from http://previewpsych.org/BPD2.0.pdf.

Bonis, B., Stamos, J., Vosinakis, S., Andreou, I. & Panayiotopoulos, T. (2008). Personalization of content in virtual exhibitions. In B. Falcidieno, M. Spagnuolo, Y. Avrithis, I. Kompatsiaris & P. Buitelaar (Eds). *Semantic multimedia lecture notes in computer science* (pp. 172–184). USA: Springer.

Callaghan, M.J., McCusker, K., Losada, J.L., Harkin, J.G. & Wilson, S. (2009). *Teaching engineering education using virtual worlds and virtual learning environments.* Paper presented at the International Conference on Advances in Computing Control Telecommunication Technologies, Trivandrum, Kerala, India.

Chittaro L., Ranon R. (2008). *An adaptive 3D virtual environment for learning the X3D language.* Paper presented at the International Conference on Intelligent User Interfaces (IUI 2008), USA, New York.

Dalgarno, B. & Lee, M.J.W. (2010). "What are the learning affordances of 3-D virtual environments?", *British Journal of Educational Technology, 41*(1), 10–32.

de Freitas, S. & Neumann, T. (2009). The use of 'exploratory learning' for supporting immersive learning in virtual environments. *Computers & Education, 52*(2), 343–352.

Dickey, M. D. (2005). Three-dimensional virtual worlds and distance learning: two case studies of Active Worlds as a medium for distance education. *British Journal of Educational Technology, 36*(3), 439–451.

Eshenbenner, B., Nah, F. & Siau, K. (2008). 3D virtual worlds in education: applications, benefits, issues, and opportunities. *Journal of Database Management, 19*(4), 91–110.

Esteves, M., Fonseca, B., Morgado, L. & Martins, P. (2009). Using Second Life for problem based learning in computer science programming. *Journal of Virtual Worlds Research, 2*(1), 4–25.

Girvan, C. & Savage, T. (2010). Identifying an appropriate pedagogy for virtual worlds: a communal constructivism case study. *Computers & Education, 55*(1), 342–349.

Hodge, E., Collins, S. & Giardano, T. (2009). *The virtual worlds handbook.* Massachussets: Jones and Bartlett Publishers.

Ibanez, Crespo & Kloos (2010). Assessment of knowledge and competencies in 3D virtual worlds: a proposal. In N. Reynolds & M. Turcsányi-Szabó (Eds), *Key competencies in the knowledge society, ed., vol. 324, IFIP Advances in Information and Communication Technology* (pp. 165–176). Boston: Springer.

Jarmon, L., Traphagan, T. & Mayrath, M. (2008). Understanding project-based learning in Second Life with a pedagogy, training, and assessment trio, *Educational Media International, 45*(3), 157–176.

Jarmon, L., Traphagan, T., Mayrath, M. & Trivedi, A. (2009). Virtual world teaching, experiential learning, and assessment: an interdisciplinary communication course in Second Life. *Computers & Education, 53*(1), 169–182.

John, D., Gatzidis, C., Boucouvalas, A. C., Liarokapis, F. & Brujic-Okretic, V. (2011). Prototyping expressive 3D social worlds. *The Open Virtual Reality Journal, 3*(1), 1–15.

Joyce, R. B., Weil, M. & Calhoun, E. (2000). *Models of teaching 6th Edition.* USA: Allyn & Bacon.

Kallonis, P. & Sampson, D. (2010a). *Exploiting virtual worlds for teachers' professional development.* Paper presented the IADIS International Conference Cognition and Exploratory Learning in Digital Age (CELDA 2010), Timisoara, Romania

Kallonis, P. & Sampson, D. (2010b). *Implementing a 3D virtual classroom simulation for teachers' continuing professional development.* Paper presented at the Workshop on Virtual Worlds for academic, organizational, and life-long learning (ViWo 2010) in the 18th International Conference on Computers in Education (ICCE 2010), Putrajaya, Malaysia

Kalyuga, S. (2007). Enhancing instructional efficiency of interactive e-learning environments: a cognitive load perspective. *Educational Psychology Review*, *19*(3), 387–399.

Keyes, D. K. (2008). *Reflecting and generating new understandings with Synectics.* Paper presented at the 18th Annual Conference of the European Teacher Education Network (ETEN18), Liverpool, England.

Konstantinidis, A., Tsiatsos, T., Terzidou, T. & Pomportsis, A. (2010). Fostering collaborative learning in second life: metaphors and affordances, *Computers & Education*, *55*(2), 603–615.

LADiE (2006). LADiE final report, learning activity design in education (LADiE) reference model project. Retrieved March 13, 2011, from http://www.jisc.ac.uk/media/documents/programmes/elearningframework/ladie_finalreport.pdf.

Livingstone, D. & Bloomfield R. P. (2010). Mixed-methods and mixed-worlds: engaging globally distributed user groups for extended evaluation and studies. In A. Peachey, J. Gillen, D. Livingstone and S. Smith-Robbins (Eds.), *Researching learning in virtual worlds*. USA: Springer.

Lucia, A. D., Francese, R., Passero, I. and Tortora, G. (2008) *SLMeeting: Supporting collaborative work in Second Life*. Paper presented at the Advanced Visual Interfaces, Napoli, Italy.

Molka-danielsen, J. & Deutschmann, M. (Eds.) (2009). *Learning and teaching in the virtual world of Second Life*. Norway: Tapir Academic Press.

Oktay, B. & Folmer, E. (2010). *Synthesizing meaningful feedback for exploring virtual worlds using a screen reader.* Paper presented at the 18th International Conference on Computers in Education (ICCE 2010), Putrajaya, Malaysia.

Oliver, M. & Carr, D. (2009). Learning in virtual worlds: using communities of practice to explain how people learn from play. *British Journal of Educational Technology*, *40*(3), 444–457.

Petrackou, A. (2010). Interacting through avatars: virtual worlds as a context for online education. *Computers & Education*, *54*(4), 1020–1027.

Prasolova-Forland, E. & Chang, T.W. (2007). *Tower of babel: facilitating multi-cultural educational activities and group work with 3D collaborative virtual environments.* Paper presented at the Internet and Multimedia Systems and Applications, Kailua-Kona, HI, USA.

Sampson, D. G. (2009). Competence-related metadata for educational resources that support life-long competence development programmes. *Educational Technology & Society*, *12*(4), 149–159.

Sampson, D.G. & Kallonis, P. (in press). 3D virtual classroom simulations for supporting school teachers' continuing professional development. In J. Jia (Ed.), *Educational stages and interactive learning: from kindergarten to workplace training*, IGI Publishers.

Smith, M. & Berge, Z. (2009). Social learning theory in Second Life. *MERLOT Journal of Online Learning and Teaching, 5*(2). Retrieved March 13, 2011, from http://jolt.merlot.org/vol5no2/berge_0609.htm.

Syamsuddin, M.R. & Kwon, Y.M. (2009). *Shared object interaction in virtual world.* Paper presented at the International Conference on Complex, Intelligent and Software Intensive Systems, Barcelona, Spain.

Talawar, M.S. & Sheela, G. (2004). *Synectics model of teaching.* New Delhi: Anmol Publications.

United Nations Educational, Scientific and Cultural Organization (2009). *ICT competency standards for teachers: Policy Framework.* Paris: UNESCO.

Vasileiou, N. V. & Paraskeva, F. (2010). Teaching role-playing instruction in Second Life: an exploratory study. *Journal of Information, Information Technology, and Organisations*, *5*, 25–50.

Vrellis, I., Papachristos, N. M., Bellou, J., Avouris, N. & Mikropoulos, T.A., (2010). *Designing a collaborative learning activity in Second Life - an exploratory study in physics.* Paper presented at the 10th IEEE International Conference on Advanced Learning Technologies (ICALT 2010), Susse, Tunisia.

Wahlstedt, A., Pekkola, S., Niemelä, M. (2008). From e-learning space to e-learning place. *British Journal of Educational Technology, 39*(6), 1020–1030.

Wankel, C. & Kingsley, J. (Eds.) (2009). *Higher education in virtual worlds: teaching and learning in Second Life*. United Kingdom: Emerald Group Publishing Limited.

Wiecha, J. Heyden, R. Sternthal, E. Merialdi, M. (2010). Learning in a virtual world: experience with using Second Life for medical education, *Journal of Medical Internet Research, 12*(1). Retrieved March 13, 2011, from http://www.jmir.org/2010/1/e1/.

Yamamoto, S., Waki, H. & Hirashima, T. (2010). *An implementation of learning environment for problem-changing exercise*. Paper presented at the 18th International Conference on Computers in Education (ICCE 2010), Putrajaya, Malaysia.

Chapter 14
Individual Differences in Different Level Mental Rotation Tasks: An Eye Movement Study

Sacide Güzin Mazman and Arif Altun

1 Introduction

Web based learning environments have highlighted the need for a better understanding of fundamental issues concerning the effectiveness of learning outcomes. To design better adaptive e-learning environments, the role of the user as an individual and their characteristics had become the research focus for researchers. Content and interface designers cautioned about taking these individual differences into account when providing e-learning content to users. Furthermore, providing adaptive learning environments is intended to address each learner with suitable content for that learner's ability level in order to facilitate learning.

Among the individual differences, spatial ability is often cited as being a good predictor of human-computer interaction performance (Chen et al. 2000; Vicente and Williges 1988). Spatial ability includes various cognitive processes and skills, such as encoding, generating, retaining, retrieving and transforming information as well as discriminating among well-structured visual images (Lohman 1993). Spatial ability is defined as the ability to formulate, to perceive and to manipulate mental images and to maintain orientation with respect to objects in space (Tartre 1990); spatial ability involves the cognition of spatial properties of things in the world like location, size, distance, direction, shape, movement, and so on. (Ahmed and Blustein 2005). Spatial ability is recognized as an important human skill set relevant to evaluating effectiveness in learning, training, working, and even playing (Rafi et al. 2005).

S.G. Mazman (✉) • A. Altun
Department of Computer Education and Instructional Technologies,
Hacettepe University, Ankara, Turkey
e-mail: s.guzin@gmail.com; altunar@gmail.com

P. Isaias et al. (eds.), *Towards Learning and Instruction in Web 3.0: Advances in Cognitive and Educational Psychology*, DOI 10.1007/978-1-4614-1539-8_14,
231

In prior research, spatial ability is found to affect Web navigation (Ahmed and Blustein 2005; Juvina and van Oostendorp 2006), mobile learning design (Li et al. 2009), and the utilization of visual cues in Web-based environments (Castelli et al. 2008; Pilgrim 2007). When measuring individual differences in spatial ability, researchers have chosen mental rotation tasks as one of the most important ones to yield strong between-person differences (Terlecki and Newcombe 2005; Collins 2010). Mental rotation is defined as the ability to quickly and accurately rotate two- or three-dimensional objects in one's mind and the ability to manipulate complex spatial information through several and sequential stages in order to arrive at a correct solution to a spatial orientation problem (Samsudin and smail 2004; Shepard and Metzler 1971). Khooshabeh and Hegarty (2010) stated that mental rotation measures a component of spatial thinking that involves imagining the movement of objects external to our bodies. It is a visual-spatial process in which mental images are represented and transformed in a visual buffer (Khooshabeh and Hegarty 2010; Kosslyn et al. 2006).

1.1 Mental Rotation Ability (MRA) as an Individual Difference

Mental rotation is one of the most important spatial abilities that produce significant individual differences (Rafi et al. 2005; Turos and Ervin 2000). In previous studies, mental rotation ability is taken as an individual difference and is investigated how it affects task performance (Juvina and van Oostendorp 2006), reaction times (Dahlback et al. 1996), problem solving strategies (Baran et al. 2007) information manipulation and visual attention (Glück et al. 2002; Just and Carpenter 1985; Kozhevnikov et al. 2005; Li et al. 2009). In addition, in various brain/behavior studies, mental rotation ability has been examined as an individual difference that affects individuals' performance in many intellectual endeavors (Barke and Engida 2001; Olkun 2003; Rizzo et al. 1998). Consequently, the mental rotation ability was emphasized as a significant predictor of success in the ability of human computer interaction (Quaiser-Pohl et al. 2006).

People with high level MRA (mental rotation ability) are reported not distracted by irrelevant visual cues with a tendency to have schematic mental images without much visual detail (Khooshabeh and Hegarty 2010). High MRA individuals can construct schematic spatial representations of figures that include metric information about their shapes but not visual details (Kozhevnikov et al. 2005), and, as a consequence, they have more economical mental code to represent a figure that permits faster execution of the rotation and comparison (Just and Carpenter 1985). On the other hand, low level MRA individuals are more likely to be affected by visual cues and, as a consequence, they encode more visual details in their mental images (Khooshabeh and Hegarty 2010); they construct more detailed representations of these figures that include both metric shape information and distinct visual cues not pertinent to a mental rotation task (Kozhevnikov et al. 2005).

1.2   Eye Movements in the Mental Rotation Process

Eye movement data is increasingly being employed to provide real-time measures and information about cognitive processing (Just and Carpenter 1976; Rayner 1998). De'Sperati (2003) cautions researchers that using reaction time in mental rotation tasks cannot expose directly the continuous spatio-temporal evaluation of mental processes since reaction time have been instrumental in characterizing a number of mental processes and sub-processes. However, it is suggested that eyes provide a window into mental life and eye movements are on-line measures of cognitive processes in general (De'Sperati 2003; Nakatani and Pollatsek 2004). De'Sperati (2003) stated that eye movements might indeed contain the amount of information that reaction time lack, as they seem to have the characteristics to continuously track both in space and time the evolution of mental events, especially those with a significant visual-spatial content. Yet, some researchers still believe that the number of studies in which mental rotation effects have been investigated using eye movement metrics is insufficient (i.e., Nakatani and Pollatsek 2004).

In an early eye-tracking study, Carpenter and Just (1978) asked participants to decide whether two objects presented in different orientations were the same or mirror-copies while recording their eye movements concurrently. They found that fixations tended to concentrate on those parts of stimuli that were presumably more informative to solve the task. In another study, Just and Carpenter (1985) recorded eye movement of individuals in a problem solving activity that had been based on rotating geometric cubes. Fixation and gaze duration data showed that people with low level mental rotation ability took longer time to rotate objects since their rotation rates were slower and of slower rotation angel because they are less efficient at mentally keeping track of their work in more demanding problems. Baran et al. (2007) investigated how people solved tangram-based geometry problems which include mental rotation ability, by recording their eye movements while they are solving problems on the computer screen. Analyzing the eye fixation duration, eye fixation count, task completion duration and transition numbers showed that participants tended to choose different strategies while solving problems with different difficulty levels. In another eye-tracking mental rotation process study, Khooshabeh and Hegarty (2010) investigated the format of mental representation of 3-D shapes during mental rotation by combination of eye tracking and verbal protocol analysis. In eye-tracking analysis, they defined Areas of Interests (AOI) that circumscribed the figures and compared the number of consecutive fixations made within each figure to the number of saccades made between the two figures to determine strategy. They found that poor and good mental rotators use different strategies in mental rotation performance.

To conclude, eye movement metrics can be used to understand some cognitive processes and to determine an individual's cognitive profile with regard to mental rotation ability. Secondly, these metrics can be extended to infer strategy use and mental rotation success among participants. However, it is not clear how individuals vary when the task difficulty levels are diverse.

1.3 Purpose of Study

This study aimed to examine whether the cognitive processes differ across different MRA levels during performing a mental rotation task. The eye movement metrics measured in this study are the fixation length, fixation count, and time to first fixation. In addition, completion times are examined across different MRA levels with differing levels of problems. Thus, the research questions are:

1. Is there a significant difference in completion time of tangram problems across different MRA levels?
2. Do the eye movement metrics differ across different MRA levels during tangram problem solving?

   (a) Do the eye movement metrics at the easy level tangram problem differ across different MRA levels?
   (b) Do the eye movement metrics at the difficult level tangram problem differ across different MRA levels?

2 Method

2.1 Study Group

In to determine the MRA levels, a mental rotation test was administered to 26 undergraduate students attending the Psychological Counseling and Guidance Department and 30 undergraduate students studying at the Computer Education and Instructional Technologies Department at Hacettepe University. Out of 24, maximum mental rotation score was found 13, and the minimum score was 1. Considering the results for this particular group of students, the group ranges between low and medium levels at their mental rotation ability. According to their mental rotation test scores, students were grouped in two levels: Low and High Mental Rotation Levels.

Considering the screened data, a total of 14 undergraduate students, ten from the Psychological Counseling and Guidance Department and four from Computer Education and Instructional Technologies Department were nominated and seven students from each mental rotation level ($\overline{X}$ =8.14 sd=2.4 for High Level; and $\overline{X}$ =3.3 sd=1.5 for Low Level) were invited to participate in the study. Since gender is reported being the most influential variable in mental rotation ability (Vandenberg and Kuse 1978; Linn and Petersen 1985), all the participants were selected among females to fix the gender effect.

2.2   Data Collection Tools

In this study, mental rotation test, digital tangram problems and Tobii T120 eye tracker were used to collect data.

Mental Rotation Test: The Paper-pencil Mental Rotation Test, developed originally by Vandenberg and Kuse (1978) and updated by Peters and colleagues (1995) redrawing figures, was used to measure mental rotation ability. This test consists of 24 multiple choice questions made up of three dimensional block figures. Each question includes a target figure on the left side and four response choices of equal size displayed on the right side. The response choices are composed of two drawings of the identical object as the target figure but rotated in a position and two distracter drawings that are either different in structure or mirror images of the target. One point is given for answers if both of the selected choices are correct but none if one is correct and other is wrong or if both are incorrect. The maximum score for this test was 24. The test is presented in 2 sets of 12 items each with a 3-min time limit for each set (totally 6 min).

Digital Tangram Problems: Tangram is a kind of moving piece puzzle, consisting of seven geometric shapes that can be assembled in different ways to create more elaborated shapes game which includes geometric pieces that can be assembled in different ways to create more elaborated shapes (Jovanovic et al. 2009). Tangrams are generally valued to as well as including rotation, comparison, placement and transformation activities and also improving individual problem solving skills, analytical thinking, geometry abilities, spatial thinking, spatial visualization, spatial reasoning and mental rotation (Baran et al. 2007; NCTM 2003; Olkun et al. 2005; Vighi 2007).

There have been two fields used in tangram problems: a problem solution field and a pieces field. Individuals are asked to recreate the target shape on the solution field using seven pieces which are different sized and shaped, either rotating them or not.

In this study, two digital tangram problems with different difficulty levels (easy and difficult) were used. Problem solution field and pieces field are determined as the two different Areas of interest (AOI) and analysis were executed separately for these two fields. Easy level tangram problem and difficult level tangram problem are shown in Fig. 14.1.

Area of Interest of problem solution field and pieces field are shown in Fig. 14.2.

Eye Tracker: Eye movement data was recorded by Tobii T120 Eye tracker, which was integrated within the panels of the monitor. The tracking system had a 120 Hz sampling rate and an accuracy of 0.5°. Participants solved tangram problems on a computer with the eye tracker. Eye movement metrics data as fixation length, fixation count and time to first fixation was obtained from eye tracker. These are the most common eye tracking metrics which are used in studies and defined as below (Oneupweb 2010);

Fixation length is the amount of the time that a particular element of a design is viewed. This may reflect the importance of that element to the user, or indicate that she or he is having difficulty extracting information.

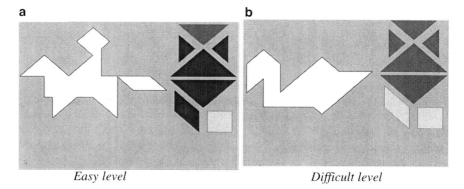

Fig. 14.1 Easy level and difficult level tangram problems

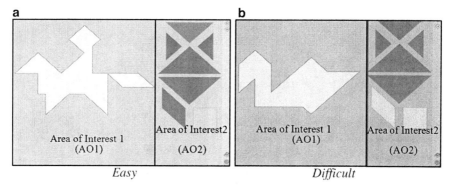

Fig. 14.2 Area of interest of problem solution field and pieces field for easy and difficult tangram problems

Fixation count is the time (individual or collective) that eyes are focused on a particular location.

Time to first fixation provides insight regarding which Areas of Interest (AOI) or element in a design attracts attention first. It can help measure how long it takes before a user finds a specific link, text or image.

2.3 Data Analysis

In data analysis, Mann Whitney U test which is a non parametric test for small sample sizes (Sheskin 1997) was executed to observe the differences between people with high level MRA and people with low level MRA in terms of their eye movement metrics during the tangram solution process.

3   Findings

3.1   Completion Time Across Different Mental Rotation Ability Groups

Difference of completion time for easy and difficult level tangram problems across different MRA groups was investigated by Mann Whitney U Test and results are presented in Table 14.1.

High level mental rotation ability group solved both of the easy and difficult level tangram problems quicker than low level counterparts. However difference is found to be significant for only easy level tangram problem ($U=8.00$, $n_1=n_2=7$, $p=.038$) but not for the difficult level ($U=13.00$, $n_1=n_2=7$, $p=.165$).

3.2   Eye Movements Across Different MRA Levels During Tangram Problem Solving

3.2.1   Differences Across Different MRA Levels in Easy Level Tangram Problem

Differences in eye movement metrics on the problem solution and piece fields at easy level tangram problem between high level and low level MRA groups was analyzed by Mann Whitney U test and results are presented in Table 14.2.

A significant difference was found on the problem solution field in easy level tangram problem between high and low level groups in terms of their eye movement metrics (time to first fixation, fixation length and fixation count). While time to first fixation on the problem solution field was found significantly higher for high level group, fixation count and fixation length on problem solution field were found significantly lower for high level group.

As participants viewed the problem field more frequently and longer, there were no significant differences between groups in terms of their eye movements on the pieces field for easy level tangram problem. Moreover, the analyses of AOI also showed that participants mostly focused on problem solution field and viewed this

Table 14.1 Mann Whitney U test result of completion time of tangram problems for different MRA groups

Difficulty level	Mental rotation ability level	N	Mean rank	Sum of rank.	U	p (<.05)
Easy	Low level group	7	9.86	69	8.00	.038
	High level group	7	5.14	36		
Difficult	Low level group	7	9.14	64	13.00	.165
	High level group	7	5.86	41		

Table 14.2 Mann Whitney U test results of easy level tangram problem

Eye movement metrics	Area of interest (AOI)	Mental rotation ability	N	Mean rank	Sum of rank	U	p
Time to first fixation	Problem solution field	Low level group	7	4.43	31.00	3.0	.004*
		High level group	7	10.57	74.00		
	Pieces field	Low level group	7	6.36	44.50	16.5	.318
		High level group	7	8.64	60.50		
Fixation length	Problem solution field	Low level group	7	10.43	73.00	4.0	.007*
		High level group	7	4.57	32.00		
	Pieces field	Low level group	7	9.57	67.00	10.0	.073
		High level group	7	5.43	38.00		
Fixation count	Problem solution field	Low level group	7	10.43	73.00	4.0	.007*
		High level group	7	4.57	32.00		
	Pieces field	Low level group	7	9.57	67.00	10.0	.73
		High level group	7	5.43	38.00		

*$p < 0.05$

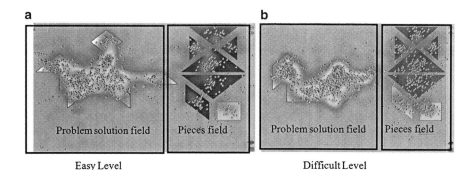

a   b

Problem solution field | Pieces field   Problem solution field | Pieces field

Easy Level   Difficult Level

Fig. 14.3 Heatmaps of easy level and difficult level tangram

field longer than the pieces field. In addition, it has been revealed out that they heavily focused on and viewed larger fields on figures in the in problem solution fields. Heat map graphics for easy level and difficult level tangram problems according to AOIs (problem solution field and pieces field) are presented in Fig. 14.3.

3.2.2 Differences Across Different MRA Levels in Difficult Level Tangram Problem

Eye movement differences on the problem solution field and piece field in difficult level tangram problem between high level and low level MRA groups were analyzed by Mann Whitney U test and results are presented in Table 14.3.

No significant difference was found between high level and low level MRA groups in terms of their eye movement metrics both in the problem solution field

Table 14.3 Mann Whitney U test results for difficult level tangram problem

Eye movement metrics	Area of interest (AOI)	Mental rotation ability	N	Mean rank	Sum of rank	U	p
Time to first fixation	Problem solution field	Low level group	7	8.71	61.00	16.0	.318
		High level group	7	6.29	44.00		
	Pieces field	Low level group	7	7.57	53.00	24.0	1.00
		High level group	7	7.43	52.00		
Fixation length	Problem solution field	Low level group	7	9.29	65.00	12.0	.128
		High level group	7	5.71	40.00		
	Pieces field	Low level group	7	8.57	33.00	17.0	.383
		High level group	7	6.43	22.00		
Fixation count	Problem solution field	Low level group	7	9.14	64.00	13.0	.165
		High level group	7	5.86	41.00		
	Pieces field	Low level group	7	8.07	568.5	20.5	.620
		High level group	7	6.93	48.50		

and pieces field in the difficult level tangram problem. However, three of the eye movement metrics (time to first fixation, fixation length and fixation count) of low level MRA group on the fields were found lower than the high level MRA group.

4 Conclusion

This study explored the differences between different MRA groups in their cognitive processes across different difficulty level mental rotation tasks using digital tangrams. Digital tangram problems are selected because they require mental rotation processes. Similar to previous studies, digital tangrams, pentominoes and other puzzle like geometric piece games were considered related to spatial abilities and pertinent to mental processes such as selecting, rotating, translating, flipping, mirroring and landing pieces (Baran et al. 2007; Olkun et al. 2005; Yang and Chen 2010).

The initial analysis indicated that participants' mental rotation scores were found to be between 1 and 13 out of 24, which can be interpreted as low. Remember that, all participants were female in groups and various research in the literature clearly revealed out that females generally had low or lower mental rotation ability than male counterparts (Linn and Petersen 1985; Terlecki and Newcombe 2005; Turos and Ervin 2000; Yang and Chen 2010).

Relatively higher level MRA group ($\overline{X}$ =8.6, sd=2.7) solved both of the easy and difficult level tangram problems in a shorter time than lower level MRA group ($\overline{X}$ =3, sd=1.58). This finding is in line with Just and Carpenter's (1985) previous study that shows people with low level MRA rotate objects in longer time because their rotation rates are slower and they spend more mental effort at keeping track of their work in more demanding problems. However, difference in completion time was found to be significant only in easy tangram problem but not in the difficult one. Since the study group had a low mental rotation ability profile, it was not surprising that no significant difference was found for difficult level tangram problem. We can speculate that studying with a higher level mental rotation ability profile group would reveal out differences at difficult level mental rotation tasks.

Eye movements differed for the groups only on the problem solution field but not on the pieces field in easy tangram problem. However, as represented in the heat map visualization tool, problem solution fields were viewed more heavily and participants took longer time in this field compared to the pieces field in both of the tangram problems. So, it can be stated that participants scanned the pieces field only for choosing the appropriate piece and don't fixate for a long time. On the other side, they mostly perform all the mental activities such as rotating, placing, decision making on the problem solution field and they fixate longer than on the problem solution field.

Fixation count and fixation length were found to being significantly lower in high level MRA group than low level group for easy tangram problem. Similarly, this finding is in line with other research in that longer fixation length and more fixation count indicate that people have more difficulty and complexity during the process and also spend more time and effort on the focused work (Cowen 2001; Just and Carpenter 1976; Poole and Ball 2005).

In contrast to fixation count and fixation length, time to first fixation was found significantly lower in low level MRA group. However, time to first fixation provides only insight regarding which AOI or element in a design attracts attention first and it could not be related with MRA or the task performance (Byrne et al. 1999; OneupWeb 2010). However it was expected to find that, individual with high level mental rotation ability has significantly lower fixation count, fixation length and time to first fixation than individuals with low level mental rotation ability, difference was found not to be significant neither in problem solution field nor in pieces field in terms of eye movements for difficult level tangram problem.

5 Future Work

This study contributed to determine the differences of cognitive processes in mental rotation tasks across different MRA level groups using the digital Tangram problem. In further research, eye movements as an indicator of cognitive processes can be investigated in different environments which require mental rotation use as different software or programs alternative to digital tangram, navigation in 3-D environments, task performance on different designed sites, information seeking behavior in hypermedia, direction/location finding on interactive electronic maps etc. Since the spatial ability is an important predictor of task performance and completion time, in further researches some adaptive learning environment should be designed to compensate for low MRA.

In previous studies, also problem solving strategies were determined by eye movements in different difficulty level questions (Baran et al. 2007), it's relation with the mental rotation ability have not been investigated. So in future works, the strategies of different level mental rotation ability groups in different level mental rotation tasks could be investigated.

This study investigated the differences between groups for two level tangram problems; yet, the differences within groups were not examined. In further studies, differences in eye movements, completion time or the task performance could be examined within groups across different level problems to determine the effects of difficulty levels on groups.

References

Ahmed, I. & Blustein, J. (2005). Navigation in information space: How does spatial ability play a part? *Proceedings of Web Based Communities (IADIS)*, Algarve, Portugal.

Baran, B., Doğusoy, B. & Çağıltay, K. (2007). How do adults solve digital tangram problems? Analyzing cognitive strategies through eye tracking approach. In: Jacko, J.A. (ed.) *HCI 2007*. LNCS, 45(52). 555–563. Dordrecht: Springer.

Barke, H.D. & Engida, T. (2001). Structural chemistry and spatial ability in different cultures. *Chemistry Education: Research and Practice in Europe*, 2, 227–239. [http://www.uoi.gr/conf_sem/cerapie].

Byrne, M. D., Anderson, J. R., Douglas, S. & Matessa, M. (1999). Eye tracking the visual search of clickdown menus. *Proceedings of CHI'99*. 402–409. New York: ACM Press.

Carpenter, P. A. & Just, M. A. (1978). Eye fixations during mental rotation. In J. W. Senders, D. F. Fisher, & R. A. Monty (Eds.), *Eye movements and the higher psychological functions*. 115–133. Hillsdale, NJ: Erlbaum.

Castelli, L., Corazzini, L.L. & Geminiani, G.C. (2008). Spatial navigation in large-scale virtual environmental: Gender differences in survey tasks. *Computers in Human Behavior*, 24, 1643–1667.

Chen, C., Czerwinski, M. & Macredie, R. (2000). Individual Differences in Virtual Environments: Introduction and overview. *Journal of the American Society for Information Science*, 51(6), 499–507.

Collins, J. (2010). Mental Rotation. Online Psychology Laboratory. Retrieved from http://opl.apa.org/ on 5 December 2010.

Cowen, L. (2001). An eye movement analysis of web-page usability. Unpublished Masters' thesis, Lancaster University, Lancaster, UK.

De'Sperati, C. (2003). The inner working of dynamic visuo-spatial imagery as revealed by spontaneous eye movements. In *The mind's eye: Cognitive and applied aspects of eye movement research*. 119–142. Amsterdam: Elsevier Science.

Dahlback. N., Hook. K. & Sjolinder, M. (1996), Spatial cognition in the mind and in the world: The case of hypermedia navigation. *Proceedings of the 18th annual meeting of the Cognitive Science Society*. San Diego.

Glück, J., Machat, R., Jirasko, M. and Rollett. B. (2002). Training-related changes in solution strategy in a spatial test: An application of item response models. *Learning and Individual Differences*, 13, 1–22.

Jovanovic, J., Gašević, D. & Devedžić, V. (2009). Tangram for Personalized Learning Using the Semantic Web Technologies. *Journal of Emerging Technologies in Web Intelligence*, 1(1), 6–21.

Just, M. A. & Carpenter, P. A. (1976). Eye fixations and cognitive processes. *Cognitive Psychology*, 8, 441–480.

Just, M. A. & Carpenter, P. A. (1985). Cognitive Coordinate Systems: Accounts of Mental Rotation and Individual Differences in Spatial Ability. *Psychological Review*. 92(2). 137–172.

Juvina, I. & van Oostendorp, H. (2006). Individual differences and behavioral metrics involved in modeling Web navigation. *Universal Access in Information Society.* 258–269. Dordrecht:, Springer.

Khooshabeh, P. & Hegarty, H. (2010). Representations of Shape during Mental Rotation. *Association for the Advancement of Artificial, Intelligence. AAAI* 2010 Spring Symposium.

Kosslyn, S. M., Thompson, W. L. & Ganis, G. (2006). The case for mental imagery. New York, Oxford.

Kozhevnikov, M., Kosslyn, S. & Shephard, J. (2005).Spatial versus object visualizers: a new characterization of visual cognitive style. *Memory and Cognition,* 33(4), 710–26.

Li, L., Ryu, H. & Parsons, D. (2009). The Influence Of Spatial Working Memory on Mobile Learning Content Design. *Mobile Learning 2009.*

Linn, M. & Petersen, A. (1985). Emergence and characterization of sex differences in spatial ability: A meta-analysis. *Child Development,* 56, 1479–1498.

Lohman, D. F. (1993). Spatial ability and *g. Paper presented at the first Spearman Seminar,* University of Plymouth.

Nakatani, C. & Pollatsek, A. (2004). An eye movement analysis of "mental rotation" of simple scenes. *Perception & Psychophysics.* 66(7). 1227–1245.

National Council of Teacher's Mathematics (NCTM). 2003. Developing geometry understandings and spatial skills through puzzlelike problems with tangrams: Tangram challenges. www.nctm. org.

Olkun, S. (2003). Making Connections: Improving Spatial Abilities with Engineering Drawing Activities. *International Journal of Mathematics Teaching and Learning.* http://www.ex.ac.uk/ cimt/ijmtl/ijabout.htm.

Olkun, S., Altun, A., & Smith, G. (2005). Computers and 2D geometric learning of Turkish fourth and fifth graders. *British Journal of Educational Technology,* 36(2), 317–326.

Oneupweb, (2010). Oneupweb Eye Tracking. Glossary. http://eyetracking.oneupweb.com/ resources/glossary/.

Peters, M., et.al. (1995). A redrawn Vandenberg and Kuse mental rotations test: different versions and factors that affect performance. *Brain and Cognition,* 28, 39–58.

Pilgrim, C. J. (2007). The influence of spatial ability on the use of web sitemaps. *Proceedings of the 19th Australasian conference on Computer-Human Interaction: Entertaining User Interfaces,* 251, 77–82.

Poole, A. and Ball, L.J.(2005). Eye tracking in human-computer interaction and usability research: current status and future prospects. In: Ghaoui C, ed. *Encyclopedia of Human-Computer Interaction.*

Quaiser-Pohl, C., Geiser, C. & Lehmann, W. (2006). The relationship between computer-game preference, gender, and mental-rotation ability. *Personality and Individual Differences,* 40, 609–619.

Rafi, A. et al. (2005). Improving spatial ability using a Web-based Virtual Environment (WbVE). *Automation in Construction.* 14, 707–715.

Rayner, K. (1978). Eye Movements in Reading and Information Processing. *Psychological Bulletin.* 85(3). 618–660.

Rizzo, A.A., et al. (1998). Preliminary findings on a virtual environment targeting human mental rotation/spatial abilities. *Proceedings of 2nd European Conference on Disability, Virtual Reality and Associated Techniques,* 213–220.

Samsudin, K.A & Ismail, A. (2004). The Improvement of Mental Rotation through Computer Based Multimedia Tutor. *Malaysian Online Journal of Instructional Technology (MOJIT),* 1(2). 24–34.

Shepard, R. N. & Metzler, J. (1971). Mental rotation of three-dimensional objects. *Science,* 171, 701–703.

Sheskin D.(1997). *Handbook of Parametric and Nonparametric Statistical Procedures.* New York, CRC Press LLC.

Tartre, L. A. (1990). Spatial Orientation Skill and Mathematical Problem Solving. *Journal for Research in Mathematics Education,* 21(3), 216–229.

Terlecki, M. S. & Newcombe, N. S. (2005). How Important Is the Digital Divide? The Relation of Computer and Videogame Usage to Gender Differences in Mental Rotation Ability. *Sex Roles*, 53, 5(6).

Turos, J. & Ervin. A. (2000). Training and gender differences on a web-based mental rotation task. *The Penn State Behrend Psychology Journal*, 4(2), 3–12.

Vandenberg, S. G. & Kuse, A. R. (1978). Mental rotation groups test of three-dimensional spatial visualization. *Perceptual and Motor Skills*, 47, 599–604.

Vicente, K. J. & Williges, R. C. (1988). Accommodating individual differences in searching a hierarchical file system. *International Journal of Man-Machine Studies*, 29, 647–668.

Vighi, P. (2007). Computer Geometry as Mediator of Mathematical Concepts. *CERME 5 Working Group 7 Final Report*. Local Research Unit into Mathematics Education, Parma University. http://ermeweb.free.fr/Cerme5.pdf.

Yang, V. J. and Chen, S. Y. (2010). Effects of gender differences and spatial abilities within a digital pentominoes game. *Computers & Education*, 55(3), 1220–1233.

Part V
Exploratory Technologies

Chapter 15
Supporting Motivation Based Educational Games Through Web 3.0

Ioana Ghergulescu and Cristina Hava Muntean

1 Introduction

The exponential technological advances over the last decade have gradually brought us in the digital era. At the same time the Web evolved from static webpages hyperlinked between them to a Web where the amount of information increased substantially and the information is published by users as well. Bringing Web 2.0 technologies, the Web has evolved towards blogging, podcasting, social bookmarking, social networking, tagging, etc. Intensive research is currently done towards incorporating Web 3.0 technologies. Web 3.0 will support a smarter, unified, personalised and semantic-based Web environment. Semantic Web involves describing data/information through metadata. The web application uses metadata in order to exchange, reuse, integrate and link existing data providing personalised content and services.

However, not only the technology has evolved, but also the learners have changed from "Digital Natives" and "Digital Immigrants" (Prensky 2001a, b) to a "Digital Wisdom" generation (Prensky 2009). Being a "Digital Wisdom" means not only using and manipulating technology easily but also making wiser decisions because "one is enhanced by technology". The technology enhances our thinking and understanding every day.

These technological developments have also partly contributed to the significant progress that has been made in the area of e-learning. E-learning environments for instance, have evolved over the past years towards adaptive e-learning systems that make use of the learner's preferences, knowledge, goals in order to adapt the delivered content. Furthermore, e-learning is continuously evolving, looking forward to new features and ideas to improve the learning process and the learning experience (Kahiigi et al. 2008). Research efforts are made to incorporate Web 3.0 into e-learning and to represent the education information through metadata.

I. Ghergulescu (✉) • C.H. Muntean
National College of Ireland, School of Computing, Mayor Street, IFSC, Dublin 1, Ireland
e-mail: ioana.ghergulescu@student.ncirl.ie; cmuntean@ncirl.ie

P. Isaias et al. (eds.), *Towards Learning and Instruction in Web 3.0: Advances in Cognitive and Educational Psychology*, DOI 10.1007/978-1-4614-1539-8_15,
© Springer Science+Business Media, LLC 2012

Despite the significant technological advances, reaching and engaging today's learners are still considered challenging tasks (Little and Page 2009), while the learning process may be considered by the students to be boring and forced. Therefore, keeping students motivated for the entire learning period continues to represent a challenge, not only in the e-learning, but in all forms of learning. However, traditional face-to-face learning involves a teacher having direct contact with the students, thus being able to analyse the whole learner's behaviour. For example, learner speaking tone and behaviour cues can be analysed in the traditional face to face learning but not in the e-learning environment that does not involve direct contact with the learner.

Meanwhile, educational games not only that proved to be effective learning environments (Gee 2003), but they can also motivate the player by bringing a layer of emotional content on top of instructional content (Berger and Müller 2009). Learning through game is not just knowing and doing. A game brings together ways of knowing, ways of doing, ways of being and ways of caring (Shaffer et al. 2005). However, despite that the gaming community has recognised the importance of emotion in creating more engaging games, current games are still lacking in integrating learner affectiveness and interaction of the non player characters with the player (Hudlicka 2009). In this context, there is a need for affective games engines, for facilitating recognition of player emotion and motivation in real time, and to generate affective adaptation to these emotions (e.g. reward adaptation, adequately response from game characters to emotions) (Hudlicka 2009).

The importance of emotion and motivation is even higher for the educational games in particular. Research has investigated the possibility to extend PlayLearn (Ghergulescu and Muntean 2009), a component that provides support for playing educational games as part of Adaptive e-Learning Systems (AeLS), with a motivation based game level adaptation mechanism (Ghergulescu and Muntean 2010).

However, as compared to measuring learner motivation in e-learning, significantly less research was conducted in order to assess and predict the player motivation in gaming. This chapter addresses the challenge of measuring and assessing learner motivation in educational games. Furthermore, the chapter illustrates how the learner motivation level can be expressed through Web 3.0 technologies.

The remaining of the chapter is structured as follows. Section 2 presents research and current trends in learner motivation assessment, educational games as well Web 3.0 based e-learning and educational games. Section 3 proposes a solution for measuring and assessing learner motivation in educational games. Furthermore, Sect. 3 presents how the motivational level can be expressed through Web 3.0 using metadata, while the last section concludes the chapter.

2 State of the Art

The research presented in this chapter falls in the following two areas: learner motivation and educational games. The latest research work in these areas is presented next. Furthermore, the introduction of Web 3.0 technologies in the two areas is presented.

2.1 Motivation

Motivation plays a significant role in the success of the learning process in general and of the educational games in particular. At the same time, motivation is a driving agent behind both participation and progression in the gaming environments (Konetes 2010). According to De Vicente and Pain (2002) the ability to detect students' motivational state during an instructional interaction can bring many benefits to the success of an AeLS. Therefore, various motivation-based solutions have been proposed in e-learning. In the same context, Hudlicka (2009) argued the need for having affective game engines not only in educational games, but also in games in general. The researchers have approached this need by introducing a motivational agent to non-player characters (Hudlicka and Broekens 2009; Merrick 2007). Various research works on defining and quantifying motivation in general are presented next. Measuring and assessing motivation in e-learning is also discussed.

2.1.1 Theories of Motivation

What do we mean by motivation? The literature regarding this term is enormous. Motivation represents a fuzzy concept, a concept that involves human's emotions, human's thought, human's believes. Motivation also represents a psychological attribute described as the energy to achieve a goal, to initiate and to sustain participation (Bandura 1994; Ryan and Deci 2000). In the learning context, motivation is referred as the energy to accomplish the goal of knowledge achievement, to initiate, and to maintain participation in the learning process.

The two most well known self-theories of motivation are presented next: self-efficacy and self-determination theories.

Self-Efficacy Theory

According to Bandura's (1994) self-efficacy theory of motivation, a person must have believes that (s)/he is capable of solving, executing and pursuing a task.

Self-efficacy represents the person's belief, self-perception of their capabilities of executing the task at a certain level of performance. It influences people actions and beliefs. Self-efficacy influences the commitment with the task, the amount of effort, the engrossment, the perception of the difficulty level, the time they recover their sense of efficacy after failure. The higher the self-efficacy is, the stronger the commitment and the engrossment are, while at the same time, the higher the speed of recovery of their sense of efficacy after failure is. Self-belief of efficacy makes people to set for themselves challenging goals and to make action plans, in this way people developing strong perseverance (Bandura 1994).

Fig. 15.1 Self determination continuum types of motivation

Self-Determination Theory

Ryan and Deci presented the self-determination theory as a new approach to human motivation and personality. According to Ryan and Deci (2000), motivation concerns the energy, the persistence, and the direction that a person is taking in his/her activities. Ryan and Deci argued that motivation is more important in real world then it is in psychology because of its consequence: motivation produces. Motivation is often treated as a singular construct, but looking closer, motivation is a quintessence of more complex constructs.

Ryan and Deci (2000) have also presented different types of self-motivation: from amotivation, to intrinsic motivation towards extrinsic motivation (see Fig. 15.1).

Amotivation represents the inability to act, or acting without intent. Amotivation results from not valuing an activity or not feeling competent. Extrinsic motivation refers to motivation in performing an activity that comes from external factors, such as rewards, money, grades that contribute to individual satisfaction that is not directly given by the activity itself. Intrinsic motivation refers to the motivation that comes from inside the individual, the pleasure and satisfaction of doing that particular activity. It reflects the human tendency to seek out novelty and challenges, to exercise capabilities, to explore and to learn.

Various motivational design models were developed and used during last decade. Among these, Keller's ARCS Model (Keller 1987), Wlodkowski's Time Continuum Model of Motivation (Wlodkowski 1978) and Malone & Lepper's Taxonomy of Intrinsic Motivation for Learning (Malone and Lepper 1987) are the most used ones.

2.1.2 Motivation in e-Learning

Since motivation represents an important factor for learning, many e-learning systems try to reach and engage learners by providing them with instructional content that motivates them. The ability to detect student's motivational state during the interaction with an e-learning system can bring many benefits to the learning process.

Table 15.1 and Table 15.2 summarise various research work on measuring and assessing motivation in e-learning. Motivation indicators, metrics used, the type of motivation measurement performed and the assessment type are presented.

The learner motivation is expressed as a standalone attribute or as a combination of motivational indicators. Various motivation indicators were assessed such as: engagement, confidence, effort, importance, expectation, attention, confusion, challenge, etc.

Various metrics are used for motivation measurement. The metrics measured include: reading time of an educational material, time taken to do quizzes/surveys, time taken to solve an exercise, number of pages read, etc. The majority of the metrics represents information about the learner interaction with the learning system. However, the majority of these metrics are system dependent or learning material depended.

The information is gathered by the e-learning system through direct interaction with the learner (e.g. questionnaire, dialog), through data analysis (e.g. log files analysis), and/or by using additional equipment (e.g. eye tracker, heart monitor, etc.).

Furthermore, learner motivation was calculated using direct computation (e.g. fuzzy logic functions, formulas) or prediction.

2.2 Educational Games

Educational games are proved to be effective learning environments (Gee 2003), but they can also motivate the players by bringing a layer of emotional content on top of instructional content (Berger and Müller 2009). Educational games clearly improve students' learning performance (Chuang and Chen 2009; Can and Cagiltay 2006), increase their motivation (Batson and Feinberg 2006), and make knowledge acquisition and at the same time knowledge assessment a more transparent process.

However, the area of educational games is not matured and challenges have to be overcome. Several approaches for measurement and assessment of player emotion and motivation are presented next.

Rebolledo-Mendez et al. (2009) have presented a motivation model based on empathy for artificial intelligence driven avatars in virtual worlds. This approach could be further incorporated in educational games based virtual worlds. The aim is to provide an avatar in the virtual world with the capability of coaching in various learning situations. The motivational model is based upon the concept of shared intentionality. In their investigation, motivation was defined as the effort spent by avatars in a virtual space. Motivation was calculated as a combination of the persistence, the competence and the help needed by the learner. Each of these three components represents a binary variable. Persistence is predicted based on actions, while the other two variables are computed analysing the player believes. However, this represents a new direction for virtual worlds and has not been implemented and tested yet.

Probabilistic models that assess student emotional reaction during interaction with an educational game were also investigated (Conati and Zhou 2002). The student

Table 15.1 Previous research on measuring motivation in e-learning

Research	Motivation indicators	Metrics measured	Measurement type	Assessment type
de Vicente and Pain (2002), de Vicente (2003)	Control, challenge, independency, fantasy, confidence, sensory interest, cognitive interest, effort, satisfaction	Student's response, student's actions, time to study a lesson, percentage of attempts, answer corectesness	Direct interaction (dialog, questionnaire)	Rule inference,
Beck (2004)	Engagement	Response time to a question, answer correctness	Log files based analysis	Item response time-prediction
Qu and Johnson (2005), Qu et al. (2005)	Confidence, confusion, effort	Time to perform a task, reading time, number of finished tasks, number of extra tasks taken, time taken to decide to perform a task	Log files based analysis, eye tracking analysis	Prediction model
Johns and Woolf (2006)	Motivation	First response time. number of hint requests	Log files based analysis	Direct computation
Arroyo et al. (2007)	Engagement, motivation	Time spent per solving a problem, help requests	Log based analysis, direct interaction (questionnaire, dialog)	Direct computation
Kim et al. (2007)	Confidence, effort	Question's response, help request, number of activities, time spent on task	Direct interaction (dialog), log file based analysis	Direct computation
McQuiggan et al. (2008)	Self-efficacy	Response time to a question. time in the "learning location", time on "learning goal", "location in the learning material", learning progression, heart rate, galvanic skin response	Log files based analysis, psychological response	Prediction

Table 15.2 Previous research on measuring motivation in e-learning

Research	Motivation indicators	Metrics measured	Measurement type	Assessment type
Takemura et al. (2008)	Importance, expectation	Linkert scale answers	Interaction (questionnaire)	Direct computation
Cocea and Weibelzahl (2009), in press	Engagement	Number of read pages, time spent on reading pages, number of tests/quizzes taken, time spent on solving test/quizzes	Log files based analysis, direct interaction (questionnaire)	Prediction
Costagliola et al. (2010)	Attention	Face posture, time spent for reading, time spent for scrolling, mouse events (e.g. number of clicks, clicking time, time moving cursor), learner message	Log files based analysis	Direct computation
Khan et al. (2009a, b, 2010)	Confidence, confusion, independence, effort	Time spent reading, solving exercise time, number of incorrect answers, number of solved exercise, help hint, number of attempts	Log files based analysis	Direct computation
Woolf et al. (2010)	Confidence, frustration, interest, excitement, help request	Learner's self-report, time between hints requests, number of hints requests	Log based analyses, direct interaction (questionnaire, dialog)	Direct computation
Munoz-Organero et al. (2010)	Motivation	Number of hints, learner actions (e.g. upload photo, learner participation in forums), time variation of total time per week	Log files based analysis	Prediction

emotional state was predicted by assessing the student interaction with the Prime Climb, an educational game for teaching number factorization, and by considering student's goals and personality. The following goals were considered: "Have Fun", "Learn Math", "Want Help", and "Succeed by Myself". These goals were evaluated via actions and questionnaires. Each questionnaire contained a list of statements of the type "I learnt math/had fun when <event>",which students have rated using a five-point Likert scale. This prediction model was continuously improved over the past years (Conati and Maclaren 2009). The model can also assess emotions like joy or distress towards the game, admiration or reproach towards the helping agent. One of their current challenge is to obtain affective labels from different other sources, apart of using judges from video-recordings of the interaction with the game and self-reports during game playing.

Rebolledo-Mendez (2006) presented that the use of tutoring systems' techniques for motivational modelling could enhance the "intelligence" of educational games offering a personalised experience for each player.

Derbali and Frasson (2010) investigated player's motivation during an educational game. Motivation assessment was done using questionnaires (after Keller's ARCS model) and electroencephalography (EEG). Thirty three volunteer subjects took part in the test. Each subject was placed in front of two computers: one for playing and one for answering the questionnaires. The results have shown that the EEG waves patterns are correlated with the increase of motivation during certain game play parts.

2.3   Web 3.0 Based e-Learning and Games

Web 3.0 based e-learning moves towards semantic metadata annotation to enable further personalisation and interchange of the learning resources. To address these aspects, researchers have already started to propose semantic adaptive frameworks and systems (Rego et al. 2010a; Rego et al. 2010b; Pandit 2010; Rani et al. 2009; Torniai et al. 2008; Yanyan and Mingkai 2008). The proposed frameworks and systems represent information on learning resources using metadata and/or ontology, in order to provide adaptive features.

Pandit (2010) has proposed an architecture for ontology based description of the learning context (i.e. in which form the context is presented), of the content (i.e. what is the learning material about), and of the structure (i.e. if the learning resources appear in isolation or else what relationship are between them: e.g. "hasPart", "isPartOf", "isBasedOn").

Saleena et al. (2010) have presented an architecture that semantically relates the learning resources. The learning resources contain metadata regarding their topics. The topics are further described using ontologies in terms of the relationship between them.

Torniai et al. (2008) have proposed a collaborative Semantic Web e-learning system in which the students tag the learning resources and contribute to an ontology, with the aim of generating feedback to the tutors about student interaction with the learning materials and between students.

The AHKME e-learning system (Rego et al. 2010a; Rego et al. 2010b) adds metadata to the learning resources using XML, in order to support adaptation based on the student's characteristics. To attach metadata, each learning resource is evaluated by the tutor/expert in terms of accessibility, legibility, usefulness for achieving the learning objective, motivation, etc. Attached metadata includes: interactivity type, learning resource type and difficulty (Morales Morgado et al. 2008).

Different approaches for reusing existing learning resources in Semantic Web have been proposed (Zhaohui et al. 2009; Brut et al. 2010). Zhaohui et al. (2009) have proposed a mechanism to adaptively manage and reuse existing learning resources by integrating e-learning databases using ontology semantics. Brut et al. (2010) have proposed a solution to extend the IEEE LOM standard with ontology-based semantic web annotations.

While Web 3.0 based e-learning moves towards semantic metadata annotation and further personalisation, the trends are to incorporate Web 3.0 in games, too (Holthe 2010; Holthe et al. 2009). New multimedia APIs and virtual machines for games engines are proposed and developed using Web 3.0 technologies. Furthermore, new multimedia presentations for games are being developed where game resources such as 3D model, videos, and sounds are described and presented using XML, and the games can be played remotely over the Internet. The user input data (e.g. mouse, keyboard, game pad, etc.) is sent to the server, which in turn renders and streams back the presentation to the user.

Metadata was attached to educational games for describing them as learning resources (Moreno-Ger et al. 2008). Metadata includes: end-user role, semantic density, learning resource type, context, difficulty, interactivity level, age range, learning time. Educational games authoring tools permit the possibility of packing and annotating games as learning objects using IEEE LOM metadata standard (Torrente et al. 2009).

Furthermore, semantics are used in educational games in order to create and manage player profiles. Metadata is used for expressing player knowledge in the game and player rewards. Based on the information collected from different games, rewarding systems over several games/sub games are created (Steinberg and Brehm 2009).

3   Describing Motivation in Educational Games Through Web 3.0

This section presents a solution on how motivation can be measured and assessed during the game play and how motivation can be described in Web 3.0 using metadata. The learner motivation may be used for further adaptation and personalisation of the game play.

3.1   Assessment of Motivation in Educational Games

The proposed solution uses two types of information collected during the game play: information on learner interaction with the game (e.g. performed actions and their duration) and information about learner thoughts/beliefs. In e-learning, information on learner interaction is gathered from log files; while information on learner's thoughts/beliefs is gathered using questionnaires and dialog based interaction (see Table 15.1 and Table 15.2). In a similar way the proposed solution uses log files for collecting information about player interaction in educational games. As in virtual worlds avatars could act as coaches in learning situations (Rebolledo-Mendez et al. 2009), information on player thoughts/believes are retrieved by embedding motivational dialogs in the existing dialogs between the players and the Non Player Characters (NPCs). NPCs are characters that appear in the game and are not controlled by the players, but instead by the game engine. A NPC can have an active role, such as: guider, a competitor, evaluator of the actual player, or can be a neutral character that does not interact with the player.

The solution of using NPCs presents the advantage of being a non-invasive method as compared to using questionnaires.

The information collected by the game system is used for assessing four motivational metrics: *TimeOnTask* (period of time during which a learner performs a specific task/activity), *NoRepeatTask* (the number of times a learner performs a specific task), *NoHelpRequests* (the number of help requests or hint requests made by the learner), *SelfEfficacy* (person's belief, self-perception of their capabilities of executing that task). The first three metrics are assessed using information about player interaction with the game, while the last metric is assessed using information about player thoughts/believes.

The first two metrics (*TimeOnTask* and *NoRepeatTask*) are task based metrics. Several tasks can be identified during a game level. Therefore, the two metrics have to be assessed for each particular task. Similarly, during a game level, a player may request help/hints with regard to different aspects of the game, thus *NoHelpRequests* has to be assessed for each of these aspects in part. Since different interactions with NPCs may be used for retrieving different kind of information (e.g. knowledge, thought/believes), *SelfEfficacy* has to be assessed only when a motivation based dialog is present during the interaction with NPCs.

By assessing each of the four metrics during an entire game level, four game level motivation states are computed: *MotivationLevel_TimeOnTask, MotivationLevel_ NoRepeatTask, MotivationLevel_NoHelpRequests* and *MotivationLevel_SelfEfficacy.* The motivation states are expressed on a two level scale, where 0 corresponds to "Demotivated" state and 1 corresponds to "Motivated" state. The motivation states corresponding to the four metrics contributes for assessing a player motivation level.

The motivation level (*MotivationLevel*) is represented as a weighted function of the four motivation states as presented in Eq. 15.1.

Table 15.3 *MotivationLevel* mapping on a five level scale

MotivationLevel intervals	MotivationLevel on five level scale
MotivationLevel $\in$ (0, 0.20)	Very low motivated (1)
MotivationLevel $\in$ (0.21, 0.40)	Low motivated (2)
MotivationLevel $\in$ (0.41, 0.60)	Motivated (3)
MotivationLevel $\in$ (0.61, 0.80)	High motivated (4)
MotivationLevel $\in$ (0.81, 1.00)	Very high motivated (5)

Practical Elaboration of Chocolate book

Fig. 15.2 Scene from an educational game

$$MotivationLevel = w1 * MotivationLevel\_TimeOnTask +$$
$$w2 * MotivationLevel\_NoRepeatTask +$$
$$w3 * MotivationLevel\_NoHelpRequests +$$
$$w4 * MotivationLevel\_SelfEfficacy \qquad (15.1)$$

where, *w1*, *w2*, *w3* and *w4* are the weights associated to the four motivation states.

The motivation level represents a number between 0 and 1 and is further expressed on a five level scale, where 1-"Very Low Motivated", 2-"Low Motivated", 3-"Motivated", 4-"High Motivated", 5-"Very High Motivated" (see Table 15.3).

To enable learner motivation assessment, educational games need to be able to record all the information required for assessment (e.g. learner actions, action duration, etc.) during the game play. Currently, the information recorded by the educational games is not complete. For example, in Fig. 15.2 can be seen a scene of the "Paniel and the chocolate-based sauce adventure" game (Burgos et al. 2009), where the player character, Paniel, revisits the Library.

Next, the report generated when Paniel is revisiting the library is presented. Although, the report records the learner action "examining the LD book", how many time Paniel examines the LD book is not recorded.

```
<?xml version="1.0" encoding="UTF-8" standalone="no"?><report>
  <processed-rule id="ReadLDBook" importance="low" time="1831"
     type="normal-rule">
        <concept>The student examined the LD book</concept>
        <text>No Text</text>
  </processed-rule>
<processed-rule id="Rocio2" importance="low" time=1831
     type="normal-rule">
        <concept>The student talks with Rocio</concept>
        <text>Second Conversation </text>
</processed-rule>
```

3.2 Describing Learner Motivation Level Through Metadata

Considering the educational game as a learning resource, this paper proposes to further describe learner motivation level in Semantic Web using Resource Description Framework (RDF)[1]. RDF is a standard model for data description, representation, and interchange on the Web. It extends the actual linking model (hyperlink) between data used on the Web by linking mining about the data and describing relations between the data. Different syntaxes are used to represent the RDF: RDF/XML, turtle, etc.

The RDF/XML syntax describing an educational game learning resource is presented next. Metadata such as title, language, creators, type, and subject, is attached to the learning resource. The flexibility offered by RDF/XML allows for other metadata to be attached in the same mode.

```
<rdf: RDF
xmlns:rdf="http://www.w3.org/1999/02/22-rdf-syntax-ns#"
xmlns:learningResource="http://example.org/learningResources/vocab#"
xmlns:dc="http://purl.org/dc/elements/1.1/" >
  <rdf: Description rdf: about ="http://game_description">
  <dc: title> Game title </dc: title>
  <dc: language> English </dc: language>
  <dc: Creator>
   <bag>
    <li> Author 1 </li>
    <li> Author 2 <li>
    <li> Author 3 <li>
    <li> Author 4 <li>
   </bag>
  </dc: Creator>
  <learningResource: type> game </learningResource:type>
  <learningResource: subject> game chocolate</learningResource:
subject>
 </rdf: description>
</rdf: RDF>
```

[1] http://www.w3.org/RDF/

Learner motivation can be described using metadata in RDF/XML syntax. For example, the learner motivation before playing the game and during a game level can be described along with other details about the learner. Learner initial motivation can be assessed using questionnaire before starting the game. The motivation questionnaire's results can be mapped on the five level scale from 1 to 5, where 1-"Very Low Motivated", 2-"Low Motivated", 3-"Motivated", 4-"High Motivated", 5-"Very High Motivated". Learner motivation for a game level assessed as described in the previous section, is represented using the same five-level scale.

The bellow code presents an example of the RDF/XML syntax expressing learner motivation assessed before and during the game for a educational game learning resource. The motivation level (*MotivationLevel*) as well the four motivation states (*MotivationLevel_TimeOnTask, MotivationLevel_NoRepeatTask, MotivationLevel_NoHelpRequests, MotivationLevel_SelfEfficacy*) computed are expressed throw RDF.

```
<rdf:RDF
xmlns:rdf="http://www.w3.org/1999/02/22-rdf-syntax-ns#"
xmlns:s="http://example.org/students/vocab#">
 <rdf:Description
rdf:about="http://example.org/courses/Paniel/6.001">
   <s:students rdf:parseType="Collection">
    <rdf:Description rdf:about="http://example.org/students/Amy">
      <s:initialMotivation> 1 </s:initialMotivation>
      <s:MotivationLevel> 2 </s:MotivationLevel>
      <s:MotivationLevel_TimeOnTask>1</s:MotivationLevel_
      TimeOnTask>
      <s:MotivationLevel_NoRepeatTask>1</s:MotivationLevel_
      NoRepeatTask>
      <s:MotivationLevel_NoHelpRequests>0</s:MotivationLevel_
      NoHelpRequests>
      <s:MotivationLevel_SelfEfficacy>0</s:MotivationLevel_
      SelfEfficacy>
     </rdf:Description>
    </s:students>
  </rdf:Description>
</rdf:RDF>
```

Furthermore, information on tasks, help/hints, self efficacy and motivation metrics (*TimeOnTask, NoRepeatTask, NoHelpRequest, SelfEfficacy*) can be described using RDF/XML syntax. An example of how *TimeOnTask* can be expressed is presented next.

```
<rdf:RDF
xmlns:rdf="http://www.w3.org/1999/02/22-rdf-syntax-ns#"
xmlns:s="http://example.org/students/vocab#"
xmlns:gt="http://example.org/gameTask/vocab#">
   <rdf:Description
     rdf:about="http://example.org/courses/Paniel/6.001">
     <s:students rdf:parseType="Collection">
     <rdf:Description rdf:about="http://example.org/students/Amy">
       <gt:gameTask rdf:parseType="Collection">
       <rdf:Description
         rdf:about="http://example.org/gameTask/makeWhiteChocolate">
           <gt:taskTime> 320 s </gt:taskTime>
           <gt:TimeOnTask> 1 </gt:TimeOnTask>
       </rdf:Description>
       <rdf:Description
         rdf:about="http://example.org/gameTask/FindKey">
           <gt:taskTime> 100 s </gt:taskTime>
           <gt:TimeOnTask> 0 </gt:TimeOnTask>
       </rdf:Description>
       </gt: gameTask>
     </rdf:Description>
     </s:students>
   </rdf:Description>
</rdf:RDF>
```

Once the measurement and assessment of learner motivation was performed, the motivation level can be used as an input for adaptation and personalization of the educational games and/or for the personalisation of other learning resources. Different types of adaptation that can be done in educational games based on learner motivation were presented by the authors in (Ghergulescu and Muntean 2010).

4   Conclusions

Nowadays, the digital technology era has arrived. Learners attempt to become a "Digital Wisdom" generation. Technological developments significantly improved areas such as e-learning, gaming and affective computing. The Web has evolved exponentially over the last decade and it is continuously extending. The Web is gradually moving toward a semantic, personalised, interoperable and intelligent Web, towards Web 3.0.

This chapter addressed new challenges for educational games: how learner motivation can be measured and assessed. Furthermore, this chapter presented how the motivation level can be expressed through Web 3.0.

In order to assess learner's motivation in educational games, we proposed to use various motivation metrics used by e-learning systems. For this purpose, player's interaction with a non-player character or/and player's interaction with the game are monitored. Furthermore, a solution to represent learner's motivation in Web 3.0 was introduced. The semantic description of player's motivation level makes use of RDF/XML.

Motivation assessment can be used as an input in the game personalisation for creating more affective educational games. By making use of the RDF/XML syntax for describing the games learning resources, the proposed solution contributes towards the interoperability, reusability and standardisation of the motivation based educational games. Furthermore, by describing learners motivation through RDF/XML syntax, other adaptive educational systems can access and reuse this information for further personalisation.

Acknowledgement This research work is supported by IRCSET Embark Postgraduate Scholarship Scheme, Ireland.

References

Arroyo, I., Ferguson, K., Johns, J., Dragon, T., Meheranian, H., Fisher, D., Barto, A. (2007). Repairing Disengagement With Non-Invasive Interventions In Rosemary Luckin, Kenneth R. Roedinger, Jim Greer (Eds.) *Proceeding of the 2007 conference on Artificial Intelligence in Education: Building Technology Rich Learning Contexts That Work* (pp. 195–202). The Netherlands: IOS Press Amsterdam.

Bandura, A., 1994. Self-Efficacy. In *Encyclopedia of human behaviour* (pp. 71–81.) New York: Academic Press.

Batson, L. & Feinberg, S. (2006). Game designs that enhance motivation and learning for teenagers. *Electronic Journal for the Integration of Technology in Education*, 5, 34–43.

Brut, M., Sedes, F., & Dumitrescu, S. (2010). A Semantic-Oriented Approach for Organizing and Developing Annotation for E-Learning. *Learning Technologies, IEEE Transactions on*, 3(4), 11.

Burgos, D., Torijano, B., Moreno-Ger, P., Torrente, J. (2009). Paniel and the Chocolate-based sauce adventure. http://e-adventure.e-ucm.es/course/view.php?id=18&lang=en_en_utf8.

Beck, J.E. (2004). Using response times to model student disengagement. In *ITS 2004 Workshop Proceedings on Social and Emotional Intelligence in Learning Environments* (pp. 13–20), Maceio, Brazil.

Berger, F. & Müller, W. (2009). Adaptivity in Game-Based Learning: A New Perspective on Story. In Ido A. Iurgel, Nelson Zagalo and Paolo Petta (Eds.) *Interactive Storytelling- Second Joint International Conference on Interactive Digital Storytelling, ICIDS 2009* (pp. 316–319). Springer.

Can, G. & Cagiltay, K. (2006). Turkish Prospective Teachers' Perceptions Regarding the Use of Computer Games with Educational Features. *Journal of Educational Technology & Society*, 9(1), 308–321.

Chuang, T. & Chen, W. (2009). Effect of Computer-Based Video Games on Children: An Experimental Study. *Educational Technology and Society*, 12(2), 1–10.

Cocea, M. & Weibelzahl, S. (2009). Log file analysis for disengagement detection in e-Learning environments. *User Modeling and User-Adapted Interaction*, 19(4), 341–385.

Cocea, M., & Weibelzahl, S. (in press). Disengagement Detection in On-line Learning: Validation Studies and Perspectives. *IEEE Transactions on Learning Technologies,* Retrieved from: http://userweb.port.ac.uk/~coceam/publications/2010/IEEE%20TLT.pdf.

Conati, C. & Maclaren, H. (2009). Modeling User Affect from Causes and Effects. *Proceedings of the 17th International Conference on User Modeling, Adaptation, and Personalization: formerly UM and AH*, pp. 4–15.

Conati, C. & Zhou, X., (2002) Modeling Students' Emotions from Cognitive Appraisal in Educational Games. In S. A. Cerri, G. Gouarderes, F. Paraguacu (Eds.) *Proceedings of the 6th International Conference on Intelligent Tutoring Systems* (pp. 944–954). Springer.

Costagliola, G., De Rosa, M., Fuccella, V., Capuano, N., Ritrovato. P. 2010. A Novel Approach for Attention Management in E-learning Systems. *In Proceedings of the 16th International Conference on Distributed Multimedia Systems, DSM 2010* (pp. 222–227), USA: Knowledge Systems Institute.

Derbali, L. & Frasson, C. (2010). Players' Motivation and EEG Waves Patterns in a Serious Game Environment. In Vincent Aleven, Judy Kay and Jack Mostow, *Proceeding of* the 10th International Conference on *Intelligent Tutoring Systems* (pp. 297–299). Springer.

Baston, L. & Feinberg, S. (2006). Game designs that enhance motivation and learningfor teenagers. *Electronic Journal for the integration of Technology in Education*, 5, 34–43.

Gee, J.P. (2003). *What video games have to teach us about learning and literacy*, New York: Palgrave Macmillian.

Ghergulescu, I. & Muntean, C.H. (2010). MoGAME: Motivation based Game Level Adaptation Mechanism. In the 10th Annual Irish Learning Technology Association Conference EdTech 2010(9 pages). Athlone, Ireland, Retrived from http://www.ilta.net/files/EdTech2010/R2_GhergulescuMuntean.pdf.

Ghergulescu, I. & Muntean, C.H. (2009). PalyLearn: Supporting Motivation through Gaming in E-Learning. In Markus Hofmann, Mark Deegen, Phelim Murnion (Eds.) *Proceedings* of the *9th Information Technology and Telecommunication Conference*. IT&T (pp. 185–190). Ireland.

Holthe, O. (2010). A Multimedia Presentation Framework for Web 3.0 Computer Game Experiences. IEEE Multimedia, 17(4), 70–79.

Holthe, O., Mogstad, O., & Ronningen, L. A. (2009). Geelix LiveGames: Remote Playing of Video Games. *In 6th IEEE Consumer Communications and Networking Conference,* Las Vegas, NV, 1–2.

Hudlicka, E. & Broekens, J. (2009). Foundations for modelling emotions in game characters: Modelling emotion effects on cognition. In *Affective Computing and Intelligent Interaction and Workshops,* Amsterdam, The Netherlands, 1–6.

Hudlicka, E. (2009). Affective game engines: motivation and requirements. In *Proceedings of the 4th International Conference on Foundations of Digital Games*, Florida, USA, 299–306.

Johns, J., & Woolf, B. (2006). A Dynamic Mixture Model to Detect Student Motivation and Proficiency. *Proceeding of AAAI'06 21st national conference on Artificial Intelligence,* Boston, *Massachusetts,* 163–168.

Kahiigi, E.K. et al., (2008). Exploring the e-Learning State of Art. *the Electronic Journal of e-Learning*, 6(2), 77–88.

Keller, J.M., 1987. Development and use of the ARCS model of instructional design. *Journal of Instructional Development*, 10(3), 2–10.

Khan, F. A., Graf, S., Weippl, E. R., & Tjoa, A. M. (2009a). An approach for identifying affective states through behavioral patterns in web-based learning management systems. In Gabriele Kotsis, David Taniar, Eric Pardede, Ismail Khalil (Eds.) *Proceedings of the 11th International Conference on Information Integration and Web-based Applications & Services, iiWAS'09* (pp. 431–435). ACM.

Khan, F. A., Weippl, E. R., & Tjoa, A. M. (2009b). Integrated Approach for the Detection of Learning Styles and Affective States. In G. Siemens & C. Fulford (Eds.), *Proceedings of World Conference on Educational Multimedia, Hypermedia and Telecommunications 2009* (pp. 753–761). Chesapeake, VA: AACE.

Khan, F. A., Graf, S., Weippl, E. R., & Tjoa, A. M. (2010). Implementation of Affective States and Learning Styles Tactics in Web-Based Learning Management Systems. *Proceedings of the 2010 10th IEEE International Conference on Advanced Learning Technologies*, Sousse, Tuneisa 734–735.

Kim, Y.S. et al. (2007). An Intelligent Tutoring System with Motivation Diagnosis and Planning. *In 15th International Conference on Computers in Education, Hiroshima*, Japan Retrieved from: http://credits.skku.edu/credits/publications/ICCE2007_Poster.pdf.

Konetes, G.D. (2010). The Function of Intrinsic and Extrinsic Motivation in Educational Virtual Games and Simulations. *Journal of Emerging Technologies in Web Intelligence*, 2(1), 23–26.

Li Yanyan, & Dong Mingkai (2008). Towards a Knowledge Portal for E-Learning Based on Semantic Web. In Advanced Learning Technologies, 2008. ICALT. Eighth IEEE International Conference on, Santander, Cantabria, Spain, 910–912.

Little, J.K. & Page, C. (2009). The Educause Top Teaching and Learning Challenges. *Educause Review*, 44(2), 30–44.

Malone, T. & Lepper, M. (1987). Making learning fun: A taxonomy of intrinsic motivations for learning. *In Erlbaum*, 223–253.

McQuiggan, S. W., Mott, B. W., & Lester, J. C. (2008). Modeling self-efficacy in intelligent tutoring systems: An inductive approach. *User Modeling and User-Adapted Interaction*, 18(1–2), 81–123.

Merrick, K. (2007). Modelling Motivation for Adaptive Non-Player Characters in Dynamic Computer Game Worlds. *ACM Computers in Entertainment*, 5(4), 32.

Morales Morgado, E. M., Garcia, F., Ruiz, A. B., Rego, H., & Moreira, T. (2008). Learning Objects for eLearning Systems. *The open knowledge society*, 19, 153–162.

Moreno-Ger, P., Spaniol, M., López Manas, E., Drobek, N., & Fernández-Manjön, B. (2008). Making Sense of Collaboratively Annotated Multimedia Metadata for (Mobile) Digital Story-Telling and Educational Gaming. In R. Klamma, N. Sharda, B. Fernández-Manjön, H. Kosch, & M. Spaniol (Eds.), *Proceedings of the 1st Workshop on Story-Telling for Educational Gaming*(10 pages). Retrieved from http://www.e-ucm.es/drafts/e-UCM_draft_119.pdf.

Munoz-Organero, M., Munoz-Merino, P. J., & Kloos, C. D. (2010). Student Behavior and Interaction Patterns With an LMS as Motivation Predictors in E-Learning Settings. *IEEE Transactions on Education*, 53(3), 463–470.

Pandit, V. R. (2010). E-Learning System Based on Semantic Web. In *Emerging Trends in Engineering and Technology (ICETET), 2010 3rd International Conference on*, 559–564.

Prensky, M. (2001a). Digital natives, digital immigrants. *On the Horizon*, 9(5), 1–6.

Prensky, M. (2001b). Digital natives, digital immigrants- part 2. *On the Horizon*, 9(6), 1–6.

Prensky, M. (2009). H. Sapiens Digital:From Digital Immigrants and Digital Natives to Digital Wisdom. *Innovate*, 5(3), 9.

Qu, L. & Johnson, W.L. (2005). Detecting the Learner's Motivational States in An Interactive Learning Environment. In Chee-Kit Looi, Gord McCalla, Bert Bredeweg, Joost Breuker, *Proceeding of the 2005 conference on Artificial Intelligence in Education: Supporting Learning through Intelligent and Socially Informed Technology* (pp. 547–554).The Netherlands: IOS Press Amsterdam.

Qu, L., Wang, N. & Johnson, W.L. (2005). Using Learner Focus of Attention to Detect Learner Motivation Factors. In *User Modeling 2005*, 70–73.

Rani, S., Ashok, M., & Palanivel, K. (2009). Adaptive content for personalized E-learning using web service and semantic web. *In Intelligent Agent & Multi-Agent Systems, 2009. IAMA 2009. International Conference on* Chennai, India, 1–4.

Rebolledo-Mendez, G. (2006). How can video-games deliver educational content in an intelligent fashion? In *Proceedings of the 9th HCT postgraduate workshop University of Sussex, UK*. Retrieved from: http://www.cogs.susx.ac.uk/users/gr20/9thHCTWorkshop2006.pdf.

Rebolledo-Mendez, G., de Freitas, S. & Gaona, A. (2009). A Model of Motivation Based on Empathy for AI-Driven Avatars in Virtual Worlds. In *Games and Virtual Worlds for Serious Applications, 2009. VS-GAMES'09. Conference in Coventry, UK*, 5–11.

Rego, H., Moreira, T., & García, F. J. (2010). Web-Based Learning Information System for Web 3.0. In Miltiadis D. Lytras, Patricia Ordonez De Pablos, Adrian Ziderman, Alan Roulstone, Hermann Maurer, Jonathan B. Imber (Eds.) *Knowledge Management, Information Systems, E-Learning, and Sustainability Research, The World Summit on the Knowledge Society WSKS 2010, Corfu, Greece,* (pp.196–201). Springer.

Rego, H., Moreira, T., Morales, E., & Garcia, F. (2010). Metadata and knowledge management driven Web based learning information systems towards web 3.0. *International Journal of Emerging Technologies in Learning,* 5(2), 36–44.

Ryan, R. & Deci, E.L. (2000). Self-Determination Theory and the Facilitation of Intrinsic Motivation, Social Development, and Well-Being. *American psychologist,* 55(1), 68–78.

Saleena, B., Salini, M., & Venkateswaran, S. (2010). A semantic approach to construct a knowledge portal for e-learning using ontology. *In Distance Learning and Education (ICDLE), 2010 4th International Conference on,* 214–217.

Shaffer, D.W. et al. (2005). Video games and the future of learning. *Phi Delta Kappan,* 87(2), 105–111.

Steinberg, M., & Brehm, J. (2009). Social Educational Games Based on Open Content. In *Intelligent Networking and Collaborative Systems, 2009. INCOS'09. International Conference on,* Barcelona, Spain, 255–258.

Takemura, Y. et al. (2008). Assessing the Learners' Motivation in the E-Learning Environments for Programming Education. In H. Leung, F. Li, R. Lau, Q. Li (Eds.) *Advances in Web Based Learning–ICWL 2007,* (pp. 355–366), Springer.

Torniai, C., Jovanovic, J., Gasevic, D., Bateman, S., & Hatala, M. (2008). E-Learning meets the Social Semantic Web. In *Advanced Learning Technologies, 2008. ICALT'08. Eighth IEEE International Conference on,* Santander, Cantabria,Spain, 389–393.

Torrente, J., Moreno-Ger, P., Martínez-Ortiz, I., & Fernandez-Manjon, B. (2009). Integration and Deployment of Educational Games in e-Learning Environments: The Learning Object Model Meets Educational Gaming. *Educational Technology & Society,* 12 (4), 359–371.

de Vicente, A. & Pain, H. (2002). Informing the detection of the students' motivational state: an empirical study. In S. A. Cerri, G. Gouarderes, F. Paraguacu (Eds.) *Proceedings of the 6th International Conference on Intelligent Tutoring Systems,*(pp. 79–86). Springer.

de Vicente, A. (2003). *Towards tutoring systems that detect students' motivation: an investigation.* Ph.D. Univ. of Edinburg.

Wlodkowski, R.J. (1978). *Motivation and Teaching: A Practical Guide.,* NEA Distribution Center.

Woolf, B. P., Arroyo, I., Muldner, K., Burleson, W., Cooper, D. G., Dolan, R., & Christopherson, R. M. (2010). The Effect of Motivational Learning Companions on Low Achieving Students and Students with Disabilities. In V. Aleven, J. Kay, & J. Mostow (Eds.), *Proceeding of the 10th International Conference on Intelligent Tutoring Systems,* (pp. 327–337).Springer.

Wu Zhaohui, Mao Yuxin, & Chen H. (2009). Subontology-Based Resource Management for Web-Based e-Learning. *IEEE Transactions on Knowledge and Data Engineering,* 21(6), 867–880.

Chapter 16
Learning from Incorrect Answers on Multiple Choice Tests

Implications for a New Teaching Paradigm

Jay C. Powell, James Bernauer, and Vishnuteerth Agnihotri

1 Introduction

There are two ways to score tests, (1) obtaining acceptable-answer frequencies and (2) considering all answers meaningful, extracting these meanings with pattern-scoring techniques. Our research shows the common practice of using only acceptable-answer frequencies to assess student learning is invalid both mathematically and psychologically (Powell 2010a).

Building on this research, we conducted an answer-by-answer analysis of the responses given on two multiple-choice tests (mathematics with 22 items and science with 20 items) taken by 11,228 students in India from Years 4, 6 and 8. Most of the items were from previous tests developed by Educational Initiatives, with some coming from TIMSS for international comparisons.[1]

The *selection proportions of every answer* on each of these tests were calculated and charted to show the changes in selection from one age group to another. This approach, Response Spectrum Evaluation (RSE), originated when a method for bypassing linear dependency to recover the performance information available from both *acceptable* (A) and *not acceptable* (¬A) answers was developed by Powell and Shklov (1992) specifically for this purpose.

---

[1] Please contact the third author for more details about test design and construction.

J.C. Powell (✉)
Better Schooling Systems, Pittsburgh, PA, USA
e-mail: jpowell@tir.com

J. Bernauer
Robert Morris University, Moon Township, PA, USA
e-mail: bernauer@rmu.edu

V. Agnihotri
Test Development, Educational Initiatives Pvt. Ltd., Frazer Town, Bangalore, India
e-mail: vishnu@ei-india.com

P. Isaias et al. (eds.), *Towards Learning and Instruction in Web 3.0: Advances in Cognitive and Educational Psychology*, DOI 10.1007/978-1-4614-1539-8_16,
© Springer Science+Business Media, LLC 2012

There was a cross-sectional administration of two tests for each age group. Change patterns indicate guessing is a small factor, in answering these tests. Mostly, students select answers based upon thoughtful interpretation. With a single administration, it is unnecessary to use statistics beyond selection proportions and proportion differences to show selection dynamics.

The ¬A answer selections provide useful diagnostic information for teachers. However, commonly these answers are collapsed into a single value zero (0) when they are scored for acceptable-answer frequencies. This practice creates an artificial dichotomy required to apply the *general linear model* (GLM), violating the underlying nonlinear nature of these data.

Six distinctive selection-pattern dynamics emerged in this study; (1) Standard, (2) Crossover, (3) Starts at Same Point, (4) ¬A Answer Dominates, (5) Scatter and (6) Miscellaneous. Each of these are illustrated with exemplary items from both the mathematics and the science test. These patterns reflect students' thought processes *in addition to* content mastery. The frequency of each type of pattern is presented and a summary of the interpretive logic provided. This logic will be discussed using child-development theory or information processing style theory with corresponding implications for classroom intervention.

Two shortcomings should be noted in the following discussion. First, these tests were given only once to these children, which precludes making polychronic individual response pattern discriminations. Second, we did not randomly split groups to obtain within-group consistency. Such refinements would be appropriate for subsequent studies. We believe that our findings are sufficiently strong to stand alone.

1.1   Theoretical Framework for Testing and Assessment

Multiple-choice tests were invented early in the twentieth Century in response to an urgent need to screen large numbers of men being inducted into the armed services as the United States entered World War I. At that time, the best model available to explain brain functioning, based upon microscopic analysis of brain tissue, was the telephone exchange.

From this interpretation of microscopic observation, Classical Test Theory (CTT) assumes that examinees know the answer or they guessed (Lord 1952; Lord and Novick 1968; Allen and Yen 2002). Given this assumption, ¬A answers *are provide no useful performance information.*

This type of testing for large groups has become routine achievement assessment. Until recently, the guessing assumption has not been challenged. There are two reasons for this oversight. First, the mathematics of *linear* analysis precludes considering non-dichotomous answers options using statistical procedures derived from the GLM. Combining both the A and ¬A answers in the analysis creates a linear dependency, rendering such analyses mathematically meaningless.

Second, the scoring process ignores these ¬A answers, making any information contained therein unavailable for assessment purposes. This linear dependency problem was solved about 20 years ago (Powell and Shklov 1992). Awareness that systematic selection of alternative answers might be occurring arose when Item Response Theory (IRT) began to show scalability of the wrong answers (Rasch 1980). Concept inventories (Halloun and Hestenes 1985) and propositional logic (Piburn 1990) testing consider ¬A answers informative for both misconception and procedural error identification.

Powell and Shklov (1992) showed that students systematically changed their answer from one ¬A answer to another ¬A answer on an age (cognitive maturity) basis following the sequence observed by Piaget (Flavell 1963). They also discovered a *cognitive-decline* pathway. Such pathways begin at age 10 (following the fourth-grade slump) and sometimes leads to leaving school prematurely.

Because changes in selection strategies are discontinuous, indicating systematic shifts in examinee thought processes, they are mathematically nonlinear. These observations, therefore, invalidate current scoring practices on mathematical grounds.

This current study goes further. It presents student data from 11,000+ students on 42 multiple-choice items from India. Primarily, we address the assumption that a large proportion of alternative answers are selected *without thoughtful consideration.*

Background studies leading up to and including the summary presentation given by Powell (2010a) were based on a reading comprehension test (Gorham 1957) that displays two developmental tracks (advancing and declining along a Piaget-like sequence).

This present study reports results where the underlying learning trajectories are more diverse than a single straight line implies. This study also demonstrates that concept acquisition, as it relates to developing understanding and concept veracity, is more complex than the simplistic approach currently employed.

Thus, this paper has three goals:

1. To document the thoughtful patterns of ¬A answer selection.
2. To connect the selection of these options to child-development theory, specifically related to Constructivist Theory as promulgated by Piaget (1985) for the role of *disequilibrium* in formulating insights, Vygotsky (1978) for the role of student participation in learning to think, and Gardner (1983) for the role in *alternative thinking styles* in differentiating answer selection, and
3. To identify the educational implications of gathering this ¬A answer interpretations to inform teaching.

1.2 Piaget, Vygotsky, and Gardner: Frameworks for Development and Learning

This paper confines itself to the *constructivist* approach in which children are assumed to create their own knowledge from their interactions with their environments. The theories of Piaget, Vygotsky and Gardner are discussed because of their

Table 16.1 Stages of Piaget's developmental theory

Stage	Age	Markers
Sensorimotor	0–2	Object permanence
		Goal-directed actions
Preoperational	2–7	Use of symbols
		Egocentrism
Concrete operational	7–11	Conservation
		Reversibility
		Logical thinking
Formal operational	11+	Abstract reasoning
		Social sensitivity

alignment with this constructivist approach. We use this perspective to provide a context for results and interpretation

Jean Piaget identified four stages of cognitive development by observing learning characteristics exhibited by his own children (Piaget 1954). Table 16.1 provides a simplified description of these stages in terms of key "markers" or characteristics that begin to emerge at various ages. The critical Piagetian concepts relevant to this paper are *disequilibrium, assimilation* and *accommodation.* Piaget argues that children and adults seek balance between what they know and what is presented by their environments.

Piaget referred to this state of balance as "equilibrium." Conversely, students in a state of *disequilibrium* experience dissonance; what they currently accept as true clashes with new experience, causing a mental imbalance and discomfort. While the natural inclination is to seek comfort, this disequilibrium offers an opportunity to learn – to break out of one's comfort zone and discover new truths through insight. Piaget suggests two possible responses to the irritant, (1) to include it in their existing mental structures (schema) or (2) to realize that their current mental structure is inadequate. Piaget used the term "assimilation" to refer to a condition when new knowledge is incorporated into existing schema and the term "accommodation" when the "irritant" refuses to fit into existing mental structures, fostering insight. Such insights can be life-changing (Powell 2010b, pp. 11–13)

Piaget's theory of cognitive development relates to our concept of building on and promoting student learning using ¬A answers seems straightforward. If learning is thought of as a continuous disjunctive process, then utilizing disequilibrium to foster assimilation or accommodation fits with our contention that *all answers* should be considered. In fact, ¬A input offers glimpses into the current stage of student cognition. This information empowers teachers to tailor instruction to specific learning needs.

Vygotsky focused more on learning than development, although both he and Piaget supported constructivist learning and the role of social experiences in learning (Vygotsky 1978). Important concepts identified by Vygotskian theory include *private speech, zone of proximal development* (zpd), and *cooperative learning.* Vygotsky viewed children's learning as progressing individually via private speech ("talking to yourself") that enables learners to slow down their thinking and therefore to reflect more fully upon inadequate and better solutions to problems. Vygotsky also saw the critical role that peers and adults can play in children's learning to achieve the next step within a proximal band of learning (zpd) that envelops their current understanding. These concepts are consistent with our contention that using all test information (rather than only correct answers) reflects more accurately how learning and development actually occur.

Finally, Gardner (1983, 2000, 2004) identified the concept of *multiple intelligences* that contrasts with the "general intelligence factor" (g) identified by Spearman (1927). While a conception of general intelligence is based on correlating abilities, Gardner's theory of intelligences recognizes the idiosyncratic abilities that individuals possess. This theory also supports the notion of looking at phenomena in unique ways, which is consistent with both constructivist thinking and discovery learning. Students select ¬A answers along developmental pathways. How students respond to test questions is consistent with Multiple Intelligence Theory based on the contention that students have unique insights. In this case, ¬A answers may not imply an absence of knowledge; rather, they signal the opportunity for teachers to develop instructional interventions that help students to discover new insights, based on their individual ways of conceptualizing and solving problems.

A common expression is "thinking outside the box" or thinking beyond commonly accepted parameters for solving known problems. However, it is also important to reflect on the inverse, "thinking *inside* the box." This latter expression implies not only trying to *solve* problems using existing methods; it also suggests that we should *find* problems to solve that have already been identified by others. On the contrary, Piaget, Vygotsky and Gardner support the idea that knowledge is not only constructed but that the very problems given to students to solve may not engender the kind of knowledge that is considered of central importance to a discipline. Based on the empirical findings in this study we argue that "wrong answers" may not only reflect strengths, limitations and creativity in student thinking, they may also provide insights into the quality of the questions themselves.

Gardner's premise also argues for a loosening of the constraints imposed by strict adherence to linear thinking and schooling, supporting convergent not divergent thinking. By loosening the constraints, new thinking *processes* will be encouraged leading to innovative ideas and insights. Rather than imposing answers on students, we should be asking more questions about how to decide when answers are ¬A. Finally, insights are rewarding to learners. Fostering them opens minds to wanting more of the same.

2 Presenting Selection Dynamics Visually

Our analytic procedure was to obtain the *selection proportions* (frequencies adjusted by group size) for every cell in answer selection data tables of each answer treated independently. The graphs show these proportions on an item-by-item and answer-by-answer basis. No more sophisticated analysis than selection ratios is used in this paper.

Differences between proportions are used to determine the statistical independence of selection ratios.

The relationships established among these graphs to classify pattern types were determined visually. This approach was augmented by considering the nature of the errors or misconceptions as these ¬A answers reflect students' thinking using *item content/process analysis*.

2.1 Mathematics: Standard Expectation (All ¬A Answers Are "Guesses")

The first two examples show items where ¬A answers (in this case; options A, B and C) start at low selection proportions and decline in parallel. We assume that if any options pairs are selected randomly, selection proportions should be statistically indistinguishable. From the theory behind current testing practice, that ¬A are meaningless, *all item response selections* should conform to this pattern (Fig. 16.1).

This item represents an easy question in the mathematics test and it showed about a 20% gain in answer acceptability from Year 4 to Year 6 ($z = 10.0$) and a 10% gain from Year 6 to Year 8 ($z = 4.7$). R_D means D is "right" and W_A is the selection of option "A" option is an ¬A answer.

3. The markings are correct on only ONE of these containers. Which one?

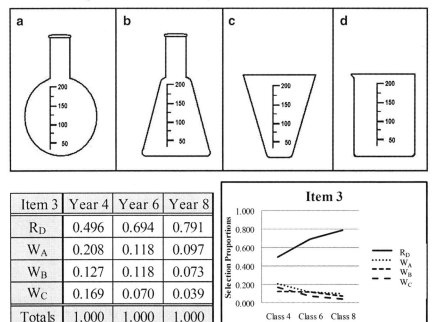

Item 3	Year 4	Year 6	Year 8
R_D	0.496	0.694	0.791
W_A	0.208	0.118	0.097
W_B	0.127	0.118	0.073
W_C	0.169	0.070	0.039
Totals	1.000	1.000	1.000

Fig. 16.1 Mathematics – Item 3

Without interviewing the students who selected the alternatives, the basis for the errors in this item is unclear. Their selection patterns are parallel enough to suggest guessing in the absence of knowledge. However only three of the nine pairs of within-age proportions are not significantly different. Using this criterion for defining randomness, there is little guessing, even in this case.

It would be interesting to determine how this question relates to Piaget's discussion of conservation of space and number in learning (Rose and Blank 1974). This problem requires the ability to associate visual stimuli with a uniform numerical scale. These students increase significantly with age in their ability to make this visual association. However, this correct answer selection may come from object familiarity and not from understanding the effects of shape upon volume. Right answers need not come from understanding (Powell and Miki 1985).

2.2   Science: Standard Expectation (All ¬A Answers "Guesses")

An obvious "easier" item since three of five selected correctly in Year 4 and nine of ten were correct in Year 8 ($z=4.5$) (Fig. 16.2).

All responses are changing in the expected direction.

Option A may reflect experience with "hard water."

Option B may indicate personal experience with water that has offensive odors or lack of experience with kerosene.

37. Ramesh was applying paint on the wall during which some of the paint fell on his hands. Instead of using water, Ramesh used kerosene oil to wash his hands.
Which of the following options explains Ramesh's decision?

    A. Kerosene is softer than water.
    B. Kerosene smells better than water.
    C. Paints dissolve in kerosene and not in water.
    D. Kerosene is more easily available than water.

Item 37	Year 4	Year 6	Year 8
R_C	0.615	0.794	0.892
W_A	0.136	0.095	0.068
W_B	0.096	0.043	0.017
W_D	0.154	0.068	0.023
Totals	1.000	1.000	1.000

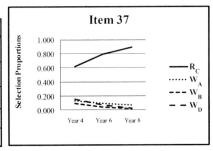

Fig. 16.2 Science – Item 37

It is difficult to determine why students chose Option D. This may be evidence for guessing. "D" was chosen by less than 1 in 20 students for each age level. Is this a good estimate of the amount of guessing occurring?

It appears that the Year 8 performance (at 89% correct) is sufficiently high to assume that the change pattern is from any wrong answer to the right one and no further information from this item would be useful.

The question of latex-based paints, which are water soluble, is not raised here. These answers must be experience-based, bringing Vygotsky's and Gardner's reasoning into the picture.

To support the random assumption, most of the answer patterns should be like this one. As a whole, there were 12 out of 42 items, which is less than 1: 3 displaying this relationship. On these grounds alone, the "wrong" options should not be ignored. This ratio is significant ($z = 3.93$) favoring systematic selection. Apparently selecting ¬A answers without thoughtful consideration is a rare event.

This conclusion is consistent with other studies (Powell 2010a).

3   Crossover

In this pair of examples, the youngest children selected an ¬A answer at a higher proportion than they chose the keyed answer. These two alternatives reversed their selection proportions as the children matured. Most of the comparisons among these proportional differences are significant.

3.1   Mathematics: (All ¬A Answers Functioning)

In this crossover response item, the right answer selection doubled from year 4 to Year 8. For the entire group, it was a difficult question with an average success ratio of 43% for the combined Year scores. Using the difference of proportions statistic with a base frequency of 1,000, the z score is 4.1 for the change from year 4 to year 8 (Fig. 16.3).

The most common wrong answer, alternative B, is a simplification. Those who selected it ignored the relative sizes of the shaded regions. In Piaget's terms, this error is an issue of conservation of size. The two shaded rectangles are of differing sizes. It may be developmentally appropriate to have about 2 children in 5 get this question correct at age 9. Why there are still 1 in 5 making this error at Year 8 is less clear. It could be a better item, if option B were $^2/_4$ instead of M to detect this developmental inconstancy.

We observe 1 in 5 children choosing alternative A at Year 4. This is an oversimplification based on visual inspection without counting. If one other square were shaded, M would be the correct answer. This assumption would make it an inversion

5. What fraction of the rectangle is shaded?

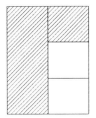

A.   5/6
B.   2/5
C.   2/3
D.   1

Item 5	Year 4	Year 6	Year 8
R_C	0.292	0.409	0.582
W_A	0.182	0.161	0.119
W_B	0.388	0.335	0.215
W_D	0.138	0.095	0.084
Totals	1.000	1.000	1.000

Item 5

Fig. 16.3 Mathematics – Item 5

of the strategy used in the choice of B. Changing this option to $^2/_4$ from M could identify children missing relative size.

Alternative D is also puzzling, but the students selected it too frequently to ignore it. Is it possible that they observed only one shaded rectangle in the diagram? The other three parts of the figure are more nearly squares. If this explanation fits the choice, it represents a misreading of the question leading to its redefinition. Redefined Terms is one of the strategies recognized in other studies (Powell 2010a). Option D might be better as 1 ⟨?⟩.

Using Montessori's (1972) or Vygotsky's approach, exploring size and shape relationships with tiles should provide the directed experiences needed to correct these errors.

3.2   Science: (All Alternatives Functioning)

While students' grasp of this concept increased in the expected direction and errors decreased, still only about two in five students got it correct in Year 8, suggesting an inadequate exposure to the homeostatic mechanisms of the human body (Fig. 16.4).

Option B suggests a simplification based on "common sense," the experience of "feeling hot" in the summer and "feeling cold" in the winter. In Piaget's formulation, this could be an Egocentric response.

Option C, which is the inverse of Option B, suggests an over-appreciation of the body's action to achieve normalcy; or perhaps it is a misreading of the question. As an inversion of the true state of affairs, it might be considered a "common misconception." Its persistence into adolescence supports this latter notion.

29. What happens to our body temperature on a cold winter day or a hot summer day?
  A. There is no difference. It remains approximately 37 degrees C°.
  B. The temperature of the body is much lower in the winter and higher in the summer.
  C. The temperature of the body is much lower in the summer and higher in the winter.
  D. The temperature of the body changes with the seasons, bur depends on body weight.

Item 29	Year 4	Year 6	Year 8
R_A	0.175	0.237	0.402
W_B	0.363	0.349	0.231
W_C	0.227	0.181	0.152
W_D	0.235	0.232	0.215
Totals	1.000	1.000	1.000

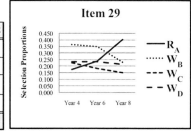

Fig. 16.4 Science – Item 29

Option D seems to attempt to find a synthesizing principle between B and C, suggesting thoughtfulness that is more multidimensional than is common among school children as discussed in Powell (2010a). This option brings with it the correct personal observation that heavier people often suffer more from the heat than the slimmer ones. The proportion of about one in five staying with this answer across the age span is consistent with our findings that the better informed think more complexly. In Piaget's approach, there is no consideration of multidimensional thinking.

Our research adds this aspect of learning, similar to DeBono's (2005) *lateral thinking*, Demetriou and Kazi (2006) *metacognition* and the *neurolinguistic programming* (Bandler and Grinder 1982) concept of *reframing*. Our research (Powell 2010c) shows this shift out of "yes/no" (2-value logic) may be detectable, where students switch from easy (narrow perspective) A answers to broad perspective ¬A answers by reading more into an item than intended by the questioner. Bond and Fox (2007, p. 22) recognize this phenomenon in Item Response Theory (IRT) studies. They explain it differently.

Did the reference to seasonal dependency lead these students to answer using additional information? If so, this item illustrates how such divergent interpretations occur. It gives rise to the need to teach reading skills in all subjects. The dynamics of these responses also suggests that scoring by patterns of answer is more likely to identify performance status.

The late crossover among answers, which occurs between Year 6 and Year 8, indicates a response pattern more complex than previous one. This item illustrates the complicated dynamics of learning that is inaccessible when only the frequency of acceptable answers is considered. This complexity may be lost entirely, if such items are discarded.

Within the two tests, there were nine items showing this crossover pattern.

4   Starting at the Same Point

In this response pattern, one of the ¬A options begins, in Year 4, at about the equivalent proportion as the right answer. There were seven such items in the combination of these two tests.

4.1   Mathematics: (All Alternatives Functioning)

This visual estimation problem proved to be moderately difficult (44%). The right answer selection rate increased somewhat more from Year 6 to year 8 than Year 4 to Year 6, but was not significant ($z = 1.61$). The overall gain was significant ($z = 2.7$) (Fig. 16.5).

Two of the alternatives (A and D) overshot the end position on the dial. Alternative A was the furthest beyond and was the most popular wrong answer. The proportional decline was somewhat larger but was also not significant. The extreme final position could be an over-generalization (OG).

7. In the dial below, the pointer turns in the direction shown. Starting from P, where would the pointer be after taking 5 3/4 turns?

A.   Between T and P
B.   Between S and T
C.   At T
D.   At S

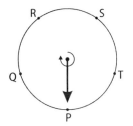

Item 7	Year 4	Year 6	Year 8
R_B	0.344	0.418	0.527
W_A	0.327	0.288	0.221
W_C	0.146	0.134	0.125
W_D	0.183	0.160	0.128
Totals	1.000	1.000	1.000

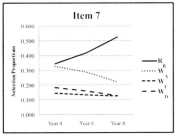

Fig. 16.5 Mathematics – Item 7

The third option (C) was an under estimate. It was somewhat more attractive than option D.

These errors show a lack of understanding of the concept of rotation. The students need more practice in this, through dance or with the help of computer interaction. Most draw programs have object rotation as one of their features.

4.2   Science: (All Alternatives Functioning)

Generally, this item shows the expected progression for both the A and ¬A answers with about two in three students answering the question correctly in Year 8 ($z=4.4$). Its unique feature, for year 4, is the selection ratios separated by 0.013 for R_D and W_A (Fig. 16.6).

Regarding option A, it is unclear why one in five Year 4 students chose this option. Perhaps they are treating the sun as the only energy source. When in doubt, ask.

Option B may reflect students seeing that mice, crickets and moths are closest to corn (narrow focus) and therefore would be the animals affected without making the proper connections to the other animals.

Option C indicates students thought that only the animals from the bottom two layers of the graph would be affected.

Both options B and C indicate that neither a full understanding of energy nor the food web has been achieved. It could mean that they do not grasp the transitive properties of graphs.

33. The food web shown here reflects the sources of energy of different living things. If the corn crop was destroyed due to bad weather, which of the animals shown above would be affected?

A. None.
B. Mice, crickets and moths only.
C. Mice, crickets, moths and birds only.
D. All the animals shown in the food web.

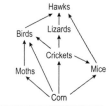

Item 33	Year 4	Year 6	Year 8
R_D	0.306	0.519	0.640
W_A	0.188	0.089	0.056
W_B	0.213	0.165	0.103
W_C	0.293	0.227	0.201
Totals	1.000	1.000	1.000

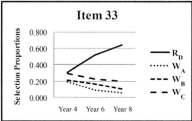

Fig. 16.6 Science – Item 33

5 Scatter

In the scatter pattern, each of the trajectories of selection appears to be independent. The answer selection processes for these items are more complex than for any of the other item types. The combination had six such items.

5.1 Mathematics: (All Alternatives Functioning)

Apparently, the order of precedence in arithmetical operations is not well understood (Fig. 16.7).

This item shows how ¬A answers can reveal the errors made. The gain is significant ($z-4.2$) but still has less than two in five students answering correctly in Year 8.

Those who chose option A solved the problem from left to right without doing the division first. This error increased significantly ($z=2.3$) from Year 4 to Year 6 and declined significantly ($z=-6.2$) to Year 8. If these selections were not thoughtful, they would not show significant changes of this magnitude. Whatever intervention was used with respect to this error, it must have occurred later than Year 6 and has not resolved the error by Year 8. Questions designed in this manner show powerful diagnostic capabilities. This item exemplifies the unreasonableness of ignoring the ¬A answers.

For option B, they treated the minus (−) sign as a multiplier (*) and solved the expression from right to left. This confusion occurred only with the Year 4 students and disappeared thereafter. Apparently, teaching intervention for this error was successful.

13. 10 + 30 ÷ 5 - 2 is equal to

    A. 6
    B. 13 1/3
    C. 14
    D. 20

Item 13	Year 4	Year 6	Year 8
R_C	0.082	0.245	0.373
W_A	0.052	0.704	0.578
W_B	0.776	0.026	0.032
W_D	0.090	0.025	0.017
Totals	1.000	1.000	1.000

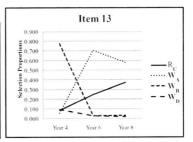

Fig. 16.7 Mathematics – Item 13

For option D, students solved it from right to left without considering precedence. Only a small number of students made this error at any level.

We suggest more practice in groups, where the students can discuss what they are doing compared with each other. Without understanding the order of precedence, these students will have difficulty with algebra where this understanding is critically important for solving equations.

The unique graphical characteristic is that the alternative answer proportions scatter disjointly. Linear mathematical models do not apply to such discontinuous data.

5.2   Science (All Alternatives Functioning)

As a thought-provoking question, this item is superb! It requires the student to analyze two separate statements for their meaning and then to synthesize the resulting relationship (Fig. 16.8).

The dynamics of the answer selection shown support this presumption. All four alternatives function as viable alternatives and each represents a different thought process.

Alternative A is remarkable in that it shows no change with age. This answer is achieved by responding only to the first part of the question. In other research (Powell 2010a), such *simplification* is the most common error.

26. Two balls, one red and one blue, are seen by Hamid through two lenses P and Q respectively. Lens P magnifies the object seen through it to DOUBLE, while lens Q makes it look HALF its original size. What can we conclude from the picture shown?
   A.   The red ball is twice as big as the blue ball.
   B.   The red ball is half the size of the blue ball.
   C.   The red ball is the same size as that of the blue ball.
   D.   The red ball is one-fourth the size of the blue ball.

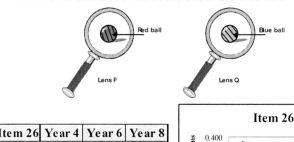

Item 26	Year 4	Year 6	Year 8
R_D	0.172	0.219	0.265
W_A	0.250	0.250	0.260
W_B	0.203	0.202	0.190
W_C	0.375	0.329	0.285
Totals	1.000	1.000	1.000

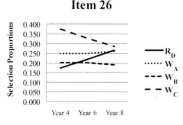

Fig. 16.8 Science – Item 26

Option B reflects size confusion, suggesting reading problems.

Option C may come from complete lack of understanding of the question and simply reading the diagram as the only meaningful data.

The proportion of A answer increases from about one in six to a bit better than one in four, which is not quite significant ($z = 1.7$). A ratio of one in four independent thinkers in middle school (Year 8) was also found elsewhere (Powell 2010a), which declined to one in five in high school. These observations may indicate the international validity of this research.

When we teach for information instead of how to think, this outcome would be the expected for such questions.

6 Wrong Answer Dominates

In this problem type, at least one of the ¬A answers had the highest selection proportion at all age levels. Four such items are present.

6.1 Mathematics: (All ¬A Functioning)

This question produced a fascinating answer pattern (Fig. 16.9). The visual analysis required is quite complicated. There are three steps to the solution. These are:

1. Realizing that the joining the blocks eliminates some corners.
2. Counting the visible corners.
3. Counting the concealed corner behind the figure.

9. A cube has 8 corners. The solid shown below is made by joining 3 cubes. How many corners does it have?

A. 24
B. 14
C. 12
D. 10

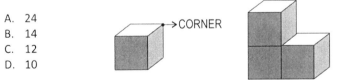

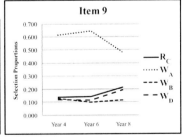

Item 9	Year 4	Year 6	Year 8
R_C	0.139	0.143	0.212
W_A	0.615	0.645	0.481
W_B	0.129	0.097	0.115
W_D	0.117	0.115	0.192
Totals	1.000	1.000	1.000

Fig. 16.9 Mathematics – Item 9

Only one in seven of the Year 4 students answered successfully. The surprise is that the Year 8 students did not do that much better (one in five).

The major error (C) was not recognizing the first step. The significant drop of the Year 8 group ($z=2.4$) means that at this level about half of them had acquired the first step skill.

This drop was not offset by a comparable upswing in the choice of the correct answer.

This item could be improved by making option D have 11 as its choice instead of 10. This change would pick up the people who had achieved the second step of the analysis and not the third step. This item illustrates levels of maturity as an increasing number of steps can be entertained.

Here is a superb situation for the use of manipulatives.

6.2   Science: (All Alternatives Functioning)

Almost no one answered this question correctly. Their results began at about one in eight and dropped by half by Class 8 (Fig. 16.10).

The wrong alternative C increased significantly ($z=2.9$) by about 20% at each level. We presume that they do not understand the spatial relationships in our solar system. If teachers explained this concept to them, they did not understand the

23. The night of July 31st, 2004 is a full moon night in Delhi. Will it also be a full moon night in Mumbai? In New York?

    A. It will be a full moon night in both Mumbai and New York.

    B. It will not be a full moon night in either Mumbai or New York.

    C. It will be a full moon night in Mumbai, but not in New York.

    D. It will be a full moon night in New York, but not in Mumbai.

Item 23	Year 4	Year 6	Year 8
R_A	0.168	0.114	0.094
W_B	0.206	0.202	0.137
W_C	0.509	0.608	0.713
W_D	0.116	0.077	0.056
Totals	1.000	1.000	1.000

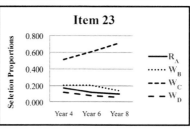

Fig. 16.10 Science – Item 23

explanation. Evidently, they have learned a misconception that because New York is opposite to Delhi on earth they can generalize this relationship to the solar system.

Of interest, one in five chose explanation (B) that is contrary to the facts.

The third option, alternative D is the opposite of C. Such scientific misconceptions led to the development of concept inventories (Halloun and Hestenes 1985).

7 Miscellaneous

This category includes the balance of the items that did not fit into the other five categories, with four such items in the two tests.

7.1 Mathematics: (All Alternatives Functioning)

Although the decline of the right answers was not significant, being only about 8%. It seems that the Year eight students had greater difficulty with rotation-comparison than did the younger children (Fig. 16.11).

On the other hand, the increase in the wrong answer (A) was significant ($z = 2.5$). The match, when measured by any simple device is ¼ of the height of the candle. The confusion between the three and the four is interesting.

8. In the picture below, about how long is the matchstick if the height of the candle is 12 cm?

A. 3 cm
B. 4 cm
C. 5 cm
D. 7 cm

Item 8	Year 4	Year 6	Year 8
R_A	0.525	0.513	0.442
W_B	0.280	0.343	0.433
W_C	0.124	0.101	0.105
W_D	0.071	0.043	0.020
Totals	1.000	1.000	1.000

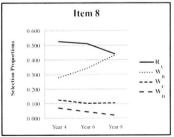

Fig. 16.11 Mathematics – Item 8

Alternative C could be identifying students who have problems with visualizing rotations, as Gardner would suggest.

Alternative D, chosen infrequently, might represent guessing.

Once again, this sort of problem should respond well to the use of manipulatives. As in the previous mathematics problem, the transfer from hands-on to pictorial representation may need some practice as well. Does familiarity with multiple choice tests cause students to stop reading at the first plausible option? Reversing option order might solve this problem.

7.2 Science: (All Alternatives Functioning)

This difficult item had one of five students answered correctly in Year 8 (Fig. 16.12).

Option A (that two of five students selected in Year 4) probably reflects a focus only on the size of the jar openings and not the "offsetting" diameter sizes of the jars.

30. Two empty vessels P and Q, as shown in the figures below, are kept outside at 4:00 pm. There was rain from 5:00 pm to 7:00 pm. The two vessels were observed after the rains.

What can be said about the LEVELS of water in vessels P and Q?

    A.   The level of the water in vessel P will be more than that in vessel Q.

    B.   The level of the water in vessel P will be less than that in vessel Q.

    C.   The level of the water in vessels P and Q will be the same.

    D.   Both vessels P and Q will be full.

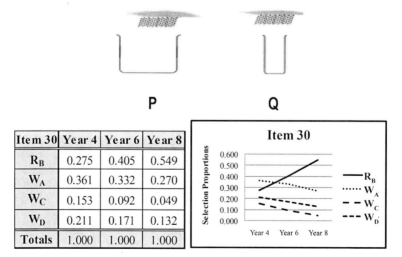

Item 30	Year 4	Year 6	Year 8
R_B	0.275	0.405	0.549
W_A	0.361	0.332	0.270
W_C	0.153	0.092	0.049
W_D	0.211	0.171	0.132
Totals	1.000	1.000	1.000

Fig. 16.12 Science – Item 30

Conversely, students who chose Option B (where the misconception *increases* with age) seem to focus solely on the relative diameters of the jars and not the jar openings size where rain enters.

Students who chose Option D may have relied the time duration and made their own estimate of the amount. In this case, option D captures those who assume that 2 hours of rain would be enough to fill them. Year 4 students may not distinguish between level and amount. This development explanation illustrates the diagnostic power of ¬A answers.

8   Conclusions and Implications

We originally presented this paper to the CELDA 2010 conference in Timisoara, Romania in October of 2010. CELDA stands for Cognitive and Exploratory Learning in the Digital Age.

We have presented 12 exemplary test items from two different tests given to the same students in India. There were three groups (Years 4, 6 and 8) taking this same test. These tests were administered only once to each group so that the within-individual changes in answer selection behaviour are not available. Thus, the dynamics revealed in this compilation represents between-individual selection behaviour across age differences.

We began with three foci for investigation:

1. To demonstrate thoughtful patterns of ¬A answer selection.
2. To connect selecting answers to child-development theory, as related to Constructivist Theory from Piaget (1985) for the role of disequilibrium to formulate insights, Vygotsky (1978) for the role of student activity in learning to think and Gardner (1983) for the role in alternative thinking styles, differentiating answer selection, and
3. To identify the educational implications of gathering this ¬A answer information to inform teaching.

8.1   Do ¬A Answers Contain Performance Information?

Current practice suggests no meaningful information can be found among ¬A answers (Lord 1952; Lord and Novick 1968; Allen and Yen 2002), implying that the direction of answer change should be uniformly from any wrong answer to the right one because these ∅A choices lack thoughtful selection.

As just stated, both these hypotheses require a single contradicting instance for refutation. We have shown that the majority of ¬A answers are chosen thoughtfully. These selections represent procedural errors, misconceptions, misreadings and insightful conclusions not anticipated in the question. Thoughtfully chosen answers are related to the ways students *interpret* questions and contain performance-specific behavioral information. Thus, our first major conclusion is that behavioral assumption justifying considering only acceptable answers to be relevant for performance assessment is *false.*

8.2 What is the Nature of this Information?

The selection of right answers does not always increase with maturity (age) and some errors can be attributed to the misconceptions taught in schools, such as item 23 (Sect. 6.2) above. This statement is true terrestrially but not astronomically. This item illustrates that "right" answers may be context sensitive, as Heisenberg (1930, 2007) makes clear in his *Uncertainty Principle.* The particularity of "right" answers is the second major finding of this research.

Having shown answer selection is thoughtful, containing performance information, the question becomes, "What is the nature of this information?"

We connected the evident rationale behind students' choices to developmental theorists holding the *constructionist* perspective. Students' answer selections pertain to their cognitive and metacognitive development. This conclusion replicates the studies reported in Powell (2010a) and in the teaching experiences reported anecdotally in Powell (2010b).

8.3 What Are the Educational Implications of This Information?

Glaser and Strauss (1967) build a case for establishing theory upon data. In contrast, Classical Test Theory ignores a major portion of the available data from tests. Furthermore, Powell and Miki (1985) showed that giving right answers and understanding the concepts behind the problems could be unrelated. Therefore, perhaps we should distrust the equivalence presumption between selecting "right" answers and "understanding the concepts" (See: Sect. 2.1).

Alternatively, both A and ¬A answers provide direct information about the thinking processes employed by students. This diagnostic information is systematically ignored during current test-scoring. Table 16.2 summarizes the results from this study.

This table gives item types. Considering individual options produces finer granularity, such as for 5.1. Concept inventories and propositional logic (Halloun and Hestenes 1985; Piburn 1990) used interviews, as did Powell (2010a), to classify alternatives.

Piaget presents disequilibrium as the driving force behind advancing cognition. Vygotsky recognizes private conversations and Gardner recognizes cognitive diversity to the same end. Powell (2010b) provides anecdotal support for the thinking/learning option.

Table 16.2 Diagnostic information from test answers

Answer valence	Diagnostic value	Text location	Description
A	1. Familiarity	2.1, 2.2	Recognizing the right answer independent of understanding the concept
¬A	1. Common misconceptions	3.2, 6.1	Culture-based errors
¬A	2. Diagram interpretation	6.1	Misreading drawing
¬A	3. Graph interpretation	4.2	Misreading charts
¬A	4. Maturity	2.1 B	Cognitive development sequences
¬A	5. Misreading	5.2	Language complexity
¬A	6. Procedural errors	5.1	Using wrong procedures
¬A	7. Rotations	4.1, 7.1	Confused visual solutions

Preschool children display curiosity leading to insightful learning. These characteristics diminish by the fourth grade (Powell 2010a). Alternatively, Powell (2010c) has shown that the transitions through Piaget's stages and beyond are driven by insights as these three theorists suggest. Hence, we can restore their natural curiosity and creativity by using the exploration of ideas and other insight-generating approaches. To achieve this end, we will benefit from additional research about cognitive advancement from the ¬A answers.

We suggest there is an important connection to learning based on wrong answers and creative insights.

The difference between an exclusive focus upon right answers versus learning from incorrect responses is illuminated by contrasting the roles of algorithms and heuristics in learning and problem solving. *Algorithms* are "step by step procedures for solving a problem" (Woolfolk 2011, p. 343) and *heuristics* are "rules of thumb" or "intuitive methods that may help to solve a problem but are not guaranteed to do so" (Moreno 2010, p. 264). Heuristics are better suited for solving *ill-defined* problems with multiple solutions. Algorithms are suited for solving *well-defined* problems with unique solutions (Tuckman and Monetti 2011).

The question arises "Is our future comprised mostly of well or ill-defined problems?" If the former is true, the current way of scoring tests is counter-productive. ¬A answers reflect correctable algorithmic errors. If our future is comprised mostly ill defined or unidentified problems, then the current scoring approach is anachronistic. It fails to provide children with the cognitive strategies they need to accommodate the future. Learning from ¬A answers is both heuristic and algorithmic. It aids in discovering novel solutions, identifying situations that test the limits of current paradigms (Kuhn 1996).

These results suggest that we should be teaching students how to think and how to learn *instead of transmitting information,* over-emphasizing content and algorithms, while under-emphasizing heuristics. Teaching for thinking and learning using subject matter as a vehicle accommodates both aspects of cognitive development. This well-established alternative dates from Socrates.

Algorithmic focus leads to narrowing cognition, particularly with the higher-scoring students (Powell 2010a). Exploratory approaches provide balance. Using all answers and scoring for response patterns will assist teachers to make improved use of test results, replacing a mind-closing form of education with a mind-opening one.

Current test-scoring practices inadequately assess students. The assumptions on which these are built are not grounded in data. These data are available from current well-prepared tests. The interpretations of the ¬A answers need to be determined and used to investigate the dynamics of learning using answer-pattern scoring.

Finally, we need to train teachers to use exploratory teaching approaches and how to use ¬A answers information to support this paradigm shift.

Acknowledgement   We extend our thanks to Educational Initiatives – India for making these test items and response data available for this study and my wife Valerie for reviewing and editing this document.

References

Allen, M. J., & Yen, W. M. (2002). *Introduction to Measurement Theory.* Long Grove, IL: Waveland Press.

Bandler, R. & Grinder, J. (1982) *Reframing.* Moab, UT: Real People Press.

Bond, T. G. & Fox, C. M. (2007). (2nd Ed.). *Applying the Rasch Model: Fundamental Measurement in the Human Sciences.* Mahwah, NJ: Lawrence Erlbaum.

Demetriou, A., & Kazi, S. (2006). Self-awareness in g (with processing efficiency and reasoning).*Intelligence, 34,* 297–317.

De Bono, E. (2005) *The six value medals.* London: Vermilion.

Flavell, John H. (1963). *The Developmental Psychology of Jean Piaget.* New York, NY: Van Nostrand.

Gardner, H. (1983). *Frames of Mind: The Theory of Multiple Intelligences.* New York, NY: Basic Books.

Gardner, H. (2000). *Intelligence reframed. Multiple intelligences for the 21st century.* New York, NY: Basic Books.

Gardner (2004). *Multiple intelligences. New Horizons, in theory and practice.* New York, NY: Basic Books.

Glaser, Barney G. and Strauss, Anselm L. (1967). *The Discovery of Grounded Theory: Strategies for qualitative research.* Chicago, IL: Aldine.

Gorham, D. R. (1957). *Proverbs Test.* Missoula, MT: Psychological Test Specialists.

Halloun, I. & Hestenes, D. L. (1985). Common sense about motion. *American Journal of Physics, 53,* (11) 1056–1065.

Heisenberg, W. (1930), *Physikalische Prinzipien der Quantentheorie* (Leipzig: Hirzel). English translation: *The Physical Principles of Quantum Theory.* Chicago: University of Chicago Press.

Heisenberg, W. (2007) *Physics and Philosophy: The Revolution in Modern Science.* New York: Harper Perennial Modern Classics. (*Full text of 1958 version*).

Kuhn, Thomas S. (1996). *The Structure of Scientific Revolutions* (3rd Ed.). University of Chicago Press.

Lord, Fredric. (1952). *A Theory of Test Scores.* Psychometric Monographs, Number 7. Philadelphia, PA. Ferguson.

Lord, F. M. & Novick, M. R. (1968). *Statistical theories of mental test scores.* Reading MA: Addison-Welsley.

Montessori, M. (1972). *Discovery of the Child.* New York: Ballantine Books.

Moreno, R. (2010). *Educational Psychology.* Hoboken, NJ: John Wiley & Sons.

Rose, S.A. & Blank, M. (1974). The potency of context in children's cognition: An illustration through conservation. *Child Development, 45,* 499–502.

Piburn, M. (1990). Reasoning about logical propositions and success in science. *Journal of Research in Science Teaching. 27,* (9) 887–900.

Piaget, J. (1954). *The construction of reality in the child* (m. Cook, Trans.). New York, NY: Basic Books.

Piaget, J. (1985). *The Equilibration of Cognitive Structures: The Central Problem of Intellectual Development.* Chicago: University of Chicago Press. (New translation of The Development of Thought)

Powell, J. C. (2010a). Testing as feedback to inform teaching. Chapter 3 in *Learning and Instruction in the Digital Age: Making a Difference through Cognitive Approaches.* New York: Springer.

Powell, J. C. (2010b). Do profoundly informed students choose wrong answers, lowering their scores? Research report Powell, J. C. (2010c). *Making Peasants into Kings,* Bloomington, IN: Author House

Powell, J. C. (2010). Do profoundly informed students choose wrong answers, lowering their scores? Research report presented to the *Psychomertic Society,* Athens, GA

Powell, J. C. & Miki, H. (1985). Answer anomalies, how serious? Nashville, TN: Paper presented to the *Psychometric Society.*

Powell, J. C. & Shklov N. (1992). Obtaining information about learners' thinking strategies from wrong answers on multiple-choice tests. *Educational and Psychological Measurement, 52,* 847–865.

Rasch, G. (1980). *Probabilistic Models for some intelligence and attainment tests.* (Expanded edition.) Chicago: University of Chicago Press.

Spearman, C. (1927). *The abilities of man: Their nature and measurement.* New York, NY: Macmillan.

Tuckman, B.W. & Monetti, D.M. (2011). Educational psychology. Belmont, CA: Wadsworth.

Vygotsky, L. S. (1978). *Mind in society. The development of higher mental process.* Cambridge, MA: Harvard University Press.

Woolfolk, A. (2011). *Educational psychology.* Boston, MA: Pearson.

Chapter 17
The Learning Potentials of Number Blocks

Gunver Majgaard, Morten Misfeldt, and Jacob Nielsen

1 Introduction

In this paper, we describe an initial exploration of Number Blocks designed to support number learning in mathematics. Number Blocks are based on the generic user-configurable modular robotic system called I-BLOCKS (Nielsen 2008a; (Nielsen 2008b). The educational goal is to support children's understanding of place value by allowing them to physically play with multi-digit numbers, the pronunciation of which is quite complicated in Danish (Ejersbo and Misfeldt 2011). The target group is children aged 5–8. Development was carried out in an experimental design process actively involving a class of 23 children and their mathematics teacher. This experiment is cross-disciplinary and combines the two scientific areas of robotics and pedagogical research. The tool combines physical interaction, learning, and immediate feedback.

Number Blocks can be labelled as a physical serious game (Majgaard 2009a). The tool is inspired by prior work in the field of physical serious games, e.g. by Papert (1980), Resnick (Rusk et al. 2008) and Majgaard (2009b). Resnick does research in LEGO Mindstorm and Pico Crickets, and he is currently working on how the learning process can become more creative and exploring. In both LEGO Mindstorm and Pico Crickets, the learner must build, program and execute their programs in sequences. During the execution, the robots give feedback and are

G. Majgaard (✉)
The Maersk Mc-Kinney Moller Institute, University of Southern Denmark,
Odense M, Denmark
e-mail: gum@mmmi.sdu.dk

M. Misfeldt
The Danish School of Education, Aarhus University, Copenhagen, Denmark
e-mail: mmi@dpu.dk

J. Nielsen
Center for Playware, Technical University of Denmark, Lyngby, Copenhagen, Denmark
e-mail: jn@playware.dtu.dk

P. Isaias et al. (eds.), *Towards Learning and Instruction in Web 3.0: Advances in Cognitive and Educational Psychology*, DOI 10.1007/978-1-4614-1539-8_17,
© Springer Science+Business Media, LLC 2012

interactive (Rusk et al. 2008). Number Blocks are different; they give direct feed-back during the building phase, and the children do not have to program the tool in a separate environment. It is our intension that the tool should support participative, creative and exploring learning processes.

Thus, the questions explored in this paper are: How can technology that com-bines building block interaction and sound modality, support place value learning? And what are the learning potentials?

The scientific method used is design-based research and action research (van den Akker et al. 2007; Lewin 1946; Majgaard 2010). The empirical foundation of this paper comprises six interventions, which took place in a second grade class during the iterative development of the system.

This paper includes an introduction to numeracy and interaction, followed by a description of the technological platform and an introduction to the way numbers are pronounced in Danish and a description of the iterative development process. Finally there is a discussion of the results and research question.

2   Theory

Comparative investigations have shown linguistically-determined differences in the conception of numbers and in understanding of place value (Dowker et al. 2008; Miura and Okamota 1989). One of the reasons for these differences is in the extent to which the words used to denote numbers reflect base ten place value system (Dowker et al. 2008).

Danish words for the numbers between 1 and 100 do not reflect the base ten place value system in two ways: (1) the words for the teens (11,12,13 ...) and the decades (20,30,40 ...) do not in any significant way relate to the names of the digits 1–10, and (2) the decades and units are spoken in reversed order compared to how they are written as digits in the base ten system. In Danish you would say 'fem-og-tres (five-and-threes)' in order to express the number 65, 'tres' (60) is an inflection of 'tre' (3), showing how the Danish number-words relate to long gone base 12 and 20 systems (Ejersbo and Misfeldt 2011). The reversed order of pronunciation of numbers between 20 and 100 also affects larger numbers such as 27,000 (in Danish pronounced 'syv og tyve tusinde' that is '7 and 20,000'). The algorithm to create larger numbers in Danish is described in Fig. 17.1.

It is broadly acknowledged that learning of mathematics can be considered an embodied activity (Johnson 1987; Nemirovsky et al. 2004). Furthermore concept formation in mathematics relates intimately to the representations that are used in work with the specific concept (Duval 2006; Steinbring 2006). The Number Block tool provides an embodied interaction with two representations that are crucial in the formation of a number concept: the number written as digit and the words used for a number. Digital manipulatives have been described as either Montessori-inspired or Fröbel-inspired (Zuckerman et al. 2005). Fröbel-inspired manipulatives are based on aesthetics and allow users to express their ideas creatively and to interact with shape and identity, whereas Montessori-inspired manipulatives allow interaction with

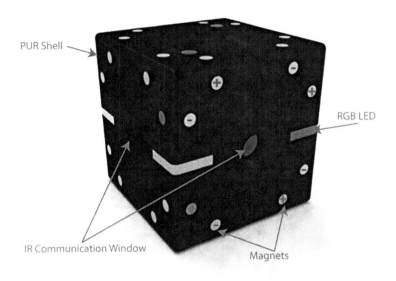

PUR Shell

RGB LED

IR Communication Window

Magnets

Fig. 17.1   The standard I-BLOCK

theoretical ideas. Number Blocks can be viewed as a Montessori-inspired digital manipulative, because it highlights interaction with the conception of numbers and the place value system (Zuckerman et al. 2005).

3   Technological Platform and the Number Blocks Tool

I-BLOCKS is a user-configurable modular robotic platform developed and tested through several prototype and application generations (Nielsen 2008b). It consists of magnetic cubic modules that can communicate with each other when connected. Each cube can communicate with up to four of its six possible neighbours and is fully self-contained with respect to power, connectors and processing. At the edges of the four communicating sides of a cube are four RGB LEDs, which can light up in 4,096 different colours. The I-BLOCKS communicate locally via infrared light, and in some cases radio (Zigbee), which allow for interaction with a computer. Each I-BLOCK makes use of a 3D accelerometer to detect its orientation with respect to gravity. This makes it able to detect which side is facing upwards.

   The I-BLOCKS hardware is encapsulated by a black polyurethane shell that has a soft rubber-like feel, with plastic fittings in top and bottom into which various sockets, connectors, sensors and actuators are integrated, see Fig. 17.1.

   The I-BLOCKS have been developed specifically to provide a general platform for exploring physical programming. An I-BLOCKS construction results not only in a physical structure, but also in a particular computational functionality which is dependent upon that particular structure.

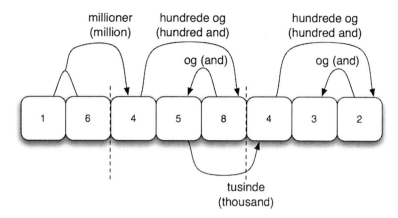

Fig. 17.2 The Danish system of pronouncing numbers

The Number Blocks implementation and instantiation of the I-BLOCKS technology allows children to explore the concept of number and the place value system in a tactile way, focusing on the way large numbers are constructed from digits and on the spoken names of these numbers. To create Number Blocks, each side of every I-BLOCK module is marked with a single digit label. Each I-BLOCK looks like a giant die. Morover six faces are not sufficient to represent ten digits, so individual modules could only represent a subset of digits. The digit number labels are glued onto specific faces of the cube, so that their value can be registered using the built-in accelerometer. When a module determines which face is currently facing upwards, it also knows which number is represented on that face.

The user connects Number Block modules in lines to create large numbers, which is equivalent to writing digits in lines on paper.

The complete Number Blocks system consists of the above mentioned number modules, a Zigbee radio communication module and a PC with a Zigbee-USB dongle, which serves as an audio playback device that convert incoming numbers into spoken numbers. The spoken numbers are consecutive playbacks of samples of recorded children's voices. A number algorithm plays the samples in the correct order. Figure 17.2 gives the correct spoken order for 16,458,432: by following the arrows from the left we get 16 -> 'millioner' ('millions') -> 400 -> 'og' ('and') -> 8 -> 'og' ('and') -> 50 -> 'tusinde' ('thousands') etc.

4   About the Research Method

The research method is based on action research and design-based research (Lewin 1946; Barab and Squire 2004; van den Akker et al. 2007). Both methods focus on iterative processes. Action research traditionally focuses on the target groups' change in behaviour, while Design-based research was developed for design of educational processes that involve digital media.

There were four step in the development and research process leading to Number Blocks: (1) Planning and making an overall plan; (2) Iterative interaction design; (3) Interviews and (4) Retrospective analysis.

In the overall planning phase, brainstorming produced many ideas for discussion. During this step it was decided to combine mathematics and I-BLOCKS. We did not decide on a specific learning goal, but a lot of ideas were aired.

Learning goals gradually emerged during the iterative interaction design phase. These were reviewed and adapted to fit national curriculum goals, theoretical hypotheses about the place value system, and to be practical with respect to our technological platform.

We held six sessions with the children, as described below. These sessions ensured that our overall ideas were appropriate for our target group, that the children enjoyed interacting with the Number Blocks, and allowed us to refine the educational content of the study and to investigate the learning potential of our technological platform.

After the six practical sessions, interviews were conducted with some of the children and with their teacher. Finally, retrospective analysis of the learning potential, design methodology, and technology used in this study is still ongoing at the time of this writing.

5   The Design Process

Our iterative design process included several 2 h sessions with our target group. The themes for the sessions were: (1) Getting to know each other and the technology; (2) Brainstorming and decision making; (3) Recording sound; (4) Testing the "Pronounce number Function"; (5) Testing the "Compare Numbers Function"; (6) The final test and putting the teacher in control.

Session 1 (06-15-10): *Getting to know each other and the technology.* The children tried an existing I-BLOCKS music application (Nielsen et al. 2008b). The goal of the session was to evaluate the potential of developing technology based on I-BLOCKS with the target group, and get to know each other, in order to make future cooperation easier for both children and researchers.

Session 2 (06-22-10): *Brainstorming and decision making.* The goal of this session was to generate ideas for the creation of suitable educational tool based on the I-BLOCKS platform. The children had ideas about how to use the blocks for mathematics, e.g. that one could add and subtract using the blocks.

Aside from brainstorming with the children, we also had a session with a group of mathematics teachers from the same school. They suggested that one could use the blocks to help children by saying numbers. They told us that Montessori had some exercises with bricks and positional notation. In an earlier brainstorm the research group had had a similar idea. We decided to design a system that supported place value and to extend the system to include number operations at a later time.

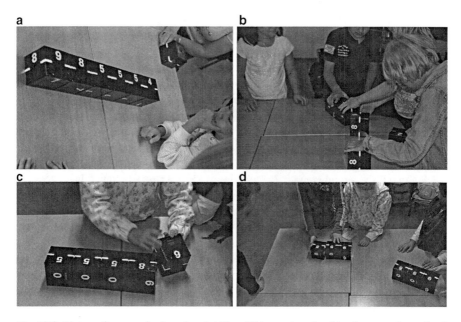

Fig. 17.3 Pictures from our final session. (**a**) The children enjoyed making large numbers. (**b**, **c**) The handy size of the blocks supported collaboration and playful investigation. (**d**) The children competed about making the largest numbers

Session 3 (08-13-10): *Recording sound and development of the first prototype*. The next step was to record the number elements sufficient to synthesise pronunciation of the relevant numbers. To involve the children as co-creators in the design process, we chose to use the children's own voices.

Session 4 (08-31-10): *Testing the initial prototype and the "Pronounce Numbers Function"*. The goal of this session was to conduct usability testing and to assess whether there was sufficient potential in the design to go ahead. Our initial observations suggested that the children were interested in creating large numbers (Fig. 17.3a). They were clearly interested in using the blocks to make as large a number as possible, either with all the cubes or with a specific selection.

Our initial concerns about the Danish number names mainly concerned the first 100 numbers but the session showed children found large numbers appealing. This came as a surprise for the teacher, since the class was only using two-digit numbers at that stage.

Another observation was that the children managed to play with Number Blocks. The session showed that the children (in groups of four) were able to create small games and competitions with the blocks (see Fig. 17.3d), without assistance from the investigators. They competed about who could make the largest number. This was a surprise in the sense that this prototype version of Number Blocks was designed without intended gameplay.

Our observations suggest that the size of the blocks supported physical play including group interaction and cooperation (see Fig. 17.3b).

Session 5 (11-2-10): *Testing the "Compare Numbers Function"*. We tested two versions for comparing numbers. If the children put a "Compare" block between two numbers, the system could tell which number was larger. This worked well, and was easy to use and understand. We also tested another version. This version could explain the difference between the two numbers. This function was too complicated for the children, because they had not yet been introduced to subtraction at that point.

Session 6 (07-12-10): *Final test and putting the teacher in charge*. This session was mainly held to confirm the findings of the previous interventions. We worked with groups of four children. In this intervention, the mathematics teacher participated in, and organized, the children's work with the blocks. The teacher did identify a number of potential uses, and spontaneously developed didactical activities involving the blocks. The pupils responded in a very natural way to these activities, did what the teacher asked just, as if it was any other form of didactical activity. This was unsurprising in that, the class seemed very positive and hard working and showed much respect for the teacher.

6   Summary of Interviews

Six of the children and their mathematics teacher were interviewed about the design process and learning potentials. The first two children were interviewed individually and after that we interviewed them in pairs, which made the more talkative. Different groups were represented in each interview. They were asked whether they had felt involved in the design process and how they perceived their participation in the technological design processes. In addition, they were asked how one could learn about the place value using the blocks. The teacher was asked about learning potential and how the blocks could be incorporated into daily lessons.

The children thought it was exciting that their voices were used as a part of the prototype. When the children were asked how they had influenced the study, it was particularly the use of their voices they mentioned. The use of their own voices gave them a special ownership of the project, which their teacher also underlined during the interview. The children could also recognise their own and each others' voices:

Child 2: "… You have listened to our ideas, to use our voices …. I can hear my own voice and it's fun … I say something with a 100 in the game" (6:44)

The teacher: "They've been looking forward to this enormously, there is no doubt about that. It has been on the top of their wish list. The children have also experienced it as exciting and rewarding to be part of the process." (teacher 1:02:52).

The children were asked how one could learn about the place value by using the blocks. This was difficult for them to explain, but they gave examples, of how they had pronounced large numbers, and how they had compared the number sizes. They also explained how they had competed to make the largest number.

The teacher thought that one obvious use of the blocks was as part of the so-called 'math workshop', where the children work in groups with physical artefacts, practical exercises, and games to improve their skills.

The teacher was asked about learning potential and if the blocks had some benefits over pen and paper. He emphasized that the blocks could 'communicate' on several channels: "They (blocks) speak to many channels at once; they (children) are faced with blocks and feel them. So it's something tangible for them, they get it aurally because they hear the sounds … It is so immediate – it is so easy to switch (the blocks) around."(Teacher, 1:06:10)

The teacher felt that the blocks appealed to both auditory and tactile channels, as well as the visual channel through the string of digits that the blocks have in common with printed representations of number. In addition, the blocks' physical form provided the teacher a good opportunity to talk with the children about figures, and the modularity made it easy to swap the digits around.

7   Learning Potential

In the following section we describe the learning potential of Number Blocks. We will argue that Number Blocks fruitful can be a way to integrate play and fun into mathematics education, and they can play an including role to support and engage pupils who typically find little or no interest in mathematics. Furthermore, the blocks' relation with the sound of number names sparked an interest to utter larger and larger numbers, and finally, the size of the blocks made them very useful for collaborative activities and allowed a different context for mathematical activities.

1. Play. The children obviously enjoyed to play with the blocks, and to put them together to form structures. The children also liked to create larger and larger numbers and to compete with each other. Children in the second grade usually work with hundreds and thousands, but in our sessions they produced much higher numbers just for the fun of it.

   It is obvious that the block format helped the children to create numbers. This came up consistently throughout the session. The children described the process as: "It is so immediate – it is so easy to switch the building blocks around" (child, 1:06:10). One of the children described the building process like this: "You can put the numbers together in new ways and go on and on" (child, 8:44).

   The playful aspect fits nicely with Vygotsky's 'zone of proximal development' in play. In play, the child can pronounce bigger numbers than s/he can when not playing and the child will behave "as if it was older". The zone of proximal development is the distance between what the child can learn by itself and what can be learned in collaboration with peers or with a teacher (Vygotsky 1978, p.86). The playful approach in Number Blocks has the potential to bring the children to play and learn in their zone of proximal development.

2. Inclusion. During the interventions, it seemed that children developed an interest in mathematics when they played with these 'digital blocks'. This is no surprise, since the interventions in the classroom represented something new and different from the typical mathematics class. The teacher's evaluation supported the impression that the blocks directly supported the so-called "weaker" pupils:

"It has helped them, I'm quite sure it has. xx finds it really hard to pronounce numbers and we get assistance from the learning support center to identify what is wrong. (…) But here she realized that if she placed a new digit in front of the number it became larger.…it became so real for her when she interacted with the blocks (…) Some of the brightest pupils, such as yy and zz, they could pronounce any of the major numbers but the rhythm has now given them a structure." (Teacher, 38:39)

Our observations and the teacher's judgment suggest that Number Blocks can be an efficient way to support mathematical activities because the typical power structure in the mathematical classroom is turned on its head, which supports the "weaker" students.

3. Rhythm and number names: by allowing an interaction with the sound of number names, the blocks sparked an interest in saying larger and larger numbers. The teacher pointed out the special rhythm in the application: "They (the blocks) have such a rhythm, take for example 99.999, it becomes quite clear for them (the children) what are thousands hundreds and so on … and they start to use the rhythm, when they say the numbers. And I think it's good for them, it becomes real for them and then they use the rhythm too … and the rhythm that has given them a structure for pronouncing big numbers. … The (system) has helped them to structure the pronunciation."(Teacher, 52:00)

The rhythm is a direct consequence of the consecutive playback of the bits of the children recorded pronunciations of the individual numbers – such as "one", "two", "ten", "twenty" and "hundred" along with the binding word "and". The software combines these different recorded bits into a structured sequence, which makes the computer's pronunciation much more predictable (rhythmic) than that of an adult.

Maybe the rhythm became important because the digital spoken numbers had a very transparent and rhythmic structure. The combination of the visual representation and the transparent rhythm of the number words, made the combination of these two semiotic registers natural when playing with the blocks.

4. Collaboration, Gesticulation and Building. The size of the blocks invited to play as a group activity. Experimentation was a big part of the overall design idea. We observed children who used their body/hands as part of a reasoning process; several times where a group of pupils were given three blocks with fixed digits, and told to find the largest possible number. Some of the children would use their hands to show how to move the blocks around, while they uttered the target number for their manipulation. This shows that the blocks can facilitate a mathematical activation of the bodily register in a structured way.

5. Bridging contexts. Creation of numbers from blocks was a new context for the children. In a 'normal' block context the children would have used blocks to build towers or quirky LEGO constructions; this can be described as a playful context. The new context for the numbers gave the children an opportunity to combine numbers and make them larger or smaller simply by manipulating the blocks. It made it clear to children that the digits were specific components. The learning tool combines a playful context and a mathematical context, and this connection between these contexts help the children to work in a new and fruitful way.

The children in second grade work normally with pen and paper. In this project, the children used their knowledge of numbers in a new context. This new context was tactile, interactive and auditory. Using knowledge in a new context made children adapt. Adaptive learning means that the child uses its knowledge in a new context. The child adapts to the new context in an optimizing manner. Bateson describes this as learning to learn or "Deutero-learning" (Bateson 2000, p.159). In this process the learner's learning strategy improves subconsciously. This is the most common form of learning, and planning and implementing of courses will often be based on this type of learning. The core elements in this type of learning are: adaptivity, optimization, new contexts, collaboration, processes of change, and qualities of interaction.

8   Technological and Interaction Insight

The development of the Number Blocks application added a few new features to the existing software framework for the I-BLOCKS. To be useful for this experiment the Number Blocks had to support a higher degree of structure recognition than earlier applications. This structure recognition is the system's ability to determine the sequential structure that a user has built. The solution was to make the 'result' or 'master' I-BLOCK record this structure when it was connected at the end of the structure, so it would transmit the correct number to the PC for playback. This solution also paves the way for new applications, such as work with letters, words, musical notes or other sequential material. Our experiments demonstrated that it is possible for the users to ignore the PC. This means that, in the case of the Number Blocks application, the PC is merely a playback device, with which the user has no direct contact – it might be placed at the opposite end of the room because of its radio connection to the master block. Conceptually speaking, the user might actually find it more natural if the actual feedback came directly from 'the master' block. We did however not get any indications on this through our experiments. Making 'the master' block do the actual audio narrative feedback would demand an electronic audio extension that would have the ability to play back sampled audio. Such an expansion is already planned and will in the future provide the possibility of working with many kinds of sample-based audio feedback.

Our studies demonstrated that the I-BLOCKS as a solid physical building-block platform has the potential to embody abstract learning material through playful interaction and collaboration. The children obviously enjoyed connecting and disconnecting I-BLOCKS, and appreciated the freedom and flexibility that the building-block approach offers through its inherent modularity. From the first intervention, we learned that the children were very curious about the actual electronic and mechanic functionality of the I-BLOCKS. They even asked us if we would take apart one of the I-BLOCKS, so they could see the components inside, which we did right away. This request showed us that the children's curiosity was not limited to play only with the content we provided them, but that they wanted to explore and understand as much about the system as possible – perhaps to be able to better exploit its functionalities. In our view, the children's extensive exploration of the system was a natural consequence of the interactive hands-on experience. The fact that the system is physical makes us relate to it in a very concrete way and to investigate it in a very concrete way – by taking it apart or handling it so as to experience its weight, material feel, smell, temperature and other physical features. The I-BLOCKS could be compared to a hand tool and it can be described as "a device for performing work on a material or a physical system using only hands". Similarly the I-BLOCKS are a tool for performing work on digital material using only hands. The digital material is immediately instantiated as physical feedback, in this case audio, and thus gives the user the feeling of working with genuine physical material.

When we work with computers, the user's curiosity is stimulated by the visual feedback provided by the screen. The screen of the screen-based technology is a window to the very soul of the device. In the users' mind the screen directly reflects the capabilities of the device – there is little point in a physical investigation of the device. All interactions are fed back through the screen. The screen is the main medium towards which we must direct our attention.

With the I-BLOCKS, the lack of a screen reduces emphasis on the user's visual senses and thus gives more importance to other senses such as touch and hearing, and it allows the user to collaborate better with other users through a common interaction with the system.

9   Summary and Conclusions

The questions explored in this paper are: How can technology that combines building block interaction and sound modality, support place value learning? And what are the learning potentials?

The I-BLOCK technology combines audio and physical interaction. This gives the learners hands-on experience with place value learning. The interactive blocks gave the children new opportunities for active participation. We believe that active participation is closely related to successful learning processes, which is supported by Wenger and Schön, who also believe that new knowledge is developed through active participation in a social context (Wenger 1998; Schön 1983). Reflection during and after the interactive learning activity also plays an important role in the learning process (Schön 1983). That's why the mathematics teacher has an important didactical role. The blocks can add new ways of participation and the teacher can add to the learning process by helping the children reflect. Our teacher felt that he did so when he guided the children through the I-BLOCK activities.

We found that I-BLOCKS contributed to the learning process in several ways: (1) The blocks combines mathematics and play; (2) They included and supported children at different academic levels; (3) The sound as a representation and the rhythm helped the children pronounce large numbers; (4) The size of the blocks made it easier for the children to collaborate and for the teacher to intervene, and the modular block concept gave the children a new perspective on building and combining digits; (5) Bridging contexts. The children were playing, interacting, building, and learning about place value at the same time. This created a new context for the learning of mathematics.

References

Barab, S., Squire, K., 2004."Design-Based Research: Putting a Stake in the Ground", The Journal Of The Learning Sciences, 13(1), 1–14. Lawrence Erlbaum Associates, Inc.

Bateson, Gregory, 2000 (1972). Steps to an Ecology of Mind: Collected Essays in Anthropology, Psychiatry, Evolution, and Epistemology. Forlaget Chicago Press. ISBN 0-226-03906-4

Dowker, A., Bala, S., Lloyd, D. 2008. Linguistic influences on Mathematical Development: How Important Is the Transparency of the Counting System? In Philosophical Psychology, Vol. 21, No. 4, August 2008, 523–538

Duval, R. 2006. A Cognitive Analysis of Problems of Comprehension in a Learning of Mathematics. Educational Studies in Mathematics, 61.

Ejersbo L. R., Misfeldt, M. (2011) Danish Number Names and Number Concepts, presented at the 7th Conference for European Research on Mathematics Education, Rzesow February 2011

Johnson, M. 1987. The body in the mind: The bodily basis of meaning, imagination, and reason. Chicago: University of Chicago Press.

Lewin, Kurt, 1946. "Action research and minority problems", Journal of Social Issues. Vol. 2, No. 4, 1946, s 34–46.

Majgaard, G., 2010. Design based action research in the world of robot technology and learning. In The Third IEEE International Conference on Digital Game and Intelligent Toy Enhanced Learning: DIGITAL 2010 (s. 85–92). IEEE Press.

Majgaard, G., 2009a. An outline of interaction types in physical serious games. Proceedings of IADIS Game and Entertainment Technologies 2009.Algarve, Portugal, pp.128–130

Majgaard, G., 2009b. The Playground in the Classroom - Fractions and Robot Technology. Proceedings in Cognition and Exploratory Learning in Digital Age. IADIS Press, 2009. Rome, Italy pp. 10–17.

Miura I. T., Okamota, Y. (1989): Comparisons of U.S. and Japanese first graders' cognitive representation of number and understanding of place value. In Journal of Educational Psychology, 81 pp. 109–113.

Nemirovsky, R., Borba, M., Dimattia, C., Arzarello, F., Robutti, O., Schnepp, M., Chazan, D., Scheffer, N. (2004) PME Special Issue: Bodily Activity and Imagination in Mathematics Learning. Educational Studies in Mathematics, 57 (3) pp. 303–321.

Nielsen, J., 2008a. User Configurable Modular Robotics - Control and Use. Ph.D. thesis, University of Southern Denmark.

Nielsen, J., Jessen, C. & Bærendsen, N.K., 2008b. RoboMusicKids – Music Education with Robotic Building Blocks. The 2nd IEEE International Conference on Digital Game and Intelligent Toy Enhanced Learning (DIGITEL), 149–156.

Papert, S., 1980. Mindstorms. Children, Computers, and Powerful Ideas. 2. Ed. Basic Books.

Rusk, N., Resnick, M., Berg, R., & Pezalla-Granlund, M., 2008. New Pathways into Robotics: Strategies for Broadening Participation. In Journal of Science Education and Technology, vol. 17, no. 1, pp. 59–69

Schön, D. (1983) The Reflective Practitioner, How Professionals Think In Action, Basic Books

Steinbring, H. (2006): What makes a sign a mathematical sign? – an epistemological perspective on mathematical interaction. Educational Studies of Mathematics 61, pp.133–162

van den Akker, J. et al., 2007. Education Design Research. Routledge.

Vygotsky, L., S., 1978. Mind in Society. The Development of Higher Psychological Processes. Harvard University Press.

Wenger E., 1998. Communities of practice Learning, meaning, and identity. Cambridge University Press

Zuckerman, O., Arida, S., & Resnick, M. 2005. Extending Tangible Interfaces for Education: Digital Montessori-inspired Manipulatives. CHI -CONFERENCE, 859–868.

Chapter 18
Toward Child-Friendly Output and Fabrication Devices

The StringPrinter and Other Possibilities

Michael Eisenberg, Kyle Ludwig, and Nwanua Elumeze

1   Introduction

Computer-controlled fabrication – the design and printing of tangible, physical objects – has seen an explosion of interest, excitement, and technological innovation in recent years. Laser cutters, 3D printers, desktop milling machines, computer-controlled sewing machines, and the like are altering our collective view of computers: instead of disembodied "electronic brains", it is now increasingly common to see computers as deeply interwoven with physical design and construction. In his popular book *The Long Tail*, Anderson (2008) describes 3D printing as "the sort of radical technology that sets the imagination soaring". (p. 247) Gershenfeld (2005), in his inspiring book *Fab*, discusses the implications of the burgeoning possibilities of personal fabrication:

> (C)onsider what would happen if the physical world outside computers was as malleable as the digital world inside computers. If ordinary people could personalize not just the content of computation but also its physical form. If mass customization lost the "mass" piece and become personal customization, with technology better reflecting the needs and wishes of its users because it's been developed by and for its users. If globalization gets replaced by localization.
>
> The result would be a revolution that contains, rather than replaces, all of the prior revolutions. Industrial production would merge with personal expression, which would merge with digital design…. Just as accumulated experience has found democracy to work better than monarchy, this would be a future based on widespread access to the means for invention rather than one based on technocracy. (p. 42)

Developments such as these have profound implications for educational computing and technology. In most educational discourse, the "computer" is seen as an entry to the Internet, or as a window to a "virtual universe" of information and abstraction; and the student is seen as someone staring at a screen (whether on a

M. Eisenberg (✉) • K. Ludwig • N. Elumeze
University of Colorado, Boulder, CO, USA
e-mail: duck@cs.colorado.edu; rushk144@gmail.com; nwanua@aniomagic.com

P. Isaias et al. (eds.), *Towards Learning and Instruction in Web 3.0: Advances in Cognitive and Educational Psychology*, DOI 10.1007/978-1-4614-1539-8_18,
© Springer Science+Business Media, LLC 2012

desktop or held in their hand). With the increasing advent of fabrication, however, we can view the computer as the heart of a newly-conceived personal workshop, and the student as a hands-on creator and craftsperson.

Indeed, the rhetoric of student-controlled fabrication is now beginning to find its way into educational research and discourse. As Lipson and Kurman (2010) write: "Educators want to serve different learning styles and offer hands-on learning: Personal-scale manufacturing tools serve today's educator's growing application of constructionist educational theory. Mainstream educators know that there is no "one size fits all" when it comes to classroom learning. Personal manufacturing tools offer students and teachers a wide range of pedagogical exercises and teaching aids." (p. 32) Later in the same paper, they add: "Personal fabrication technologies provide a powerful educational tool that offers students the driver's seat in the design and engineering process.... Computers and low-cost, small-scale manufacturing technologies, when integrated into science and technology classes, help educators craft physical models to help demonstrate educational concepts." (p. 60) Likewise, Berry et al. (2010) observe: "The next generation of personal digital fabricators now make digital fabrication in schools feasible and practical for the first time.... Low cost, versatility, and ease of use make this technology accessible to K-12 educators and students and can facilitate the introduction of engineering design and manufacturing concepts into early education."

Despite the exhilarating possibilities of educational fabrication, however, there are still frustrating barriers to be overcome before these devices and systems can become commonplace in children's lives. Design software is still too difficult for children (indeed, for many adults) to use; the various devices themselves are often too expensive, risky, or unwieldy for youngsters to play with; there is little in the way of supporting infrastructure (literature, websites, social networks, classroom or neighborhood laboratories) available to children interested in physical construction. Perhaps most important, there is a *cultural* shift that is needed: the designers of fabrication tools and systems need to re-interpret their products for children, and the educational technology community needs to expand its imaginative vision beyond the by-now-traditional combination of screen and Internet. A detente is called for.

This chapter is an exploration of several tentative-but-plausible ideas for creating "fabrication devices and techniques for children." The essential turn in this exploration is to begin with the sorts of materials and construction projects that children have traditionally enjoyed, and to bring the affordances of computational fabrication into that realm. Rather than thinking in terms of "industrial fabrication," then, the goal here is to think of "playful, informal fabrication." In a sense, the cultural shift being suggested is analogous to a similar, earlier shift that took place in the realm of computation: just as computers evolved from the industrial behemoths of the 1960s into the handheld browsers, e-book readers, phones, and game players of the current decade, we need to move our expectations about fabrication from the putatively "serious" world of adult professionals to the more playful (but in our view no less "serious") world of children's activities.

The remainder of this chapter is structured as follows: in Sect. 2, we describe a working prototype of a child-friendly fabrication device, the *StringPrinter*, intended as an example of the sort of innovation that we are advocating. The StringPrinter (Ludwig et al. 2010) is an early work-in-progress, but it illustrates the potential of a design stance that emphasizes fabrication for children. Indeed, our larger goal here is not to highlight the StringPrinter in particular, but rather to use it as a springboard – a starting point – for broader discussion. Sect. 3 unpacks this discussion, as we present a wide variety of plausible innovations for children's fabrication. Much of this section is frankly exploratory and (at times) perhaps a bit futuristic; the overall intent is not to promote any one single project, but rather to spark the collective imagination of the educational technology community. The final section discusses current related work in the area of educational fabrication; we also outline our plans for the StringPrinter and other projects in children's fabrication technology.

2   The StringPrinter: Purpose and Design

We begin, then, by focusing on one of the most venerable (and perhaps the humblest) of children's craft materials: namely, string. Children have of course long enjoyed pastimes such as "cat's cradle", played with nothing but a loop of string and (at least) two pairs of hands[1]; while a variety of children's craft books, both old (e.g., Winsor 1915, pp. 76–77) and recent (e.g., Campbell 2008, p. 66), illustrate how to tie knots. In the literature of mathematical education, there have been numerous compelling uses of string for the creation of mathematical models of curves and surfaces. Cundy and Rollett's (1961) classic book *Mathematical Models* is an excellent introduction to this genre of work; still other marvelous sources of mathematical string crafts include (Millington 2004; Pohl 1986).

This, in fact, is an interesting place to begin our exploration of children's fabrication. Let us imagine, then, that we can treat string (for crafting purposes) as a material that can be retrieved from an output device. In this case, the output device will not create or alter the string itself, but will merely decorate it with user-controlled color patterns.

A string-decorating device would actually be a useful addition to the tool chest of children's crafts. In all of the traditional sources on string crafts, the material is assumed to be uniformly-colored: that is, the student's projects cannot make use of varied color patterns along the length of the string itself. The ability to vary the coloring of the string or yarn in projects of this type should allow for an infinitely wider range of possible projects, and should allow string crafts (particularly of the mathematical sort) to serve as a much more aesthetically appealing medium than it does at present. (See also Eisenberg (2002) for an early discussion of this idea).

---

[1] A cartoon from 1858, by the artist John Leech in the British magazine *Punch*, depicts adults playing cat's cradle (called "scratch cradle" in the cartoon's caption). The cartoon can be found on the Web at: www.john-leech-archive.org.uk/1858/snowed-up.htm.

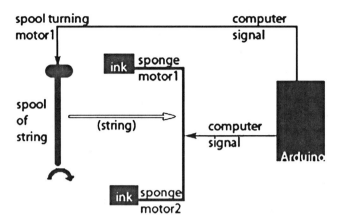

Fig. 18.1 Schematic and design of the StringPrinter

It is with this goal in mind – adding a novel output device to the repertoire of children's crafts – that we created our first prototype of the StringPrinter. The basic design of the StringPrinter is shown in the schematic in Fig. 18.1. Essentially, the device consists of a computer-controlled inking device that can apply ink selectively to portions of string as the string is pulled through the device. The inking device employs motors that push ink-soaked sponges against the string; the motors close and open under computer control. Of course, this brief description effectively finesses many of the finer parameters that went into the construction of the device: the materials chosen for the various elements (primarily, acrylic plastic); the mechanical means for conducting liquid ink to the sponges, and for retrieving and recycling ink for later use; the programming of the computer controller (in this case, implemented in an Arduino device). Space limitations preclude a fine-grained description of all these construction choices, but a video of the current working prototype can be found on the Internet.[2]

Figure 18.2 shows several photographs of the current device, highlighting distinct aspects of its construction. In the upper left of the figure, a full-color photograph of the entire device is shown; in addition three similar photographs are shown, tinted to emphasize specific portions (upper right, the paths by which fluid ink is conducted to the sponges; lower left, the ink spool, Arduino controller, and funnel for retrieving unused ink; and bottom right, the framework and sponge-controlling motors for the device). Again, the overall function of the device is to permit the user to specify a pattern for decorating string of the following sort: "2 cm blue; 1 cm white; 3 cm blue; 1 cm white; 4 cm blue..." and to produce a length of string with that decorative pattern. Much as one might think of a standard ink jet printer as a "paper decorating device", then, the StringPrinter is a "string decorating device".

---

[2]The video can be found at: http://www.youtube.com/watch?v=33UV5E37RKU.

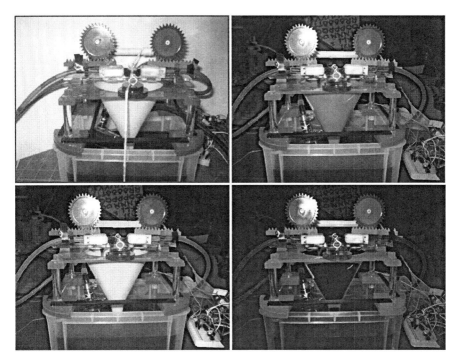

Fig. 18.2   The StringPrinter. At *upper left*, a photograph of the device. At *upper right* and *bottom*, we highlight the fluid pathway for the ink, in *blue*; at *bottom left* we highlight the funnel, string spool (toward the *upper center* of the photograph) and Arduino controller (*bottom right* of the photograph), all in *yellow*; and at *bottom right* we highlight the framework and sponge-controlling motors of the device (in *red*)

As already noted, the current StringPrinter implementation is a prototype only – and an early one at that. The device is currently controlled solely by an Arduino microcontroller, and the user can specify patterns of ink application by manually pushing buttons that are read by the Arduino; a full software interface, to control the device from a desktop computer, is currently under development. There are still other limitations to the current device: it only applies one color of ink at present (e.g., one cannot decorate a length of string with multiple colors), it is rather slow, and the resolution of ink application is on the order of between 1 and 2 cm. Much more work has to be done on the current device before we can employ it in pilot tests with children. Still, the purpose of the current device is to illustrate a *style* of design – namely, a style in which children's craft materials can become the focus of computer-controlled fabrication. Even in its present primitive state, the StringPrinter is capable, we believe, of expanding the possibilities of mathematical string crafts. Figure 18.3 shows a couple of sample projects done with the printer. At left, a length of string with varying lengths of decoration (some employing one "length unit" and others two) can be seen; at right, a longer decorated string has been placed in a frame to display a central white square against a background of blue.

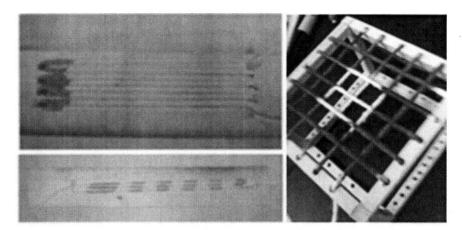

Fig. 18.3 StringPrinter projects. At *left*, lengths of custom-decorated string have been wound back and forth around opposite rows of pegs to produce (one or multiple) vertical stripes; at *right*, custom-decorated string inserted into a square frame to produce a central white square

3 Beyond the StringPrinter: Fabrication in Education, and in Children's Culture

The StringPrinter of the previous section is – we concede – a prototype targeted both at a rather specific material (i.e., string) and at a specialized, if beautiful, corner of children's mathematical crafting. The larger point of this effort is not so much to produce a commercial-quality fabrication device, but rather to illustrate the theme of child-friendly fabrication. In this section, we discuss a variety of potential design ideas building on the themes highlighted by the StringPrinter. The reader is encouraged to think of this section as an outline of many rough ideas–ideas which could conceivably be carried forward into working devices and techniques for children's construction and engineering projects.

3.1 Arranging or Placing the Materials of Children's Crafts

One way of viewing a fabrication device is as a tool for taking existing materials in "raw" form and placing those materials in complex patterns according to computer control. We might thus imagine a version of "child-friendly fabrication" characterized by the positioning or arrangement of craft materials.

To take a specific instance, a time-honored sort of classroom craft project is to begin with a collection of standard-sized multi-colored pieces: buttons, beads, mosaic stones, or even jellybeans might be used for this purpose. The pieces are then placed on a two-dimensional surface to create patterns or representational artwork; in effect,

Fig. 18.4 Two vase-like constructions made from multicolored beads. The construction at *left* (made by Jeff LaMarche) is created from Perler beads, which are cylindrical beads that can be fused together by the heat of an iron. The construction at *right* was made with Pixos, which are spherical beads that stick together in water; in this instance, the shape was made by pouring dry Pixos into a vase-shaped mold, adding water, and then (after a time) removing the mold

the various pieces are being used as discrete tangible pixels, analogous to the pixels of a computer screen. It would be plausible to create fabrication devices that can perform complex "pixel-placement" projects of this sort; this would enrich – but not supplant – children's crafting. For instance, one might have a "button-placing machine" that, given supplies of standard buttons or discs of specific colors, places those items in a two-dimensional array to serve as a background pattern for children's work. Ideally, the design software to create the patterns would be simple enough for children to use: thus, a child might create part of a button-art project via output device (using design software to specify the pattern to be placed), and might create other portions of the project (perhaps using specialized buttons or other pieces) with her own hands.

The previous paragraph described a scenario in which children's craft materials (e.g., buttons or beads) are arranged via computer control. One might go even a bit further and imagine devices that fabricate objects via placement in three dimensions – rather than only two, as in the previous example. Figure 18.4 illustrates where we are headed with this idea: the figure shows a pair of constructions made in our lab (unaided by machines!) using multicolored beads. The construction at left uses Perler beads, which can be fused together by the heat of a handheld iron; the construction at right was made from Pixos, which join together into solid masses when moistened. In both cases, it is clearly possible to use the beads not merely as "tangible pixels",

Fig. 18.5 A computer-controlled paper-tape spooler device has been placed on the table of a desktop laser cutter. The basic idea of the device is that it permits users to progressively spool lengths of paper tape that can be cut or engraved by a moving laser. Details of the device's construction can be found at the Instructables.com website, at: http://www.instructables.com/id/Scrollable-Laser-Cutting-Addition/

but in effect as "tangible voxels" that could conceivably be placed by a suitably constructed children's fabrication device. A bead-printer in this expanded sense could translate screen representations of 3D objects into physical versions, printed out by the arrangement of numerous colored beads in successive vertical layers. One might think of such a device as a discrete, child-friendly version of a 3D printer, with the added advantage (beyond the capabilities of standard single-material printers) of creating objects in multiple colors.

3.2   Cutting or Engraving the Materials of Children's Crafts

The previous subsection described potential directions for what might be called "fabrication-via-placement". Another way of thinking about children's fabrication is to use an output device to cut, slice, or engrave materials (e.g., through the use of a computer-controlled laser, as in standard desktop laser cutters).

A number of classroom craft materials are good candidates for this sort of project. Consider, for example, the venerable classroom supply of ribbon. One might imagine creating a device whose role is to cut customized patterns in long strips of ribbon via computer control. The basic idea here is to use a computer-driven laser to "draw" complex high-resolution patterns of holes into the material. Figure 18.5 shows a photograph of a recent prototype along these lines constructed by a team of graduate students in our laboratory. The students created a computer-controlled device that moves a spool of paper tape within a desktop laser cutter, allowing the cutter to create patterns in the tape. (In this case, the paper tape is playing the same

Fig. 18.6 A length of paper tape, spooled by the device in Fig. 18.5, in which a succession of diamond-shaped holes have been cut

role as spools of ribbon in our description). Figure 18.6 shows a photograph of a length of paper tape in which patterns have been cut using the device.

The paper-tape-cutter of Figs. 18.5 and 18.6 is (like the StringPrinter) a prototype, but it suggests a type of design that might well be employed for classroom fabrication. That is, we could imagine a small-scale "ribbon cutter" (or "paper tape cutter") geared toward children's crafts, and accompanied by software that allows children to specify patterns to cut into the material. These patterns might be repetitive "frieze" type patterns, as in the photograph of Fig. 18.6; or they might be specialized patterns such as snippets of cut-out text. Such an output device might also be used to customize materials used in mathematical crafts such as paper weaving (cf. Wigg and Hasselschwert 2001, p. 316), in which strips or paper tape are folded or woven into complex constructions.

Nor are ribbon or tape the only craft materials that could be employed in this sort of cutting/engraving fabrication device. Another possible choice might be the common (we resist the adjective "lowly") popsicle stick. These wooden "craft sticks" are routinely used in children's construction projects; being made of wood, they could easily be cut or shaped by a small-scale, specialized laser-cutting device. Children could thus build with sticks into which specialized holes (or, again, text) could be cut; the sticks might be shaped along the edges to produce construction sticks with complex boundaries. In short, then, a classroom "popsicle-stick-cutter" would be a delightful tool for children's crafting.

3.3 Extruding or Reshaping the Materials of Children's Crafts

The previous subsections began by examining standard materials of children's construction – beads, buttons, ribbon, popsicle sticks – and imagining ways in which fabrication devices could arrange, cut, or engrave these objects. Still other children's craft objects might be extruded or shaped by innovative fabrication devices.

To take an example along these lines, consider the humble plastic soda straw – again, a staple of children's constructions. In many classroom projects, straws are used much like wooden construction sticks – they are assembled as struts in larger patterns and structures. Often, the straws are connected by threading string (or pipe cleaners) through the length of the straw, and tying together the ends of the string (or pipe cleaners) to link adjacent straws. One advantage of straws over wooden sticks is that the former can be easily bent into curved shapes. If the reader is in any doubt as to the remarkable versatility of plastic straws as a crafting medium, an Internet image search on "plastic straw sculpture" (using one's favorite search engine) will prove an astonishing experience.

For children's work, it is quite conceivable that a fabrication device could be constructed to heat and bend plastic straws into specified curved configurations (say, a circular arc, or V-shape, or one cycle of a sine wave). Such a device alone would, in effect, expand the artistic range of this most-informal children's medium. Even the classic "cube made out of drinking straws" could be made more interesting if the straws themselves were fashioned into curved arcs. A still more ambitious fabrication device might be able to join straws together at their ends, or to fashion custom-made construction straws out of inexpensive plastic material, or (returning to the ideas of the previous subsection) to cut or engrave straws in complex patterns.

3.4 Decorating or Coloring the Materials of Children's Crafts

It should be pointed out that the most familiar of all modern-day "output devices" – the desktop inkjet printer – does not so much output paper as it does decorate paper. That is to say, an inkjet printer (much like the StringPrinter) takes in plain or undecorated material and then elaborates that material with printed designs. Thus, one of the primary purposes of a standard output device can be described as the decoration of a physical substrate.

Children now routinely make use of inkjet printers to make various types of papercraft projects (though even here, it is worth bearing in mind how rapidly color printers have blossomed into classroom-ready devices; 25 years ago a computer-controlled color printer was an expensive artifact, for professional use only). At the same time, there are other types of craft materials, besides paper, that are common to children's projects and that could be decorated or embellished with child-friendly output devices.

Two materials of this sort are the soft sculptural materials made from (in the first case) a mixture of sawdust and glue, and (in the second case) cornstarch and baking soda mixed with water. Both these media are familiar to classroom arts-and-crafts teachers, and both are capable of being shaped into creative sculptural constructions. The former mixture is a kind of homemade wood putty; the latter more like a simple sort of soft clay, suitable for baking into hardened forms. In either case, it is conceivable that an output device could be constructed to tint or decorate the plain mixture (using, e.g., dyes or food coloring) in complex computer-controlled patterns while the material is still soft and pliable. The idea here is to think of "fabrication" as a matter of custom-decorating the raw material with which children work.

To conclude this extended daydream: there are numerous ways to think about computer-controlled fabrication – as a matter of physical arrangement of existing pieces, or cutting material, or reshaping material, or decoration. We have no doubt that there are still other modalities of fabrication that we have overlooked here; we make no pretense of completeness in this list. And – to continue in this self-deprecatory vein – most likely, some of the suggestions in this section for creating novel fabrication devices wouldn't pan out if attempted; but perhaps others would pan out spectacularly well. The larger point, again, is that the landscape of children's crafts is abundantly populated with materials – buttons, straws, ribbons, homemade clay – that are off the collective radar of the "serious" fabrication industry, much as children's activities were invisible to early computer designers. There is a wealth of potential research and development in this area – and a lot of fun to be had by both designers and children alike – in re-imagining fabrication through the lens of children's crafts.

4 Related and Ongoing Work: The Growth of Child-Friendly Fabrication and Output

The work and ideas described in this chapter are influenced by several lines of existing research. It should be clear that, from the standpoint of educational philosophy, our examples draw strongly on the "constructionist" tradition in which learning is grounded in the design and creation of content-rich artifacts (see, for example, Papert 1991 and Noss and Hoyles 2006). By and large, we see fabrication devices not exclusively, or primarily, in the role of "teaching skills", but rather in the role of providing children with expressive, challenging activities and interests. For this reason, we have not (in this chapter) highlighted the use of fabrication devices to teach standard content in areas such as arithmetic or algebra, though such uses are certainly plausible. Instead, we see fabrication as furthering children's idiosyncratic, creative intellectual lives (cf. [Eisenberg 2011]).

This is not the occasion to revisit long-standing arguments about the merits and problems of the constructionist viewpoint. Nonetheless, the connection between fabrication and the constructionist educational philosophy is (to our way of thinking) quite natural. The tools with which children can build are now much more powerful than those available just a decade or so ago. It is time to revisit educational constructionism in the light of these new technological developments.

Indeed, the growth of fabrication promises to have educational impact beyond the world of children, or classrooms, alone. Most prominently, there is a recent explosion in affordable 3D printing that, we believe, heralds an increasingly democratized climate of personal construction. Examples such as the Makerbot (www.makerbot.com), RepRap (reprap.org), and Fab at Home project (Malone and Lipson 2007) collectively point the way toward a near future in which all sorts of people – professionals, hobbyists, amateurs, and youngsters – have access to high quality personal fabrication devices and techniques. Moreover – and here, the analogy with the early home computer industry breaks down somewhat – this budding revolution in personal fabrication is supported by an infrastructure of Web-based services and information. Even for those without access to a fabrication lab, sites such as ponoko. com and shapeways.com advertise their ability to print out high-quality customized objects from computer specifications. Other sites, such as that associated with *Make Magazine*, offer advice, forums, and information to the apprentice user of fabrication devices; and still others, such as thingiverse.com, allow users to present and share their best 3D construction work.

In short, 3D printing is well on its way toward a prominent presence in home technology – including, without question, educational technology. Still, to return to our overall theme, it has been the argument of this chapter that 3D printing is only one (very powerful) element of a much larger potential landscape of child-friendly fabrication. We have 3D printers – how about "printers" for string, or straws, or popsicle sticks, or buttons, or beads? A suggestion of the type of innovation that we are advocating here is found in the marvelous "Eggbot" device created by Bruce Shapiro (egg-bot.com); this is a device that decorates eggshells and spherical surfaces with complex patterns under computer control (it thus falls into the "fabrication-as-decoration" category of the previous section's informal taxonomy). Still other researchers are exploring children's projects using other types of fabrication tools such as commercial desktop paper cutters (see for example the project description at www.DigitalFabrication. org). These are wonderful developments, but what is really needed is a much greater, longer-term collaboration between the largely disparate worlds of children's arts-and-crafts (on the one hand) and fabrication technology (on the other).

We intend to do at least some additional development on the StringPrinter (including some software development for controlling the device from a desktop "string-decorating" interface); and we hope to pursue at least one or two of the sample ideas described in this chapter. There is evidently no lack of work to pursue, and opportunities for a wide range of researchers and participants of all ages and backgrounds. As an initial step, we happily invite readers to pursue any of these ideas in their own design work, or to make up still other projects for children's fabrication.

Acknowledgments This chapter is a substantially extended version of (Ludwig et al. 2010). The work described here was supported in part by the National Science Foundation under award no. IIS0856003. Thanks also to Ted Chen, Ann Eisenberg, Gerhard Fischer, Mark Gross, Clayton Lewis, and Andee Rubin for wonderful conversations on the subject of this paper. Jeff LaMarche constructed the "vase" at left of Fig. 18.4, and invented the original idea of a "3D bead printer". The vase at right of Fig. 18.4 was constructed by Jane Meyers and the first author. The paper-tape-printer is the work of Russell Winkler, Mossaab Bagdouri, Susan Hendrix, and Michael Coury.

References

Anderson, C. [2008] *The Long Tail* (Revised edition.) New York: Hyperion.
Berry, R. *et al.* [2010] Preliminary considerations regarding use of digital fabrication to incorporate engineering design principles in elementary mathematics education. *Contemporary Issues in Technology and Teacher Education*, 10(2), pp. 167–172.

Campbell, G. [2008] *The Boys' Book of Survival*. Buster Books, London, UK.

Cundy, H. M. and Rollett, A. P. [1961] *Mathematical Models*. London: Oxford University Press.

Eisenberg, M. [2002] Output devices, computation, and the future of computational crafts. *International Journal of Computers for Mathematical Learning*, 7(1), pp. 1–44.

Eisenberg, M. [2011] Educational fabrication, in and out of the classroom. In *Proceedings of Society for Information Technology & Teacher Education* (SITE 2011), pp. 884–891.

Gershenfeld, N. [2005] *Fab*. New York: Basic Books.

Lipson, H. and Kurman, M. [2010] Factory@Home: the emerging economy of personal fabrication. Whitehouse Office of Science and Technology Policy. Available at: www.mae.cornell.edu/lipson/factoryathome.pdf.

Ludwig, K.; Elumeze, N.; and Eisenberg, M. [2010] "The StringPrinter: First Steps Toward Child-Friendly Fabrication Devices" (reflection paper). In *Proceedings of IADIS Cognition and Exploratory Learning in Digital Age (CELDA 2010)*, Timisoara, Romania, pp. 300–302.

Malone, E. and Lipson, H. [2007] Fab@Home: the personal desktop fabricator kit. *Rapid Prototyping Journal*, 13:4, pp. 245–255.

Millington, J. [2004] *Curve Stitching*. Norfolk, UK: Tarquin Publications.

Noss, R. and Hoyles, C. [2006] Exploring mathematics through construction and collaboration. In Sawyer, K. (ed.) *Cambridge Handbook of the Learning Sciences*. New York: Cambridge University Press, pp. 389–405.

Papert, S. [1991] Situating constructionism. In Harel, I. and Papert, S. (eds.) *Constructionism*. Norwood, NJ: Ablex

Pohl, V. [1986] *How to Enrich Geometry Using String Designs*. Reston, VA: National Council of Teachers of Mathematics.

Wigg, P. and Hasselschwert, J. [2001] *A Handbook of Arts and Crafts. (10th edition)* New York: McGraw-Hill.

Winsor, H. H. [1915] *The Boy Mechanic, Book 2*. Chicago: Popular Mechanics Press.

Index

P. Isaias et al. (eds.), *Towards Learning and Instruction in Web 3.0: Advances in Cognitive*   317
and Educational Psychology, DOI 10.1007/978-1-4614-1539-8,
© Springer Science+Business Media, LLC 2012

CPSIA information can be obtained at www.ICGtesting.com
Printed in the USA
LVOW100232070612

285043LV00004B/53/P